CIRCLES AND SQUARES

CIRCLES AND SQUARES: THE LIVES AND ART OF THE HAMPSTEAD MODERNISTS

Caroline Maclean

BLOOMSBURY PUBLISHING
LONDON • OXFORD • NEW YORK • NEW DELHI • SYDNEY

BLOOMSBURY PUBLISHING
Bloomsbury Publishing Plc
50 Bedford Square, London, WC1B 3DP, UK

BLOOMSBURY, BLOOMSBURY PUBLISHING and the Diana logo are trademarks of Bloomsbury Publishing Plc

First published in Great Britain 2020

A catalogue record for this book is available from the British Library

ISBN: HB: 978-1-4088-8969-5; EBOOK: 978-1-4088-8967-1

2 4 6 8 10 9 7 5 3 1

Typeset by Newgen KnowledgeWorks Pvt., Ltd, Chennai, India
Printed and bound in Great Britain by CPI Group (UK) Ltd, Croydon CR0 4YY

FSC www.fsc.org
MIX
Paper from responsible sources
FSC® C020471

To find out more about our authors and books visit www.bloomsbury.com and sign up for our newsletters

To Ben, Gwen and Henry

CONTENTS

Map viii
Prologue xi

1 Ben, Barbara and Winifred 1
2 Back at the Mall Studios 23
3 Molly, Jack and Wells 51
4 Gropius, Moholy-Nagy and Breuer 83
5 Herbert and Ludo at the Mall Studios 117
6 The Rise of Surrealism and the Fall of Unit One 135
7 The Moores in Parkhill Road 159
8 *Axis* and *Circle*: From Belsize Park to Fawley Bottom 177
9 MacNeice, the Coldstreams and Auden: Keats Grove and Upper Park Road 199
10 Mondrian and Calder: Parkhill Road 217

Epilogue 233
Acknowledgements 249
Illustration credits 251
Selected Bibliography 255
Notes 259
Index 285

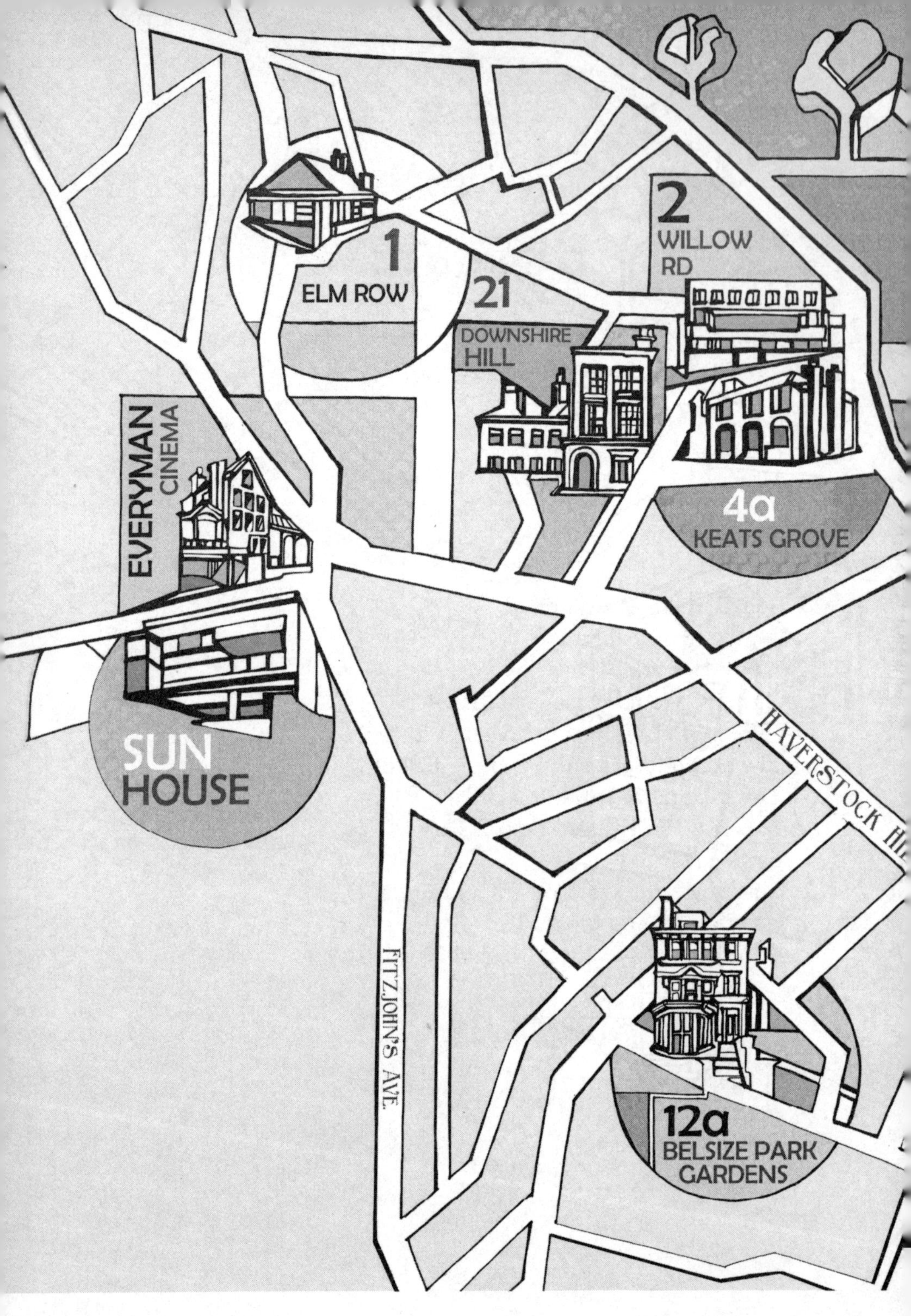
1
ELM ROW
2
WILLOW
RD
21
DOWNSHIRE
HILL
EVERYMAN
CINEMA
4a
KEATS GROVE
SUN
HOUSE
HAVERSTOCK HI
FITZJOHN'S AVE.
12a
BELSIZE PARK
GARDENS

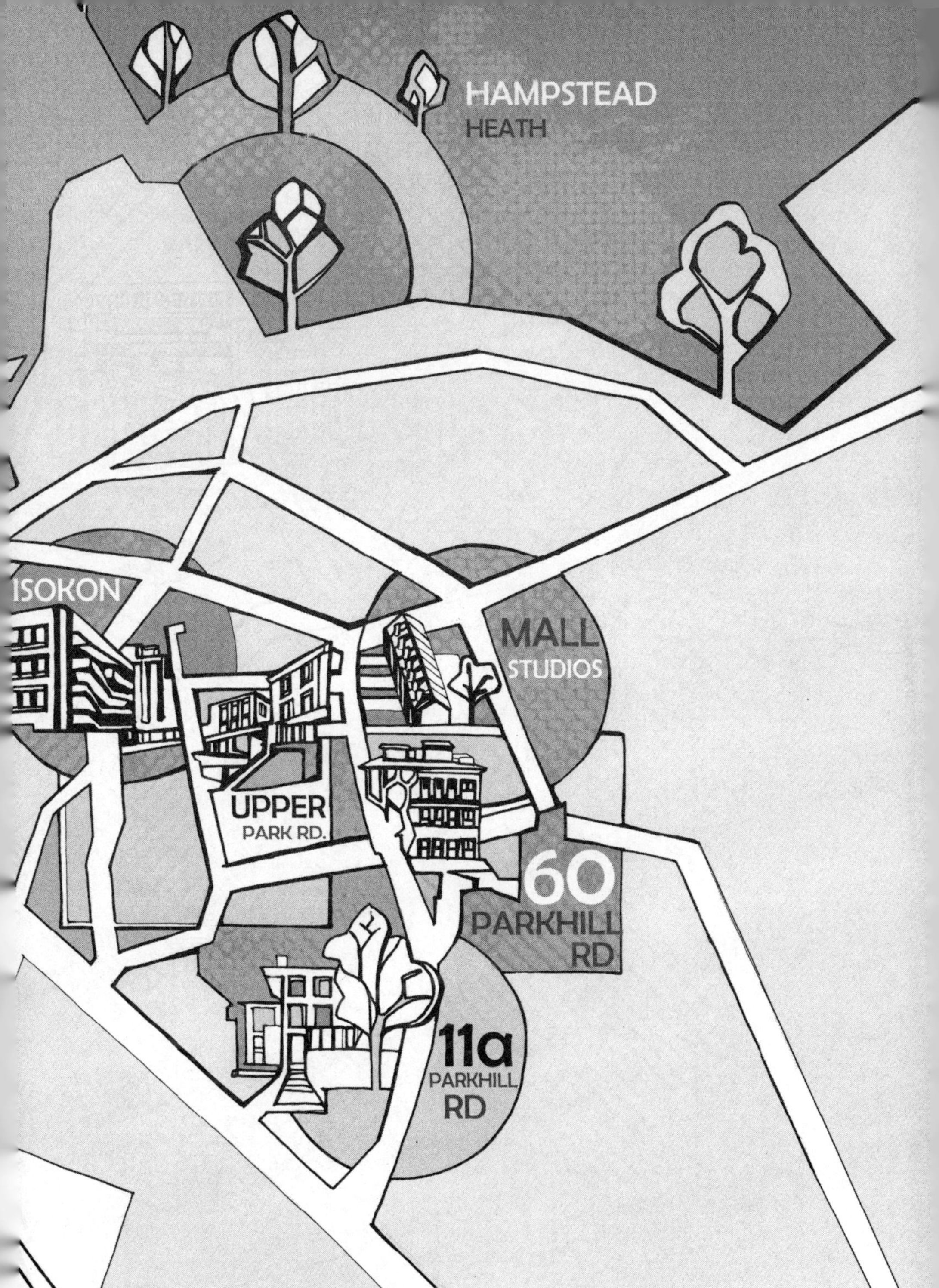
HAMPSTEAD
HEATH
ISOKON
MALL
STUDIOS
UPPER
PARK RD.
60
PARKHILL
RD
11a
PARKHILL
RD

PROLOGUE

'Your dear head is like the most lovely pebble ever seen'

On 12 September 1931 Ben Nicholson made his way from Cumberland to Happisburgh, a small village on the north-east coast of Norfolk.[1] He was joining Barbara Hepworth and a few of her friends for a two-week holiday in a farmhouse by the sea. His wife Winifred stayed at home with their new baby and two small children. Barbara had sent him a last-minute invitation and a photo of the house. The beach, she told him, was a 'ribbon of pale sand as far as the eye can see' and the land was flat but for a 'little hill with a tall flint Church & a lighthouse'. The trees were all 'bowed to the West', the birds 'dominate all' and she felt she had 'wings on such flat earth'. The Moores, she added, would be so pleased if he could come.[2] Ben didn't need much persuasion. Barbara was delighted and sent him details of trains and buses; then as an afterthought she wondered 'what you eat!! You must advise me when you arrive.'[3]

Once he had arrived in Norwich he followed Barbara's instructions and took the local train to North Walsham where he was picked up by one of her friends, Douglas Jenkins, the only one with a car. Ben was rather 'an eyeful' in his light-blue linen cap, light-blue linen jacket, rather crumpled trousers and sandals.[4] The North Walsham road is flanked by fields and the sky and sea fill the rest. Church Farmhouse is to the north of the village on Blacksmiths Lane, a long thatched brick building with large windows looking out to sea.

Ben was living with his wife, the artist Winifred Nicholson, in Bankshead, a stone farmhouse in Cumberland, and she had just given birth to their third child, Andrew, that July. With three small children, Kate aged two, Jake aged four and Andrew a few weeks old, both Ben and Winifred had been finding it difficult to get much work done. So when the invitation came to spend some time working alongside their new friends from London, Winifred generously agreed that he could join them. Ben and Winifred had met Barbara and her husband the sculptor Jack Skeaping earlier that year and they admired both their energy and their work.

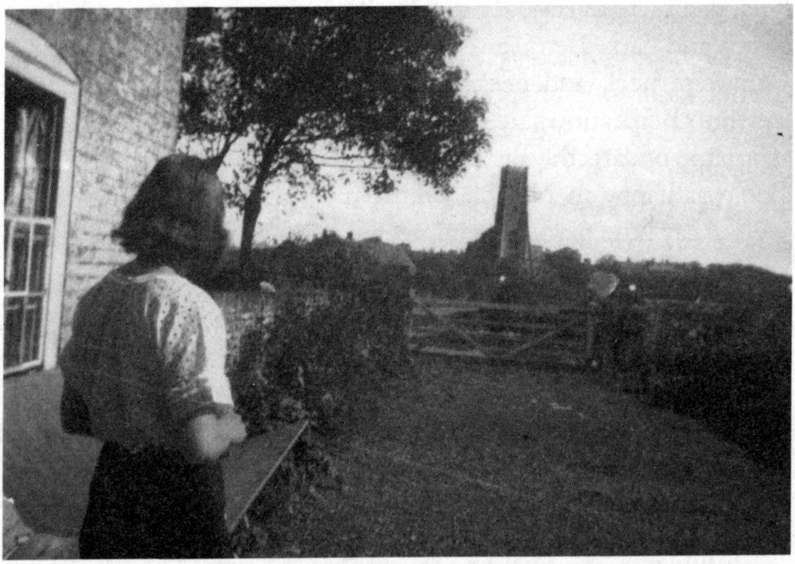

Barbara in Happisburgh, Norfolk, 1931

For the first week, Barbara's husband Jack stayed in London. The farmhouse was occupied by Ben, Barbara, her two-year-old son Paul, Harry (Henry) and Irina Moore, the artist Ivon Hitchens, Barbara's friend Douglas Jenkins and his fiancé Mary Stannard. The weather was fine, and Barbara remembered that she and Henry carved while her son Paul played on the beach.[5] Ben recalled that 'we all took our clothes off and played cricket and other games on the sand.' The only person not at ease with unclad cricket was Ivon Hitchens, who insisted on remaining 'in all his jerseys, coats and a hat'. The 'funny thing was', remembered

Ben, 'I think he was the only person who was embarrassed.'[6] The letters and photos show them playing games, bathing, collecting stones and dancing to records as well as working. Barbara wrote that we 'talked and walked, we bathed and played cricket, then we worked and danced'.[7]

One of Moore's favourite games was to sing along to a record featuring songs without lyrics, and to try and join in at the right moment, much to everyone's amusement. And on rainy days they held games tournaments involving shove ha'penny, quoits, table tennis and darts. Ben was extremely competitive, and Douglas and Ben were neck and neck one evening after a series of matches, much to Ben's annoyance. But then when Douglas finally beat him in a game of darts the air was cleared and they became firm friends.[8] Ben was happy in Norfolk and told his mother-in-law that they were a 'gay little party'. He compared them to the 'free and creative' artists in Paris, telling Winifred that they were 'alive & vital – you know like we thought of Derain & Picasso in Paris, with the same imagination & power & purpose'.[9]

For two weeks they led a carefree existence, but there was also a more significant relationship evolving. Ben had 'never seen anything so beautiful' as the look on Barbara's face while she was carving, and Ben's head, Barbara thought, was like the most 'lovely pebble ever seen', worn clean like the stones left by the sea. Barbara believed that 'if a pebble or an egg can be enjoyed for the sake of its shape only, it is one step towards a true appreciation of sculpture.'[10] Her feelings for stone, sculpture and Ben were intertwined. Ben took a series of tasteful photographs of her naked back during the holiday. In some she is sitting on the beach and in others she is sitting on a bed in the farmhouse with the light catching her side like Ingres' *Valpinçon Bather*. By the time Jack arrived during the second week Barbara and Ben had fallen in love and so Jack went back to London.

After two weeks of bathing and working, talking and dancing, Ben went back to Winifred and the children in Bankshead, leaving the rest of the group at the farmhouse. He wrote from the train on his way home so that his love would reach Barbara by the morning, promising to think of her 'lots tonight' and encouraging her to

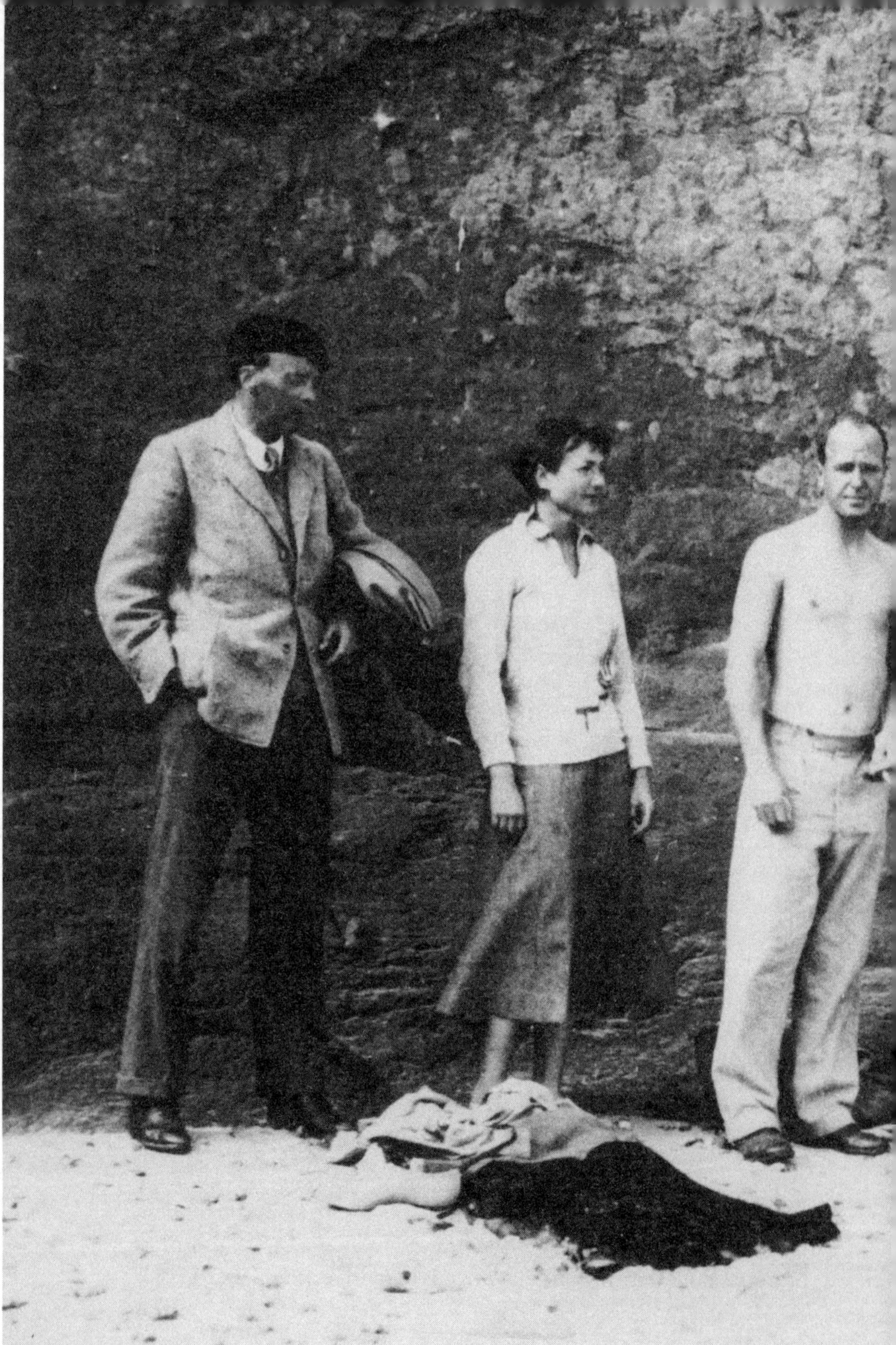

On the beach at Happisburgh: Ivon Hitchens, Irina Moore, Henry Moore, Barbara Hepworth, Ben Nicholson and Mary Jenkins (originally Stannard)

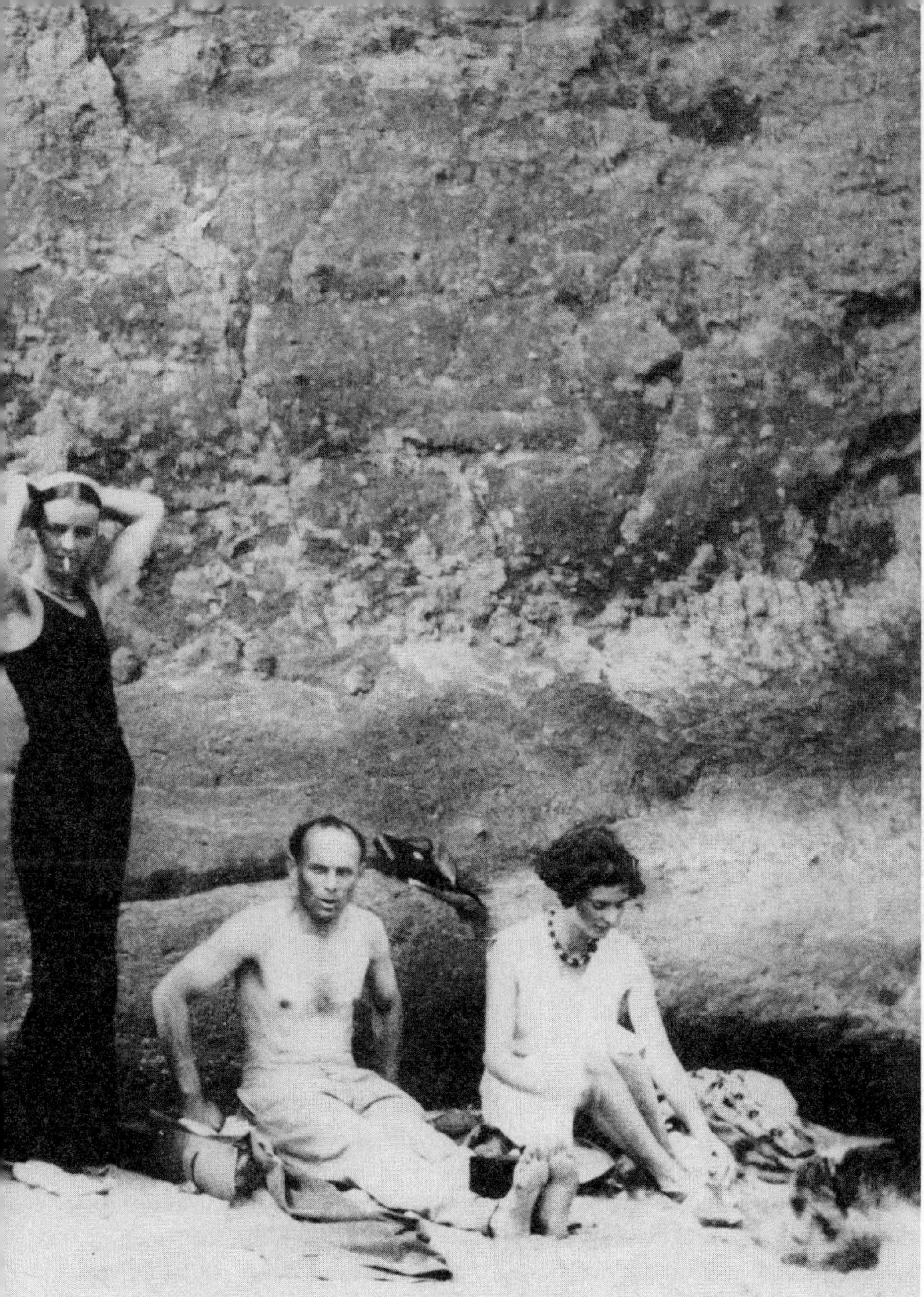

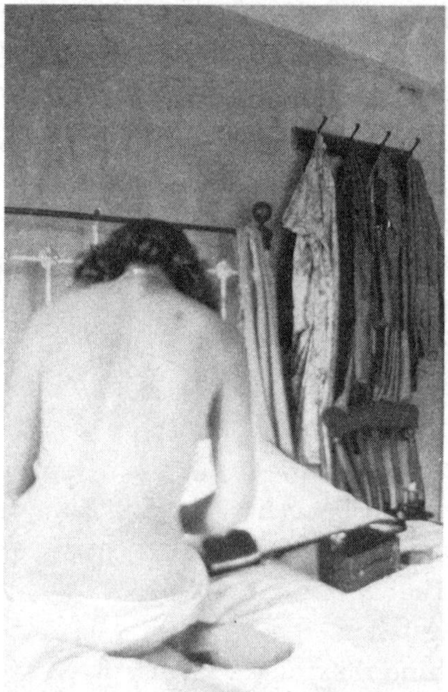

Barbara in the farmhouse, by Ben

have a 'gay happy sleep & all tomorrow – to work at your carving'. Barbara was miserable after Ben left and couldn't help crying. Paul, aged two, had never seen her cry before and it made him laugh. Everything seemed a little unreal to Barbara in Ben's absence; there were 'fairy clouds scudding across the sky', but the horses still came to drink from the pond and they had some 'fine games along with the tears'. She cheered herself up by putting 'Lady in Spain' on the gramophone and dancing with Paul.

During the two weeks Ben and Barbara had discussed new ideas for their work and Barbara felt that something 'very big' would emerge from their plans. Their work, she thought, was associated with 'infinity' and she had 'never felt anything like it before'. When she got the letter Ben had written on the train she wrote back straight away: 'dear I must write just once to tell you how I love you – if you think not I never will again.' In case this was the only chance she got, she wrote that she loved him just as she loved the leaves on the trees and that all 'that has happened is for ever & ever, & always'. She added that he must be so happy to be home because he loved Winifred and the babies so much. Ben replied swiftly that he loved her very much, he loved everything about her, including the new sense of time she had given him. They were fascinated by the perception of time through art. In his contribution to the exhibition catalogue for Unit One, a group of eleven artists, sculptors and architects who several years later stood for a 'truly contemporary spirit', Ben described his search for 'an idea which is complete, with no beginning and no end and therefore giving to all things for all time'.[11] But in the autumn of 1931, once their feelings were out in the open, Ben and Barbara's letters became more poised and they began to paint pictures for each other in words.

Barbara told Ben about a moonlit walk when a boat came in very close, going fast in the wind on a 'heavy green sea' and a lovely moon behind the church that changed from 'a pale silvery to a curious dull red'.[12] Barbara liked to go for an early morning bathe and on one of her final mornings she found a stone 'grey like a sea bird' that she packed carefully among her clothes. She saw a vision of a farm worker in a blue smock outlined against the grey sky, taking a bull into the field, and this inspired her to go into Happisburgh and buy a blue smock for Ben.[13] He was extremely pleased with it. They were getting ready to go back to London and Barbara and Harry packed up four crates of Norfolk stone to take with them. By the end of the Norfolk trip Barbara was longing to be in her studio and do some work because of all the 'lovely things' that had happened.[14]

1
BEN, BARBARA AND WINIFRED

'something momentous has happened'

William Nicholson tried to dissuade his son from following in his footsteps and becoming a painter. As a young man, Ben wanted to be a poet and his father suggested he do both, like Blake. But growing up with parents who painted (although his mother Mabel gave up to look after the family), and in a household full of 'lovely spotted mugs & striped jugs & glass objects', Ben chose art. He went to the Slade in 1910, where he became friends with Paul Nash, but left after a year, having spent most of his time playing billiards at the Gower Hotel. Not until he travelled around Europe in 1912–14 did he begin painting in earnest. He sent home some of these early experiments. His father paid the 80-franc postage but didn't know what to say about them. Firmly rooted in the realist tradition, William was 'frightened' by his son's pictures. They were abnormal and seemed to be 'the work of an untrained eye, both in colour and form'. If you want to be a 'great Painter', his father urged, you must '*Draw draw* – only *draw*.'[1]

Ben first met Winifred Roberts at her aunt's house in Boar's Hill, Oxfordshire, in the summer of 1920. Winifred was the eldest daughter of the Liberal politician Charles Henry Roberts and Lady Cecilia Maude Howard, daughter of John Howard, the 9th Earl of Carlisle. Hearing Ben before she saw him, Winifred 'knew in an instant that this was the person I would be marrying – and so it turned out'. That August Winifred sent Ben a book on Gauguin, visited him in his Chelsea studio and invited him on a family holiday to Cornwall and Devon where they went sketching together. Winifred remembered drawing 'in pencil sitting by the side of the road'.[2] Within a few months they were engaged. They got married at St Martin-in-the-Fields in November 1920, Ben in tails and Winifred, as she put it, in a 'long dark brown woollen dress chosen by him, like a monk, without any ornament' and holding a bunch of dark red roses tied with a dark blue ribbon that she remembered not liking very much.[3] Winifred's grandmother, the Countess of Carlisle, supported them with a generous allowance of £500 a year.

For their honeymoon they visited Venice, Florence, Rome, Naples, Amalfi, Pisa, Portofino, Rapallo and Genoa and then they settled in a house above Lake Lugano in Switzerland in late December. Winifred's father had bought the Villa Capriccio, which they rented back from him and eventually bought themselves. The house had two studios, enough bedrooms for five people, two sitting rooms, a kitchen and a bathroom. They hung photographs of Gauguin and Rousseau's works on the wall, as well as photographs of the family, including one of Ben's mother Mabel. She had died from the flu epidemic in 1918 while Ben was in America. Ben had been very close to his mother and as they said goodbye, for what would turn out to be the last time, she gave him a note that read: 'Goodbye my darling boy, I will miss you more than you would ever believe possible. You are one of the great successes of my life, and have only been a source of continuous pleasure to me always.'[4]

Winifred believed that she was unable to have children because she had been told after a childhood operation that 'all that made it possible' had been cut and when she told Ben he did not seem to mind. Their time in Lugano was productive, Ben wrote to a friend: 'O Lord, have we worked – yes we have.' The darkest room in Lugano was painted blue and turned into Ben's studio. They had sitters come to the house, or they rode their bicycles (bought for them by Winifred's parents) for 'long speditions' into the countryside, as Ben called them, and painted all day. The country was good to paint, Winifred said, with 'austere mountains

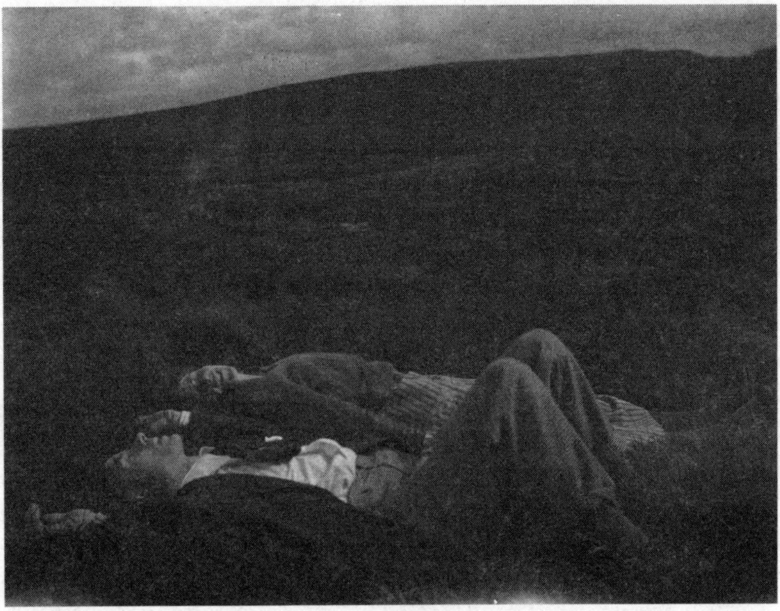

Ben and Winifred Nicholson, Westmorland, early 1920s

and patterned vineyards, terraced down the hillside with knobbly willow trees and funny fig trees and springing fruit trees'.[5] They made trips to Como and Milan where they saw contemporary Italian art including de Chirico, Savinio, Carrà and Morandi. And they acquired a dog they called Nipper, who mostly followed Ben and Winifred's vegetarian diet of soup.[6]

They spent their summers in London and Cumberland and on their way between England and Italy they often stopped in Paris, which Winifred found 'electric with renovation – at every turn there was a genius and transformation. Its creative energy was not to be believed, so we always went back to Villa Capriccio and brooded on our ideas.'[7] Ben was very taken with a Picasso with a particular shade of green, and he liked Derain and Matisse but he thought the rest had lost the 'pt of painting' and were modern but 'dated, local. It is all froth.' Winifred claimed that they had done more painting since being in Italy than they had ever done before: 'Ben has done 14 oils and some drawings. One or two of them have got some funny new things in them, leading to new developments. We do absolutely nothing but paint all day, eat supper and tea at 6.30 wash brushes and prepare canvases, go to bed and dream painting. Sometimes we go for a walk to look for new painty things.'[8] They had 'cobalt green with our coffee for breakfast' and 'rose madder for supper', she told her friend.[9] Steffy, their maid, was taught to treat their studio as 'sacred & unapproachable', but she helped wash their brushes at the end of each day, which was a 'great saving of energy'.[10] In the winter of 1923 Ben gave Winifred a pot of lilies of the valley in tissue paper that she placed on the window sill. Behind it she saw 'azure blue, Mountain, Lake, Sky, all there – and the tissue paper held the secret of the universe. The picture painted itself.' Winifred painted with more freedom and spontaneity in Lugano, even using her fingers to paint *Window-Sill, Lugano* as her brushes had been packed up. Ben later destroyed most of the work he had produced in this period.

By the end of 1922 Ben and Winifred had begun to have enough of Lugano. They wanted to be in London, they wanted to play tennis, to 'bang a bouncy ball' and to go dancing, and

Ben wanted new brightly coloured clothes. They were also both becoming more interested in cubism. Winifred painted a mandolin, and said, 'you can't have an abstraction without a mandolin'. Ben thought it was so damn good he scrubbed out his own work.[11] The villa was also proving expensive to run, Ben wanted to 'live simpler' and they were concerned by the rise of fascism in Italy and the restrictions on travel.[12] Their time in Switzerland had been formative for both of them. Winifred believed the landscape had freed Ben; the mountains and the sky had given him, she said, a 'balance of space', whereas she had been given a 'sense of rainbow' from the 'golden light of the sun'.[13] Their sense of joy did not stay with them on their return to England. Winifred became increasingly despondent about not having children, and they discussed the possibility of adoption if their first exhibition went well. It was held in Paterson's Gallery in May 1923. All of Winifred's paintings sold but none of Ben's did. They did not pursue adoption, and in 1923 they bought the grey stone farmhouse called Bankshead in Cumberland, overlooking Irthing Valley to the south and close to Winifred's parents' house, Boothby. They enlarged the windows for more light, turned the barn into a studio for Ben and moved in the following year, in 1924. There was no electricity or running water; instead they had a well and pump outside. Winifred loved cooking at her 'altar', the open hearth. Even though he hadn't sold anything at the exhibition with Winifred, Ben was slowly becoming better known. He had a one-man show in March 1924 and the *Daily Mail* claimed that his father must be horrified by his son's 'experimenting' with 'irregular geometric shapes … here and there decorated with round spots'.[14] But a bad review in the *Mail* did not deter Ivon Hitchens from inviting Ben to join the Seven and Five Society, a group which had been set up in 1919 and originally included seven painters and five sculptors. By February 1926 Ben had become chairman and changed the rules to get rid of 'the duds', and to bring in Winifred and his father's second wife, Edie Nicholson, with whom he had been in love many years before.

A less well-known influence on the lives and art of Ben and Winifred during this period was their belief in Christian Science, based on Mary Baker Eddy's *Science and Health with Key to the Scriptures* (1875). Ben had first come across it in the States and he had even recommended it to his mother when she wrote to tell him she had caught the flu. Christian Science had evolved in New England in the late nineteenth century, and had become increasingly popular on both sides of the Atlantic. The central belief was in the primacy of the spiritual as opposed to the material world, and the idea that illness was an illusion that could be cured through common prayer. Winifred's friend Margaret 'Bunty' Nash (married to the war artist and surrealist Paul Nash) was an enthusiastic supporter and she encouraged Winifred to explore it. Margaret also supported the suffragette movement, had been part of the Women's Tax Resistance League and was a founder of the Committee for Social Investigation and Reform, to help house prostitutes from urban areas.[15]

The Nicholsons had spent time with the Nashes in Dymchurch in Kent in 1923, and then again in Cumberland in 1924. Ben knew Paul from his year at the Slade. The Nashes' marriage was becoming increasingly strained in the early 1920s. Paul had been an official war artist in 1917–18 and he suffered a breakdown in 1921. Margaret had severe anxiety and Christian Science helped her. It made a distinction between the 'mortal mind' and the 'divine Mind' and one of its main tenets was the attempt to rise above corporeal desires as well as corporeal sickness and ill health. The move away from the physical body anticipated the move away from the figurative and the eventual shift towards abstraction in Ben's work. Christian Scientists also believed that it was wrong to have negative feelings and thoughts towards those you love, something that became increasingly difficult for Ben, Barbara and Winifred in the 1930s.

After many years of believing that she could not conceive, Winifred became pregnant towards the end of 1926. Her doctor described it as a miracle and Winifred believed it was because of her new faith in Christian Science.[16] Margaret Nash had suffered a miscarriage at the end of 1924 and asked Winifred to pray for her, which she did, reading repeatedly the passage from St Mark's Gospel, 'Suffer little children to come unto me, and forbid them not,' and Winifred believed this was, in part, responsible for her pregnancy. And then when she was seven months pregnant, she experienced another miracle. While arranging a joint exhibition of her work at the Beaux Arts Gallery she fell through an open trap door on to a concrete floor in the basement below. The doctors said that she had broken her back and might not survive the night, and so Ben was allowed to sleep in the ward with her. He sat beside her in St George's Hospital reading the 23rd Psalm. After five days in hospital she was well enough to go home and a month later, on 16 June 1927, she gave birth to their first child, Jake. Although her recovery was extraordinary, Winifred never fully recovered her posture after the fall. After seeing the exhibition at the Beaux Arts Gallery Helen Sutherland wrote to Winifred that it was a 'beautiful show' and that the new paintings had 'a lovely thing in them, a new mystery and gaiety combined – earthly and unearthly'.[17]

In the mid-1920s Ben and Winifred split their time between Bankshead and Chelsea before moving to Dulwich in 1927. They weren't always in the same place at the same time, and Ben was sometimes in London while Winifred was in Bankshead. She told him that even if her days were lonely, her nights were very lovely, as that was the time they spent together in her dreams. Ben told her he could enjoy 'the King's Rd & its cinemas & buses' knowing she was not there 'regretting every moment'.[18] Ben painted *1924 (first abstract painting, Chelsea)* in the studio at 97 King's Road. It clearly echoed Winifred's colour palette and her ideas about colour forming structure. It was also a period in which they spent time with the artist Christopher 'Kit' Wood. Born in Knowsley, near Liverpool, Kit had trained at the Académie Julian in Paris in the early 1920s and knew Cocteau, Picasso and Diaghilev. He was introduced to Ben and Winifred by the artist Cedric Morris in 1926 and when they first saw his work in his studio flat in Chelsea Winifred was delighted, calling him 'England's first painter'. His vision, she said, 'is true, his grasp real, his power is life itself'. Kit's work was deceptively simple; he liked to create the impression that he got there by accident. Cocteau explained that you don't *think*, but *live*, in front of Kit's canvases, just as you might walk down a street, or smell a bunch of flowers. Ben wasted no time asking Kit to became a member of the Seven and Five Society and he enjoyed spending time with the 'Nickies', both in Cumberland and in Cornwall during the summer of 1928. Ben and Kit shared a passion for what they felt was 'true' art that depicted the world through innocent eyes rather than those of a trained artist. Their delight, then, is no surprise, on stumbling across the work of Alfred Wallis on a day trip to St Ives from Feock where Ben, Winifred, Jake and Kit were staying. Ben and Kit simply walked past the open door of his tiny cottage on Back Road West, a cobbled street set back from St Ives harbour, and saw, nailed to the walls, pieces of wood of various sizes painted with ships and boats and strings of cottages, all at jaunty angles. The largest nails held up the smallest paintings. Wallis used household and boat paint, which meant his palette consisted of 'lovely dark browns, shiny blacks, fierce greys, strange white and a particularly pungent Cornish green'.[19] And he painted on anything he could find: cardboard, old wooden boxes, the walls of his house and the furniture. The naivety of his work captivated Ben and Kit. They introduced themselves and thus began a friendship and patronage between Ben and Alfred Wallis that lasted many years. Ben included Wallis in the March 1929 Seven and Five Society exhibition to show true art to the contemporary art world.

After the birth of their second child, Kate, in July 1929, Ben and Winifred moved back up to Cumberland. Although Ben was getting some painting done, he was growing tired of the constant needs of young children and was desperate for some uninterrupted time for his work.[20] In May 1930 Kit offered to include Ben in an exhibition in Paris, but this only heightened his mounting desperation: Kit sold twelve paintings and Ben didn't sell any. Ben was reaching a crisis point. He and Kit argued, not just over the exhibition, but because Winifred and Ben were distressed to witness

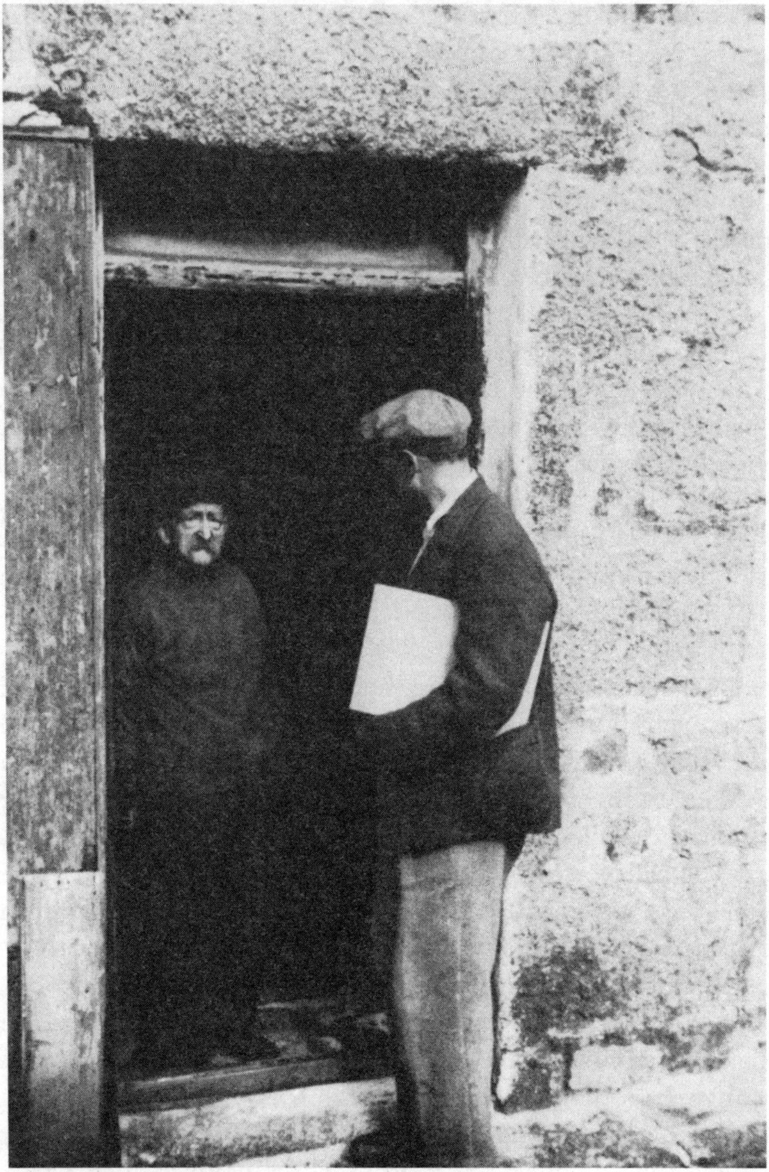

Alfred Wallis standing in his doorway in St Ives with Ben

Kit's opium-fuelled existence in Paris. They tried to persuade him and his friends to convert to Christian Science, but that did not go down well. Kit wrote to his mother that his life was 'unlivable, so the Nicholsons think. I think the same of theirs.'[21] Ben and Winifred were completely unprepared, however, for the news later that summer that twenty-nine-year-old Kit had committed suicide at Salisbury railway station on 21 August. They were so shocked that, together with Jim Ede, Assistant at the Tate Gallery they commissioned a private detective to investigate. The report was inconclusive. It gave details of Kit's final hours travelling from Paris to Southampton and then to a hotel on the Isle of Wight. Having stayed out all night Kit asked for several whisky and sodas at the hotel bar and the waiter found a six-chamber revolver in his overcoat pocket when he hung it up. Kit took a boat and then a train to get to Salisbury where he had lunch with his mother and sister before jumping in front of a train at 2.10 p.m. The jury at the inquest delivered a verdict of suicide while of unsound mind. Ben and Winifred had not realised the full scale of Kit's addiction and the sharp deterioration of his mental state. They spent the following months promoting Kit's work. Ben discussed the possibility of putting on an exhibition with Kit's mother and he asked Jim Ede to write a biography of Kit, although it never materialised. Ben felt that he could have parted with 'almost anyone but him' but that Kit had been freed from his 'frightful struggle'.[22] Winifred wrote to Wood's partner Frosca Munter after his death about the 'zest and vitality' of the friendship between Ben and Kit and how 'wonderful pictures turned up, all out of nowhere. The vision in them true and alive, and always daring further ahead with highest courage.'[23] Kit Wood and Alfred Wallis were extremely significant influences on Ben and Winifred in the 1920s, but more important was the role they played in each other's work. As well as freeing up Ben's use of colour and light, Winifred combined the 'poetry of life' with the 'touch of reality'.[24]

In April 1931, Ben's fortune changed. He was included in an exhibition at the Bloomsbury Gallery with the potter William Staite Murray and a young sculptor called Barbara Hepworth.

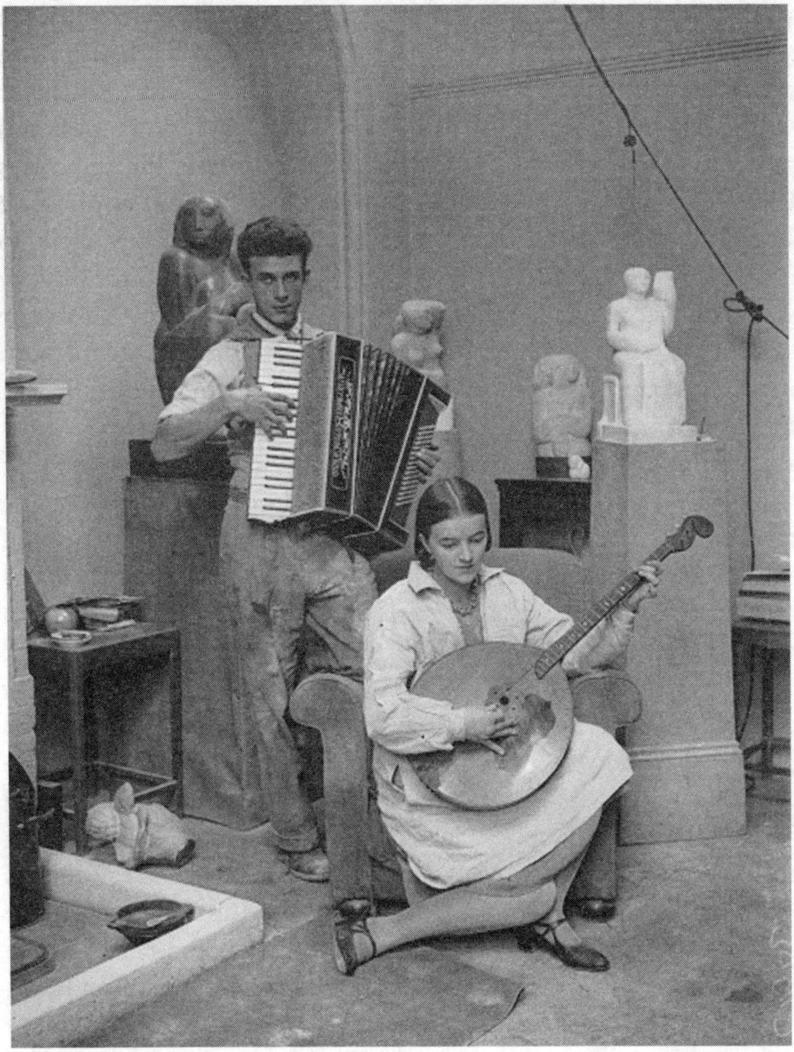

Jack and Barbara playing musical instruments

□

Jack Skeaping and Barbara Hepworth appeared happy; they were stylish, young and successful. They had both been top students at their art schools, Barbara at Leeds and then the Royal College of Art, and Jack at the Royal Academy. They were both in the final four for the prestigious Prix de Rome scholarship, to study in Italy for three years. Although Jack won the scholarship, Barbara got herself the West Riding scholarship so that she could go to Italy anyway. The competition task was to create a bas-relief to be placed above the main entrance of a hospital. It had to be modelled in clay and suitable for casting in bronze. Hepworth decided to play it safe with a traditional composition to please the judges. However, the result was static and 'stony' and difficult to imagine in bronze.[25] She grew increasingly disillusioned as she was working on it and wanted to smash it and withdraw from the competition. When she lost she went to see some friends and said 'God – give me a drink, will you? Something strong. And a fag.'[26] She hadn't met Jack Skeaping yet, but Harry Moore had told her that he was 'quite fascinating' and she expected they'd meet 'some day'. And then she asked for another whisky.

It is possible that Barbara first met Jack in London before she went to Italy. She had certainly heard that he was tall, dark and handsome and that he loved to dance. If they did not meet in London they definitely met in Rome. After two months of living alone, aged twenty-one, Barbara wrote to her old friend Harry, saying she was lonely. And so Moore arranged for her to meet Skeaping, who had just recovered from appendicitis. They met at the railway station and Jack believed it 'was inevitable that we should fall deeply in love'. Barbara dressed in old-fashioned smocks and parted her hair exactly down the middle, and had a long coat with astrakhan collar and cuffs, and a pillbox hat. Jack took Barbara to his favourite places including Siena, Volterra and San Gimignano, and he spent more time looking at her than at the art. The light seized Barbara after three years of London smog and, although she didn't get around to producing any sculpture, what she saw sustained her for many years.[27] About a year after they met, they married in the old Palazzo Vecchio in Florence on 13 May 1925, with a couple of students from the British School in Rome as guests.

They returned to London in the autumn of 1926 leaving their monkey Pipi and many sculptures behind. Barbara had carved her first piece from life, *Dove*, and Jack had carved a head of Barbara, which he believed was one of his best works. In London they lived in a studio in Chalk Farm, until Barbara's friend Leo Walmsley offered them his basement flat in St John's Wood to rent. It was a terraced house, not far from Acacia Road, with four storeys, and the basement had been built out into the garden with skylights. Barbara and Jack used this as their studio

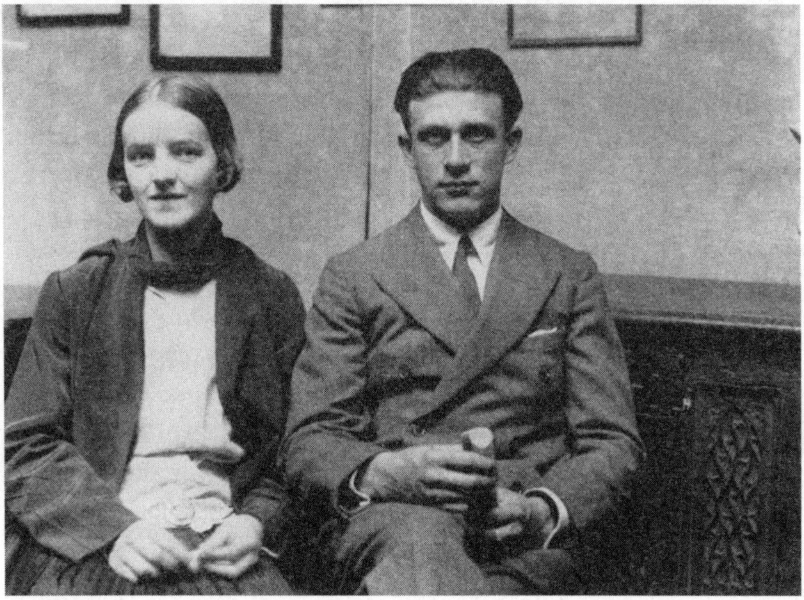

Barbara and Jack in 1928

and built an aviary along one wall, filling it with budgerigars, canaries, Java sparrows, lovebirds and doves. The birdseed spilled out and attracted mice, which became quite tame.[28] Barbara was pleased with her almost abstract, bill-less and featherless doves from this period.

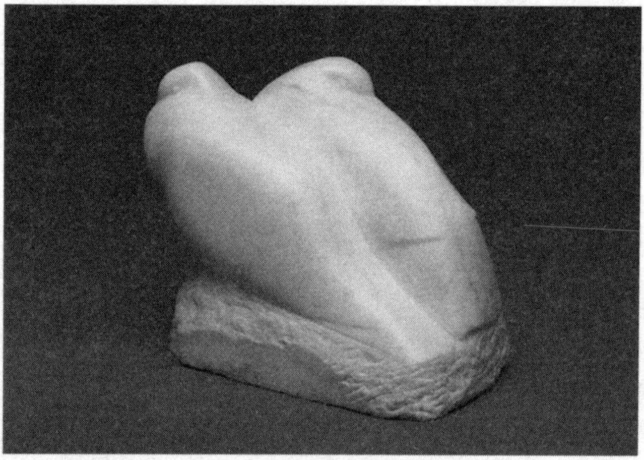

Barbara Hepworth, Doves, *1927*

Barbara and Jack held a joint exhibition in their basement studio (in order to avoid a gallery fee), for which Barbara wore her 'most exotic frock'. The Greek collector George Eumorfopoulos stayed for a long time and bought sculptures by both of them including *Seated Figure* (1927) from Barbara. After the visit she went 'bounding up the basement stairs' to tell their friends, and Jack went to buy a bottle of wine so they could celebrate. Altogether Eumorfopoulos had paid 'hundreds of pounds'. Jack bought an aquarium and some Japanese goldfish and they acquired marble and wood; Jack planned to create a life-size racehorse. By September 1928, the Beaux Arts and the Lefevre Gallery in London were showing pieces by Hepworth and Skeaping. Not long afterwards, Barbara and Jack found a studio to rent in Belsize Park. Through a wooden gate and down a muddy overgrown path, just off Church Road (now Tasker Road), they lived at 7 Mall Studios, at the end of the row, with a little more space and privacy than the other studios. The twenty-foot-high window was a welcome relief after the basement flat in St John's Wood.

The Mall Studios in Belsize Park were originally built for gentleman artists living in Parkhill Road. Designed by Thomas Batterbury and described as 'avant garde' in a contemporary journal, they included small waiting rooms, costume rooms, a lobby and 'other necessary conveniences'. They had three skylights each and large north-facing windows for consistency of light throughout the day. The roofs were varnished 'open timber', covered in red tiles, and the chimney pots bore the 'monograms of the respective owners'. The shelves and moulded corbels were carved from Portland stone and the dados, or lower parts of the wall, were originally painted different colours from the higher parts to offer a background to pictures.[29] Artists, including George Clausen who lived there in the late nineteenth century, could walk across their gardens to their studios after breakfast.

Hampstead and the surrounding area has attracted artists, writers and intellectuals since the early eighteenth century.

Shelley, Byron, Keats, Reynolds and Constable all delighted in its rural peace, the rugged beauty of the heath, only three miles north of the city. Constable was pleased to be able to avoid 'idle callers' but still 'get a message in an hour'. Gainsborough called the Bull and Bush (on North End Way) a 'delightful little snuggery'. Ford Madox Brown painted his canvases of Victorian life, *Work* and *Autumn Afternoon*, on the Mount, Heath Street.[30] By the 1880s the census and directories show that Belsize Park was inhabited by a mix of tradesmen, merchants and professionals, but also architects and authors. Belsize Park was an area of 'above-average prosperity, but the mixture is not untypical'.[31] In 1900 the parish of Hampstead became a metropolitan borough covering Belsize Park, Primrose Hill, West Hampstead, South Hampstead and most of Hampstead Heath. It included parts of Kilburn and Cricklewood too.[32]

In the early twentieth century Henry Lamb lived on the top floor of the Vale Hotel and not long afterwards Stanley Spencer

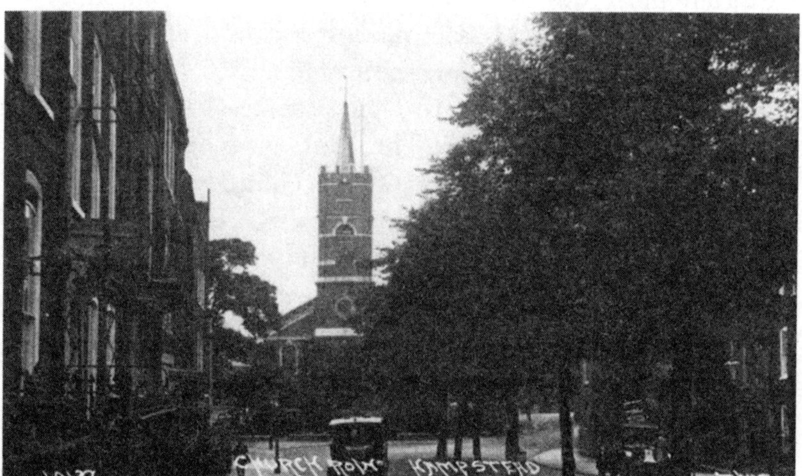

Church Avenue, Hampstead

took over his rooms and painted *Resurrection* there in 1924. Mark Gertler moved to a studio in New End, Hampstead, in 1915 and painted *Merry-Go-Round* the following year. D. H. Lawrence lived in Byron Villas in the Vale of Health in 1915 and Katherine Mansfield and Middleton Murry moved to 17 East Heath Road in 1918. With the economic decline in the 1920s and the carving up of larger houses into flats and lodgings, more artists, writers and European émigrés could afford to live there: in London, but not quite of it. The poet and editor of *New Verse*, Geoffrey Grigson, moved to Keats Grove, and he remembered Hampstead in the 1930s as 'not an expensive place to live. It had its big houses for sure, its grand houses, but within easy distance of the tube station and the bus terminal plenty of Regency corners and little villa houses falling into shabbiness or decay and costing little to rent (or buy if you had the money).'[33]

With the economic downturn the Mall Studios were converted into combined living and working spaces. Barbara and Jack were not the first artists to move into the converted Studios. Cecil Stephenson moved into number 5 in 1919 and lived there until 1965. Stephenson studied at Leeds School of Art (as did Hepworth and Moore) and then the Royal College and the Slade. His early work was figurative but it became abstract in the 1930s, most likely due to his modernist neighbours. In 1938 Alexander Calder gave a performance of his wire circus in Stephenson's studio where the audience sat on crates, drank beer from a barrel and watched the little figures and animals perform circus tricks.

Despite their success Barbara and Jack found working alongside one another difficult. Barbara wanted to work with no interruptions, whereas Jack enjoyed breaking up his working day. Barbara told a friend later that 'I'm not fit to live with unless I can do some work – even an hour a day keeps me civilized.' She was relieved to be a sculptor and not a painter because 'in anger or despair' she could 'work off steam roughing out & swear

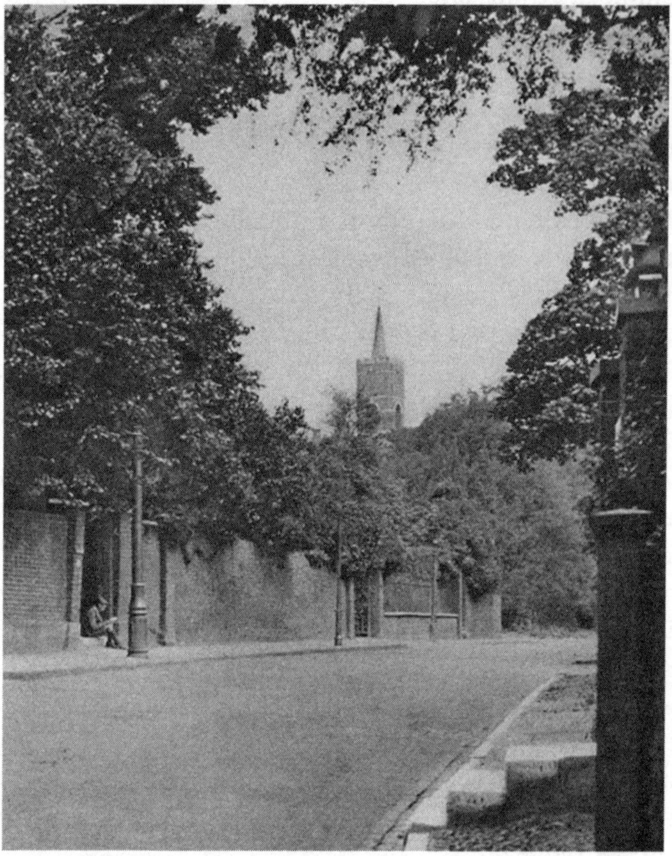

Frognal Lane, Hampstead

horribly sometimes'. The risk for painters, Barbara realised, was that they could take a rag dipped in some turpentine and 'swipe out all they've done' and that is a 'fearful shock'. Although her work was exhausting she felt that it was nourishing in a durable way unlike anything else.[34]

In order to get away from the studio, Jack began riding with the King's Battery of the Royal Horse Artillery in St John's Wood, where he met Eileen Friedlander, 'an attractive and sexy-looking character' as well as an accomplished horsewoman. He bought his own horse and Barbara complained that it 'used to breathe through my kitchen window!'[35] Jack avoided Eileen 'like the plague', convinced that his marriage would 'collapse like a pack of cards'. But then he agreed to go on a weekend riding trip to the garrison town of Tidworth in Wiltshire, which was a '"fly" opener' for him. After the trip Barbara caught them together one afternoon in the studio and Eileen leapt, half dressed, out of the back door and over the fence into the monastery next door. A monk who was reading his breviary on a bench below carried on reading while she dressed (so the story goes) and then showed her the way out.[36] Barbara claimed that there was no ill feeling between them, she just didn't see what was happening right in front of her and quite suddenly they were 'out of orbit'. Barbara said Jack was always kind to her and they remained friends.[37]

Despite this smooth account, these early years of their marriage were not easy. After the birth of their son Paul in August 1929 things did not improve. Jack confronted Barbara because he believed she had been having an affair with one of their friends in response to his infidelity. In Moore's account, he and Barbara had had a 'little flirtation' at Leeds but the only clue Jack gave was that the person was not an artist.[38] Barbara carried on working when Paul was a baby. She carved *Infant* in Burmese wood when he was a few months old. The polished plump legs and raised arms of the sculpture echo the form of the wood but also capture the vulnerability of a sleeping baby.

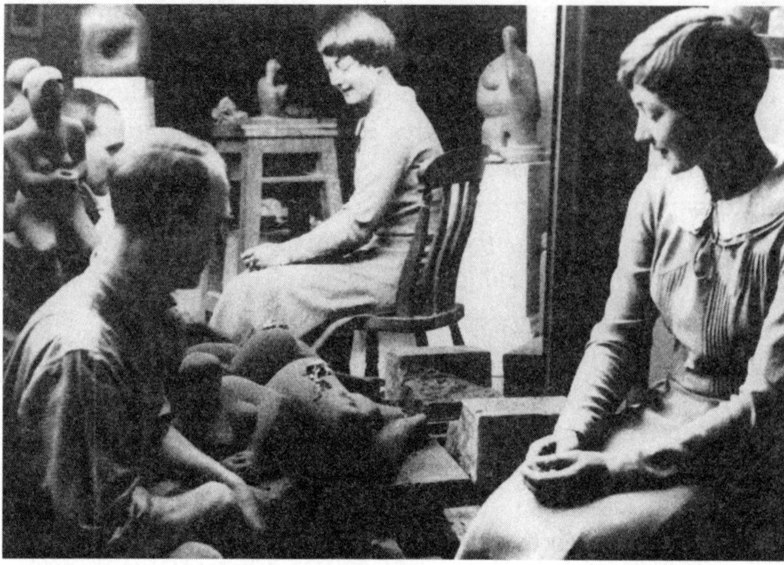

Henry and Irina Moore in the studio at IIa Parkhill Road, Hampstead

Barbara and Jack had found the Moores a place to live at 11a Parkhill Road, just around the corner from the Mall Studios. It was a ground-floor studio and bathroom with curved outdoor steps leading to a two-roomed flat above. Barbara, Jack, Henry and Irina spent a lot of time together in the late 1920s and the four of them would sometimes hire a model for an evening's drawing at Jack and Barbara's studio. Once the drawing was finished they opened a bottle of wine and played shove ha'penny, a game Henry was very good at.[39] In the summer of 1930, Moore suggested they all go to Happisburgh because he had become familiar with the area after his family had moved to Norfolk in 1922. So the two couples, with Jack and Barbara's one-year-old baby plus Ivon Hitchens, rented Church Farmhouse. It was such a success they decided to do it again the following year and Barbara invited Ben to join them. During the first trip Jack described how 'Henry, Barbara and I used to pick up large iron-stone pebbles from the beach which were ideal for carving and polished up like bronze'. When Henry and Jack went fishing,

Henry took a piece of 'iron-stone and rasp' and sat at one end of the boat 'filing away continuously' and checking his line occasionally to see if he had caught anything.[40] In the autumn of 1930 Barbara and Jack held an exhibition at Arthur Tooth & Sons Gallery and the *Sunday Times* called them brilliant young sculptors, praising their 'direct carving'. They exhibited forty-seven pieces in twenty-five materials, seven of them in Norfolk ironstone.

Their careers were taking off but their marriage was foundering, and this was the moment they met the Nicholsons. Although Barbara had seen Ben's work at his one-man show at the Lefevre Gallery, they were physically brought together by the show at the Bloomsbury Gallery in April 1931, where Ben and Barbara were both exhibiting. The two couples got on well, so well that Barbara felt that 'something momentous has happened' when they first met and told Ben she had experienced a 'feeling of Power'. The couples spent at least one evening at Barbara and Jack's studio in Belsize Park. The path to the studio was not that easy to find and from the outside it looked like a small cottage, but inside, the light from the double-height window flooded the room.

After that evening Ben lent them some of his pictures, and Barbara was delighted when she woke up and saw them 'looking marvellous' on their wall. She told Ben that they had affected her very deeply, even though she wasn't sure why she loved them so much. Barbara also introduced them to the Moores on Parkhill Road. It was a significant moment for Ben and Barbara to have met. Ben was suffering from a crisis with his work and Barbara was suffering from a crisis in her marriage. After one of their evenings together Barbara wrote to Ben to say how much she and Jack had enjoyed Ben and Winifred's visit and their talks, and to thank them for giving them a solution to a problem that had been worrying them for a long time. Although we do not know the solution, we do know that the problem was their marriage. If Ben and Winifred had not been in town during those weeks the 'horrible blank' Barbara felt would have been much worse.[41] She thanked Winifred separately for her help with the 'Jack problem', sent her some 'woollies' for the new baby and hoped she (Barbara) would now achieve some sort of 'poise and quiet again' instead of the nightmarish feeling of running after an express train.[42] Of course, the poise and quiet she was looking for were from Ben.

2

BACK AT THE MALL STUDIOS

'Barbara and I are the same'

The weeks following the Happisburgh holiday were not easy for Winifred back in Cumberland. It is hard to imagine how she coped with the new baby and two small children and being told by her husband that he had fallen in love with a successful sculptor ten years younger than her. And the rules of her faith meant that she was not supposed to hold any ill feelings towards those she loved. You must 'control evil thoughts', the Christian Science manual proclaimed, or 'they will control you'.[1] A few days after he got back home from Norfolk to Bankshead, Ben wrote to Barbara that Winifred had lost her clarity and that things were very difficult for her. Ben and Winifred had a 'Christian Science practitioner' called Mrs Ferguson whom they turned to for advice from time to time. Winifred contacted Mrs Ferguson about Ben's affair and she wrote back with some ideas to help them, but Ben was not happy with her emphasis on 'adultery' and 'cruelty' to the children. He was baffled by the way that people 'fetter themselves up' with ideas.

Although Mrs Ferguson clearly offered Winifred support, it did not give her the confidence to condemn Ben's behaviour and he seemed unable to see the reality of the situation for Winifred. 'Winifred's ideas are so funny,' Ben wrote to Barbara. 'She tries suddenly to make some desperate decision & says if I love you I must go away with you' and then changes her mind and says 'I could not see the children again...' Winifred's unhappiness is painfully apparent, and it is not surprising that she felt conflicted at times. Ben, on the other hand, believed that by staying true to his feelings, everyone else would be happy, eventually. A close friend described how they '*thought* they were freeing themselves' from bourgeois constraints, and 'they *thought* there was no such thing as jealousy' but 'it didn't seem to work out that way'.[2] Other friends were more openly critical. The art patron Helen Sutherland, who had known Winifred and Ben for many years and supported both their careers, came up with a 'Ben Theory'. He was, she decided, 'almost entirely lacking in the power of seeing objectively' and instead held on to his own 'wonderful subjective truth', so everything became 'a bit of a fog'. She felt that he was 'really wonderful' but that he was also quick to condemn 'the morality of the whole world', leaving himself alone as the moral force for right. She suspected it was all 'nonsense to a very great extent' as 'too much individuality does become madness – tho' it is the way of genius too'.[3]

About a week after Ben had returned, Barbara went home to Hampstead from Norfolk and felt that she was 'coming into a new world instead of being unhappy'.[4] She contacted a solicitor about divorcing Jack and decided to break a joint contract they held with the Arthur Tooth & Sons Gallery. Dudley Tooth agreed to release her from the contract, and she took the opportunity to tell him that her work was becoming increasingly abstract. This seemed to go down well and they discussed the possibility of a solo show in a year or two. As her marriage came to an end, her art was opening out in a new direction. Her turn to abstraction was also a response to the ideas in Eddy's *Science and Health*.[5] A Christian Scientist artist should turn away from the visible and material world and instead depict abstract ideals. Thought, Eddy wrote, will 'finally be understood and seen in all form, substance, and colour'.[6] Barbara was delighted with these new ideas and with her liberation from the gallery. She felt 'absolutely free – as regards work' and her joy in her newfound freedom spilled over: Winifred was 'splendid' and she thought of her and her injured back and the babies every day.[7] However, her talk with Jack about starting divorce proceedings didn't go quite as planned; he was unwilling to sever ties too quickly. With Ben, Barbara felt a 'beautiful strange thing' in the room as they worked, whereas Jack 'arrested' her thought and so she hoped that he wouldn't get a studio too close by.[8]

Despite his apparent conviction, Ben was dealing with complex emotions. He was captivated by the 'free & living idea' that he had found at Happisburgh and believed that this lovely idea would free Winifred too, even if it would be a 'painful process'. He decided to move to London in order to give everyone and everything time to 'find the right thing'. Ben liked to imagine Barbara in her studio, in 'that room & the approach to it', but decided that the solution was for him to live alone for a while and to get a teaching job in order to be financially independent as well as to take his share of looking after the children.

After another week of trying to work through the 'painful process', Ben made arrangements to move to London and Winifred took the children to her parents in Boothby for a while. Ben told Barbara he would be in London soon, when the right moment struck, and that he simply loved her letters and 'everything about you much much more than I have ever loved anything'. He was looking forward to their getting a lot of work done together. Barbara admitted that she woke up early to wait for the postman, and that she wished she could fly across to Bankshead for a moment. She was longing for him to be in London and then added, as a good Christian Scientist, that she hoped Winifred would come too. She told Ben that she was holding a Norfolk reunion at the studio and that he would be much missed. One of things Ben did before he moved was to send Barbara a photograph of his mother, which she told him was very beautiful.

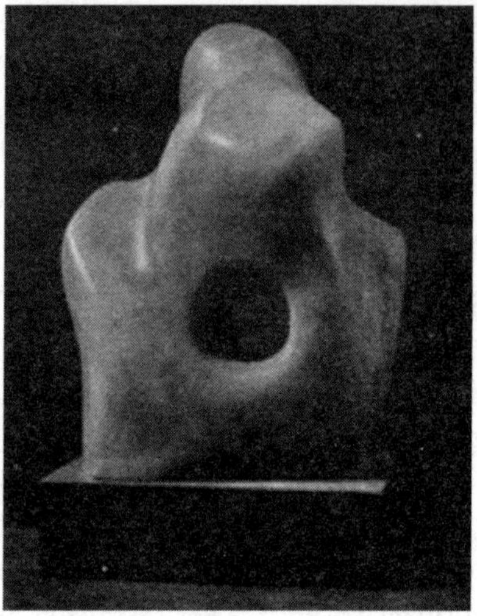

Barbara Hepworth, Pierced Form, *1932*

After staying in Chelsea for a couple of weeks Ben found a studio in Parkhill Road, around the corner from the Mall Studios. On 27 October 1931 Barbara wrote that the 'solution is very near at hand' and that she could feel Winifred's 'beauty all about us', so 'today is all radiance'.[9] This period coincided with one of the most important moments in Barbara's career. She decided to pierce a hole in a small abstract sculpture made of pink alabaster now known as *Pierced Form*. She described the act of piercing the delicate pink stone as a moment of intense pleasure, unlike anything she had experienced while making figurative sculptures. It marked a shift towards the more tactile and haptic qualities of her work. A review of Moore's work had somehow given her the idea, and Moore, in turn, was inspired by her pierced form. It became a central motif for both artists for years to come. By opening up sculptural form to involve interior space Hepworth transformed twentieth-century sculpture. She said later that the ten-inch sculpture formed the basis of all her work.

Winifred was a resourceful, competent woman and rather than wait around in Cumberland to see if Ben would come back, she took the children to London in November. Realising that Barbara and Ben were now living around the corner from each other in Belsize Park she couldn't bear to be in London, knowing they would be visiting all their old friends. She considered moving to Paris but decided the exchange rate was too 'heavy' and she wondered about going to Lamorna in Cornwall, only to conclude that it might be too cold for the children over the winter. And then in December she found the Watchhouse in Fishbourne on the Isle of Wight. She wrote to Ben to tell him how much the children were enjoying themselves, that Kate in particular enjoyed making 'puddly pies' on the beach.[10] She also sought advice from an old art-school friend who had been to see Ben and Barbara. She was desperate for any light that she could shed on the situation as she felt it was too difficult for her to see things clearly herself. She wondered if Barbara could make Ben happier than she could, and whether it was a 'forever thing' and if it had a 'good feel about it'.[11] Her friend either never got the letter or didn't know how to reply.

Ben couldn't stay away from his family for long and went to the Isle of Wight for Christmas. When he got there everybody was 'very sweet' to him and gave him a 'charming welcome'. It was the 'quietest & stillest place' he had ever seen, the sea was smooth and there was a 'creek with a point' that he sketched through the arched window for Barbara. Straight after Christmas he went back to London. This time when he left, Winifred was more open to the idea of 'complete freedom' with no sense of the 'divisions of people'. She even toyed with the idea that she and Barbara should live together for a year without Ben, which delighted him: 'I am all for it! Especially if I can have Jake + Kate.'[12] Winifred changed her mind, however, and realised that she was too sad even to look at a lovely patchwork blanket that Barbara had sent for Christmas. She used it in one or two of her paintings but then decided to give it away as she couldn't bear having it around.[13]

A few weeks later, Ben was back again on the Isle of Wight. Barbara felt at peace in Hampstead, but, as the days went by,

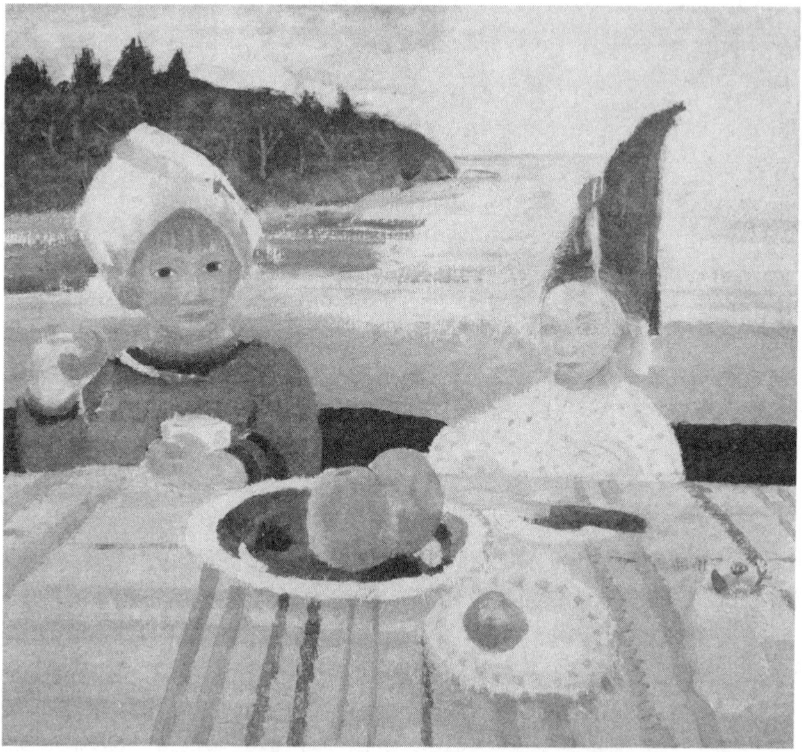

Winifred Nicholson, Kate and Jake, Isle of Wight, *1932*

she told him she was longing to hear his voice. So in one of her letters she enticed him with news that there were plans to build squash courts in Upper Park Road in Belsize Park. In early February 1932 he was back in London again, still in Parkhill Road. Barbara had felt anxious in the studio alone, so Ben put locks on the windows for her. On the day he left again, he scattered spotted hankies for her to find in bed that reminded her of pebbles on the beach.[14] At this stage the rhythm of transition between Ben's two worlds appeared relatively smooth. Barbara liked to imagine Ben on the sleeper train and being met by Winifred at the other end.[15]

Ben moved back and forth throughout that year, with Winifred and Barbara showing remarkable grace and poise. By the end of March Ben had moved into the Mall Studios with Barbara,

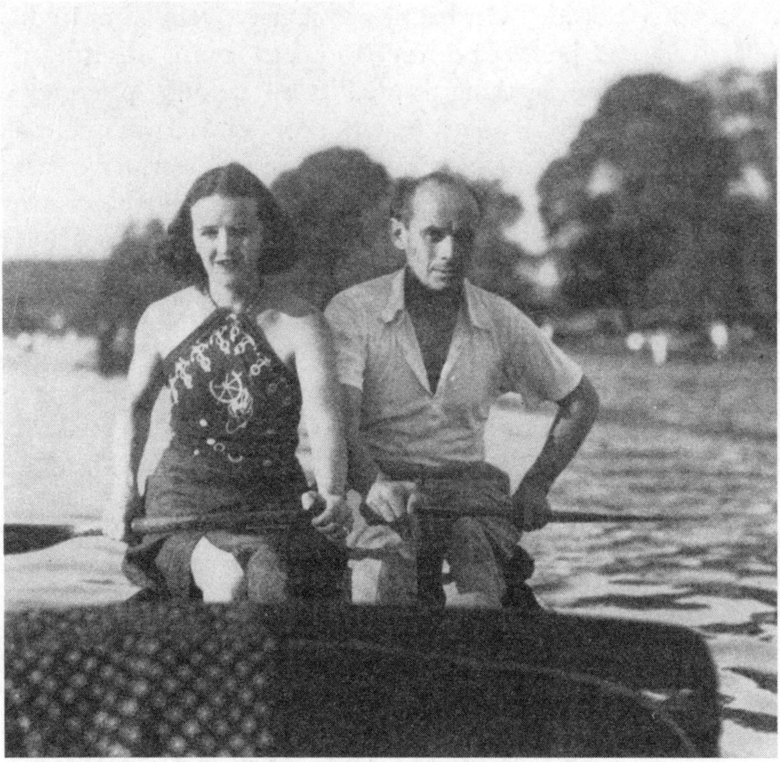

Ben and Barbara rowing on the Serpentine

although he continued to rent 53 Parkhill Road. Winifred turned to her friends for solidity when things became too much and she felt 'stretched on drifting sands' and needed 'rocklike qualities in other people'. She was keen that the children should not be infected with the bitterness of what she called 'changing love' and wanted to teach them something more beautiful and permanent.[16] She briefly wondered if she should move to America but the logistics were too complicated, so in May she moved to Cornwall, a place that held many memories for her and Ben. If she was looking for a way to entice Ben to join her and the children, her move was wise; Ben was there like a shot. She rented Penpillick House, near Par, on the south coast. The house was 'pretty & gay with sunlight pouring in whatever the weather outside'. On his first visit they were all out when he arrived, and he walked from room to room, admiring the brightness with everything painted in 'his' colours, 'pale grey & white … pale buff … yellow & dark browns'. He was impressed by Winifred's ingenuity in rigging up boxes with striped curtains for chests of drawers. Even the oilcloth on the table had narrow white lines and pink squares, making the crockery look a 'bit of a dream' on top of it. Ben was delighted to be there. Jake, almost five, was extremely thoughtful and good company, and Kate, nearly three, was lovely with such a 'pretty cheeky little face'. She handled words as though they were the 'most precious things in the world' and when Ben called her a silly goose she replied 'me – not a goose, you – a goose'. Andrew, now ten months old, was 'dark brown & completely serene & happy'. The bedroom in Cornwall was 'white & clean & simple' and Winifred had set up a perfect studio for him to work in.

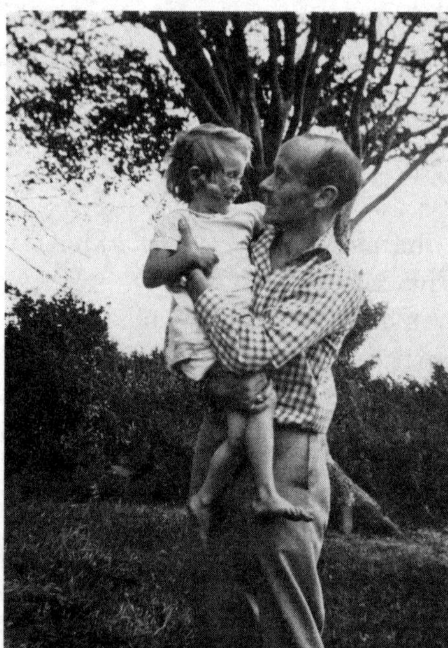

Ben and Kate in Cornwall

Winifred was being 'such a dear', but Ben was worried about Barbara alone in London. She was initially happy to have some space and felt happy and peaceful lying in bed listening to a blackbird singing in flight from tree to tree. She cleaned the studio, turned the furniture and dug the garden to get it ready for planting up. Ben, with his natural buoyancy, felt certain that everything would work and wrote to Barbara that 'I feel completely & utterly clear myself about my relationship to [Winifred] & to you.' His clarity spread so that he felt that 'everyone else in the world, must inevitably get it, also'.[17] This was somewhat ambitious. The first few days had been smooth at Penpillick House, but on day three he and Winifred had a 'first class A1 super storm' and Ben nearly packed up and went back to London. He and Winifred managed to work things out and made plans to hire a car to drive to St Ives to visit Alfred Wallis, taking Jake with them.[18]

Despite her initial resilience, Barbara missed Ben and so characteristically threw herself into her work. She had enrolled Paul at a local nursery before Christmas which gave her about five hours to work, with a short lunch break. She described sawing the 'bottom off that piece of blackwood to make it stand up' but then realised that it wasn't straight and wouldn't stand up 'at all!'[19] She was also enjoying experimenting with printmaking. Then towards the end of May she wondered if she and Ben could steal a few days away in Happisburgh together. She felt that it would make them 'so well' and she missed that 'sweet line on your forehead made by your beret'.[20] Ben agreed that if they sold some work and borrowed his dad's car they could go to Happisburgh.[21] But they didn't have any money. Although Winifred gave Ben money occasionally he no longer had the full benefit of her family income. His father helped out sometimes but the rent for the Mall Studios was £75 per annum. Ben wrote to all his contacts that summer asking if anyone would like to buy his work. Winifred's art-school friend E. J. Hooper bought a painting for £12, Helen Sutherland sent £50 for a proposed new 'School of Painting', in which Jack Hepworth (Barbara's cousin) was the only student. And in July Jim Ede bought a painting from Ben for £22. This was a generous amount and Ben wrote to say that it felt more like £222 and to thank him for giving them the liberty to work again. The Great Crash and the subsequent economic downturn had affected artists, and Ben and Barbara had resorted to breaking into a small money box for their bus fares, and they had run out of credit for their food bills.[22]

Cornwall suited Ben and Winifred. By the end of July 1932 they were getting on well. They took Jake sailing with the Brumwells (Ben knew advertising executive Marcus Brumwell from the tennis club in East Dulwich) near Falmouth and the whole family travelled in a ponycart to bathe at Par in 'such lovely sea and sun and air'. Ben was spending a lot of time with Jake, and had renewed his friendship with Alfred Wallis. Jim Ede was buying up a lot of Wallis's work, with Ben acting as intermediary. Wallis would tie up his latest work into 'parcles' and send them to Ben. At one point the orders became overwhelming and the smell of paint put Wallis off his food.

Towards the end of the summer Winifred asked Ben not to visit for a while because she was in the middle of some 'enthralling work' and did not want to be interrupted. She also thought he needed some uninterrupted time to work. She made it clear that she respected his feelings for Barbara and believed they had reached a level of understanding that had taken them all to a higher plane. She thanked him for all the 'hard things' they had gone through because it had taught her courage. However, it does not appear that Ben kept his distance, as her next letter suggested a renewed intimacy. 'There was a beautiful thing about wasn't there,' she wrote, 'behind things in the white sea – in our room as the night drew down on the hills – in the purpose deep in your eyes – and I feel it in my heart like Peace.'[23]

Barbara didn't hold back on letting Ben know about the fun she was having in London when he was in Cornwall. She played tennis with Helen Ede, she went to the Palladium to see Louis Armstrong, she heard Ethel Bartlett play Bach and she wore her 'lovely new red print frock' to watch ballroom dancing at the Astoria. Ben wondered vaguely which Jack she went to the concert with. Despite her gadding about, Barbara missed Ben terribly. She missed his paints in her studio as much as she missed him, so she thought she'd have a go at the 'intriguing game' of painting herself. The results, she found, were 'far too fussy & muddled & dirty colours & nasty textures'. In order to get the hang of it, she decided she would have to devote her entire life to it.[24] When she missed Ben, Barbara tended to phone him in Cornwall more often. This annoyed Winifred, who accused her of trying to persuade Ben to come back to her.[25] Ben seems to have agreed and asked Barbara to avoid phoning unless it was an emergency. Barbara was adamant that she didn't want to 'upset things' and hoped that 'the 3 of us can manage this alright'.[26] However, her desperation mounting, she came up with a plan to visit him in Plymouth for half an hour and then to return on the last train.[27] Ben thought it was an expensive idea but he was up for it if it would help her at all. It would make more sense, he suggested, for them to go to St Ives the following week instead. Barbara's friend, art patron Margaret Gardiner, had mentioned that they ought to have a child together, as it would be such a beautiful thing. Ben thought that was a sweet thing to say. None of them would have imagined the reality of what was to come.

Barbara was beginning to question some of the central ideas in Christian Science. She was disappointed that Science did not 'admit the necessity of sex harmony'. She wondered why they should 'cut out the most lovely thing that God has created'. In the same way that it would be impossible to cut out the 'strength and urge' that forces a flower out of the ground or to ignore 'the rhythm of the seasons & the heat of the earth & sea & sands', it would be impossible to ignore the warmth and creativeness of human sexual relations. She wondered, then, if she felt this way because she was simply on a lower plane than Winifred.[28] However, she also playfully thanked Ben for a drawing of his room as she needed the 'lie of the land' in case she tripped in the dark during one of her nocturnal visits.[29] This seems to have been a lovers' joke, but it also owed something to Christian Science's attachment to some kind

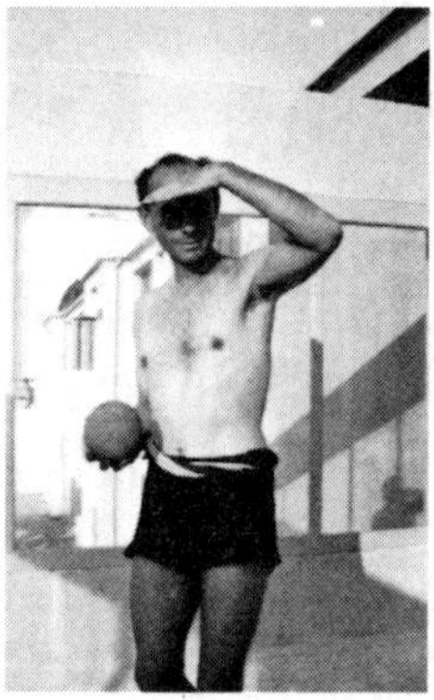
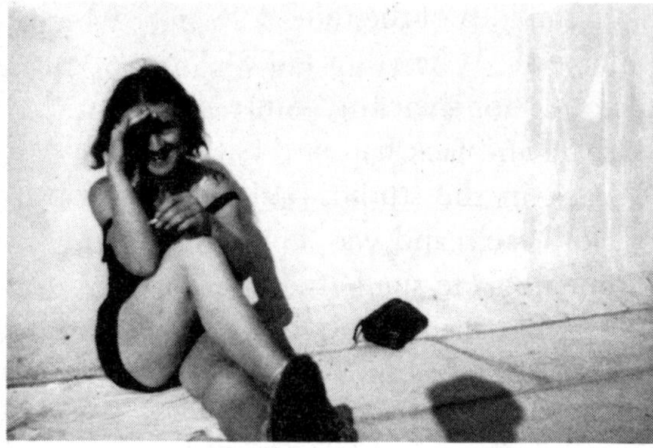

Ben by Barbara in Dieppe *Barbara by Ben in Dieppe*

of thought travel. They certainly all called upon each other for thought-help to cure common ailments. Barbara thanked Ben for his help with her cough, and he often asked for help with aches and pains. Illness in Christian Science was considered an illusion, a symptom of an underlying spiritual condition, and to cure it the divine Mind must overcome the mortal mind. In other words, if a doctor tells you that you are ill it makes you worse because the belief feeds the illness.

Barbara and Ben did not meet up in Plymouth or St Ives that July, but in August they took a short holiday to Dieppe. The photos show Barbara looking girlishly happy on the modernist beachfront and sitting against a wall in the sun next to Ben's shadow, complete with his distinctive beret, as he took the photo. In Dieppe Ben was inspired by the reflections he saw in the window of a shop called Chat Botté or Puss in Boots. When he got back to London he painted *Au Chat Botté* in which he replaced the footwear with a jug and bowl and a bust of Barbara. He played with the two-dimensional nature of the canvas so that the red letters of the shop name were painted on the surface of the glass, and yet the word 'Dieppe' is tucked behind the jug. The reflections create three intersecting planes and break through into a kind of 'imaginative world in which one could live'.[30] Years later Ben explained to a friend how he'd 'always liked the idea of the reflection being more actual than the object reflected'.[31] When they got back to London they began preparing furiously for their first joint exhibition at Tooth's Gallery, where Barbara and Jack had been so successful two years earlier.

Back in the studio, Barbara was working on a head carved out of acacia and was 'knocking lumps' out of it when Moore popped by. He suggested that she have another go at the lower half of her blackwood 'big torso'.[32] There is a touch of anxiety in Ben's letter from Cornwall as he urged her to go gently with the torso, as it is such a 'very lovely thing'. Couldn't they, he asked, 'have a go at it together at the end of some very good working day?'[33] Ben said he would love to see 'old Harry', but perhaps he would have preferred 'old Harry' to leave Barbara's sculptures alone. Two days later she was happy with the acacia head, and felt she had learnt so much from the process that she 'can't have known anything before'. The idea that had 'mistily' suggested itself had now freed itself from inside the wood.[34] Barbara agreed to leave the torso alone for when they were next working together. Many of the pieces in the exhibition were produced as they worked alongside one another, so there were strong overlaps and connections between them.

As the exhibition drew near tensions rose. Barbara sent some presents for the children after the trip to Dieppe, only for Winifred to return them. In retaliation Barbara put away a red necklace that Winifred had given her and was waiting for the right moment to send it back.[35] Barbara was very upset at the thought that the children would not know her, or know anything about her. But her work was going too well for her to remain upset for long. And for Winifred, too, the storm passed. She had her own plans in the pipeline: days before the opening of Ben and Barbara's exhibition in London she arranged for herself and the children to move to Paris.

All the hard work paid off, and the exhibition at Tooth's Gallery was a great success. Ben's paintings of mugs and jugs and mythical fish were described by Paul Nash in the *Weekend Review* as having the charm of 'old walls or pavements stained

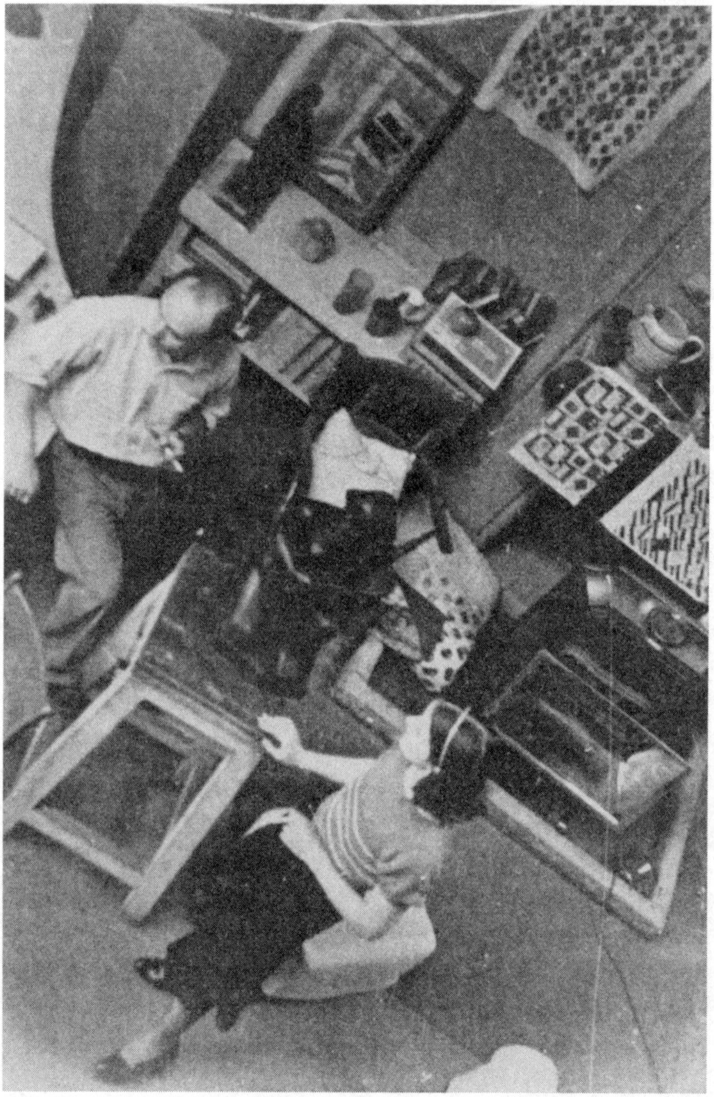

Ben and Barbara in the Mall Studios

and scoured, encrusted with exquisite lichens'. And Barbara's sculptures, wrote Nash, seemed like 'stone worn by the elements through years of time'. All in all, the exhibition achieved a 'delightful unity'.[36] Herbert Read, who was on his way to becoming one of the most significant contemporary art critics, had agreed to write the foreword to the catalogue for the exhibition. He focused on the relationship between the artist and their material, which, he argued, had been lost over the centuries. 'Stone and wood', he wrote, 'yield their essences to give form a concrete significance.' Hepworth's sculptures 'recede into a symbolic world of abstractions' and should be enjoyed for their 'freedom … force and … contemporaneity'. The critic Adrian Stokes went one stage further and described Hepworth's sculpture as becoming the thing itself. It is not a matter 'of a mother and child group represented in stone. Miss Hepworth's stone *is* a mother, her huge pebble its child.'[37]

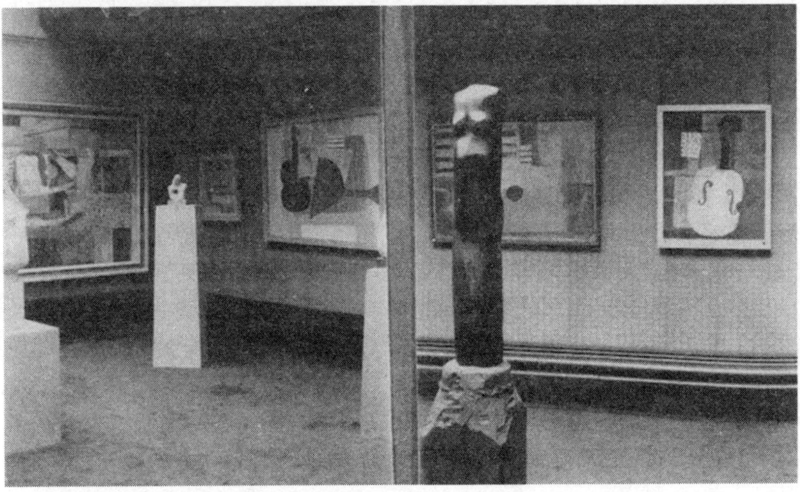

Photographs from Barbara Hepworth's album of the exhibition Carvings by Barbara Hepworth, paintings by Ben Nicholson *at Arthur Tooth & Sons in London (October–November 1932)*

Ben and Barbara also gave their own accounts of their work to promote the exhibition. In *Studio* Barbara explained that she preferred direct carving because she liked to feel the 'resistance of the hard material' and was 'happier working that way'.[38] And Ben exploded the need for one-point perspective in painting: 'there is no reason we should be limited to a fixed viewpoint once we have discovered that in life itself there are an unlimited number of points of view.'[39] Together they sold an enormous £300 worth of work.

Winifred had meanwhile moved the children to a second-floor flat in Paris at 48 quai d'Auteuil, right on the Seine, with views of the Eiffel Tower. Like the move to Cornwall, it had a powerful effect on Ben, who wrote immediately to ask when he might visit. Winifred replied that he could come and stay in mid-December if he brought a camp bed with him. Ben was there by 15 December. Ben described the Citroën factory lighting up the sky, the outdoor cafés selling ice cream and stalls with Christmas toys and decorations that looked like something in a fairy tale. He had little desire to go and see any paintings or to make use of his introductions, but he was keen to work and wrote that Winifred was 'profoundly happy'. She even had a 'nice intonation in her voice' when she said Barbara's name. He couldn't remember a more harmonious time in their relationship.[40] Their harmony was apparent when Ben and Winifred went shopping in Paris separately and by chance bought the same lino print for each other. Winifred's tennis was getting very good too; Ben thought she now played a 'very pretty stroke'.[41]

Barbara was not sure what to do for Christmas. She lit a fire in the studio and, although there was a beautiful 'silver light' and a sweet-smelling air, she felt as though her 'head had been severed' because she missed him so much.[42] In the end she and Paul spent Christmas with her cousin Jack and his family in Saffron Walden. She described a drive they took with 'silver winding roads & trees casting lines of shadow' and seeing a horse tethered next to a tent with a woman 'in such a deep red jacket & blue skirt sitting by a fire & cooking'. But everything made her think of Ben.[43] Barbara was generally not very keen on the fuss made over Christmas and she was longing for things to return to normal so that she could get back to work. Not to be outdone by Winifred, however, she was perfecting her tennis skills and that Christmas she learnt a new and 'amusing movement – like dancing with the ball as a most perfect partner'. She had also given up smoking and had stopped wearing lipstick as Ben didn't like makeup. She was thinking of having lessons to improve her French in preparation for visiting Paris. In the meantime Ben was trying to find a way to bring Barbara over to Paris more permanently. He was making use of his contacts in Paris to see if there were any cheap rooms they might rent together.[44]

Barbara was particularly sad not to spend New Year with Ben, and decided to spend it alone so that she could send him a special 'think' for the first day of the year. In the end she changed her mind and went for supper with Jim and Helen Ede on Elm Row up the hill, where they had a 'charming' dinner party and talked about Ben and Winifred in Paris. As she walked home she saw a 'thin silver moon'; there was a cool air blowing and lots of young people in party frocks were wishing everyone a happy new year. Barbara's other news was that her divorce was finally going through. Even though Jack hadn't liked the 'feel or thought of it' in the autumn, he had finally come around to the idea.

During the first week of January 1933 Barbara had to field calls from the *Daily Express* about the divorce, and Ben Nicholson had been named as a co-respondent. Articles also appeared in the *Sunday Express* and the *Daily Herald*. She felt sick with worry, particularly about how her parents would react as they had not told their friends about the separation. She had also just started teaching the daughter of the musician Arthur Bliss, work which she both enjoyed and needed financially. She was (needlessly) worried they would sack her because of the newspaper scandal. Jack Skeaping, it turned out, was the one to comfort her. He told her not to say anything to the journalists, and reassured her that if the newspapers made it look rotten on the outside he and she knew that what they were doing was right on the inside.

While Barbara was coping with the news of her divorce being made public, Ben was delighted to have met Braque in Paris. Ben thought he was a 'dear', a 'big & simple person', a 'most beautiful thought' who understood things immediately. He showed Braque photographs of contemporary work from London, but it was over Barbara's work that he grew most animated, exclaiming 'mais, oui!' about many of them.[45] Ben had just done 'a largish ptg' and thought that it might be the best he'd done. It was four feet by four feet, 'pretty abstract' and with a 'French light in it'. He thought it was 'very mysterious' but 'after all why not?' He had started to put sand in the 'ground' of his paintings, collected from the Seine. Braque had been mixing sand into his paint for years, as had Paul Klee. As well as creating an obvious texture, when Ben was 'scraping parts of the ptg the sand had set so hard' it made 'sparks like a toy gun' and broke the blade.[46]

Ben also went to see Picasso in his studio that spring and was struck by his 'good nature' and his 'laughing eyes'; he thought he was generally bursting with good health. He said Picasso's latest painting, hung on a grey panelled wall, was the second greatest pleasure he had had in Paris, after perfecting his new tennis stroke. Ben was spending more time in Paris than in London and so in April Barbara joined him there. They went on a drawing trip to Avignon and Saint-Rémy-de-Provence and then back to Paris where they visited Brâncuși in his studio. Barbara was mesmerised by the 'great eternal column of wood' and the 'earthbound shapes of human heads or elliptical fish' and the 'soaring forms of birds'. She looked back on this visit as transformative: it gave her a 'miraculous feeling of eternity mixed with beloved stone and stone dust'.[47] They also visited the Arps in the suburbs of Paris. Sophie Taubier-Arp showed them Jean Arp's abstract relief sculptures and her 'space' paintings which were divided up into grids. Barbara was interested in the way Jean Arp fused landscape and form. Ben also introduced Barbara to Picasso and she loved the light in his studio that streamed in over 'roofs and chimneypots' and on to the large canvases, 'from which emanated a blaze of energy in form and colour'.[48] Ben wanted to create a kind of 'Paris–London liaison'.

Ben began incising his canvases with the blunt end of his paintbrush in 1933. Braque had been doing it for some time and Barbara had begun incising her sculptures with suggestive lines in her recent work, as in *Seated Figure* (1932–3) and *Sculpture with Profiles* (1932). In some of Ben's work the lines connect abstract shapes, but in *St Rémy, Provence* (1933), he depicted two figures about to embrace, carved out in white lines on a black surface. A third figure hovers between them, appearing to face both of them and the viewer simultaneously, in an echo of their embrace. Barbara was also experimenting with new techniques in 1933. She met the Bauhaus artist Lászlo Moholy-Nagy on one of his visits to London, and he introduced her to the process of photograms, in which objects are placed on light-sensitive paper. She had a lot of fun placing her head on the paper to produce her profile and felt she had discovered a 'beautiful new world of light and form'.[49]

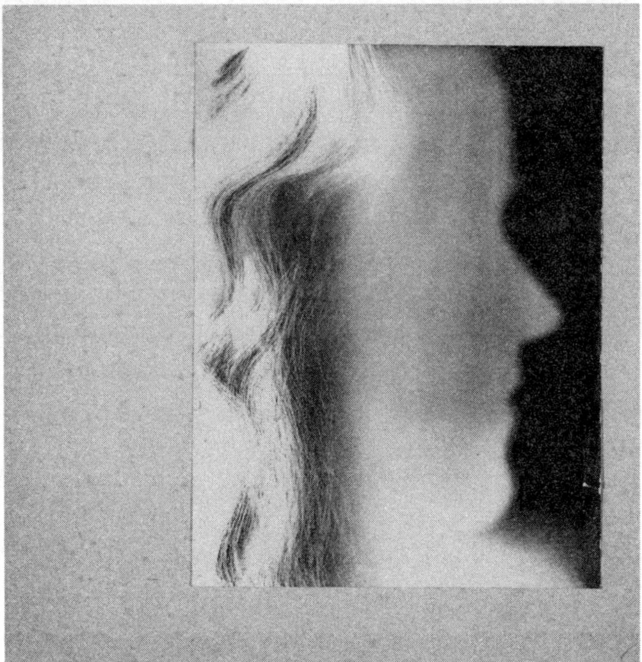

Barbara Hepworth, Self-portrait photogram, *1932–3*

If piercing the pink alabaster had been a breakthrough for Hepworth in 1931, Ben had the most important breakthrough of his career in Paris in December 1933. He was incising a piece of board covered in some 'kind of plaster preparation' and by accident 'a piece came out where two lines crossed'. Instead of feeling frustration, he was interested in the different planes and 'developed this lower level further'. This became his first 'relief'. He said later that he had been ready for the accident, or what Barbara called 'carving out', at that moment.[50] Barbara had been 'longing for it to happen for ages', and it must have felt in some ways that their two art forms were merging. Her only regret was that she had not been there when it happened. She sent him new packs of razor blades from London to use with his brushes and wished she could see his new work.[51] The fact that she couldn't made her reluctant to send him one of her new photograms, but she did post him a copy of Moholy-Nagy's *60 Photos* that explained the process.[52] Ben accused her of not playing the game.

Ben carved an 'amusing' thing in mid-December that looked like a 'primitive game', and so when Jake and Kate came into the studio they rolled a marble around it.[53] Ben was thinking about games that winter as he had come up with a new version of table tennis that he called 'Tablehazard' or 'Bridgepong' and that he hoped would be bought up by a sports equipment company. He had replaced the net with a platform that resulted in the ball rolling off it at unexpected places on to the opponent's side. After a demonstration from Ben's brother Kit and their friend Adrian Stokes, Slazenger were interested but Ben did not take it any further as he was in Paris.

When it became clear that Ben was planning to stay in Paris for Christmas in 1933, Barbara became increasingly distressed. She wrote him a long letter that she destroyed and sent a shorter one that simply said, 'I feel very blue … I love you – quite desperately.'[54] In the end Ben decided to return to London just after Christmas. The journey itself was part of the reason he came: he would travel by aeroplane. Barbara was very envious and pointed out that the weather was perfect for it. Ben spent a 'miraculous' day in Paris with Winifred, and then took his first flight 'above the white clouds for 2 hours'. He reported it as the 'happiest day I have ever experienced'.[55] Not long afterwards, Barbara became pregnant.

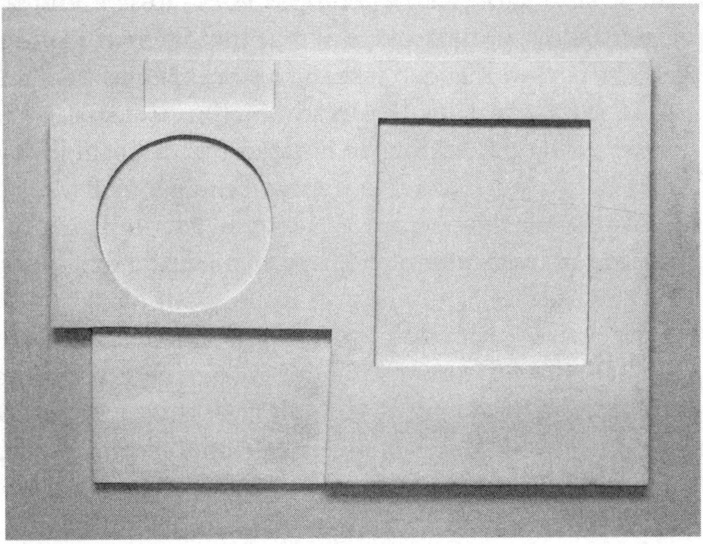

Ben Nicholson, 1934 (relief), *1934*

At first, Winifred was unaware of the pregnancy and the first few months of 1934 were relatively calm. It appears that Barbara simply indicated her pregnant status with a dot drawn inside a circle on her envelopes. She felt unable to do much heavy sculpting and turned her attention to prints and drawings. Although she did not feel well and was looking forward to eating a square meal again, the idea of their baby struck her as beautiful and mysterious. Her letters from that summer are easy and happy; she mentioned making 'crackly brown cakes' with Paul, sunbathing in the garden, the architect Wells Coates bringing friends round, 'Herb and Ludo' (Herbert Read and his partner Margaret Ludwig) coming for dinner and having tea at the Edes'.

In February Ben began to paint his pressed layers of wood a dazzling white. One of the pieces he made was a panel from a dining table that he had carried home with him on the 24 bus to Belsize Park. There is some speculation about why he started to paint his reliefs white, including suggestions that he had been inspired by his proximity to two of Le Corbusier's houses in Paris, Villa la Roche and Villa Jeanneret, or by the publication of Theo van Doesburg's *Manifesto of Concrete Art* (1930), which stated that white was the most spiritual colour. Whatever triggered this decision, his visit to Mondrian's studio on 5 April confirmed his departure into pure abstraction. He was captivated by the 'feeling of light' in the space and felt that he had visited a 'hermit's cave' where lions go to have thorns taken out of their paws. After the visit he sat in a café at the pavement's edge with traffic whizzing by, feeling a great sense of quiet and repose.[56]

Barbara hoped that Ben would tell Winifred about the pregnancy before he came over for the opening on 10 April of the exhibition of works by Unit One, the group that had been set up by Paul Nash along the lines of Abstraction-Création in Paris. He did tell her and, unsurprisingly, it created enormous difficulties. Winifred felt that the previous weeks they had had together had a 'feeling of finality like a last chapter'. She went back to Cumberland that summer with the children and asked Ben not to contact her for a year. Helen Sutherland wrote to Ben on Winifred's behalf, telling him that he would be unable to move between two families and that he would have to choose. She said that the idea of pure love might exist in heaven, but in real life 'greed selfishness jealousy exclusiveness judging and so on & so on' get in the way.[57] Now that she was pregnant, Barbara changed her name by deed poll, fusing Hepworth and Nicholson. This meant that many of their contemporaries believed they were married in 1934, although their wedding did not take place until four years later.

On 3 October Ben accompanied a heavily pregnant Barbara to the cinema to see if the 'bangs and crashes' of the gangsters and cowboys would bring on the birth. Then they had supper with their friend Margaret Gardiner in the studio and played a game of cards before Barbara became a little withdrawn and went to bed.[58] They were renting the basement flat of 3 Church Road, around the corner, for the birth and new baby. Not long after she had gone to bed she scribbled a note for the nurse to take to Ben saying that the 'waters have just come away & first pain started'. The nurse thought she was 'quite mad' for letting him know, but Barbara wanted Ben to understand what was happening and to do what he thought best about 'being here'. Her note told him to get a 'decent sleep' but then she had a change of heart and wrote on the envelope 'please come over'.[59] She had been surprised during the pregnancy by how active the baby had felt, as though it was 'playing a tennis match inside me'. The reason for this, it turned out, was that instead of one baby, there were three.

Ben called Margaret at four in the morning to say there was a boy and a girl and 'I'm not quite sure yet what the third is.' When Margaret said 'It can't be true!' he replied, 'I bet you a bag of sweets it's true' and rang off.[60] The babies were tiny, and a note in Ben's hand records them as Rachel 2 lb 13¼ oz, Sarah 3 lb and Simon 5 lb 12¼ oz. The birth of the babies was astonishing, but Barbara suddenly 'knew fear for the first time in my life, as I was very weak, and wondered how on earth we were to support this family on white reliefs and the carving I was doing'.[61] She became desperate in the weeks that followed and Margaret said she cried 'for days on end. She couldn't stop.'[62] The size of the babies meant that the doctors feared for Rachel and Sarah in particular. The midwife stayed on for the nights and Barbara's sister Elizabeth helped during the days. Ben was convinced that he had predicted the triplets with the relief he finished the day before they were born, which included two circles and a square. Calder wrote to congratulate them on the Nicholson-Hepworth production line, and Paul Nash congratulated them on their 'trinity'.[63]

Ben went back to Paris when the babies were two months old, and although Winifred relented about not seeing him she did not want him to stay in the flat with them; instead he found a place near by. Winifred bought seven-year-old Jake some pet

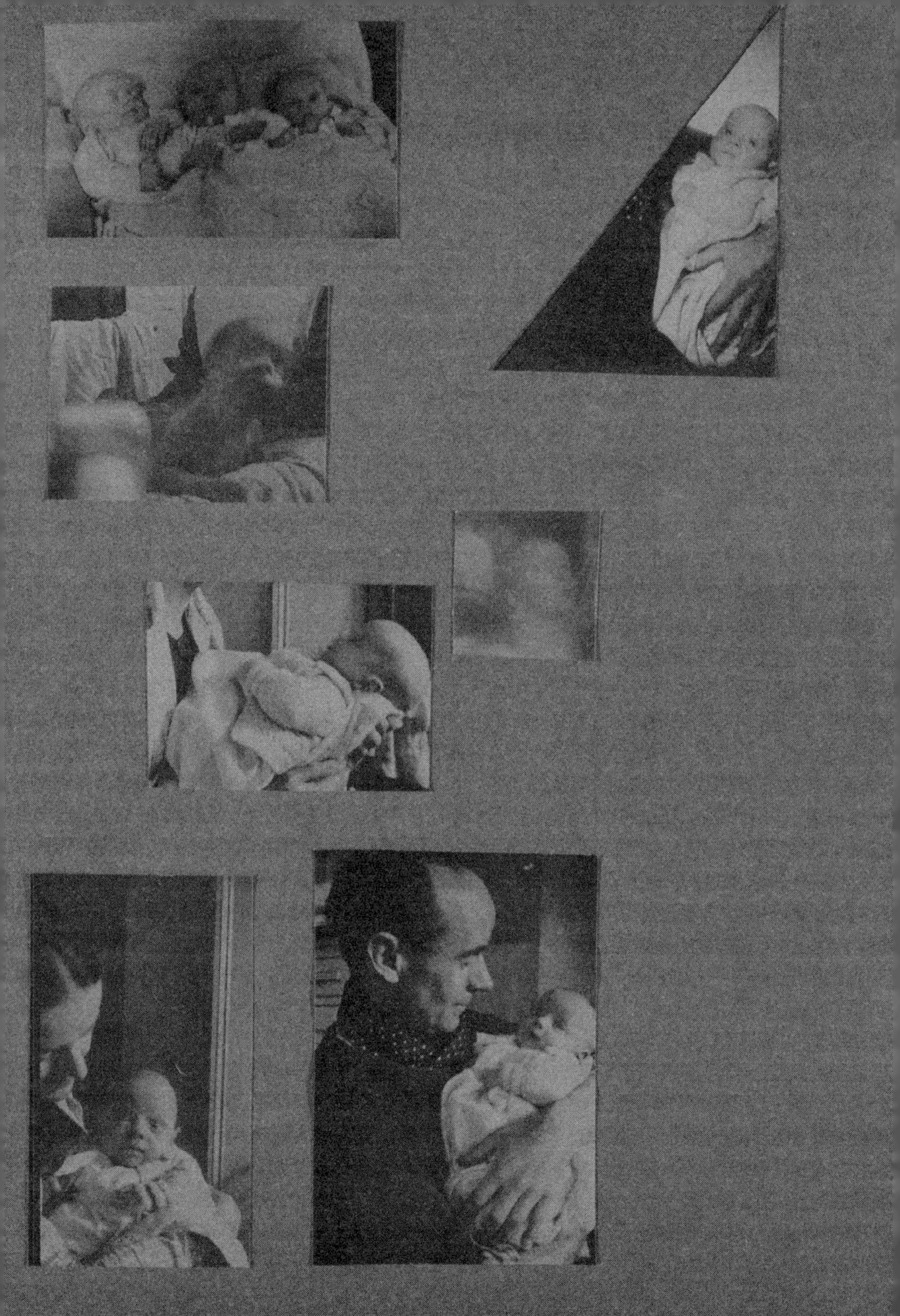

Page from Barbara's photo album

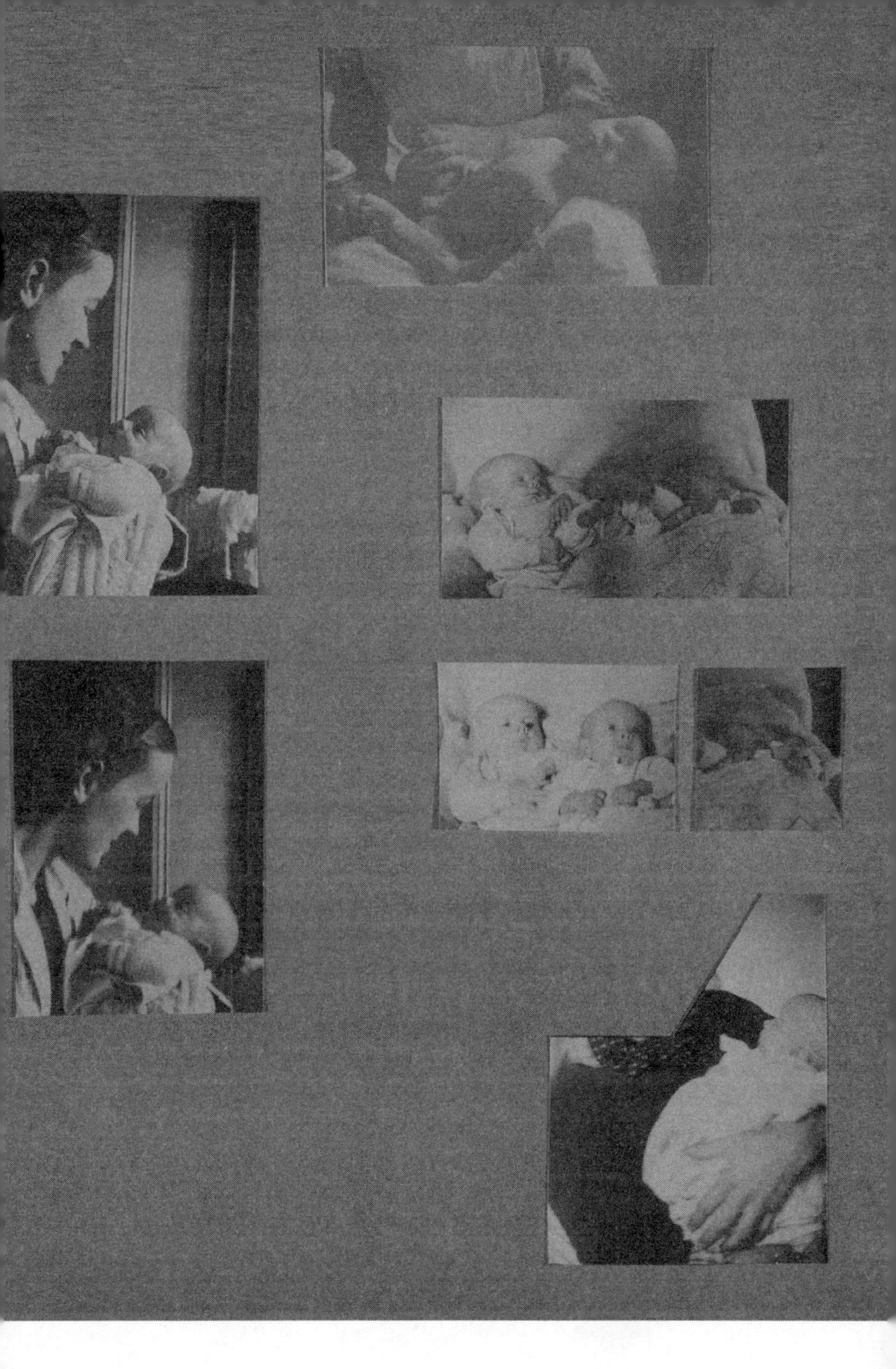

doves, perhaps as a way to cheer him up after he had been told about the triplets. Jake asked if he could go to school in London and see Ben on Sundays, and when Winifred said that would be difficult, he said, 'Ben likes his painting better than you, & better than me.' Up until this point Winifred had assured Jake that Ben would come back.[64]

Barbara's letters are full of details of the babies: their weight, their smiles, their lovely eyes and the joy they brought her. But the nurses who were helping were struggling. Sarah and Rachel were too small to be allowed out and that meant staying indoors for much of the time. By December Barbara was still anxious enough to look for a more permanent solution. She found the Wellgarth nursery training college in Golders Green and felt reassured by the idea that she could call an ambulance and the babies could all be taken there if the situation deteriorated rapidly. She visited the crèche at the training college and thought it was well designed with a lot of light and balconies outside the rooms that give 'maximum sheltered air'. The nursery offered to look after all three babies at a discounted rate of £5.50 instead of £9.90 a week. Barbara was not ready to take such a drastic step but she was reassured by having the option. When the babies were about three months old she arranged things with the nurses so that she was able to spend a few days in Paris with Ben after Christmas and they went to see Mondrian together. On her return her desire to work again was strong and she decided to paint the studio white. It was very 'roughly done', she said, and needed a third coat, but she had 'hidden so many things' she didn't like and so it now felt peaceful.[65]

Even though he was in Paris Ben seemed keen to keep the babies at home. Barbara could not stand the idea of being separated from them, but the basement flat on Church Road was damp and cramped and the 'gas is leaking the boiler's leaking & the window's falling in!!!!' The responsibility of reaching a decision on her own was 'awful'. The logical side of her told her to send the babies to Wellgarth, but the emotional side of her couldn't do it. She believed they would become 'much hardier' at Wellgarth as they would have 'more sun & air & skilled diet' and she was worried that if things continued as they were she would become ill. Herbert Read encouraged her to send them to the nursery as he believed 'in the Russian method' of bringing up children collectively.[66] Barbara even worked out that it was cheaper to send them to the nursery than to employ nurses at home. However, the burden of making the decision was too much, and even though Ben said that he would support her in whatever option she chose, she told him she couldn't decide alone, particularly as one of the nurses had told her that she didn't think Rachel would survive the transition.

Towards the end of January 1935 Rachel had 'started to bloom'. Barbara was 'deeply happy' and wanted the babies with her all the time. She was also 'deeply unhappy' about not being able to work. When Ben eventually returned at the end of January they decided together to send them to the nursery, aged about four months. Margaret Gardiner, who was already assisting them financially, helped with the fees and Barbara now had time to work and also some time for herself. After months of looking after the babies she went out to dinner, played tennis, sunbathed in the garden and went to the cinema. The year 1935 was also the height of the explosion of abstraction and Ben and Barbara were at the heart of the excitement and controversy around the Unit One exhibition and the publication of *Axis*, the first art journal dedicated to abstract art. The babies flourished at the nursery, looking lovely in their dressing gowns with their eyes 'moving sideways just above the bed clothes'. As they grew older, Simon liked to bend over to touch his toes over and over again, laughing all the time.[67] A short film when they were a little older (they stayed at Wellgarth until they were at least one) shows the toddlers marching around in the grass and pushing toy prams with Ben and Barbara looking on.[68] Barbara now imagined a time when she and Ben might have the 'perfect' set-up with '2 studios adjoining'.[69]

In 1973, Barbara looked back fondly on the mix of family life and work, with the children 'brought up in it, in the middle of the dust and the dirt and the paint and everything'. She worried later about having sent them to a nursery, but when they were back with her she had her methods for keeping her focus. If she was 'in the middle of a work and the oven burned or the children called for me, I used to make an arrangement with music, records, or poetry, so that when I went back to the studio, I picked up where I left off'.[70]

3
MOLLY, JACK AND WELLS

The 'ever-open Lawn Road flats'

As Ben and Barbara were working out how to take care of the triplets while living in two cities and sustaining two careers, another experiment in living was taking place around the corner on Lawn Road. Designed by the architect Wells Coates, a modernist white block of flats that looked a bit like an ocean liner was built over the winter of 1933 and the spring of 1934. The Lawn Road flats, known as the Isokon, were built to free people from the clutter of daily life, to release them from household chores.[1] They did not need to cook or clean so that they could focus on more important things like art, politics or love. As the flats were being finished Ben wrote to Wells that they looked 'v. fine from my tennis courts'.[2]

The idea for a new style of living had arisen from conversations between Wells Coates, engineer Jack Pritchard, who was working for the Venesta Plywood Company, and his wife, Rosemary 'Molly' Pritchard, a bacteriologist who later trained as a psychotherapist. Jack wondered in retrospect if the flats would ever have been built if he had 'the experience I have now' but concluded that even with all the 'stupid mistakes' he had made he was very glad they 'took the plunge'.[3] Jack and Molly bought the plot of land in Belsize Park in 1929 for £1,500 and initially planned to build a house for themselves, or possibly two houses with a nursery school on the site. But as they became increasingly interested in European architecture and new styles of living, they came up

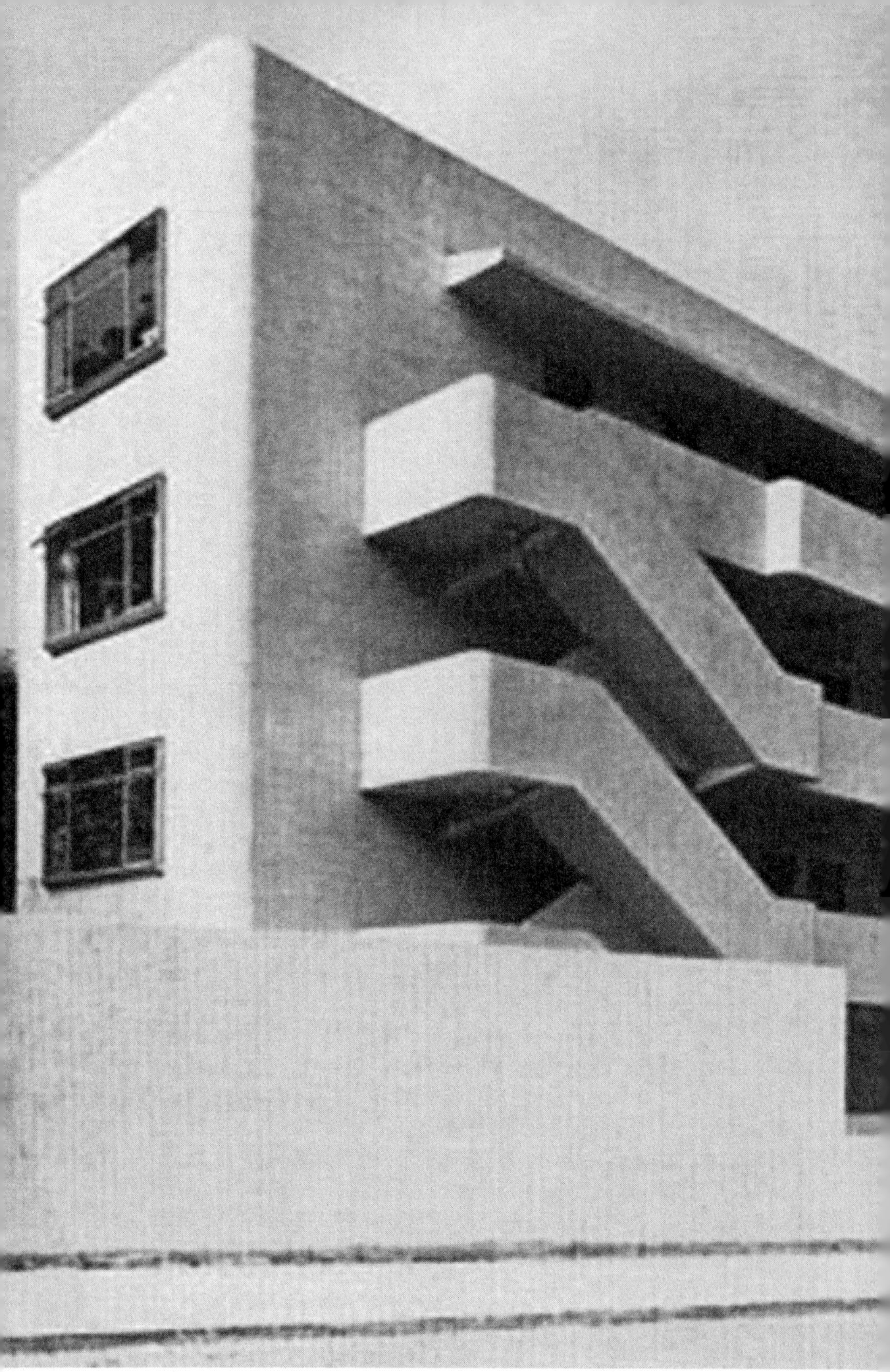

The Lawn Road Flats, also known as the Isokon

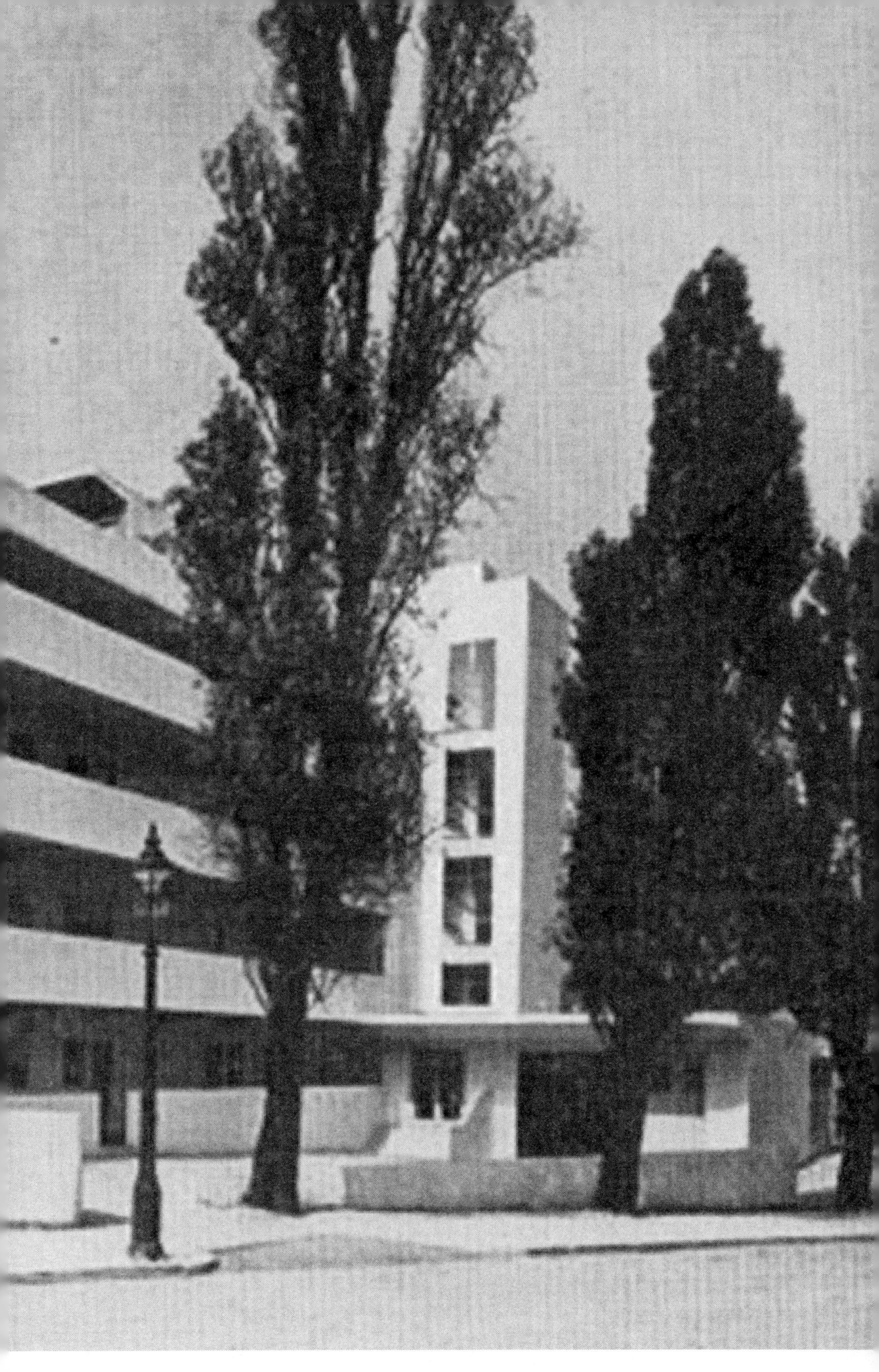

with the idea of a serviced block of flats with a penthouse and roof garden on top for themselves. In her speech at the opening of the building in April 1934, Molly explained that they had asked themselves 'how do we want to live?' and then 'what sort of framework must we build around ourselves to make that living as pleasant as possible?'[4] The intention, she said, was to provide 'good living' for people, and to spread the design across the country so that families could live in semi-communal buildings with nurseries on site for their children. The concept was utopian but the reality was less tranquil. Love and architecture were closely entwined: the Pritchards believed in open marriage and Molly was in a relationship with both Jack and Wells.

Wells was handsome and charismatic. He had a chevron moustache and 'crisply waving hair', wore sharp suits and drove a Lancia Lambda. Brought up in Japan, he liked to cook Japanese food and sit in the lotus position. In the early 1930s he was becoming quite a well-known figure on the architectural scene. In 1933 he set up the English branch of the International Congresses of Modern Architecture, known as MARS, the Modern Architectural Research Group. Wells had also designed the new sound studios for the BBC building in Portland Place and the popular circular bakelite wireless for Ekco in 1934. The Isokon, however, was his first proper building project. To show his international roots he liked to borrow a phrase from Count Herman Keyserling's *Travel Diary of a Philosopher*, that the man whose eyes have been 'trained in the East' will only 'rarely want to open them in the West'. The truly cultured man, he believed, must be 'an artist of living' through his 'eyes, voice, hands and movements'.[5]

Alternative living was familiar to Wells. By his own account he was 'passionate, mystical, proud, inquisitive and fearless', but he also felt something of a misfit.[6] Wells's father, Harper Havelock Coates, was a professor of philosophy and comparative religion at Aoyama Theological College in Tokyo and his mother, Agnes Wintemute, was co-founder and principal of one of the first missionary girls' schools in Japan. Before moving to Japan she had studied architecture with Louis Sullivan, known as the 'father

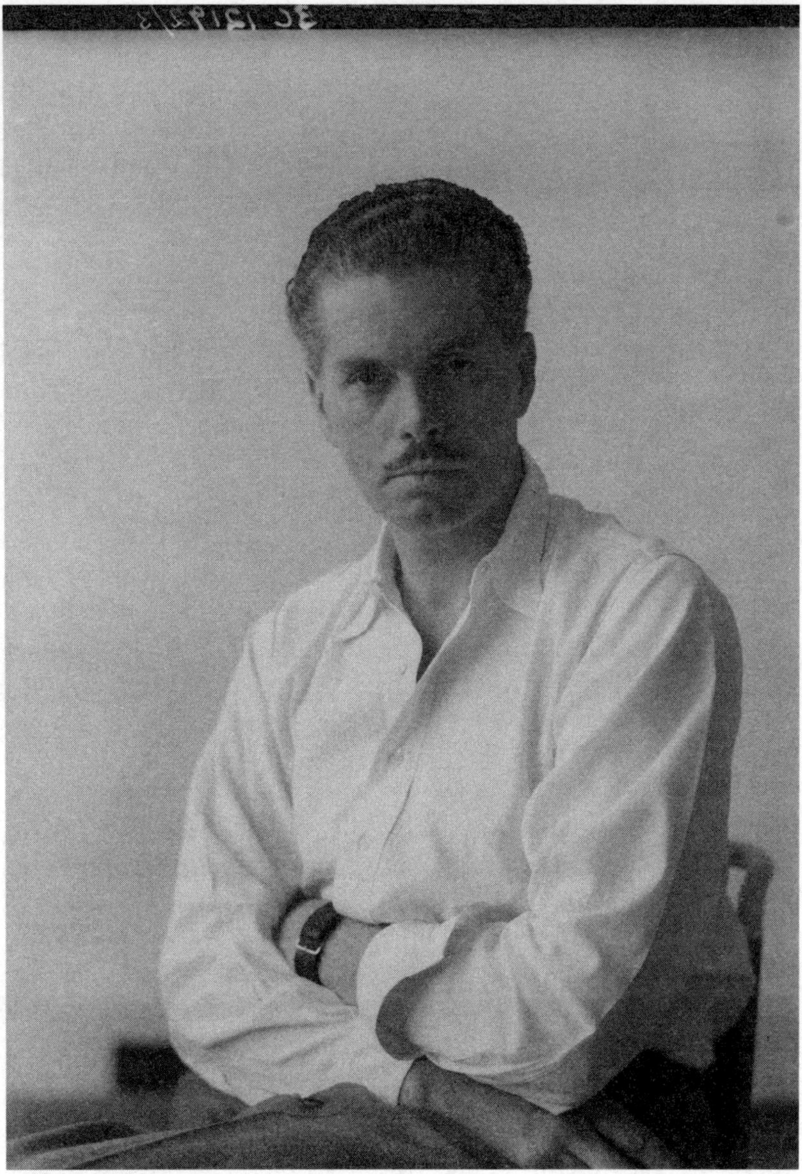

Wells Coates

of skyscrapers', in Chicago. Coates learnt a range of traditional skills in Japan that he liked to list. They included papermaking, printing, rearing silkworms, spinning, weaving and boat building as well as the ritual of serving food. When he was seventeen, his parents decided to move back to Canada, and he and his father turned the journey into a four-month cruise during which they visited China, Indonesia, Burma, India, Egypt and Europe. He went back to Canada to study engineering in Vancouver and then enlisted in the army. After a brief stint as a gunner with the Canadian Field Artillery he enrolled with the Royal Naval Air Service. Once the war was over he returned to finish his engineering degree in Canada before receiving a scholarship to study in London where he completed a PhD on 'The Gas Temperature of the Diesel Cycle' at the University of London in 1924.

Wells began hanging out at the actress Elsa Lanchester's club, the Cave of Harmony on Charlotte Street, where he met an elegant left-wing student from the London School of Economics, Marion Grove. They began a relationship in 1925 and mingled with other regulars at the club including Evelyn Waugh, Paul Nash and the dancer Rupert Doone. Marion was studying political science with the influential political theorist Harold Laski and she was a member of the Communist Party. She was tall, slender and beautiful, with fashionably short hair, but she was more interested in books than clothes and referred to herself as a 'gobbler of print'. Marion and Coates's relationship was tempestuous and when after a few months she broke things off he felt it was like 'losing one of my eyes'.

To try to mend his broken heart he and a friend from the University of London, Alfred Borgeaud, went to Canada to search for a new 'strategy for living' to combat the 'evil destructive forces of civilisation'. They were young and idealistic and decided not to tell anyone of their plans. They took editions of T. S. Eliot, Marianne Moore and Wyndham Lewis as well as a typewriter, £50 in bank credit and £5 cash. To save money they decided to 'beat trains', which meant hiding between the carriages. They had travelled about 2,000 miles when tragically Borgeaud lost his grip as the train jolted over the Coquihalla Pass near Hope and he was killed. Traumatised and distraught, Coates returned to London and looked for Marion again. He went to the 1917 Club in Gerrard Street, a left-wing group he and Marion had both once joined. She left him a letter at the club apologising for rejoining it just when he wanted to use it. They got married in August 1927 when Marion was twenty-two and working with Francis Meynell and David Garnett at the Nonesuch Press. Wells was ten years older and he set about designing their flat at 32 Doughty Street in Bloomsbury. It became a showcase for his early work: he put aluminium sheeting over the fireplace, bought some simple furniture from Heals and asked their friend John Banting to paint designs on the curtains and cupboards.

In 1928 Wells took a job designing fittings for the silk company Crysède. He designed a new façade for the first shop which opened in Cambridge in early 1929. He used curved aluminium and veneered plywood for the interiors and the woodwork was coated with metal paint. Then the manager for Crysède, Tom Heron (father of Patrick Heron, who became an artist), left to set up Cresta Silks and asked Wells to design the interior of their first shop on the Brompton Road in Knightsbridge as well as the Welwyn Garden City factory. Wells and Marion moved first to Porthmeor Square in St Ives, and then, when he joined Cresta, to Welwyn Garden City. The new brand was a great success and they opened shops in Knightsbridge, Bournemouth and Brighton. Patrick Heron later explained that the large lettering on the shop was 'totally abstract' from the front, and only visible as you walked along the pavement. The result was 'very beautiful, very brilliant'.[7] The *Architectural Review* were so impressed by Wells's clean designs they featured the Cresta interiors in their February 1931 issue. This led Wells to Jack Pritchard, who got in touch to ask if he could use them in his advertising for Venesta. Wells came to Jack's office at Venesta and they quickly realised their shared passion for modernist design, new styles of living and plywood in particular. Wells told Jack that he knew straight away that they

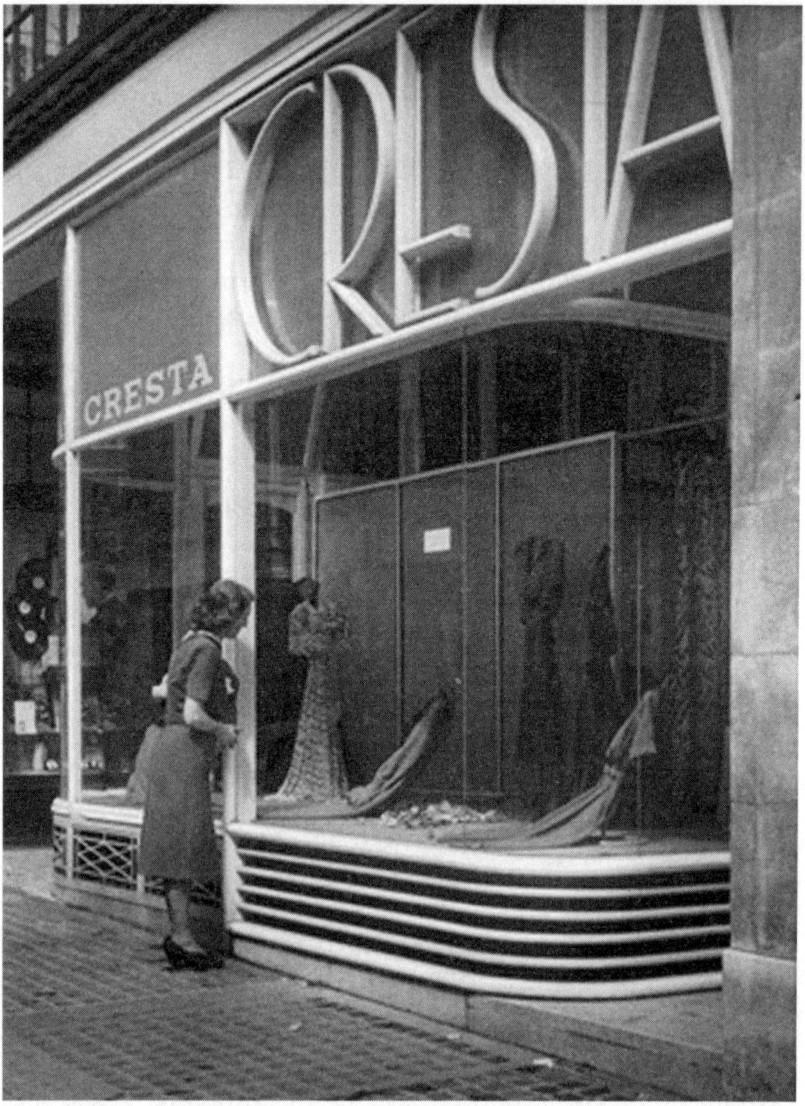

Cresta Silks in Knightsbridge

were destined to work together one day. He even told Jack that he reminded him of his old friend Borgeaud.[8] Meanwhile Wells and Marion had a new baby, Laura, born in 1930. The pregnancy had not been straightforward and so the doctors advised Marion to move to the country with the baby. They went to Sussex and Wells was optimistic that he could be there at weekends. His letters, however, were hasty and unpunctuated: 'love love love Must rush and get things done' or 'Impossible get to you Sunday writing love'. Marion understood, but suggested he sometimes 'dropped the reins and amble along. Yes?' And by early July 1931 she decided it was time she 're-entered adult life' and that she and Laura should move to a flat in London. Wells was not keen as it would cost, he thought, about £200 a year. But by mid-July Marion was desperate: 'I am humiliated, I am afraid, I rage and despair at the same time... What has happened? For God's sake what has happened?'[9] Wells relented and they found a basement flat, 12a Belsize Park Gardens, a five-minute walk from Lawn Road.[10]

Jack Pritchard was the kind of person who 'made things happen, often against the odds'.[11] He was more practical than Coates and yet, paradoxically, he had a utopian streak. He believed that new buildings could lead to new lives, even to a better world. He was born in Hampstead in 1899, on the 'less fashionable side of Finchley Road', at 6 Compayne Gardens, the youngest of four children. His father, Clive Pritchard, was a barrister but in 1902 he was elected mayor of Hampstead and the family moved across the Finchley Road, and up the social ladder, to Maresfield Gardens. Jack was dyslexic, so he struggled at primary school and did not read until he was eleven. He was sent to boarding school at Oundle in Northamptonshire where the progressive headteacher F. W. Sanderson encouraged his interest in engineering.

At the end of his schooling Jack sat a psychology test with the Pelman Institute. Founded in 1898 the Institute was a popular way of determining mental strengths and weaknesses and offered courses for ailments such as 'brain fag', 'indefiniteness' or 'want of energy'. Jack's results revealed a good visual memory and a healthy dose of ingenuity and inventiveness, but also a mental laziness to be overcome by reading the 'right' books. His results suggested that he might be suited to engineering, so he applied for engineering and economics at Pembroke College, Cambridge. While there Jack put his inventiveness into some lighthearted fun as a member of the Teapot and Pavement Club. This involved sitting on the pavement and reading the news aloud so that passers-by or thirsty lecture-goers could drink a cup of tea and listen to the news. On another occasion they advertised a talk by Arthur Conan Doyle at the Guildhall, Cambridge, and, mocking Doyle's fascination with the paranormal, Jack pulled a string at the required moment to reveal a notice that read 'We very much regret that Sir Arthur Conan Doyle has failed to materialise.'[12]

Jack and Molly met during their first week at Cambridge, punting on the River Cam with a group of friends. Molly was more reserved and more intellectually inclined than Jack, but they both felt an immediate attraction. Molly grew up in Streatham and then Kensington and her father was a solicitor. Encouraged to be musical and artistic during her childhood, she felt herself the black sheep of the family and a 'naughty and disagreeable child' and believed that her mother had sent her to boarding school when she was nine as her presence was 'too upsetting'. Molly thrived at school, inspired by a science teacher who held up a prism to a ray of sunlight to show them the colours of the rainbow. After prep school in Surrey she went to Godolphin and Latymer in Hammersmith and then won a scholarship to read medicine at Girton, the first women's college in Cambridge. She and Jack were very much at the heart of Cambridge society, a vibrant scene of May balls, boat races, fast cars and nude bathing. During his finals Jack was anxious not to miss a friend's wedding and so he hired a small aeroplane to take off just after his last exam, selling tickets to a handful of family and friends to pay for it. He finished the exam and they made it on time.[13]

After university, Jack worked for the Michelin Tyre Company, run by a humorous and 'comfortable buffer' in Clermont-Ferrand in the centre of France, for six months before moving back to London. An unusual first job for a Cambridge man, it had a big influence on Prichard's later career. He learnt the art of scientific management, or the breaking down of operations into a series of units and recording the time of each.[14] After a couple of years of selling advertising space for various magazines he joined the Venesta Plywood Company in 1926 as a market investigator. Molly received a first in Natural Sciences from Cambridge and between 1921 and 1924 trained at Charing Cross Hospital in London where she became the assistant pathologist. She then moved to the drug manufacturer Glaxo, working on the benefits of cod-liver oil.

Molly and Jack got married in 1924 at Kensington Register Office and lived in Paddington before moving in 1926 to 79 Platt's Lane, a four-storey house in Hampstead. Their first son Jonathan was born that same year followed by Jeremy in 1928. They were both interested in theories of parenting and education and were influenced by Molly's mother, who had worked at the infant welfare clinic in Marylebone, set up in 1907. They decided to follow a strict regime where the 'child must be fed by the clock, pot trained from the start, and never picked up except for nappy changing or feeding'. They later decided that this was a 'bad mistake' and wished they had been more 'lenient and affectionate'. After the children were born Molly continued her studies and took courses in psychology and psychopathology at University College London. Through a mutual friend from Cambridge she met Beatrix Tudor-Hart in the late 1920s.

Beatrix had read classics at Newnham College, Cambridge, and then studied psychology in Vienna and nursery school education at Smith College in Massachusetts. She was brought up in Paris and spoke six languages. When Molly and Jack met her she had just been teaching at Dora and Bertrand Russell's new progressive school in Beacon Hill, near South Harting in Sussex. Jack was much impressed by Beatrix; she was a 'fine tall girl, handsome and intelligent' and 'passionately concerned with education'. She invited Molly and Jack to stay in her father's villa in France and during the holiday she and Jack became lovers. In 1929 Beatrix gave birth to Jack's daughter, Jennifer. With three small children, and a relaxed attitude to marriage, it made sense for Beatrix and Molly to set up a nursery school on the top floor of the Pritchards' house in Platt's Lane. They called it the Children's Group and as well as being extremely convenient it gave the children a 'splendid start'.

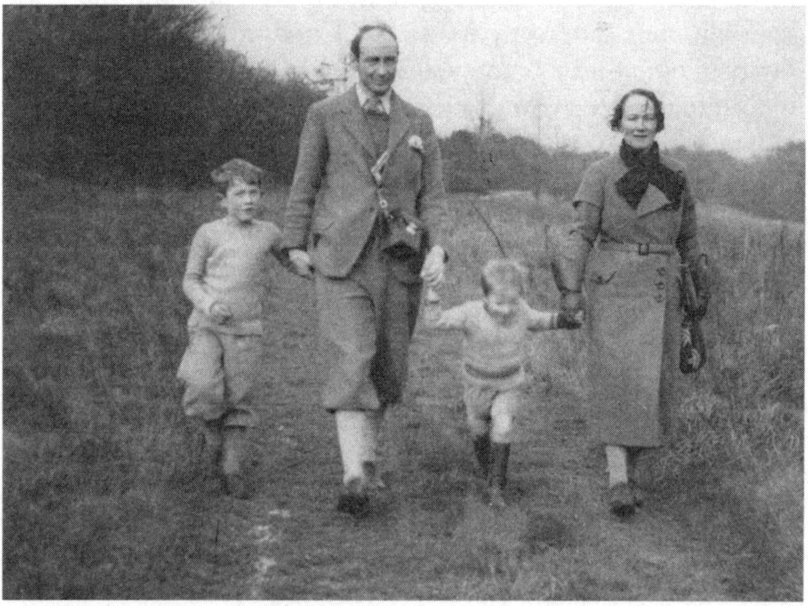

Molly and Jack with their children Jonathan and Jeremy

Having been impressed by Bertrand Russell's book *On Education* and by what they had heard from Beatrix about the school, Jack and Molly decided to send their boys to Beacon Hill. Set up in 1927, the school took children as young as two. It claimed to fill young people with 'constructive hopefulness', rendering them conscious of the 'great things to be done in the world', rather than churning out 'listless individuals'. Morality and reasoning were not imposed but learnt through experience. Molly and Jack felt that Dora Russell was a 'veritable mother-figure' and the family atmosphere she created was very real.[15]

Dora Russell was a radical as well as a mother figure. She was a feminist and a birth-control campaigner and had helped to set up the Workers' Birth Control Group in 1924. She and Bertrand had been members of the Heretics Society at Cambridge and Dora had become the secretary of the English Section of the World League for Sexual Reform, a group that advocated sex education and free contraception. The League promoted the idea that sexual pleasure was healthy and desirable and should be 'legitimately obtainable in any and every form provided there is no interference with the rights of others'.[16] Despite their progressive views and high ambitions for the children, it was harder to run a school than they imagined. They had considerably underestimated the costs, so just before the school opened Bertrand went to America to give a series of lectures in order to make more money. Left to run the school, Dora quickly realised that the children had no 'quiet love or concern for creative things'. She wrote to Bertrand that she was so overwhelmed she felt like crying. She decided the children must be homesick and forgave them their disruptive behaviour. She changed her mind: a month later she wrote to Bertrand that they were 'sadists'.[17] Bertrand urged her to hire another teacher to help out and in retrospect he thought they were mistaken in 'several things'. Many of the children had been sent to Beacon Hill as they were unsuited to mainstream schooling. The Russells were also ill equipped to deal with multiple illnesses, especially when the school suffered a chickenpox epidemic. Left to their own devices, they concluded, young children 'turn to bullying or destruction'.[18] Their own child Kate described the opening of the school as the moment their idyllic family life was destroyed.

However, in the early 1930s, the Pritchards, like the Russells, believed that children needed to work out discipline for themselves and they liked the fact that classes at Beacon Hill were not compulsory. Jack was delighted by the sight of a young boy up a tree, reading a maths book. Later the Pritchard boys went to Bryanston, under the headship of T. F. Coade, who had 'many good ideas'. But Jack felt they 'had not at that stage fully learned the importance of the family – a common mistake in the 1930s. I think we sent the boys to boarding school too early and did not give them enough of the family background that is so important in development.'[19] At the time Molly and Jack believed they had chosen a utopian community for their boys and this freed them up to consider their own living arrangements.

□

In the spring of 1930 Jack went to Paris for Venesta to report on their sister plywood furniture company, Luterma. As well as office and railway furniture Luterma had begun to make plywood hatboxes, bags and suitcases and were experimenting with lunchboxes and collecting bags for botanical specimens. While he was investigating uses of plywood, Jack met Louise Goepfert, who went on to found the Rochester Folk Art Guild in upstate New York. In Paris she was working at Gurdjieff's Institute for the Harmonic Development of Man. Through Louise Jack spent an unusual evening with Gurdjieff at the Grand Café in Fontainebleau drinking Armagnac. They returned to the Institute and went to the Turkish baths dug out of the hill. Jack found himself trapped in a hot corner unable to move past the 'very large Gurdjieff'. After a cold shower and a slice of cold potato dipped in curry powder he went back to Paris.[20] Although he was not overly impressed by the guru himself, the Institute at Fontainebleau gave Jack another taste of alternative lifestyles.

Jack suggested to Molly that while he was away she might like to invite Wells to dinner and let it be known that their views on marriage were very relaxed. Molly was open to the idea but was worried that her flirting would not work: 'suppose he didn't want to flirt with me. I should feel snubbed and awkward.' It turned out that he was very happy to flirt and they embarked on an affair. And so they began to discuss the possibility of building more than one house on the Lawn Road site, one for the

Pritchards and one for the Coateses, and a nursery too. They had also considered a house for Beatrix and Jennifer, but Beatrix and Jack were currently not speaking as Jack had refused to spend one night a week with her and Jenny.

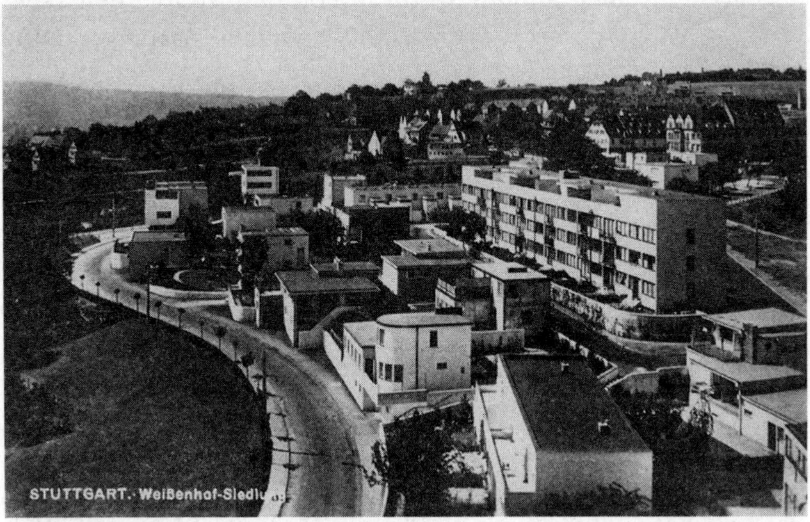

Weissenhof Estate Stuttgart, 1927

In April 1930 Molly and Wells planned to join Jack in Europe for an architectural tour of Germany. Molly was ill and unable to travel, so Wells and Jack went alone to Stuttgart to visit the popular Weissenhof Estate built for the Deutscher Werkbund exhibition in 1927. This was a housing complex organised by Ludwig Mies van der Rohe with twenty-one buildings designed by seventeen architects, including two by Le Corbusier and two by Gropius. The prototypes were all designed as workers' housing, although in reality they were out of the price range of the average worker. The trip cemented the partnership between Wells and Jack and when they got back they set up Wells Coates and Partners in order to design and build 'dwellings for modern people'. They were both keen to start building on the Lawn Road site, but they could not raise the £2,000 needed for each house. In February 1931 they turned their company into the

Isokon Company, so named because Coates used 'isometric unit construction' or units of the same measurements in his drawings and Pritchard liked 'the Russian type of name'. Molly was also pleased with the new name. Wells was the architect and Jack was in charge of planning, marketing and advertising, but together they were committed to 'modern industrial design, based on the principle of conspicuous economy'. They were united in their anti-Victorian modernist belief that 'decoration is desecration'.[21]

Inspired by the trip, Wells set to work designing two 'Isotype Dwellings' on the Lawn Road plot of land. These evolved into four or five houses of various sizes. Molly and Jack were 'bowled over' by the designs. They had previously asked Molly's sister Jill and her husband Harry Harrison to design a house which would have been a 'charming little neo-Georgian house that gave a nod to the modern', but Wells's design blew theirs out of the water. Although united in their design preferences, cracks began to appear between Jack and Wells when it came to practicalities. Jack made the mistake of asking about the issue of waste disposal and Wells almost tore up the plans because Jack had discussed his design 'on the same level as dustbins'. Wells told him that he had 'put all my heart and soul into this job, for it's the most important I have ever done'. He had only shown Jack and Molly the drawings when they were 'clearly drawn, tight, logical, scientific' and all he heard through the window was a 'mumble grumble about dustbins and their position'.[22] Jack also wondered about the possibility of dividing up the site into separate dwellings at a later date. Wells was passionately against carving up land into little pieces. The 'idea of property', he told Jack, where 'this little garden is for you m'dear and this tweeny little wishy bit is for me so there! – is *dead*, dead, dead ...'. Wells's vision was one in which every 'actor in this drama' has a room to sleep in, a room to work in and a place to eat. Other than that everyone can enjoy the sun on the roof garden and the garden is a place for everyone, 'like a park' or 'our little playground'.[23] Wells was committed to the idea of collective living.

After the success of the Weissenhof Estate trip, Wells, Jack and Russian-born architect Serge Chermayeff went to visit Erich Mendelsohn in Berlin and then on to the Bauhaus in Dessau in March 1931. Wells and Serge had worked together on the Broadcasting House designs; Serge later went into partnership with Mendelsohn and in 1934 designed the ultra-modernist De La Warr Pavilion at Bexhill on Sea in East Sussex. Wells, Jack and Serge almost didn't make their train to Dessau from Berlin. Mendelsohn had entertained them extremely well the night before, beginning with 'green' cocktails, followed by cherry cobblers (gin and brandy) and then a visit to a Russian restaurant involving a few blinis and a considerable amount of vodka. They dragged Wells to the railway station the next morning and managed to jump on the last carriage as it was leaving the platform. Gropius had resigned three years earlier from the Bauhaus, the school of design he set up in Weimar in 1919, so when they got there the place was pretty much abandoned due to political difficulties and yet it 'looked fine amid the unkempt grass, and at least we could look round the building'. Some unearthed film footage shot by Jack shows Wells and Serge striding ahead towards the buildings, the camera sweeping 'back and forth across the vast glass curtain wall, cantilevered steel-frame balconies, flat roofs and grey and white concrete facades'. Pritchard didn't know it yet but 'both the Bauhaus and Walter Gropius were to have an enormous influence on much of my future.'[24]

During the planning stages of the Isotype dwellings, Molly mentioned to Wells and Jack that she supposed that land in London should really be used for more than one family. Wells jumped at the idea and said he always knew the right thing to do was to build flats. So, although the 'decision was much more the product of a general discussion' among all three of them, 'it was Wells who kept up the pressure'.[25] By August Wells had confirmed that he would 'proceed on these lines'.[26] Although Molly and Jack were still captivated by the small houses, once they saw the initial plans for the flats they 'were completely and utterly convinced that it was right to do it' and thought the 'whole thing was very beautiful'.[27]

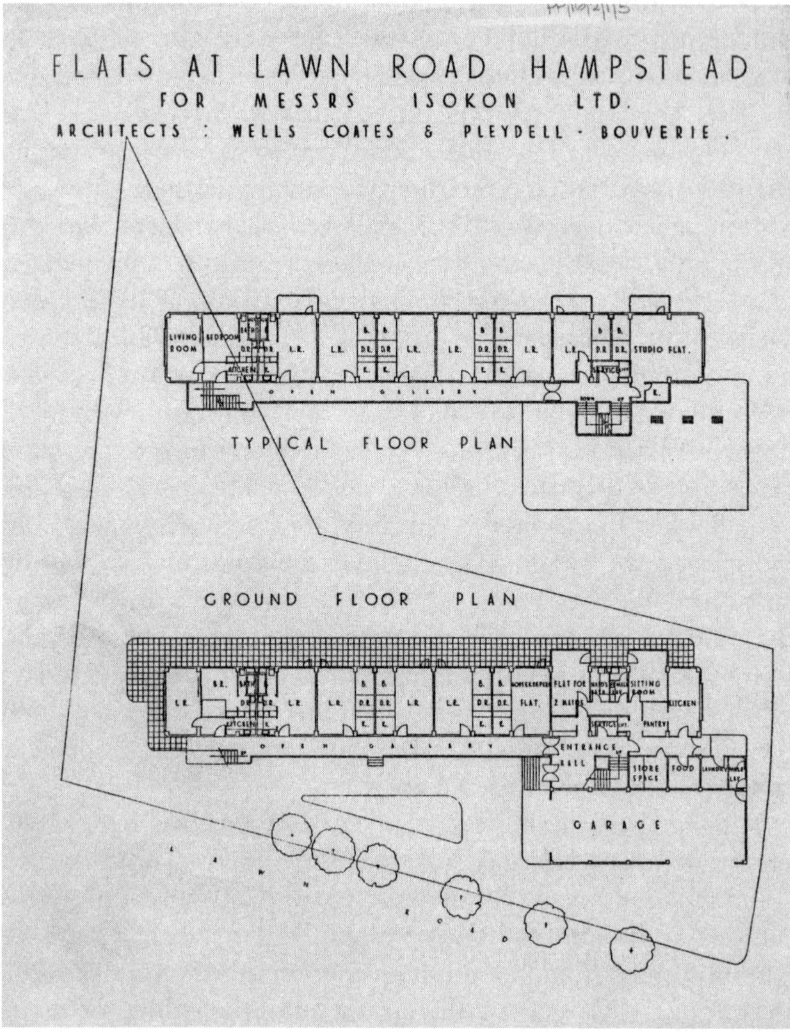

Floor plans for the Lawn Road Flats, Wells Coates, 1933

The early designs were beautiful, but they also required more money. Molly drew up an advertisement to drum up support. They decided to target young professionals with few possessions, on an income of about £500 per year. A draft of the ad stated that everything 'unnecessary, ugly, inconvenient and "labour-making"' would be eliminated and everything essential would be 'in exactly the right position'.[28] They would offer bedmaking, clothes washing, shoe polishing, window cleaning, dusting and meals provided by a central kitchen. And so by the spring of 1932 Molly and Jack were ready to set out exactly what they wanted. They asked Wells to create a block with twenty one-room flats, a few two-room flats, staff quarters, a central kitchen, a laundry room, a roof garden and balconies where possible because sunbathing was such a popular pastime in the 1930s. They also wanted a lounge for visitors and a garage for about eight cars. Their estimated cost was about £6,500 but Wells said it would cost more like £8,000–£9,000. The final building costs eventually came in at £14,850.

By June 1932 Coates had created a mock-up of one of the 'minimum' flats, measuring about eighteen feet by ten, for the Exhibition of British Industrial Art in the Home at Dorland Hall in Lower Regent Street. The modernists had taken over the exhibition: Chermayeff designed a weekend house and Ambrose Heal designed a dining room. Wells's mock-up had the desired effect: they let twelve of the flats with deposits paid before building work had begun. Jack would have preferred to exhibit designs for Isotype houses at the exhibition, but in the end he agreed 'it gave us an awful lot of publicity'.[29] Jack's long-term plan was to move affordable housing away from a Victorian red-brick Peabody atmosphere and towards light, modern houses that made efficient use of space. The Peabody Trust, set up by the American banker George Peabody in 1862, promoted comfort and happiness for the 'poor and needy' of London through model dwellings. Some Peabody ideas were still useful to Jack and Wells, for example having walkways on the outside of the building from which each flat would be entered. But the structural decisions were new: the external walls were to be concrete, which had not been used for domestic housing in Britain before. Wells had seen reproductions of Russian blocks of flats built with concrete and he had met Lubetkin in Paris,

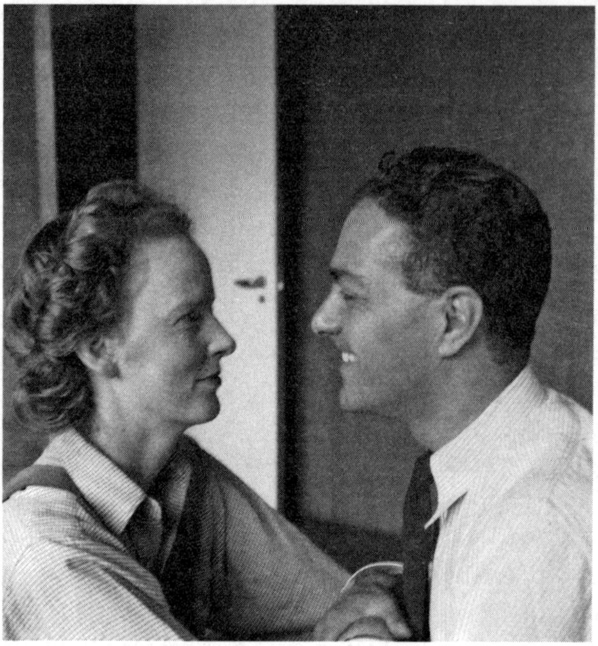

Ursula and Ernő Goldfinger

but this was the first concrete block of flats in Britain. The finished design included twenty-two single flats, four double flats and three double studios. The one-bedroom penthouse and adjoining apartment for the children was completed later when the Pritchards found the extra funds.

The Isokon Company had competition. The Georgian-born Berthold Lubetkin was already part of the Modern Architectural Research Group started by Wells and Philip Morton Shand, and in 1932 Lubetkin set up the Tecton Group. Their first commission was the Gorilla House at London Zoo, followed by the Penguin Pool with its elegant interlocking spiral ramps. Lubetkin drew upon the expertise of structural engineer Ove Arup, an expert in reinforced concrete. In the same way that Wells and the Pritchards were planning to influence the lifestyle of the inhabitants of the Isokon, Lubetkin's behaviourism investigated the ways animals were shaped by their environment. But some of the penguins caught 'bumblefoot' or bacterial infections caused by micro-abrasions from the concrete, so they were later rehomed. The walkways are now simply admired for their architectural ingenuity. The Tecton Group also designed structures for both Whipsnade and Dudley Zoo and then in 1935 they won the commission for Highpoint, a block of flats in Highgate that was later joined by Highpoint II to complete the pair of modernist towers with views over London. Ernő and Ursula Goldfinger moved into Highpoint I in 1935 before moving into 2 Willow Road, one of three modernist houses built by Goldfinger in 1938–9. Ursula and Margaret Gardiner enjoyed swimming in the Hampstead ponds together.

Ernő knew Lubetkin from Paris and was a fan of the Penguin Pool at London Zoo, but didn't like living in Highpoint very much; he thought it awkward having to walk through the living room to get to the other rooms of the flat. Ernő and Ursula married in 1933 and moved to London in 1934. They rented in Markham Square, just off the King's Road, and then in Springfield Road in St John's Wood, and Ernő rented an office in 7 Bedford Square. They moved to Highpoint in July 1935 and Ernő began work on a design for a salon in Golders Green with Moholy-Nagy. It did not come to anything in the end but Ernő's furniture designs were going well, including a range of wooden toys and furniture for children. He came up with the idea of a 'Growing table' where you unscrew the legs and make them taller as the child grows. He had also begun designing houses with Gerald Flower and their first house was built in Broxted, Essex. Ursula decided it was time to release some of her family money so they could buy land and build their family home. In 1936 they found a site on Willow Road in Hampstead for £3,885 and cleared the three Georgian cottages on it. At first Ernő wanted to build flats but then decided on three modern terraced houses. The plans were not popular with the Hampstead Heath and Old Hampstead Protection Society. The President, Henry Brooke (who later became Home Secretary), wrote that the 'atmosphere' of the approach from the Heath to Downshire Hill would be 'irretrievably' damaged. Roland Penrose and Lee

Miller, who lived around the corner on Downshire Hill and were friends with Ernő and Ursula, supported the Willow Road plans. And Julian Huxley, the zoologist and brother of Aldous, wrote to the *Daily Telegraph* that the Protection Society should spend more time preventing the 'sham Tudor and nondescript villa architecture' that was sprouting up along the borders of the heath and to leave the 'true twentieth-century British style' alone.[30]

The plans for 1–3 Willow Road were put up in the bar at the Isokon and Goldfinger pointed out that he was echoing and updating the Regency and Queen Anne style and proportions of the surrounding houses. The plans were given the green light. The houses had three stories at the front and four at the back because they were built on a slope and the central one, belonging to Ernő and Ursula, was the largest. They were all built with a concrete frame and exterior walls made of traditional brick. Unlike Corbusier, Ernő preferred to leave materials showing. Each house had a cast concrete spiral staircase and some of the rooms were lined with plywood. The studio space in the central house had a raised step for models and a storage space for paintings in the drawers beneath. The partitions between the dining room, the studio and the living room could fold back to open out the space. Ernő believed that bathrooms and WCs should be small, as space is for living.

Returning to the construction of the Lawn Road Flats, by mid-July 1932 the building-contract bids were in. They decided to go with the lowest, an East London building firm, Messrs George Barker, whose bid came in at £13,587 and a total construction period of twenty-four weeks. Jack and Molly were excited by Wells's design but Jack was 'bewildered and hardly dared think about what we were undertaking'.[31] After cutting out a few of the specifications, for example saving on roofing materials and the metal trims to door and window frames, they brought the cost down to £12,500.[32] They came to an arrangement by which the building firm would be paid £1,000 every two weeks, but they were less clear about the financial arrangements with Wells.

Jack and Molly had £5,000, but that was not enough to keep the project afloat so they took out a loan at a very high interest rate. They quickly realised their mistake and found a better one. However, alongside their financial naivety and anxiety, friction was growing between Wells and Jack. Wells was under a lot of pressure and felt uneasy making promises he might not be able to keep. He could not, for example, promise that all the cupboards would open on both sides if they formed a partition between the 'kitchenette' and the 'dining recess'.[33] The main cause of friction was money, not Molly's affair with Wells. Wells needed money up front and in November he asked for a 'small sum on account' for 'staff and overhead' because the bank was 'closing in on me'.[34] Jack felt he was paying everybody and seeing no progress. By February 1933 he was so frustrated that he asked the Isokon company solicitor, Graham Maw, to write to Wells. Maw got straight to the point and asked Wells if he would 'keep to a schedule' and 'produce the goods'.[35] Wells told them that their 'unsympathetic' and 'big-stick' business letter was pointless. If they did not have faith in him, he suggested they proceed without him.[36]

Wells himself then became frustrated with the slow progress. He wrote to Molly, rather than Jack, to complain that his plans were going to waste. He had designed 'unit plyboxes' for storage and clocks for all the flats but they had come to nothing as Jack couldn't make up his mind about whether to use them. Wells suggested that they get together to find a way forward and thanked Molly for 'honestly trying to help', reassuring her that he had 'no personal feelings' about any of it. He reminded her of his various triumphs, perhaps hoping that she would remind Jack. He mentioned Broadcasting House, his role as vice chairman of the architects committee for the Dorland Hall exhibition and as chairman of MARS.[37] He was annoyed that Jack seemed to think he was not working hard enough and suggested that he come and sit in his office for a day.

By May Wells was promising, somewhat rashly, that the 'Isokon Lawn Road flats will go to schedule'.[38] Jack was relieved, but the newfound harmony did not last long. Wells was unhappy with an order of mahogany and he took it out on the contractors. Jack had to smooth things over and told Wells that there was 'no reason why you should be rude'.[39] Wells was confident that building work would begin as soon as he returned from holiday on 21 August and, in buoyant mood, he expressed the hope that they would work on bigger building projects in London.[40] Now it was Jack's turn to hold things up. He had been under the impression that London County Council needed to sign off on the project and he found their vagueness 'disconcerting'. Wells urged the builders to go ahead but Jack made them wait. As winter set in they lost two weeks of construction time because they were not allowed to set concrete when the temperature was below 39 degrees Fahrenheit (4 degrees Centigrade). It also meant they held back payment to the building contractors just before Christmas.[41] On 17 January 1934 they finalised the details for the penthouse. Although it is difficult to imagine them all living at such close quarters, Wells, at this point, asked about renting one of the flats 'if its not too expensive!' He had also found another site for them to develop into a block of flats.[42] Molly and Jack promised to reserve a flat for Wells and asked him to think of important people they might invite to a cocktail party in the specimen flat when it was ready.[43]

Jack was under the impression that, even with the delays over the winter, the tenants would be able to move in by Easter. Wells explained that, in addition to the two weeks lost in December, on some days work had not begun until 10 a.m. or even noon and had been stopped early before the temperature dropped. He also pointed out that the contractors had spent longer on the foundations, in order to check that the soil could withstand two tons per square foot weight. They had moreover been forbidden to put electric service pipes in the structural floor. The frost, he added, was an 'act of God' and there was nothing he could have done about it.[44]

Molly and Jack were anxious on two fronts. The delays meant that they were unable to recoup their costs through rent and they were worried about negative publicity when tenants found they were unable to move in. Wells was struggling financially and complained that it was a 'bit thick' that he had not been paid for three months.[45] Jack retaliated by asking Wells about the 'little debt of a hundred and something pounds'.[46] The financial strain was causing a rift. Wells was fed up with being asked for drawings, details and conferences, extra staff for supervision and completion without being 'adequately paid according to our verbal arrangement'.[47] And the penthouse plans didn't help. Jack and Molly wanted plywood walls and floor throughout and a seven-foot extension to their living room, but that meant that Wells would have to move the central service lift so that it could emerge inside their kitchen. The changes cost £800 with £5 going to Wells for the new designs.[48]

Wells's financial situation put extra pressure on his already strained relationship with Marion. He was obsessed with work and, according to Marion, never wanted to come home. She was torn because Wells gave her the most joy she had known with anyone, but also the most pain. She was angry that he was 'over stimulated' and was 'never there'. Unlike their flat in Doughty Street, he hardly decorated their flat in Belsize Park Gardens – he just covered it with the 'cheapest white lining paper'. When the lease on the Belsize Park flat came to an end they decided to live separately. Marion took Laura to Jersey where her parents lived, and then moved into a flat on Abbey Road, NW8. Wells moved to his offices in Victoria and then designed himself a studio flat in Yeoman's Row, SW3.[49] He sent money sporadically, but it was not enough to live on and so Marion took a secretarial job at the publisher Jonathan Cape and found a Swiss girl to look after Laura. This was the best thing she could have done. It meant she no longer felt she was becoming a 'grass-green-greying widow' in her mid-twenties. Through her work, which she enjoyed very much, she met the novelist Anthony Powell. They began to meet regularly and although he had had a series of affairs, he later described his great passion for her. Powell said Marion reminded him of Rubens's *Chapeau de paille* (*Woman in a Straw Hat*) and 1934 was a period of extreme happiness for them both. Even though Powell paused his writing during their affair, Marion edited *Sea Sequel to the Week-end Book* that year, an anthology of poetry, songs and games for the 'sea-going traveller'. Their affair became the love affair with Jean Duport that haunts the protagonist in

Powell's twelve-volume *A Dance to the Music of Time*. Marion's daughter remembered her mother in the 1950s, 1960s and 1970s rushing out to buy a copy whenever a new volume came out.[50]

Despite the financial wrangling and emotional entanglements the flats were slowly emerging on Lawn Road. They were angled away from the road to avoid building over two railway tunnels under the site, giving them an exaggerated sense of perspective. Jack remembered an elderly lady who walked by as they were being built and asked him why they had such small windows. He explained they were the kitchen windows and would keep things cool, whereas the 'sitting rooms were on the other side, with large windows facing south-west to get the sun'. She said that was 'a wonderful idea' and then, with a 'happy smile', added that she still hated the building and carried on walking.[51]

The flats were not suitable for families (apart from the penthouse), and they were not affordable by working-class people. They were intended for middle-class professionals who might otherwise live in digs. Each flat, the advertisement stated, would be kitted out with 'floor coverings, light fittings and a radiator, a sliding table, divan with over-lay, wash basin with mirror and glass shelf, hanging cupboard with a long mirror, and a dressing table with drawers and cupboards underneath, electric cooker, refrigerator, sink and refuse bucket, and additional storage space'.[52] All you have to do, the ad claimed, was bring 'your rug, armchair and favourite picture'. And, despite Wells's concern about the practicalities, it turned out that laundry, window cleaning and shoe cleaning were all on offer, as were meals 'at moderate prices'. There was an irony in the fact that Molly, Jack and Wells wanted to free people from the chaos of their lives when their own lives were far from simple. 'We cannot burden ourselves with permanent tangible possessions,' Wells wrote in the *Listener*, as we already have 'our real new possessions of freedom, travel, new experience – in short, what we call life'.[53] Some tangible possessions were on offer though: bookshelves, cupboards, chairs, an electric fire and a combined wireless and cocktail cabinet could all be bought on hire purchase. The Isokon Company also produced a range of plywood furniture. Wells designed book units that could be joined together by a sheet of plywood to create a desk, and Pritchard designed a desk and cantilevered chair made from a section of a plywood Venesta tramcar seat.

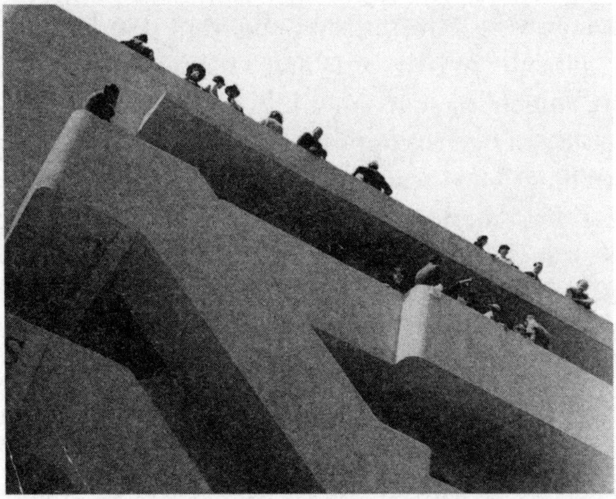

The opening of the Lawn Road Flats, 9 July 1934

Relations between Wells and Jack hit rock bottom in April 1934 when Wells sold Isokon housing plans to a building firm called E. & L. Berg. Even though he didn't completely copy the designs, he copied the methods. 'You and I', Jack wrote to Wells, were 'within an ace of cementing a most formidable combination.' He added that Berg would simply build the designs for money whereas at Isokon they would have built the whole idea. Wells had 'broken faith' and Jack felt they would be unable to 'work together in the future'.[54] But by the middle of May they were discussing the numbering of the flats, and then the position of the letterboxes and door handles. The manager of the newly opened cinema at the Everyman Theatre in Hampstead asked to put up a poster in the lobby. And then, a month before the grand opening of the building, Wells threatened the Isokon Company with the 'usual procedure for debt collection'. Jack took 'great exception' to Wells's 'impertinent letter' and, in bullish mode, suggested that

Wells's accountants could 'take any legal action' they liked but that they would do the same back 'for your little debt to me'.[55] Nothing came of these legal threats, and days before the opening ceremony Wells confirmed that a sign saying 'Lawn Road Flats' would be an 'attractive method' of finishing the building, much better than putting lettering 'over the front door'.[56]

The Conservative MP for Islington East, Thelma Cazalet, was invited to 'launch' the flats on 9 July, and in 'democratic fashion' broke a bottle of beer, as opposed to champagne, against the side of the building. They served smoked salmon, egg-and-anchovy and cheese-and-gherkin sandwiches for about 150 people. Molly made the speech, a diplomatic choice given the tension, and she called it 'the most modern building in England', not only in terms of its design but as 'a revolutionary idea for living'. Rather than seeing city living as 'complicated, expensive and dirty' they wanted to provide 'good living' for young people who were working in the city, before they had families. She urged everyone to 'spread the news of these flats among your friends' so that they could fill them up quickly and build flats in 'Manchester, Birmingham, Nottingham and so on'.[57]

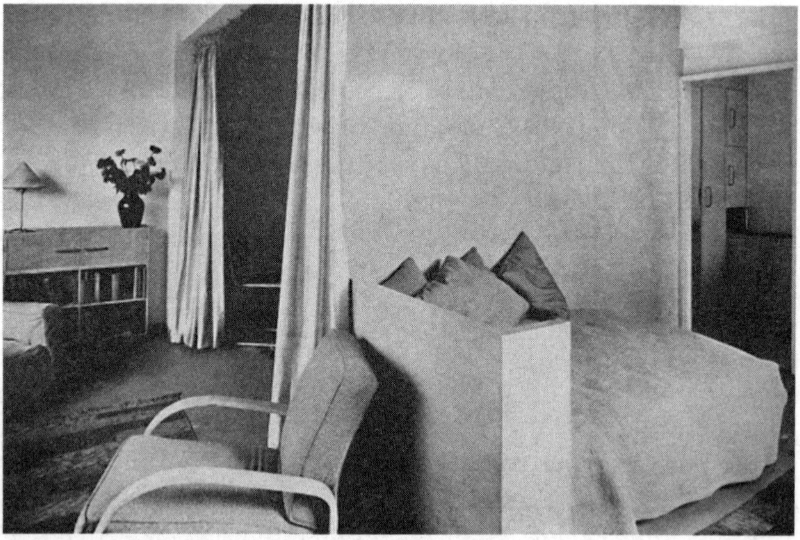

Furnished studio living room in the Lawn Road Flats

News of the opening of the flats was picked up all over the UK. The *Observer* congratulated Mr Coates on 'the logic of his planning and the beauty of his smooth, lean, elegant design', explaining that one does not want to feel 'dominated by one's surroundings'. The *Yorkshire Observer* seized on the ship metaphor, describing the building as a 'dazzlingly white' modern liner with 'exterior landings as decks' for communal sunning. It went on to add, however, that there was a distinct lack of 'quarrelling' and 'muddle' space. The *Birmingham Post* called them 'Hotel-like Homes' and the *New Statesman and Nation* pointed out that as long as you didn't have a family you could live in 'perfect comfort'. In fact, the writer continued, they wouldn't mind being one of the industrious 'human bees' in one of those 'soundproof cells'. The *Daily Mirror* reviewer spotted that most of the flats were occupied by single men but thought perhaps that was because women preferred to decorate their own homes. Some papers were concerned about making housewives redundant, but the *Cabinet Maker* was most distressed by the inbuilt furniture, which would no doubt erode the taste of the general population.[58]

And so, by the summer of 1934, the flats were occupied. But not all of the tenants were happy in their new homes. One of the first inhabitants was the Honourable Ralph Edward Gathorne-Hardy, a friend of Winston Churchill's. He wrote to complain that a landlord who advertises his building as 'the first attempt at providing modern living arrangements' should be careful to provide better comforts than a 'Mornington Crescent lodging house'. Twice a week since he moved into number 21 he had not had any hot water, and the lock on the door made it 'almost impossible' to get into or out of his flat. The doors were 'not the shape of the openings they intend to close' and although the design is 'admirable' there must have been 'a good deal of cheese-pairing [sic] in the joinery and interior decoration and arrangements'. He concluded: 'my bath <u>must</u> be hot, my doors <u>must</u> open and shut, my paint <u>must</u> remain on the walls.' He refused to pay any more rent until these things had been fixed.[59]

Wells was amused by the letter and wrote to Jack that Mr Gathorne-Hardy was 'exaggerating minor complaints', but agreed that 'cheese paring' had taken place and that he had warned Jack that 'trouble would occur'. He promised to go over the whole place with the builders by the end of November before the contract period was up.[60] The troubles were not confined to flat 21. The boiler room flooded and Jack had to bail it out himself in the middle of the night. The floors in some flats were bubbling up in blisters, and plaster was coming off the walls in flat 22.[61] A 'dark coloured fluid' was dripping out of the light socket in flat 30, where the plaster had a 'decidedly mottled appearance'. This was particularly unfortunate as the tenant of number 30 was very sociable and strangers were 'constantly seeing this particular flat'.[62] 'Ponds of water' were accumulating on the balconies, some of the balcony rails were breaking and the basement pantry needed better ventilation.[63] There were even problems with the furniture: the rods in the cupboards were not very strong and if too many clothes were hung up the sockets cracked.[64]

Despite all this, the flats were filling up. The art critic Adrian Stokes moved into flat 23, the novelist Nicholas Monsarrat into flat 29, the Austrian ethnomusicologist Professor Erich von Hornbostel into flat 6 and the German illustrator R. A. Brandt into flat 26. The German architect Arthur Korn who had been forbidden to work as an architect in Germany moved into flat 24. But on 18 October 1934 the most high-profile new tenant moved into the Isokon: the founder director of the Bauhaus, Walter Gropius, and his wife Ise. Not long afterwards, Wells discovered that Jack had asked Gropius to take over the design side of the Isokon. That was the last straw. He wrote to Jack in dismay:

> You have chosen to place your next work in other hands. The information has come to me by the most circuitous and hurtful routes – hurtful I mean to my own position. (In spite of this, you have expressed your pleasure at the success of

> the scheme, and so far as I know, you have no outstanding complaints to make).

Wells went on to say that he was sure Gropius's work would be very good and that he had worked with him but that he hoped that Jack and Molly would 'realize what I have done for you both'. He wanted to make it clear that despite their 'statement to the press and to private individuals, you know perfectly well that you have not "inspired" the Lawn Road Flats, but that the whole idea of the small flats on that site was mine. I don't give a damn, and in the long run it is no harm at all, but that is my view.'[65] Molly replied that she thought Wells was being 'unkind' and that one germ of the idea had been dropped by Wells and one by her and the 'idea came to us both independently'.[66]

4
GROPIUS, MOHOLY-NAGY AND BREUER

Bauhaus in Britain

On a visit to London in May 1934 Gropius's wife Ise asked him how much happier he thought they could be in London compared to Berlin. He was wondering the same thing and whether he'd cope with 'unsalted vegetables, bony women and an eternally freezing draught?!'[1] He was in London because Philip Morton Shand, critic for the *Architectural Review*, had persuaded the Royal Institute of British Architects (RIBA) to hold an exhibition of Gropius's work. They had arranged for Gropius to stay with the architect Maxwell Fry in Chiswick by the Thames. Ise didn't join him as they couldn't afford travel for them both, so she stayed behind with their dog Ali who, Ise told him, joined her in bed every morning, sniffed around looking for Gropius and 'finds it unsatisfactory! So do I!'[2]

Barbara Hepworth, pregnant with the triplets, wrote to Nicholson that Gropius was in town, that he had a 'most interesting show on' and that he was, she believed, 'the real thing'.[3] The evening after the exhibition opening at RIBA, Morton Shand arranged for Gropius to give a talk on modern architecture and planning to the Design and Industries Association. Gropius's English was not very good and he was reading a speech translated by Morton Shand that he had given earlier that year. He had practised it in front of Ise in Berlin, but he was still nervous and sounded as though he did not understand what he was saying. The talk set out his belief that architecture and art should be an integral and necessary part of life, rather than an adjunct. The audience, most of whom were already aware of Gropius's work, were extremely supportive and when they had finished applauding there was a sense of 'wild excitement'. Gropius was 'shaking with emotion' as he turned to thank Maxwell Fry.[4] Fry thought Gropius had 'the utmost clarity in broken English' and that he spoke with 'humility and authority' in ways that gave them all 'strength and assurance'.[5] Gropius appreciated that England was a place where one didn't need to shout to be heard. Jack Pritchard was in the audience and they met 'for a moment' afterwards.[6]

When Gropius got back to Berlin he wrote to the organiser of the exhibition, Morton Shand, to say how pleased he was that the trip had not been 'in vain' and that he had been seriously considering 'looking for work in England'.[7] Although very much part of the establishment, having been educated at Eton, King's College, Cambridge and the Sorbonne, Morton Shand was passionate about modernist architecture. He was determined to find a way to bring the founder of the Bauhaus to London. Egged on by Shand, Pritchard wrote to offer Gropius a job designing fifty flats in West Didsbury, Manchester. It would be a joint project with Maxwell Fry, who went on to build the Sun House in Frognal the following year with architect and designer Jack Howe. Fry wrote to Gropius that he had never dared to hope that he might work with him and gave him some more details about the site. It was about three acres at the end of a cul-de-sac with fine trees and a lovely view to the south. The River Mersey was at the bottom of the garden, heavily 'embanked and not visible'. Expanding on the Belsize Park project, Pritchard suggested that they build 'bigger flats than at Lawn Road' with a 'preponderance of 2 and 3 room flats & some even larger with a few 1-room bachelor flats on top'. The fee would work out at about '£225 to £250' for both of them, and the whole project would take them about three months.[8]

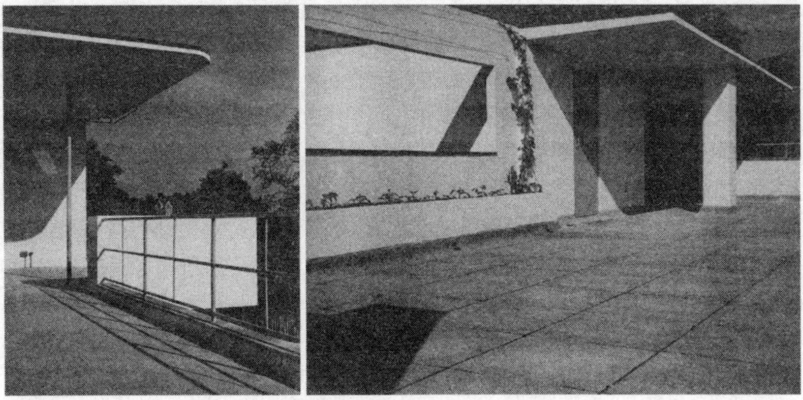

The Sun House, Frognal Way, Hampstead

Gropius wrote back immediately that the site in Manchester 'seems to be very suitable' and that he was 'looking forward very much to our common work'.[9] Pritchard had also offered to put 'one of our flats at your disposal' for six months, or for as long as the project took.[10] Gropius was very grateful as that 'will make the beginning much easier for me'.[11] He and Ise would have to leave their furniture behind in order to give the authorities the impression that they would return. An almost fully furnished, serviced flat in Lawn Road was exactly what they needed. Gropius was torn over leaving Berlin, but he was pleased to put some distance between Ise and Herbert Bayer, the handsome Bauhaus designer and typographer with whom she had been having an affair since 1930. Jack later admitted that he wouldn't have had the courage to ask Gropius if Morton Shand had not persuaded him. Jack was thirty and embarking on his first building project and wondered 'who was I' to even think of asking such an important person.[12]

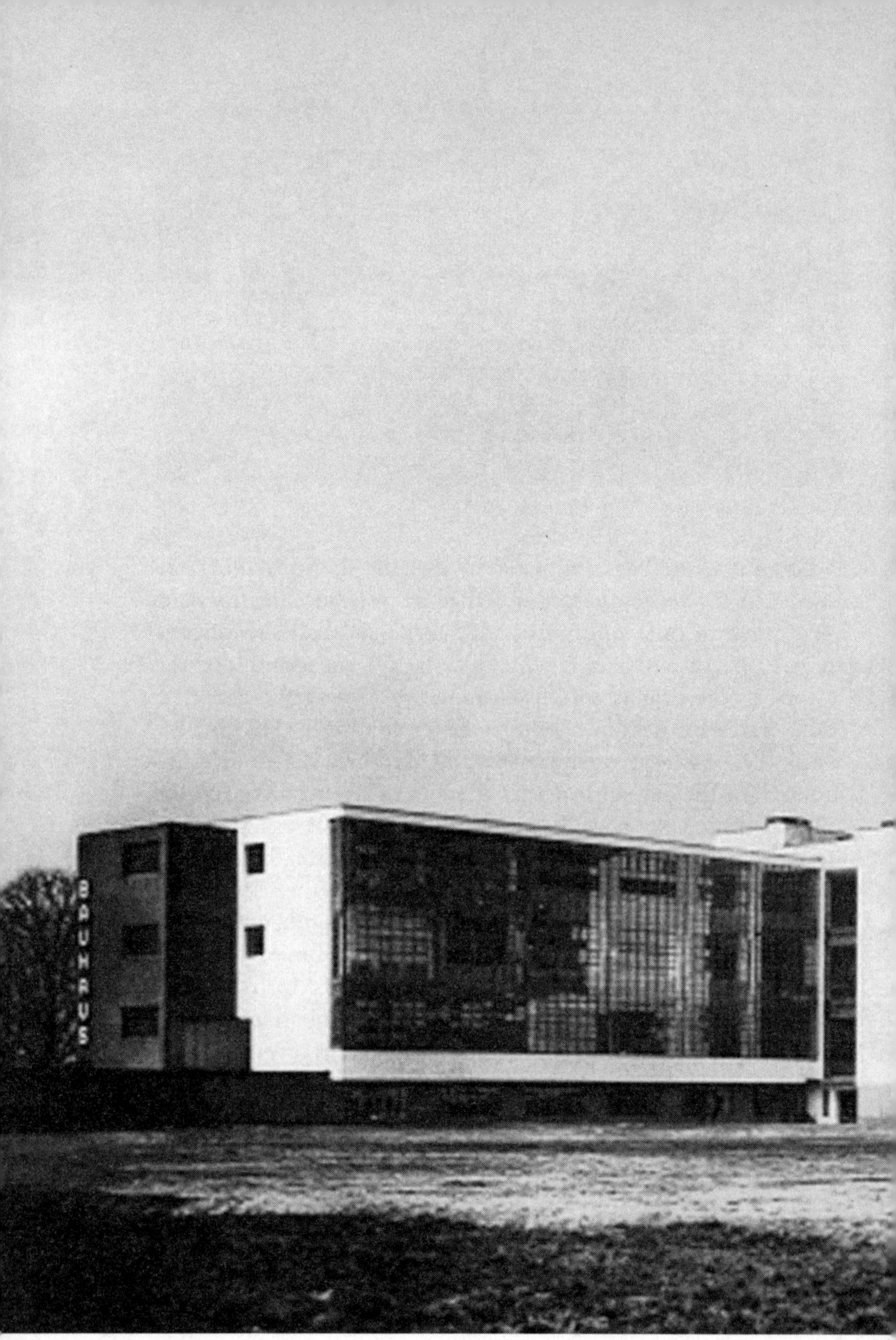

The Bauhaus campus in Dessau, designed by Gropius, 1925–6

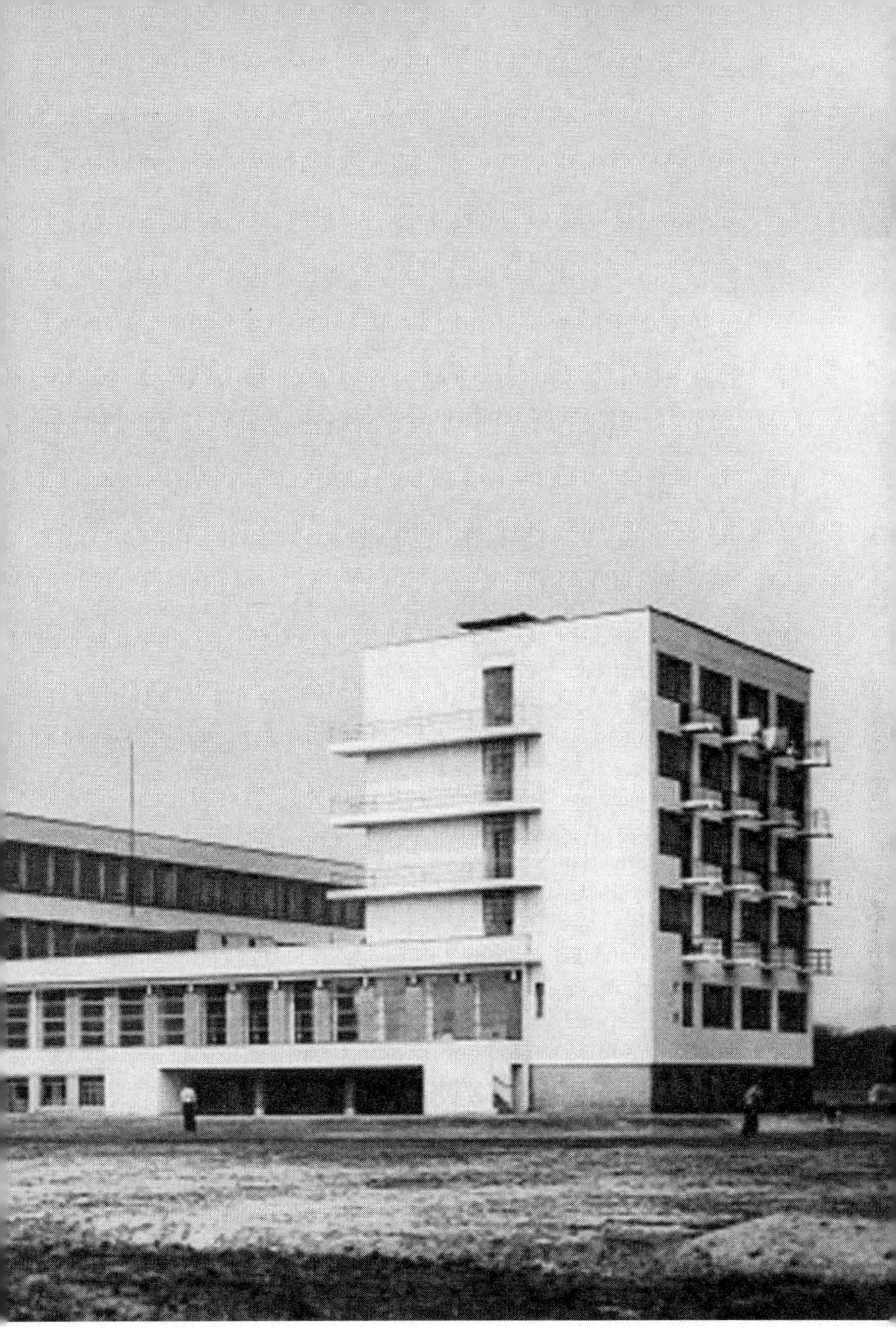

Gropius, aged fifty-one, was at the height of his career and yet was facing deep uncertainty about the future. An optimistic, enthusiastic man, he had built up the Bauhaus over the previous decade, bringing in a teaching faculty that included Paul Klee, Josef Albers, Moholy-Nagy and Kandinsky. He had had a series of turbulent love affairs, and his first marriage to Alma Mahler, with whom he had a daughter Manon (Mutzi), had ended in 1918 when he discovered Alma's affair with the writer Franz Werfel. Gropius met Ilse Frank in May 1923 when she was already engaged to her cousin, a manager at the family ironworks. She and her sister Hertha had attended one of Gropius's lectures in Hanover, and Gropius spotted Ilse in the front row through a gap in the curtain before he took the stage. She was hard to miss; she was extremely attractive and wore a black rayon cape and a black silk hat. Although they failed to meet that night Gropius arranged things so that he could stay in Hanover a little longer and she invited him to dinner with her family.

A week later Gropius asked her to cancel her wedding. She was captivated and overwhelmed and went to visit him in Weimar where she was intrigued by the Bauhaus style of living. And then they arranged another trip to Cologne where, Ilse put it, as if 'on another star, we were completely united'. By July Gropius was growing impatient: 'I am not a man who can wait! I storm through life and whoever cannot keep pace will remain by the wayside. I want to create with my spirit and with my body; yes – also with my body; and life is short and needs to be grasped.'[13] When he thought he had lost her he sent her a farewell present of an almost complete set of *Le Charivari*, a nineteenth-century magazine with illustrations by Daumier among others. This did the trick, and Ilse told her cousin that the wedding was off the night before it was supposed to take place. By August 1923 Ilse had moved to Weimar with a 'little suitcase' in her hand and agreed to change her name to the more modernist 'Ise'. They were married two months later.

Working in Berlin in 1933 became increasingly difficult for Gropius, and Ise was Jewish. Like Mies van der Rohe, Gropius was suspected of 'disloyalty and embezzlement' by the Nazi police.

In December that year he wrote to the Ministry of Propaganda to try to clear his name. The Dessau magistrate claimed he had 'strong communist tendencies' and that he had 'exploited Bauhaus products for his personal gain'. Specifically, he was charged with taking a 'Bauhaus door knob' and issuing a general licence for it to the Berlin company S. A. Loevy. Gropius argued that he had designed the door knob in his own private studio, that he had never belonged to any political party and that the accusations of communism were 'a false, malicious fabrication'. He was of 'pure Aryan, German origin', he added.[14] The following month he wrote to Herr Professor Hönig, at the Reich Chamber of the Creative Arts, because he was in a 'depressed state' after hearing him lecture. Hönig had discussed what he called 'packing-case architecture' which would be rejected by the new Reich. It would be a disaster, Gropius wrote, if the new architectural movement were lost and he was convinced in his innermost being that its 'power, intellectual penetration, and truthfulness' would spread across the world. Gropius was extremely proud of his work and was

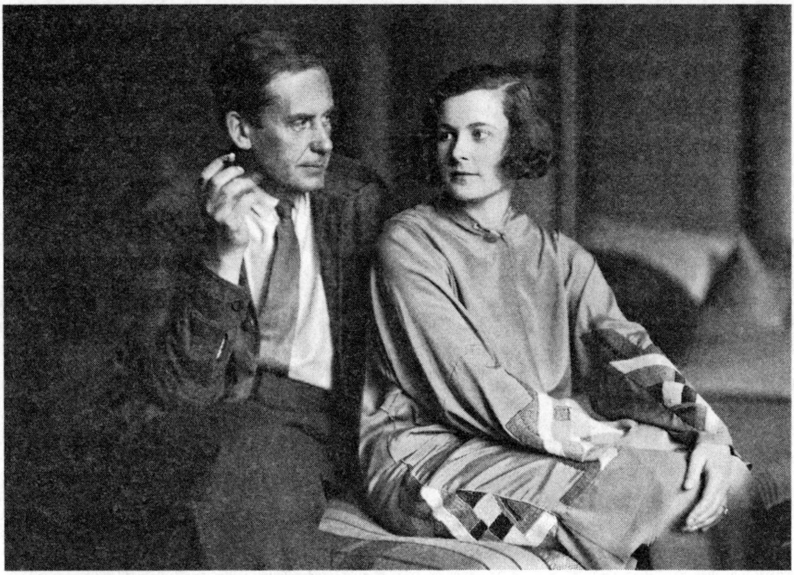

Walter and Ise Gropius, soon after their marriage

insulted by the label of 'structural cubes with flat roofs'. He argued that his contribution was sociological as well as structural and would benefit the 'broad German masses'. After giving all he had to Germany he now felt an 'outlaw' and he appealed to Hönig's humanity and purity of intention to prevent the suppression of new German architecture. He could not, he concluded, for all these reasons, remain silent.[15]

Gropius's complaints were ignored and most likely put him at greater risk. Tensions were rising in Berlin in the summer of 1934, with a series of executions and Hitler's declaration in August that he was adding the role of head of state to his existing role as Chancellor, followed by the Nuremberg rally at the start of September attended by about 700,000 Nazi party supporters. Gropius was invited by the Italian Minister of Culture, Dino Alfieri, to take part in a conference on theatre in Rome in October. Hönig granted permission for Gropius and Ise to attend and also granted them authorisation to stay in England afterwards until 30 April 1935 to work on a 'small housing construction'. Gropius stressed that he was still keeping his apartment in Berlin and that his architectural practice would be run by a former student while he was away. They left for Rome on 1 October and visited Giotto's frescoes in Assisi on their way. The conference was large and grand and, as the honoured German guests, Ise and Walter were given special treatment by Alfieri, who took a particular shine to Ise. They were seated in a box next to Mussolini's at a performance of Franchetti's *La figlia di Iorio*. Gropius's speech at the conference was based on his theory of 'total theatre', which meant that the audience were involved in the performance as much as possible. He and the Berlin director Erwin Piscator had come up with a theatre design that placed the performers at the heart of a series of concentric rings.

Instead of going back to Berlin and then on to London, Gropius and his wife asked the conference organiser, casually, if their tickets might be rerouted via London. The secretary answered 'yes, why not' and so they went from Rome to Milan to Zurich, and then on to London on 18 October. A month earlier Morton Shand had confirmed that everything was 'signed and sealed' for their arrival.[16] But just to cover his bases Gropius had written to Fry on 18 September to say that he would arrive with Ise on 18 October and wanted to make sure he didn't need to 'settle details' with Pritchard. Fry reassured Gropius that his work permit was sorted out and that 'a flat at Lawn Road is being reserved for you.'[17]

On 18 October Gropius and Ise arrived at Victoria railway station. Morton Shand, Fry and Pritchard were all there to greet them and Pritchard was surprised to see that Gropius had Ise with him. Flustered, he told 'Max and Morton' to keep them chatting on the platform while he rushed off to find a telephone to ask Molly to arrange a double flat for them instead of the studio they had prepared. Pritchard was nervous as he wanted to impress the Bauhaus director with his new model of living at the Isokon. They had polished the sliding partition in the studio with two coats of wax, put up a new curtain rail and selected the curtain material, all with Gropius in mind. But Molly smoothed things over and made arrangements so that Walter and Ise could have flat 15 at the north end of the building. Gropius and Ise had asked a friend in Rotterdam to transfer some money for them for their travels, but other than that they were allowed to take only twenty Reichsmarks out of Germany. Thus they arrived at Lawn Road with very little money and very few possessions.

Pritchard was delighted to have Gropius at the Isokon, but he was also anxious about the financial commitment and wrote to Fry that he had been 'taken by surprise' by the arrival of Gropius with his wife and was now 'landed' with providing food and accommodation for both of them.[18] He didn't let on to their new guests, and on their first weekend Jack and Molly took Gropius and Ise to see Stonehenge. On their way Jack recalled that they saw signs saying 'Take Courage' and 'You are now entering the Strong country' and Ise and Walter were both amused and relieved to discover that these were beer advertisements rather than motivational posters. About six weeks after they arrived,

Pritchard must have sensed an unease and wrote to Gropius to say that he and Molly wanted to apologise for their rudeness in not having offered them a formal invitation to stay at the Isokon. He reassured Gropius that they could stay as long as they liked, or as long as their permit allowed. It was a real pleasure, he said, to have them under their roof.[19]

Gropius was keen to expand the theories of the Bauhaus in England but he did not have the appetite, energy or financial means to set up a whole new British Bauhaus. He was very keen, however, to get on with some building projects. As well as the block of flats in Didsbury, the Isokon Company was planning another block in Birmingham on land belonging to Jack's old economics professor from Cambridge, Philip Sargent Florence. The costings for the Manchester and Birmingham projects did not add up in terms of the rent they would recuperate. Jack was frustrated and embarrassed, as both projects had to be shelved.

Just before Christmas Gropius was invited by Leonard and Dorothy Elmhirst to visit their estate in Devon, Dartington Hall. They had been inspired by a visit to the Bauhaus and had set up a primary and secondary school with adult educational programmes on site. They wanted to teach people traditional industries including cider making, textile weaving, forestry and saw milling as well as art, music and dance. Gropius wrote to a friend in Berlin, the architect Martin Wagner, that it was a 'kind of British Bauhaus'. They were interested in having Gropius convert their barn into a theatre. Although Gropius was very keen, and sent them the design for his 'total theatre' that he had presented at the conference in Rome, in the end the Elmhirsts stuck with their original architect, William Lescaze. But they did send a generous cheque at Christmas as a 'welcome' to Gropius and his wife. Gropius told them it was a great surprise and delight, and it meant a lot to him to find people who were really interested in what he was doing, like 'a fairy tale'.[20]

The first few months in London were difficult for Gropius. He had no fixed income and after six months he had to write to Pritchard to admit that they were still not in a position to pay any rent. Jack replied immediately that it was 'happiness and a privilege to have you both at Lawn Road. I only wish that the accommodation was better.' He told Gropius there was no shame in not being 'on your own legs' as it was *his* fault that 'Manchester fell through'. He assured Gropius that they would continue to cover their expenses until something changed, at which point they could let a flat to them.[21] And then on 19 April 1935 Gropius received a telegram from his ex-wife Alma Mahler-Werfel telling him to board the first plane to Vienna. She did not give details of their daughter Manon's condition, but it had become extremely serious. Manon had polio, contracted during a visit to Venice in 1934, and her mother had taken her to Vienna for specialist treatment. Gropius could not get the paperwork and the permissions he needed in time to get there before she died. He did not even make it to her funeral as Alma did not respond to his request to delay it. He and Ise managed to get to Berlin the day after she died, but he was then denied permission to cross the border into Austria to see her grave. Unable to grieve properly, Gropius returned to England with Ise on 7 May 1935. His ties to Germany were slowly being cut.

There was a brief moment early that year when it seemed that Gropius might be employed by the Royal College of Art. He was invited to come to the College by Frank Pick, who was not actually a member of the appointments committee but was chairman of the Council for Art and Industry that had been set up to improve design standards. Ise acted as translator at the meeting and there was some suggestion that Gropius might be brought in as an adviser, or to teach some classes. Art education specialist E. M. O'Rorke Dicky even hoped they might set up a Bauhaus in place of the RCA. But the British art world was essentially conservative and the College was reluctant to employ an 'alien architect'. The Impressionist landscape painter Percy Jowett was appointed principal to replace William Rothenstein shortly afterwards. Gropius still had vague hopes of returning to Berlin, and he had kept up contact with Eugen Hönig, who was still president of the Reich Chamber of the Creative Arts. Hönig came to London with a colleague, Carl Christoph Lörcher, an architect and member of the Nazi storm troopers. They had lunch with Gropius at Lawn Road and Ise remembered it as a convivial occasion.

Gropius's profile was raised in London in June 1935 with the publication by Faber and Faber of his book *The New Architecture and the Bauhaus*, with a cover designed by Moholy-Nagy. Frank Pick had written the introduction but Gropius was worried and asked him to change the reference to a 'period of crisis' in Germany to a 'period of transition'. He feared that otherwise the German authorities would withdraw his permission to work in Britain. A month later Pritchard bought a six-month option on thirty-three acres of land near Windsor. This was the most ambitious project undertaken by the Isokon to date, and the one that almost came to fruition. The plan was for a luxury block of flats on St Leonard's Hill, next to Windsor Great Park, that could offer a 'country gentleman's life near London'. The flats would look over Windsor Castle, as well as Eton College, about two miles away and so they sought royal permission, which was granted. It was to include two blocks of flats, a nursery with a fully qualified member of staff, a swimming pool, tennis courts, a communal restaurant and a residents' lounge and ballroom. The cost was estimated at £225,000. The idea was to house 500 people in one acre and to leave the surrounding land as a park. Pritchard began fundraising for the scheme but the stress became too much and he fell ill. He regretted asking his brother's company to advertise the project, as their campaign was bland. When the project fell through he felt ashamed and told Gropius that he must think him a 'broken reed' and that he had been invited to London for nothing.[22]

Gropius's English was still not very good, despite having lessons with a private tutor. And he and Ise continued to be baffled by the English themselves. They couldn't understand open fires that roasted you on one side and chilled you on the other while pumping smoke into the already smoggy atmosphere. One 'eats the particles', he remarked. He also couldn't bear the way English people prepared food so as to get so little pleasure out of it. He put it all down to some kind of 'puritan self-punishment'. Yet he really liked what he called the sentimental 'anti-Muse' world of London and the attractive qualities of the people.[23] A year after arriving at the flats he and Ise asked for a few extra furnishings. They asked for a sofa to match the 'Fauteuil', a lampstand, a writing board fixed to the wall and two more stools. They also wondered if they might exchange the large bed for a smaller one, and the round table with a rectangular one. These things, he said, would 'bring about a great improvement of the flat'.[24] Then, as the weather got colder, he requested a nine-shilling electric fire from Best & Lloyds, and Jack picked up the bill.[25] It can't have been easy for the director of the Bauhaus to have to ask for a lamp and stools and an electric heater. Gropius suggested that they could stop having catered meals at the flat, but Jack would not hear of it, at least until Ise recovered from her illness. Ise was suffering from gynaecological problems that had troubled her for many years.

In October 1935 Jack offered Gropius the official position of design controller for the Isokon Furniture Company with a salary of £165 per annum and a share of the profits. Although Jack and Wells had designed various pieces of furniture including Jack's Experimental Chair No. 2 and Wells's book units, cocktail cabinet and radio, the official Furniture Company was not launched until 1935, with Gropius at the top. As well as aligning a famous Bauhaus designer with the company, it also solved the awkward financial situation: Gropius's salary was equivalent to the rent on the flat. In the end Gropius only designed three things as design controller: an aluminium wastepaper basket, a table and a flatpack set of bookshelves.

With the new year came news of another death in Germany. Ise's sister Hertha had suffered from epilepsy and had become increasingly weak and unwell. She died on New Year's Day 1936. Ise went back to Berlin and brought Hertha's ten-year-old daughter Ati back to live with them at the Isokon. Lonely and confused and speaking very little English, at first Ati stayed in one of the bedrooms in the flat attached to the Pritchards' penthouse as their boys were boarding at Beacon Hill. Ati remembered it as a plain white clinical room with leaden grey skies outside. Ise enrolled her in various classes in English, art and music, and when the Pritchard boys were home from school they took her swimming in the Hampstead ponds. She was more shocked by the nudity than by the cold water. Eventually the Pritchards persuaded the Gropiuses that she would do very well to join the Pritchard boys at Beacon Hill. Having visited some other English boarding schools en route Ati was delighted to see the 'half-naked children' racing 'randomly over the lawns', completely ignoring the adults. She heard sounds of 'wild cavorting' from an outdoor swimming pool and loved the school from the moment she got there.

Gropius completed only a handful of building projects during his time in London. He and Fry were commissioned by the Hungarian filmmaker Alexander Korda to design a new film laboratory in Denham, Buckinghamshire. It transpired, however, that there was very little for them to do: the frame had already been built and the Kordas were inconsistent in their briefings and so mistakes had been made. Gropius was furious and vowed he wouldn't touch another of their projects even if they offered him 500 buildings to design. Although it was frustrating, the job paid £700, which allowed Gropius and Fry to set up their own architectural practice in Victoria. Their first residential commission was for playwright Benn Levy and his wife, the actress Constance Cummings, at 66 Old Church Street, Chelsea. The result was the asymmetrical sparkling white modernist house adjoining the Chermayeff and Mendelsohn villa owned by Levy's cousin. Not long afterwards, Gropius designed a country house in Shipbourne, near Sevenoaks, for the left-wing politician Jack Donaldson and his wife, the biographer Frances Donaldson. The house was unusual for Gropius in that it was clad in Canadian cedar wood and had an exterior sleeping porch and outdoor staircase.

The biggest project that came to fruition when Gropius was in London was the Impington Village College in Cambridgeshire, still going strong as a secondary school and sixth-form college today. Pritchard described the moment that he introduced Gropius to Henry Morris, secretary to the Cambridgeshire Education Committee in 1934 at Lawn Road as 'orgasm!' because their views on education were so in tune.[26] Morris had written a report for Cambridge county council suggesting that every village in Cambridgeshire should have a hall dedicated to education and the arts for all ages. That way, he argued, schooling would never end. Fry and Gropius set about designing Impington Village College in the summer of 1936. It involved a long 'promenade' down the centre of the building so that students and teachers could meet and mingle, and it had bright, airy classrooms with floor-to-ceiling windows. When Morris saw the designs he told a friend they were pure 'architectural seduction'. Pritchard managed to raise £1,200 for Gropius's fee from private sources. Supervised by Fry and architect Jack Howe, it was completed in 1939, after Gropius had left England. Pevsner called it one of the best buildings in England, 'if not the best'.

□

Gropius was keen to bring more of his Bauhaus colleagues to London. Morton Shand met Moholy (as he liked to be called) at a CIAM (International Congress of Modern Architecture) conference in 1933 and encouraged him to come for a visit. Moholy's first wife, the photographer Lucia Moholy (née Schulz), moved to London in 1933 and found work as a photographer and lectured at the Central School of Art and Design on the social history of photography. She and Moholy had been students at the Bauhaus and worked together on various experimental projects, including photograms. Gropius was so impressed by Moholy's energy and fresh approach that he was one of the first students to be promoted to a teaching post. Moholy was interested in light, transparency and movement, but he did not limit himself to one medium. He worked with plastic, collage, paint, metal, film and photography and produced sculpture, set design and advertising. He saw little difference between fine art and commercial art. Gropius described him as an 'unprejudiced, happy child at play' who ventured into new 'experiments with the curiosity of a scientist'.[27]

Although they were no longer a couple, Lucia Moholy arranged for them both to study the Kodak dye-transfer method of printing when László was visiting London, which meant learning how to make full-colour photographic prints. Moholy had recently taken a post as creative director of *International Textiles* in Amsterdam, but in January 1935 when the contract ran out he and his new partner, the writer and actress Sibylle (who became Sibyl in London) Pietzsch, made another trip to London. Both having been married before, their divorces had just come through and they decided to marry in London. During this visit Gropius encouraged him to make the move permanent. So in May 1935 Moholy, Sibyl and their eighteen-month-old daughter Hattula moved into the Isokon. They stayed for a few months and then moved to 7 Farm Walk in Temple Fortune where there was space for Moholy to have a studio. Their second daughter Claudia was born in London in 1936.

The European dimension of the Isokon Company was expanding. Moholy's advertising skills were put to use straight away. He took over from the original advertising company for the Isokon Furniture Company, F. C. Pritchard, Wood and Partners, which belonged to Jack's brother. Jack was initially worried that as well as firing his brother's company he had made a mistake employing Moholy, because he worked so fast that he feared the results would be 'facile'. He soon realised, however, that Moholy had grasped the ethos and outlook of the company very quickly and that he had the ability to understand and execute a project simultaneously. Moholy rapidly set to work creating the Isokon Company 'trade mark', an S-shaped plywood chair, based on the young designer Gerald Summer's iconic Isokon chair, cut from a single sheet of bent plywood. The ad had the words 'For ease. For ever' underneath.[28]

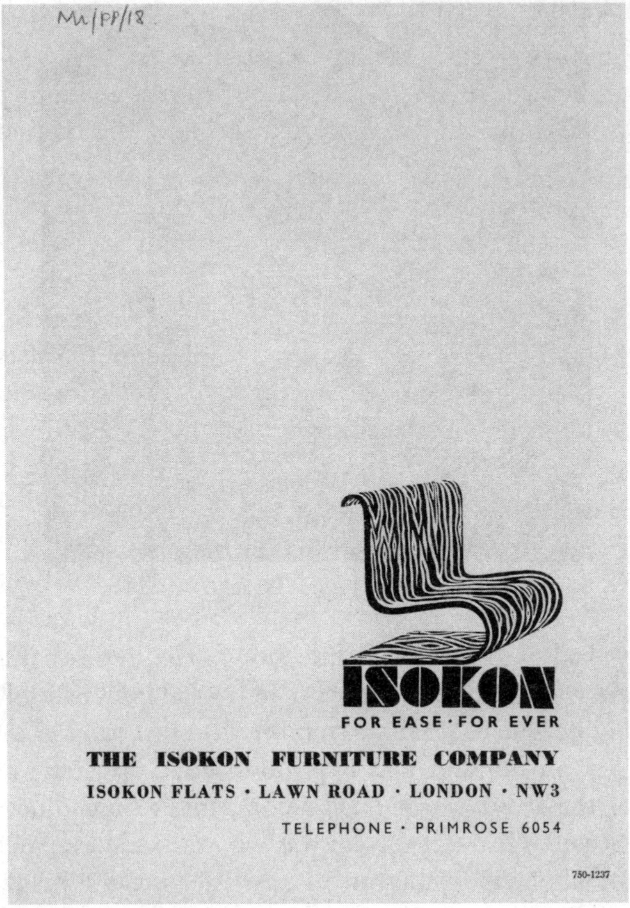

The Isokon Furniture Company 'trademark',
László Moholy-Nagy, 1936

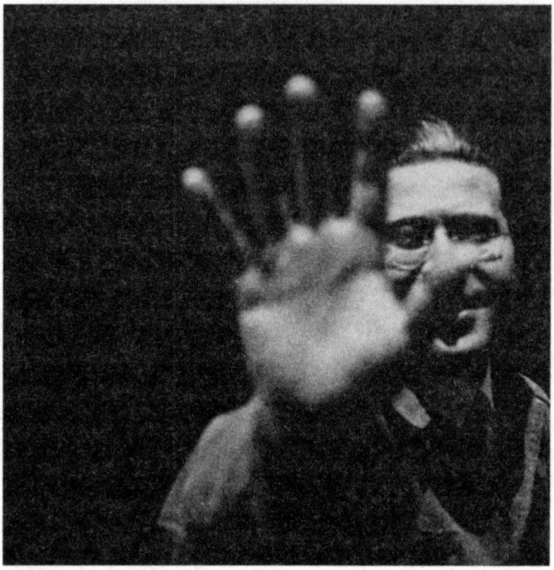

László Moholy-Nagy by Lucia Moholy

Moholy 'had a magnificent, infectious grin' beneath his small round glasses and he liked to wear industrial boilersuits. He also seemed to be able to hold down more than one job at a time. He had arrived in London with a position lined up at the London office of the *International Textiles* company, whose offices were on the Strand. Through this he was recommended to Alexander Simpson, who was establishing a new menswear shop in a six-storey building on Piccadilly. The idea behind the shop was to offer well-cut, affordable clothes, ready to wear. Moholy, and his friend and colleague from the Bauhaus, György Kepes, who had also recently arrived in London, were given the task of designing the interior decor, the window displays and the advertising material. The displays were modern and extraordinary. Moholy arranged for three aircraft (a Flying Flea, a Gipsy Moth and a Supermarine seaplane) to be brought into the building and hoisted up through the central staircase to the fifth floor. The planes were replaced by boats for the next campaign. He adopted modern materials, using plywood screens and transparent free-standing price labels in the displays. As the opening approached Moholy did not come home one evening and, although she was used to him working late, Sibyl eventually went down to Piccadilly to find him. It was getting light and as she walked into Simpsons she saw him standing barefoot, feet bleeding, up a ladder hooking fishwire over the sports-section display. A group of reporters were staring up at him as he explained his theory of 'asymmetric advertising', which involved a 'mild electric shock to the eye' in order to make the familiar unfamiliar. He told them to look over at his wife's face to see what he meant. Sibyl persuaded him to leave the displays and they walked along the Strand, him still barefoot, until they found a taxi and he fell asleep on the way home.[29]

Moholy was also commissioned to design advertising material for London Transport, Abdulla cigarettes and Imperial Airways when he was in London. Imperial Airways wanted a campaign that would highlight the luxury and the accessibility of air travel, so he constructed a mobile exhibition that ironically could travel in a railway carriage. For London Underground he promoted their new pneumatic doors operated by air engine arms, for improved speed and safety. He was also commissioned to take photographs for three books published by Harry F. Paroissien, Mary Benedetta's *The Street Markets of London* (1936), Bernard Fergusson's *Eton Portrait* (1937) and John Betjeman's *An Oxford University Chest* (1938). Like his film shots, the photographs are taken from unusual angles with strong diagonals and curious compositions. The Eton portrait takes the well-known symbols of the school and makes them unfamiliar again: a pair of upturned top hats; school scarves and hats hung on a brick wall and a close-up of the 'caviar of Eton' that turns out to be banana, ice cream and wafers.

In 1935 John Grierson, the Scottish documentary filmmaker, introduced Moholy to the film producer John Mathias. Grierson had seen and admired Moholy's film *A Lightplay: Black-White-Grey* (1930). Moholy called it a 'moving painting': it explored the movement and light effects of his sculpture *Light Prop for an Electric Stage*, originally designed for the theatre.[30] Grierson used a thirty-second sequence of the film for the opening of *The Coming of the Dial*, a film to promote the automation of the telephone system for the General Post Office in 1933. On Grierson's recommendation Mathias commissioned Moholy to co-produce a fifteen-minute film about lobsters. It was funded by fellow Hungarian Alexander Korda, whom Moholy knew from Vienna. Moholy and Sibyl went to stay with Mathias's wealthy family in Sussex while they were filming and Sibyl noticed the 'clannishness of the men, the coldness of the women, and the drilled, unnatural politeness of the children'.[31] Moholy's delight is obvious from the start of the film, from the abstract lines of withies being woven into lobster pots by the fishermen to the sparkling light on the water, and a sequence worthy of David Attenborough where the lobster extrudes itself from its old shell in order to grow a new and bigger one. He built tension into the film with low-angle shots of the sailors in a storm and loved ones watching anxiously from shore. The final sequence is abstract and funny: a shiny lobster rips through a menu listing a range of lobster dishes.

The success of this documentary was followed by another short film in 1936 called *The New Architecture at the London Zoo*. Funded by the Museum of Modern Art (MoMA) in New York and the Architectural Department of Harvard, it showcased Lubetkin's Penguin Pool and Gorilla House at London Zoo and the Elephant House and Giraffe House (now demolished) at Whipsnade. The idea was to show the ways Tecton architects deployed reinforced concrete to create, as the MoMA press release put it, a 'new theory of modern housing for wild animals' and spaces that provide a 'hygienic, organic setting'. The Kordas were also producing the adaptation of H. G. Wells's *The Shape of Things to Come* and they asked Moholy to create an abstract sequence for the film, called *Things to Come*, released in 1936. From November to December 1935, Moholy worked at night to fit around his day job. He used a supply of Rhodoid, a kind of plastic used on the sets, which Naum Gabo also liked to use for his sculptures. Moholy wanted to create a utopian city of 'superhuman dimensions' where houses had no walls but were 'skeletons of steel'. In the end only ninety seconds of his sequence made the final cut.[32]

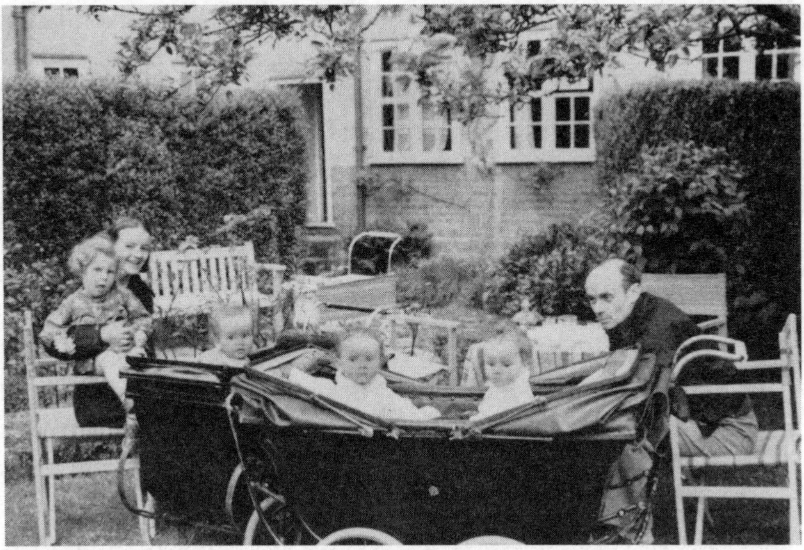

Ben, Barbara and triplets in the Moholy-Nagys' garden; Barbara holding Hattula

Juggling so many jobs began to take its toll and Moholy was granted two months leave from Simpsons in the summer of 1936. At about the same time a British picture agency offered him the job of filming and photographing the Berlin Olympic Games. Going back to Berlin was a shock. He saw an old Bauhaus student dressed in SS uniform who reassured him that he was simply 'playing the game' and then he visited his old landlady who had destroyed thirty pieces of his early experimental figurative work. When Moholy protested, her husband threatened to call the police. Moholy left Berlin immediately, giving up the job and vowing never to return. He shifted his allegiance to London. He exhibited in the *Abstract & Concrete* exhibition in 1936 and with the Artists International Association. He was a committee member of the Modern Architectural Research Group (MARS) and he held his first one-man show in London at the London Gallery in December 1936. He enjoyed discussing his work with Hepworth, Nicholson and Moore in the Mall Studios and Parkhill Road. A family album includes photographs of Ben and Barbara and the triplets in Sibyl and Moholy's garden in Temple Fortune. One picture shows the triplets peering out of their prams while a smiling Barbara holds Hattula on her lap. Sibyl believed that Ben's paintings 'posed a visual problem' related to Moholy's 'space modulation'. And Hepworth's sculptures 'sought a new organisation of space displacement and multiple volume' which Moholy had tried to solve in his early sculpture.[33] Herbert Read wanted to include him in an Artists' Unit that would form part of a kind of British Bauhaus, but it never materialised. Moholy had a greater appetite for a new British Bauhaus project than Gropius. There was much discussion, but a lack of funds and a conservative climate thwarted the vision.

By the spring of 1937 Moholy had become 'tired and melancholic' and as they sat watching a cricket match on Hampstead Heath he told Sibyl that 'painting is not enough' and 'not even exhibitions are enough'. In fact, he decided, no money or 'satisfaction of shows and public recognition can equal teaching'.[34] Frustrated by his own work and by the lack of vision in England he went to the States at the beginning of July 1937 to discuss setting up a new Bauhaus funded by the industrialist Walter Paepcke, in Chicago. Moholy was more impressed by the British 'notion of the weekend and taking tea' than by their 'vitality, visual awareness and imagination'.[35] By 13 August he cabled Sibyl that he had 'signed five-year contract for Bauhaus. Opening October eighteenth. Liquidate everything. Details follow.' She wrote back on 16 August from London, 'Congratulations. Drop name Bauhaus. Identification with Germany and past program unwise. Suggest American School of Design. Love.' He returned: 'Your opinion re school name wrong and uncalled for. Official name New Bauhaus. Inform London press.'[36] Any marital tension was diffused by the excitement of their new venture. In the end they combined the names: 'The New Bauhaus: American School of Design'.

□

Gropius persuaded Marcel Breuer to join the growing number of Bauhaus exiles at the Isokon in the summer of 1935. Hungarian-born Breuer had been one of the first students at the Bauhaus but he had also worked briefly at an architecture firm in Paris where he met Le Corbusier. He had returned to the Bauhaus in 1925, aged twenty-three, to join Albers, Kandinsky and Klee on the faculty, and it was here he designed his famous tubular chair, inspired by his bicycle handlebars. After setting up an unsuccessful architectural practice in Berlin he took off for a while, bicycling around Europe and Morocco in 1931. And then at the end of 1932, the year the Bauhaus was shut down, Breuer started work again as a designer in Zurich for architectual historian Sigfried Giedion's new furniture store, Wohnbedarf. Breuer also worked on various architectural projects. And along with Corbusier and Alvar Aalto they designed furniture including Corbusier's LC4 reclining chair, a shorter lounge chair, nesting tables and aluminium chairs. But Breuer was unhappy and anxious in Zurich; he wrote to his friend Ise Gropius, in May 1934, that there was a 'fog over everything' and he felt that war was inevitable. When he heard about the Gropiuses' lives in London he wrote to them on Christmas Day that it sounded like a 'fairy tale'.[37]

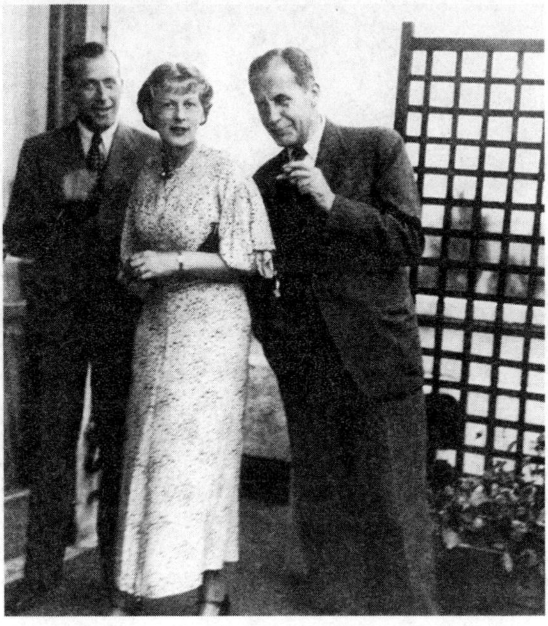

Breuer, Ise and Walter Gropius on the terrace of the Lawn Road Flats

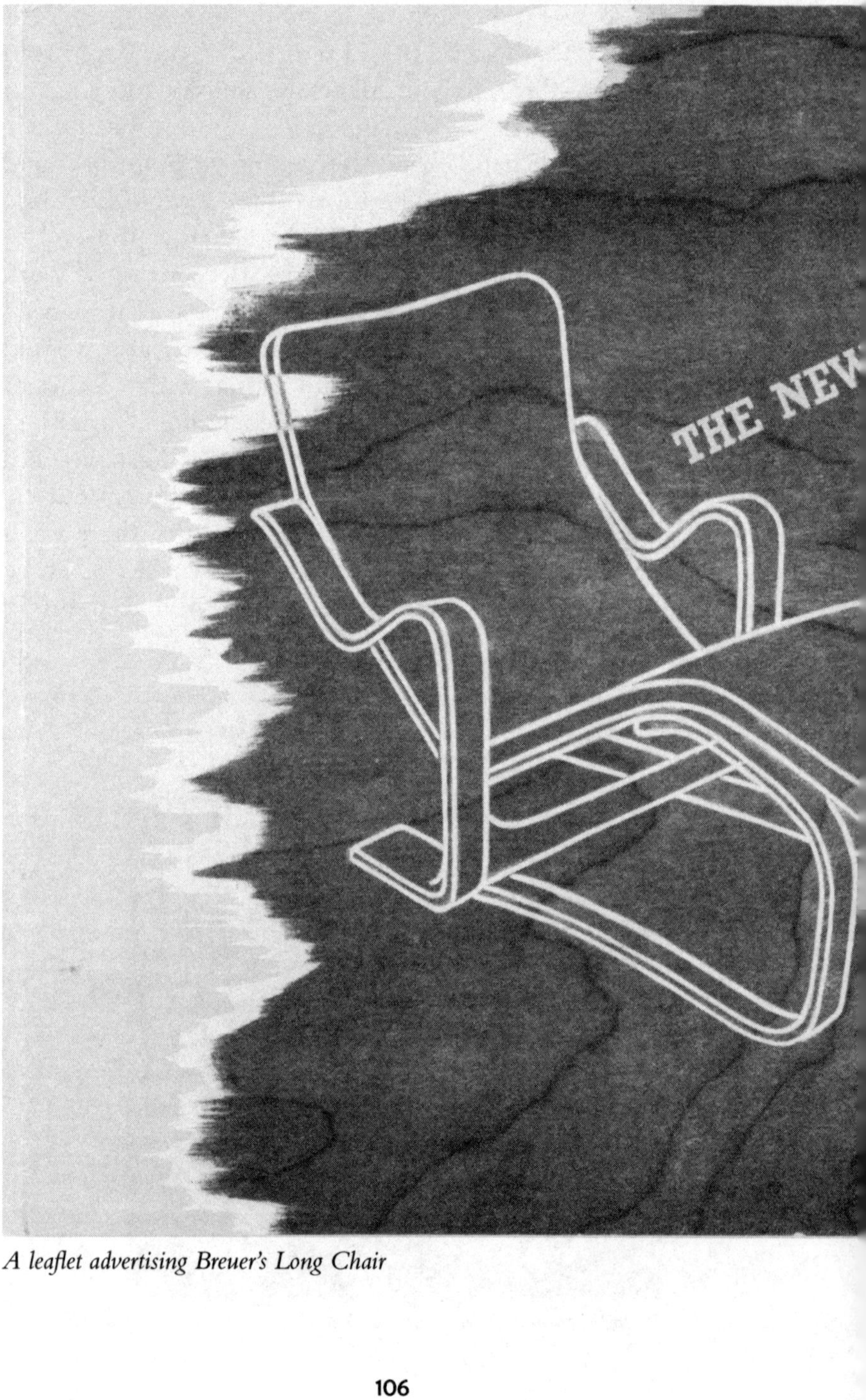

A leaflet advertising Breuer's Long Chair

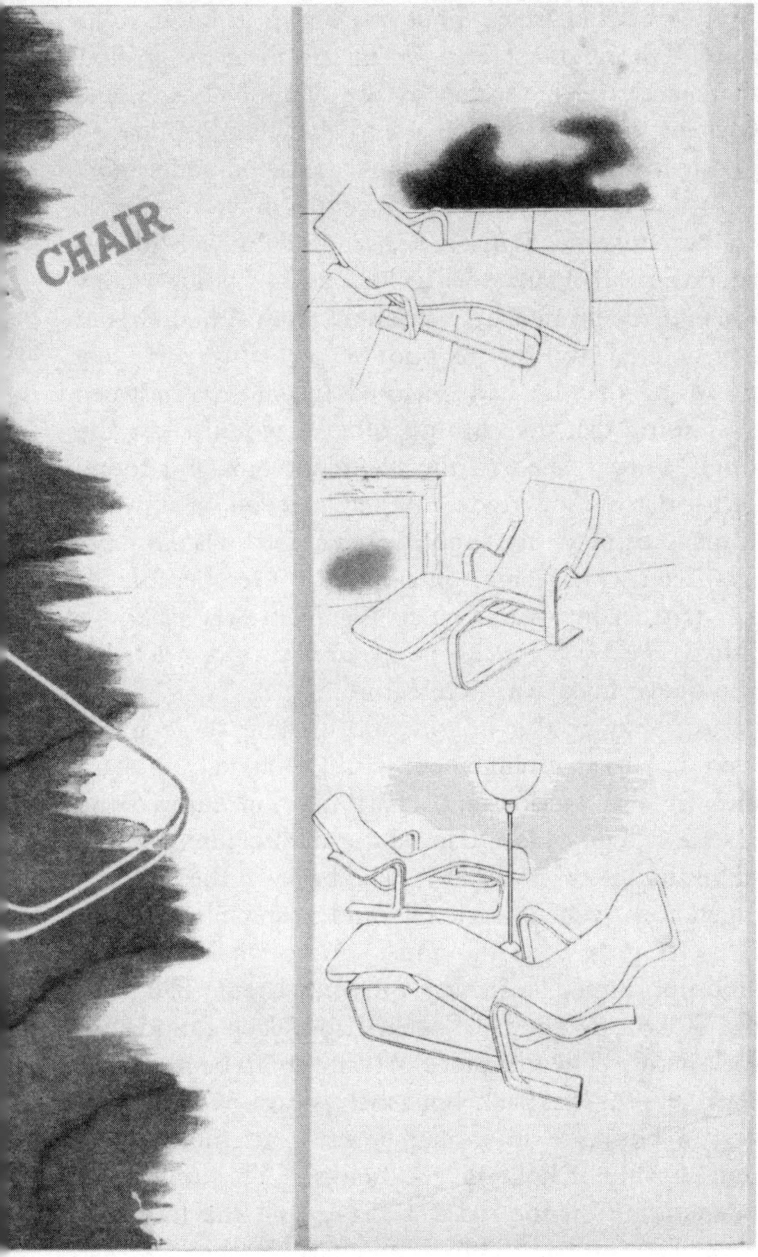
CHAIR

Even so, Breuer was uncertain about moving to London, so he came first for a short visit. He stayed in flat 16 at the Isokon, which had recently been vacated by the Moholy-Nagys, and he liked what he saw, so he went back to Zurich and Budapest to organise his move. In advance of his arrival he addressed a parcel to Carola Giedion, who had recently moved to Lawn Road with her husband Sigfried. Carola and Sibyl Moholy-Nagy opened the parcel and were so furious on finding a copy of *Mein Kampf* they immediately threw it away. When Breuer arrived they berated him for his poor sense of humour, only for him to reveal that he had enclosed his money between the pages assuming that the customs officials would allow the book through. They rushed to the basement bins and found the book with the money inside.[38] At Lawn Road he was in a good position to bring designs and designers to the Isokon and Gropius was keen to have him on board. By October Breuer had set up a partnership with Francis Reginald Stevens Yorke, who published *The Modern House in England* in 1937, a detailed account of modern European architecture.

Breuer was happy at the Isokon, and, despite some initial difficulties coming to an arrangement with Pritchard over salary and royalties, he was sociable and charming and enjoyed the communal style of living. He also loved the architecture, the 'airy rooms' and 'restful views' and later looked back on the building itself as a 'generous wench, a friendly and hospitable one'; he wished all 'pretty girls were the same'.[39] Although Breuer and Pritchard did not immediately hit it off, once Breuer had been hired as the Isokon designer in January 1936 Jack found him 'easy to work with'.[40] The first piece of furniture to be marketed by the Isokon was the 'flat pack' bookshelves from Wohnbedarf, advertised as 'a bookcase in a carton', easily assembled in '3 minutes' and capable of holding '100 books'.[41] The units were adaptable depending on the space available and the furniture was cheap because you had to build it yourself. In the new year Breuer moved to 4 Tregunter Road in Chelsea, in part to be closer to Yorke's house and studio.

Breuer designed one of his most famous pieces of furniture in his role as designer at the Isokon: the plywood Isokon Long Chair. Based on his earlier aluminium version, it became, almost instantly, a design classic. It embodied his idea that furniture should be 'free in space'. Moholy lost no time advertising it, claiming it was a 'better aid to digestion than any medicine under the sun'. Pritchard added the idea that it gave you the 'amazing sensation of the principles of Archimedes without being in water!' The first bulk order for ten Long Chairs was for an indoor swimming pool in a new block of flats in Pimlico, Dolphin Square. The order was not a great success. The chairs were glued with Scotch glue and the heated tiled floor by the pool meant that the chairs soon became 'an embarrassing collection of veneer'.[42] They quickly found a new type of glue. By the mid-1930s Isokon furniture was being sold at Heal's, John Lewis and Dunn's of Bromley. Molly Pritchard furnished her Harley Street office with it.

As well as working for the Isokon, Breuer had a number of private clients including Dorothea Ventris, a modern art collector who lived in Highpoint I in Highgate with her young son. Breuer designed a number of bespoke pieces for her flat including an asymmetrical dressing unit in her bedroom, drawer units with red laminated tops and a tubular-steel serving trolley for the dining area. She was delighted with the results and thought Breuer had the colour sense of a painter.[43] The truth was, Breuer did not really see himself as a furniture designer and preferred to include furniture as part of the design of a building. In early 1936 he put his ideas to use when, with Yorke, they created a modernist vision of a new town for the Cement and Concrete Association at the Ideal Home Exhibition at Olympia. Breuer and Yorke had several commissions outside London too, Gane's Pavilion in Bristol, to showcase the domestic furnishings made by P. E. Gane Ltd, and the Sea Lane House in Sussex, built in 1937. But in the summer of 1935 three of the most important artists and designers from the Bauhaus were working for the Isokon Furniture Company. They released a press statement to capitalise on it: 'The ideas developed by Professor Walter

Gropius at the Bauhaus at Dessau are the inspiration behind the new organisation for the design and manufacture of furniture in Great Britain.' Furniture need not be heavy, it stressed, but rather, by bringing together British and Bauhaus, old and new, 'traditional English comfort' would be achieved through 'modern forms and materials'.[44]

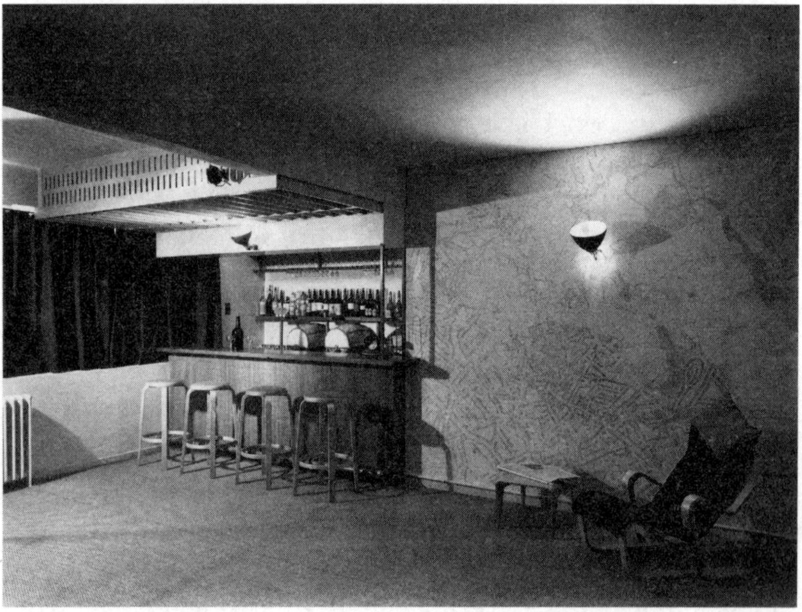

The Isobar, designed by Breuer and Yorke

□

Jack wanted to create a members' club feel to the Isokon and to give it an edge over the other recent modernist building in north London, Highpoint. And so, once the basement was watertight and other issues in the flats had been ironed out, he wrote to the occupants to tell them he was opening a 'club for the tenants of the flats and their friends'. Some redesigning was necessary, so Jack told Wells he wanted to move the existing kitchen and larder to make space for a restaurant and to turn

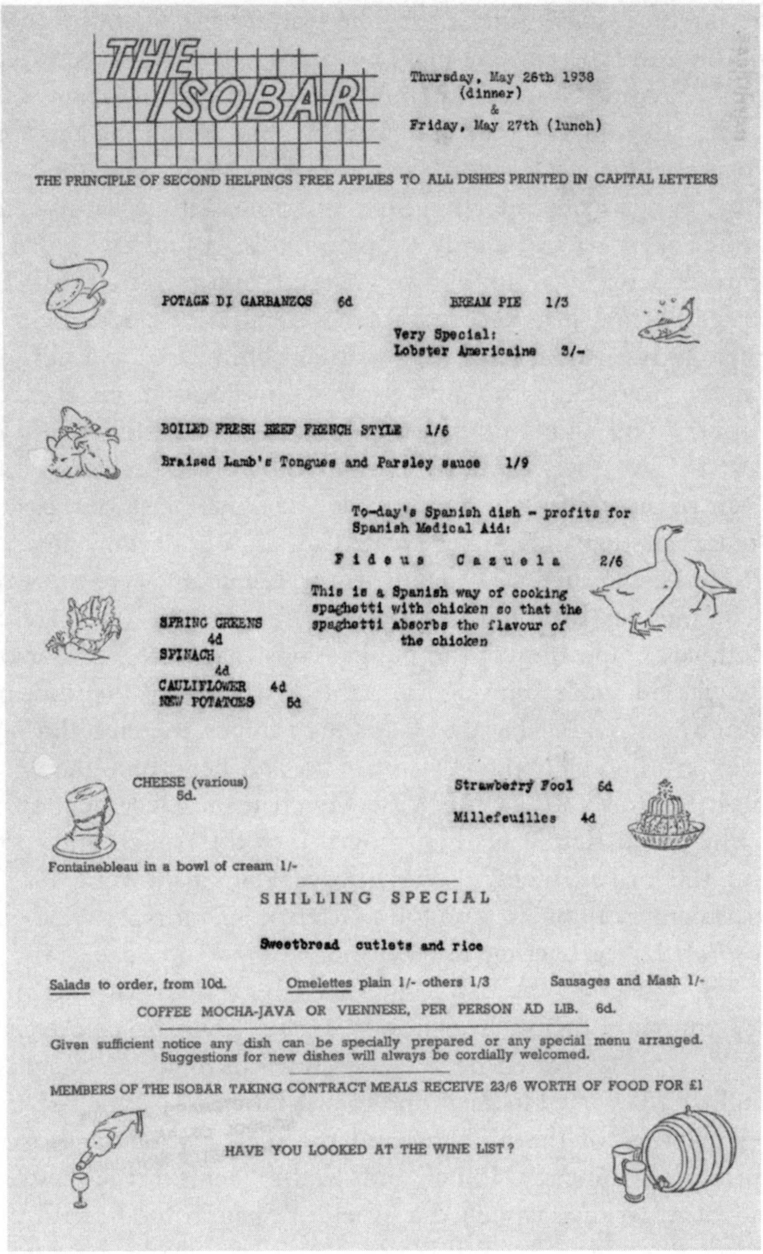

THE ISOBAR

Thursday, May 26th 1938
(dinner)
&
Friday, May 27th (lunch)

THE PRINCIPLE OF SECOND HELPINGS FREE APPLIES TO ALL DISHES PRINTED IN CAPITAL LETTERS

POTAGE DI GARBANZOS 6d

BREAM PIE 1/3

Very Special:
Lobster Americaine 3/-

BOILED FRESH BEEF FRENCH STYLE 1/6

Braised Lamb's Tongues and Parsley sauce 1/9

To-day's Spanish dish - profits for Spanish Medical Aid:

F i d e u s C a z u e l a 2/6

This is a Spanish way of cooking spaghetti with chicken so that the spaghetti absorbs the flavour of the chicken

SPRING GREENS 4d
SPINACH 4d
CAULIFLOWER 4d
NEW POTATOES 5d

CHEESE (various) 5d.

Fontainebleau in a bowl of cream 1/-

Strawberry Fool 6d

Millefeuilles 4d

SHILLING SPECIAL

Sweetbread cutlets and rice

Salads to order, from 10d. Omelettes plain 1/- others 1/3 Sausages and Mash 1/-

COFFEE MOCHA-JAVA OR VIENNESE, PER PERSON AD LIB. 6d.

Given sufficient notice any dish can be specially prepared or any special menu arranged. Suggestions for new dishes will always be cordially welcomed.

MEMBERS OF THE ISOBAR TAKING CONTRACT MEALS RECEIVE 23/6 WORTH OF FOOD FOR £1

HAVE YOU LOOKED AT THE WINE LIST?

Isobar menu, 26 May 1938

the existing pantry into a bar. The porter's flat would become an office and the existing maid's lavatory and porter's bathroom would become lavatory accommodation for the restaurant.[45]

The Isobar, designed by Breuer and Yorke, opened in November 1937. The idea was to create a focal point for local artists, designers, architects, writers and politicians, a place where they could meet and discuss utopian ideals, or just have a drink. Breuer's design was inspired by meteorology and he installed a barograph in a glass case with a photograph of clouds behind it. Molly was the head of the 'weather committee', and her job was to provide up-to-date weather conditions from the Air Ministry. The whole thing was a joke on the British obsession with the weather. Members could lounge on Breuer's Long Chair or dine at Isokon dining tables, or perch on stools next to Breuer's nesting tables. They created an outdoor decking area for use in the summer. The menus in the restaurant were unusual, including, for example, crayfish, Turkish kebabs and pigeon. Members could browse the publications that were laid out on Breuer's side tables, among them the *New Yorker*, *Vogue* and the *Architectural Review*. Despite Jack's high hopes, the club did not break even and Thomas Layton, who had been brought in to run it, left to set up Layton Wine Merchants in December 1937.

Philip and Kathie Harben moved into the Isokon and took over the management of the Isobar. Philip had worked as a documentary filmmaker on John Grierson's *Drifters* (1929) about the North Sea herring fishery, and he went on to become a television chef on the BBC. He has been credited with the first 'TV moment' on his live show, *Cookery*, when he cracked an egg that was so rotten he and the crew collapsed into helpless laughter. They lived in flat 7 on the first floor and Kathie became the manager of the building and the secretary of the Isokon Furniture Company. Philip and Kathie held themed events and early on they launched a 'week of Spanish food', with the proceeds going to Spanish Medical Aid. This involved a dinner with Henry Moore, Herbert Read and Louis MacNeice in the Pritchards' flat which was a 'great success and the Spanish cooking admirable'. Supplies had come from a Spanish restaurant in Soho, brought to them by a Mr Salsoma on the 24 bus.[46] The dinner raised almost seven pounds and the Hampstead Spanish Relief Committee wrote to thank them for the 'splendid help' they had given.[47]

The restaurant under Harben had high ideals, turning food into an art. The menu explained:

> The pepper in the mills is Telecherry Black; the bread is made to the Isobar recipe from stone-ground flour; the coffee is blended to the Isobar formula and made in individual Melior coffee-pots; Delhi rice (8 years old and hill-grown) is always served with the famous Isobar curries (which are made in three strengths), whereas Valencia rice is used for risotto; the anchovies served in the Club are imported direct from Collioure, Pyrénées Orientales; the pâté-de-foie-gras is imported from the Dordogne – the best truffle country, and considered by Frenchmen as the home of the best foie-gras; virgin olive oil, also specially imported, is used in the marinades for making the Isobar Terrine of Hare and Terrine of Pigeon. This oil is also used for all deep frying.
>
> By a special arrangement with firms in Covent Garden the Club is able to obtain such vegetables as fennel, salsify, celeriac, sweet potatoes etc. Also Autumn raspberries, and in Winter fresh asparagus, peaches, apricots, new potatoes etc.

In July 1938, Jack was pleased because he got a bit of a 'scoop'. The Isobar was going to exhibit prints from the Contemporary Lithographs company, set up by John Piper in 1936, before they were exhibited at the Leicester Galleries. The exhibition included prints by Duncan Grant, John Piper, Raymond Coxon, Edward Wadsworth and Vanessa Bell. Instead of making ordinary reproductions, Jack explained to one of his tenants, Paul Reilly, the artists draw their pictures directly on the stone so that, 'in effect, the pictures that are run off are originals'. Jack organised a dinner for 20 July to celebrate the exhibition with a welcome talk by poet and printer Francis Meynell and a short talk on the technical side by John Piper.[48]

The success of the Isobar led the Pritchards, the Harbens and the journalist Raymond Postgate (who went on to start the *Good Food Guide*) to form the Half Hundred Club, a club that would combine 'good and imaginative dining with economy'. The club had twenty-five members, all of whom could invite a guest, and ten dinners were organised per year, costing no more than £1 a head for food, wine and service. A two-shilling impoliteness fine was exacted if members failed to give notice that they were unable to attend and members were required to be 'seriously and intelligently interested in food and drink and to possess no religious, political or other taboos or unsociable characteristics which may impede conversation'.[49] The first meal, cooked by Harben, included terrine of hare and olives and Norfolk capons roasted in espagnole sauce. Ben Nicholson became a member early on and the zoologist Julian Huxley organised a meal at London Zoo where they ate bison tail and silverside of nylghau (antelope) with a Cumberland sauce and creamed fennel. Members were encouraged to keep the meal to themselves as it would embarrass the 'Zoo Authorities'.[50] Another meal was devised to be 'the most disgusting menu that even a British hotelkeeper could conceive'.[51] On another occasion Postgate came up with a bizarre menu where the mashed potatoes were dyed the colours of the flag of Jamaica and the soup was turned blue by using methylene. Breuer apparently rang Pritchard in the middle of the night when he saw his urine had turned blue.[52]

Gropius had been in discussion with Joseph Hudnut, the dean of the Harvard School of Design, for a few months about the possibility of teaching there. He was reluctant to commit to anything as he was still toying with the idea of returning to Germany, and more importantly he was keen to build, not teach. And then on 22 October 1936 the president of Harvard University, James Conant, came to London and arranged to meet Gropius. They got on well. Discussing education and aesthetics, they hardly mentioned the possibility of Gropius teaching at Harvard at all. Gropius thought Conant had a 'brilliant personality' and by December had agreed to go on condition that he could open his own architectural company and would not have to lecture. Gropius told his friend Adolf Sommerfeld that he had begun to 'draw a line under my English balance' and that he was gearing himself 'to the new thing' even though he was longing 'for the old Germany and the friends there, who are scattered to all winds'.[53] When he told him Jack was not surprised, but he was very sorry, and he hoped that Gropius would continue to work for the Isokon from the States.

There was a large gathering for Walter and Ise's farewell dinner on 9 March 1937. One hundred and thirty-five guests piled into the Trocadero Restaurant in Piccadilly including Geoffrey Faber, Henry Moore, Herbert Read, Julian Huxley and H. G. Wells. Moholy designed the 'bill of fare'. They started with oysters, followed by turtle soup and cheese straws, boiled Scottish salmon with lobster sauce and then Aylesbury duckling with apple sauce. For pudding they had iced nectarine melba. Herbert Read gave the final toast in which he said that Gropius was 'the man in whom the very spirit of modernism is concentrated'. Other ages may have had poets or philosophers, he said, but this is an age of 'immense technical progress, an age that has witnessed the final triumph of the machine'. In Gropius, said Read, America has found 'the genius most suited to the task of creating the plastic forms of a new civilisation' and that everyone at the dinner wished him Godspeed.[54] Gropius complimented his colleague Maxwell Fry in his speech, saying they had worked in 'complete harmony' and that Fry would make such headway in the architecture of the future that posters would read: 'Maxwell Fry built us towns, Oxo builds the body'. Over the years, he continued, the Atlantic will be 'less and less of a barrier' as the two countries have so many 'common tasks'. But the 'balance and poise' of the average Englishman is the real achievement and the reason 'everybody envies you', Gropius concluded.[55] His diary entry three days later on 12 March 1937 simply read: '9 0 Abfahrt USA'. Molly and Jack accompanied Walter and Ise to

Waterloo where they took a train to Southampton to board their ship to America. The brief possibility of a British Bauhaus was over.

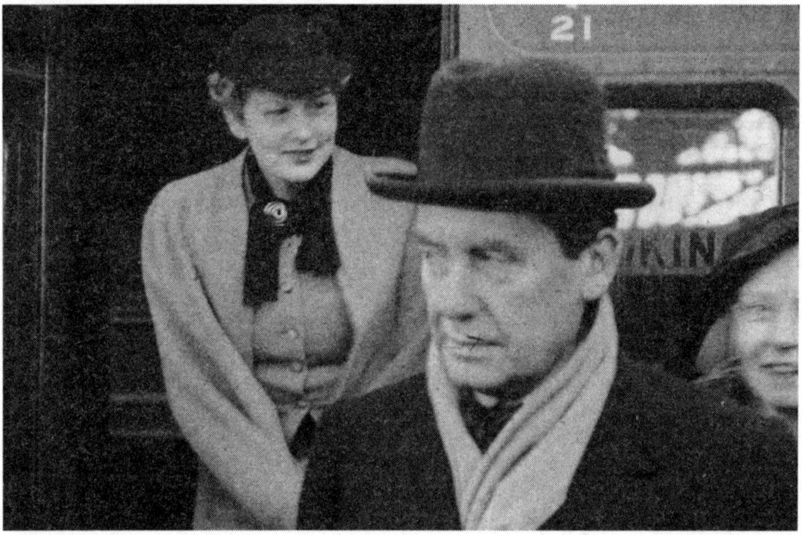

Ise and Walter Gropius leaving London, 12 March 1937

Jack's friend the architecture and design historian John Gloag wrote to congratulate him on the 'very considerable part' he and Molly had played in making it possible for English architecture to have 'such a wonderful injection of foreign genius'. He didn't know many people, he said, who would have 'taken such a modest back seat' at the dinner.[56] One reason for keeping a back seat was to hide his frustration with a room full of people who had failed to find a way to keep such a significant architect on British soil.

5
HERBERT AND LUDO AT THE MALL STUDIOS

'How I miss Herbert. I often find myself wondering what he would have thought about work that I have just been doing'[1]

The man who became the voice of British modernism arrived in Belsize Park in the summer of 1933. Herbert Read left his wife Evelyn and his son John in Edinburgh and resigned from his post as professor of fine art at the university. He had fallen in love with a twenty-five-year-old viola player, Margaret Ludwig, or 'Ludo' for short. Before she realised why he had disappeared Evelyn called the police, and this marked the start of a serious decline in her mental and physical health. Read and Ludo had nowhere to live in London, so Henry and Irina Moore, who were away in Kent, lent them their flat in Parkhill Road. Ludo was unsure about living with Herbert straight away and at first she stayed with a friend's mother. It wasn't long before she moved in and she enjoyed practising her viola with all of Moore's 'little early wood carvings' around her. She became attached to one of them in particular which they nicknamed the 'butter girl', a boxwood figure from 1932, and she longed to own it, but they didn't have any money and 'never thought of possessing anything' anyway.[2] The Moores' flat was 'on the frontier' between the worlds of Hampstead and Camden Town and just a few yards along the road from the Mall Studios. Read, Hepworth and Moore had all studied at Leeds, and it is no surprise that this Yorkshire trio spent a lot of time together in

London. Read was a huge advocate for them both as well as for Nicholson. Things became more complicated when surrealism arrived in London in 1936, complete with Dalí in a diving suit, and Read's affinities split.

When Henry and Irina needed their flat back, Herbert and Ludo moved into number 3 Mall Studios where they stayed for almost five years. Ben came round shortly after they had moved in, had a look around, left and came back with a round cork mat, still wet with scarlet paint. Ben had decided that the distance between the top of the picture hanging above the mantelpiece and the ceiling was too great, so he and Herbert moved the red circle 'up the white wall until they found the exact place for it to stay'. Read called it a single 'accent of colour, perfectly placed'.[3] Barbara remembered the cork mat in her statement for the Unit One catalogue: 'Objects that we place near to each other, in their different aspects and relationships create new experience. A scarlet circle on the wall, a slender white bottle on a shelf near it, a bright blue box and lovely-shaped fishing floats that rest in the hand like a bird.'[4]

Ludo remembered the path up to the Mall Studios as 'slightly smelly – you know, smelly greenery, London greenery, which I didn't like very much'. But, once inside, 'there was this lovely room in front of you, with a huge window, a little garden outside and a monastery garden beyond.' There is now a large fig tree outside the window, but it is still full of light and greenery. It was very nice, Ludo remembered, having the Catholic church at the end of their 'long, little garden' because, as a Catholic, she could nip in to say one prayer and then, 'there you were' in Kentish Town ready to do some shopping or go to a movie.[5] Read built a wooden hut at the end of the garden and wrote his only novel in it, *The Green Child*, over the summer of 1934. This, he said, was the best summer of his life. The current owners, architect Robert Maxwell and artist and architect Celia Maxwell Scott, described how Robert accidentally burnt the hut down. He built a fire of dead leaves in a wire basket and the flames spread to the dry creepers covering the back fence. There is now a modern studio in its place.[6]

Read grew up on a farm in the Vale, North Riding, which seemed to him, as a boy, to be a 'basin, wide and shallow like the milkpans in the dairy'. His early memories are flooded with colour: yellow cornfields, soft blue and purple moorland. Inspired by Wordsworth, Read believed that our lives are an 'echo of our first sensations' and for him these were being dunked in a trough of rainwater by his father, falling asleep on the warm flank of a newborn calf, helping to skin a freshly slaughtered pig with the end of a candlestick, smoking dried pear and clover leaves in the orchard, crushing his little finger in the granary machine and the humiliation of not being able to milk a cow or make the 'kuk-kuk' noise to 'urge a horse on gently'. The first ten years of his life took place in this rustic idyll, but then, when Herbert was ten, his father died. Read remembered waking in the night with a terrible earache and being told the next day his father was dead. The house 'became muted and silent' and then the farm was sold. Read and his eldest brother were sent to the Crossley and Porter School for Orphans on the moors, overlooking Halifax.[7]

Read's life, at this point, 'grew detached' and seemed to float away 'like a leaf on a stream'. His memories from school were hazy, although he did set up a literary magazine with the support of his head teacher. But then, when he was fifteen, the school cast them 'willy-nilly, out into the world', armed with a local examination certificate. He went to Leeds to join his mother, and got a job in a bank, spending his free time at the local library prepping himself for his application to university. In 1912 he signed up at Leeds University for classes in French, English, history, law, political economy, social economics and geology. Most of his fellow undergraduates were training to become teachers and bank clerks. He also signed up with the university Officer's Training Corps, which gave him a free summer holiday in the fresh air.[8]

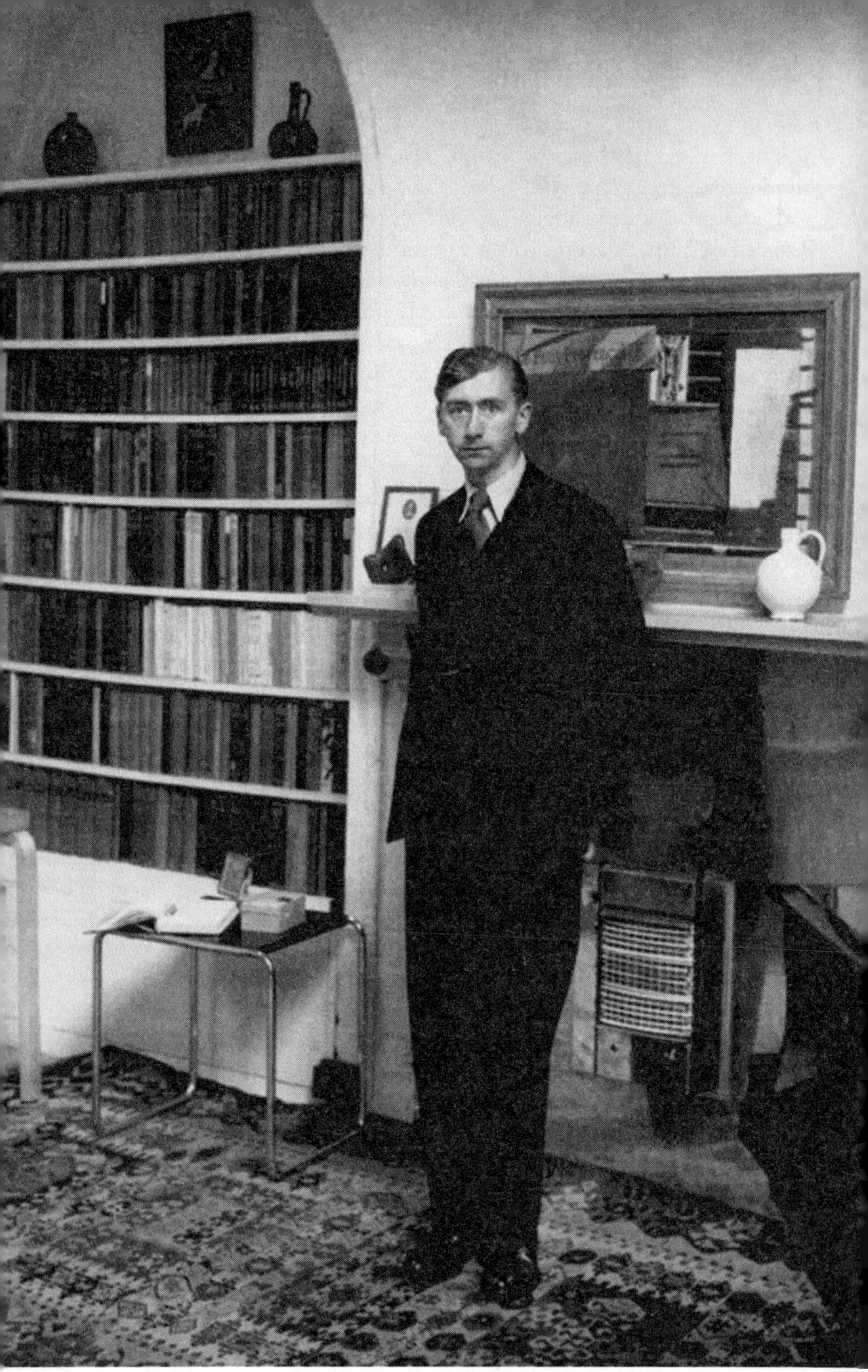

Herbert Read at 3, the Mall Studios

It was a good time to be a student at Leeds. Michael Sadler had become vice chancellor in 1911 and his liberal views on art and education transformed the spirit of the university from, as Roger Fry put it, 'a rather sullen suspicion of ideas to a genuine enthusiastic and spiritual life'. Sadler showed what '*can* be done, but rarely is, by education'.[9] His private art collection included works by Gauguin, Constable, Fantin Latour, Puvis de Chavannes, Philip Wilson Steer, Augustus John and William Nicholson. In 1911 Sadler's son came back from the Allied Artists' Association exhibition at the Royal Albert Hall with six woodcuts by an artist he hadn't heard of but whose work he liked very much called Wassily Kandinsky. The young Sadler wrote to Kandinsky to ask if he could reproduce them in his new quarterly review, *Rhythm*. Father and son were so intrigued that they decided to visit the artist and his partner Gabriele Münter in Murnau, a small town outside Munich. During their visit they saw some of Kandinsky's early paintings on glass, influenced by the Bavarian craft known as Hinterglasmalerei, and they discussed the possibility of Sadler translating into English Kandinsky's recent book *Über das Geistige in der Kunst* (1912). It was published in 1914 as *The Art of Spiritual Harmony*, now translated as *Concerning the Spiritual in Art*, one of the most important texts on modernist aesthetics of the twentieth century. The book included Kandinsky's famous theories relating to synaesthesia and the idea that colours create vibrations and moods in the soul. It explored the way that the expression of inner 'need' might result in abstract form. In other words interior thoughts and feelings are best represented through abstract art. Abstraction, for Kandinsky, was not an experiment but a necessity.

The young Read spent time at the Sadlers' grand, somewhat austere home, Buckingham House, on Headingley Lane in Leeds. Here he met the art critic for the *Sunday Times*, Frank Rutter, who also ran the Leeds City Art Gallery and the Leeds Arts Club. The club had been set up in 1903 by the Yorkshire schoolteacher, theosophist and intellectual Alfred Orage and the Yorkshire textile manufacturer Holbrook Jackson. It had quickly become a centre for modernism. Discussions involved radical politics, abstract art, spiritualism, feminism and philosophy. Speakers included W. B. Yeats and G. B. Shaw, and in 1913 Rutter organised an exhibition including works by Van Gogh, Cézanne, Matisse, Gauguin, Toulouse Lautrec and an early Picasso. Sadler donated Kandinsky's *Fragment for Composition VII* to hang at the headquarters in the Georgian town house on Blenheim Terrace. As well as introducing him to abstract art, Rutter took Read to the studios of artists in the Camden Town Group in London, including Charles Ginner, Robert Bevan and Harold Gilman. They were modern, if not modernist. The critic Charles Marriot noted in 1911 that they painted music halls, hansom cabs, coster girls, back gardens and even back bedrooms.[10] They painted life as it really was, shabby rooms with dust caught in shards of light. The visits opened Read's eyes to the way that art could be relevant to everyday life and he felt that he had been introduced to the 'professional' atmosphere of paint.

Two traumatic things happened during Read's time at Leeds. Britain declared war on Germany in August 1914 and his mother died of cancer four months later. At the start of the new year Read became a second lieutenant in the Yorkshire Regiment, the Green Howards, and was posted to Wareham in Dorset. He had little time to grieve for his mother during the first months of the war and this led to a sense of unreality and confusion: 'Was she really dead? Or had her death occurred only in one of my obsessive nightmares? I did not dare to give expression to this real state of uncertainty, but as the months passed, there came no confirmation of her existence.'[11]

He met Evelyn Roff, a botany and zoology student, during a debate on morality at Leeds. He was immediately drawn to her calm and rational intellect, which reminded him of his mother. And then in November 1915 he and his regiment were sent to the Ypres Salient where they experienced the realities of the front: 'primitive filth, lice, boredom and death'. He felt 'inexplicable unreality' when he saw the first man killed and 'did not know whether to laugh or cry'.[12] Read was awarded both the Military Cross and the Distinguished Service Order for his bravery and leadership, but declared himself a pacifist. A pacifist who held military decorations and an anarchist who could make organisations work, Read's ability to hold two opposing positions helped in the art world too.[13] He described himself as a circus rider with his feet 'planted astride two horses'. Later in life he hung a 'pure abstraction' by Nicholson and a 'surrealist fantasy' by Paul Delvaux next to each other. 'By chance', he said, the colours harmonised and if there was any contradiction in their form, 'it must correspond to a contradiction in my own mind, for both appeal to me with equal force.'[14] His son, the writer Piers Paul Read explained that Read had a sense that he had been saved during the war for a purpose, and he made that purpose modern art.[15]

A month before the end of the war Read's younger brother Charles was killed at Beaurevoir. In a poem full of grief and anger he railed against the 'supreme sacrifice' and pleaded that we 'be frank for once' as 'foisted platitudes cannot console sick hearts'.[16] We left the war just as we entered it, Read wrote later, 'dazed, indifferent, incapable of any creative action'.[17] Read and Evelyn were married in 1919 at the Register Office in North Bierley, West Yorkshire, with Evelyn's father and Read's remaining younger brother William as witnesses. Judgements are easy to make in retrospect, but their levels of antagonism ran high from the start. 'You are wildly, tragically wrong,' he wrote from France, and she told him he was 'artificial – self conscious – cynical – unsympathetic' with no 'zest for life'. He, in turn, called her a 'Puritan Rat'. Of course, there were tender moments too. Read wanted to define the 'precious' thing between them that held 'a world of wonder and joy'.[18]

Rutter and Read set up *Art and Letters* in 1917 with Rutter sending contributions to Read in France during the war for consideration. Read joked to Evelyn that the magazine was opposed to realists, romanticists and even 'Abstracts (poor me!) who do not relate their art to life at all'.[19] The *Times Literary Supplement* praised the journal for being 'agreeably free' from 'extravagance and affectation'.[20] Read had been impressed by Eliot's *Prufrock and Other Observations* and wanted him to write for them, so when Read was home to receive his investiture from the Palace in 1917 they met. Although Eliot was initially shy they became firm friends.[21]

Read got a job at the Treasury after the war, but the civil service didn't suit him. He and Evelyn discussed moving back to Yorkshire and she reluctantly encouraged him to resign. Ford Madox Ford, however, urged him to stay in London and to 'try to forget that you come from the Sheeres [Shires] at all... Whitechapel is really a better lieu de naissance.'[22] Before they had to make a decision he spotted a job in the Ceramics Department at the Victoria and Albert Museum, which they offered to him. He quickly got his eye in and published over twenty articles on English pottery and the first modern classification of the field, *English Pottery* (1924). And then Alfred Orage, editor of *The New Age*, who now lived on Keats Grove just next to Hampstead Heath, offered him the job of editing some of the critic T. E. Hulme's philosophical essays, and Eliot invited him to write for the *Criterion*, launched in 1923. At last, Read's intellectual thirst was being quenched. But he was still not satisfied; he never much liked Hulme's philosophy, and in particular the tendency to 'order everything' into 'one single ... authoritative unity'. Hulme was primarily a critic and a poet, but Read was not keen on his fondness for drawing parallels between politics, religion, art and literature.[23]

The big question for Read was whether to pursue a career in the verbal or visual arts. His marriage was growing increasingly turbulent and, being in Eliot's shadow as a critic, he was feeling stifled. He began to cut himself off from his wife and his son, afraid that if he waded in too deep he would 'drown'. Clearly, it was also a very difficult time for Evelyn. She wrote fragments of notes in her diary: 'Beginning of Anxiety symptoms. Too strained & strenuous a time... Too much silence'. By 1930 Read had reached a crisis. After delivering the Clark Lectures on

Wordsworth in 1929 he felt he could 'no longer be a disciple of Eliot' and he was thinking of leaving his wife.[24]

In 1931 Read was offered the Watson Gordon professorship of fine art at the University of Edinburgh, one of the first art history posts in Britain. It felt like a chance to come out of Eliot's shadow, to have a change of scene and maybe even to renew his marriage. Some of his friends were concerned that it would kill his creativity. The imagist poet Richard Aldington wrote to warn him about how the English bourgeoisie get hold of an artist and make a 'professor out of him' in the way they 'buggered poor old Tom Eliot up'. He believed there was 'masses of stuff' in Read that was simply awaiting expression but then, sticking the knife in, he wondered if he'd 'rather be a first-rate critic than a second-rate novelist'.[25]

Read could not avoid the romanticism–classicism debate among critics in the 1930s. Eliot argued that classicism was complete, adult and orderly whereas romanticism was fragmentary, immature and chaotic.[26] Hulme, fed up with the state of poetry, argued for a classical revival because beauty does not have to be infinite and free, it 'may be in small, dry things'. Writers, he went on, like architects, must get the 'exact curve' of the thing. It may have been a debate rooted in aesthetics, but it also served to refresh the rhetoric of the Conservative Party as the ordered, sensible party, unlike the 'romantic' Liberals.[27] Preferring to bridge oppositions rather than create deeper divides, Read searched for a new way to write about art. At first, he aligned himself with romanticism and all the immature fragmented chaos that went with it. He was very clear, however, that this was not, in his mind, at odds with the modern or the abstract. Romanticism for Read was neither a period nor a style but a 'psychological attitude'. It was an attitude of 'inspiration, daring and originality', unlike classicism, which he felt was characterised by 'derivation, conformity and timidity'.[28] Read later included Le Corbusier, Brâncuși asnd Ben Nicholson in the romantic camp, as well as Luciano di Laurana, Bernini and Piero della Francesca. Read's romanticism was in some ways a matter of taste and could be shoehorned into whatever he found most appealing.

At first, in Edinburgh, Herbert and Evelyn were pleased to have escaped London, and his new post allowed him one term off a year to write. But it did not solve all their problems. Read was withdrawn and Evelyn was suffering from a thyroid disorder and felt increasingly isolated. They spent more money than they meant to on the move, and rented a 'large, ugly, but comfortable mansion' at 9 Tipperlinn Road in Morningside. Read felt that their social life was conventional, and his inaugural lecture was not a great success. He announced that art must be at the centre of everything and should 'dominate our lives' so that 'there are no longer works of art, but art only'.[29] His lectures were an eclectic mix, bringing together ancient Greek art, Eric Gill, Brâncuşi, Zadkine, Moore and Hepworth, but his teaching was somewhat shambolic. One student remembered Read as disorganised and unsure of himself, while others remembered students showing up having come from the pub and throwing bread rolls around.

The most fun they had in Edinburgh was at the salons organised by Marc-André Raffalovich and his partner, the poet John Gray, who had known Aubrey Beardsley, Walter Pater and Oscar Wilde. It was at one of their gatherings that their lives changed for ever. One Sunday lunch Read sat next to the young viola player Margaret Ludwig, and she, without knowing he was married, thought, 'I am going to have that man.' Ludo was eleven years younger than Read, 'small, dark haired, dark eyed and with a very deep voice'. She was half-German, and she spoke slowly and made 'capricious remarks with an air of intense solemnity' while Herbert, 'head slightly to one side, watched her with delighted amusement'. Ludo had arrived in Glasgow aged seventeen or eighteen and pursued the violin and viola before going to Cologne, where she was taught by the Catholic composer Walter Braunfels. She returned to do a degree in music at Edinburgh and converted to Catholicism. Read took her a bunch of white lilac and garlic in her studio after the lunch. She looked stylish in a green silk flapper dress and patterned stockings. Read encouraged her to come and practise on their grand piano, much to the displeasure of his eight-year-old son John, who stuck out his tongue at her when she came in. Ludo apparently did the same back.

Read was hatching plans to create a Scottish Bauhaus in Edinburgh, with a gallery, film workshop and space for experimental projects, but it never got off the ground. He was also given an honorary degree from Leeds University in 1932 and Evelyn went with him to receive the award. For the ceremony she chose to wear a garish outfit including bright red gloves, which Read took as an insult. The gloves, of course, were merely a symptom of a larger malaise. They tried to have one more family holiday on Islay in the spring of 1933, but by June Herbert and Ludo had planned their escape. They went to stay with friends in Cologne and Read wrote to resign from his post at the university. Aldington congratulated him, telling him he'd feel enormous relief and will 'go like a race-horse now'.[30] Evelyn and John moved to a flat in Edinburgh, and although friends encouraged her to go back to teaching, she became increasingly unwell. At one point she locked herself into her bedroom and refused to eat. Years later, when John left to join the army in 1941, she was placed in an institution, first in Edinburgh but later in York, Norfolk, Shropshire and finally Stafford. She remained in institutions for the rest of her life.

By the time Read arrived in Hampstead, aged thirty-nine, he'd had a career at the Treasury, received the DSO, been a professor of fine art at the University of Edinburgh, edited T. E. Hulme's essays, published *The Meaning of Art* (1931) and *Form in Modern Poetry* (1932) with Faber, had a column in Eliot's magazine the *Criterion* and a weekly arts column for the BBC's *Listener*. Not long after their move to the Mall Studios, Roger Fry put him up for the editorship of the *Burlington* magazine, a post he held until 1938. Fry wrote to the art historian Kenneth Clark, who became director of the National Gallery in 1934, that there was a general consensus that Read was the best man for the job, 'in spite of my great distaste for his writings and his general *weltanschauung*. He seems to have wide general interests and all-round curiosity, which is more to the point than great learning along narrow lines.'[31] Fry was scathing of the 'tendency to accept with uncritical enthusiasm everything which proclaims itself modern and up-to-date' and Read was keen to distance himself from the 'painter critic'.[32] In fact, Read owed a lot to Fry, both for his job at the *Burlington* and for his theories of art. Fry had praised Kandinsky above all else at the Allied Artists' Association exhibition in 1913 and Fry's idea of 'pure visual music' was on the cusp of defining abstraction. The move to abstract modernism had been set up by Fry and Read embraced it.

By leaving Edinburgh without a trace Read caused great distress to his family, but his move to London contributed to an exciting new chapter in modernism. Herbert and Ludo became a kind of social glue in the modernist art world. Although Herbert was quiet in company, he and Ludo gave a lot of parties. The poet and editor Geoffrey Grigson remembered their studio as a place of 'extraordinary entertainment' where people of different nationalities and generations mixed:

> Braque might be there, or Jean Hélion, from Paris, or Eliot gayer than his reputation, actually singing 'Frankie and Johnny'. The exodus from Hitler's Reich having begun, one might walk into the solemn dignified company of Gropius to find oneself face to face with slow-smiling Moholy-Nagy from the Bauhaus (furniture all round to match, as far as could be found). Ben and Barbara from next door would be there, and the Moores from down the road…

They sometimes played a game where they pulled out a roll of wallpaper, blank side up, and pinned it to a long table. Each player took a coloured piece of chalk and together they drew 'something like a sixteenth-century chart, with headlands and straits and reefs and islands and whales and mermaids'. Then each player took turns, eyes shut, to sail a line from the harbour at one end, trying to 'avoid being wrecked on one or other of the obstacles'. Poets, according to Grigson, 'weren't dabs at visual form', and Nicholson and Moore won every time.[33] Ludo and Herbert also enjoyed going to the 'cookery club' at the Isokon, although they once ate 'something like rook pie' which Ludo 'didn't like at all'. They both got on very well with Gropius. But Ludo was distracted by his broken 'baby talk' and she preferred talking to him in German when 'he was himself'.[34]

One of the few things that Ludo and Herbert argued about was furniture. They had a large white sofa made by a 'special modern furniture shop' between Regent's Park and Camden Town that they both loved. They also had one of Breuer's 'lovely steel chairs' and a 'beautiful stove'. But Ludo did not like their round table 'covered with linoleum' and their 'rather nasty' little 'plywood stools' that she tripped over. She liked to keep a stash of Woolworth's plates to smash dramatically during their fights.[35] Their curtains were printed by Nancy Nicholson (Ben's sister) from linocuts by Ben, the woodwork was painted pale blue, the walls were white and the floor was white linoleum. They had pictures by Alfred Wallis and sculptures by Hepworth and they liked to play Cole Porter's 'Miss Otis Regrets' on the gramophone. Munza Braunfels, Walter's daughter from Cologne, moved into the small bedroom off the main studio and she became de facto cook and chauffeur. Herbert and Ludo slept on the covered platform above.

Read enjoyed writing his novel *The Green Child* in their second summer at the Mall Studios. It was a strange, mystical story about a Yorkshireman (Oliver) who returns to his childhood home and notices that the stream is running uphill. He follows it and rescues a strange pale green-skinned girl from the clutches of a miller. During the fight the miller is killed and Oliver and the green child follow the stream to its source where they slip through the water and enter a world below. It is a calm world, devoid of passionate emotion, with a precise social order and 'universal harmony'. The man and child join the harmony by becoming abstract sculptures. Jung later wrote to Read that he had read the novel 'right through in one day' and that it had given him 'a rumbling in the depths that kept me awake for the better part of a night'.[36] Read was pleased that Jung (whose work he later edited) had spotted all 'sorts of symbolism' he 'hadn't realised was there'.[37]

Read met Moore for the first time in April 1931 when he reviewed Moore's solo exhibition at the Leicester Galleries and asked if he could visit him in his studio. Henry and Irina gave him supper and Read was characteristically silent while looking at the sculptures and drawings. The next morning Moore received a letter expressing Read's huge admiration, and when he read the review in the *Listener* Moore was 'absolutely staggered … at the amount of appreciation and understanding he'd got out of that experience'. Read liked the fact that Moore was in the business of creation rather than representation. Hepworth met Read around the same time and she enjoyed his silences because it meant she 'began to look at the work through his eyes'. He responded, she thought, to the 'sensuality of what lay underneath the skin', and allowed the 'creature' within the sculpture to speak to him.[38] Read was passionate about modern art and felt betrayed when writers or artists toyed with traditional form. Stephen Spender thought that this inhibited Read's poetry because a 'free verse imagistic style' excludes 'a great deal of your experience'. Spender, aged twenty-five, became friends with Read in 1934 after Read had given him a favourable review in the *Adelphi*. Spender joined some of the gatherings in Moore's studio in Parkhill Road, where they met after a day's work at six o'clock to discuss art. Spender remembered a discussion on movement, and looking at a 'circle or a square or something' in Nicholson's work and noticing that it seemed to move.

For one of their many dinner parties Herbert and Ludo invited the Moores and the Woolfs in 1935. Virginia Woolf was not in a good mood when she arrived, having just had a row with her brother-in-law, Clive Bell. She was 'parched and throbbing' on arrival at the 'vast comfortless studio' where 'none of the charm of Bohemia mitigated the hard chairs, the skimpy wine, & the very nice sensible conversation'. Ludo was annoyed that Virginia asked when she came in if it was a stable. Leonard Woolf's palsy, Ludo noticed, was quite pronounced as he ate his soup. Respectable Bohemia, Woolf felt, was 'a little cheerless'. However, the evening went 'decorously. Steel chairs, clear pale colours; talk of pots; brainy talk; specialists talk. Read devitalised: possibly his look – a shop assistant.' But the evening was stimulating enough that Woolf was unable to write the next morning and could 'only correct'.[39] Read thought Woolf 'remarkable, but the cattiest woman I have ever known'.[40] She never quite forgave him for moving from her publishing house, the Hogarth Press, to Faber & Faber when Eliot became an editor there in 1925.

Eliot threw a party for Herbert and Ludo, her sister Maymay and her old friend Munza. He recounted the evening with the 'two stout German girls' to the Woolfs who were delighted by it: Virginia gave a 'long hyena shriek' at the shenanigans they got up to. Eliot had gone to Gamages, a department store in Holborn Circus famed for its stock of toys and games. He bought sugar cubes that let out small toy fish on being dropped into coffee, as well as fireworks, and chocolates filled with soap. Eliot described how the German girls, loving chocolate, ate greedily but then 'began to foam at the mouth'. At this point they 'set on' him and 'almost tore his collar off' and he cried, 'Mind my falsers!'[41] The evening went downhill after that and they forgot about the fireworks and 'exploded them on the doorstep' as they left. The tale was so funny Woolf wanted to kiss Eliot, but instead 'L made cigarettes. Tom drank whisky. I mused and was at my ease.' The relaxed atmosphere as Eliot recounted his tale led him to admit that he had wanted to send all his work to Woolf but thought that she wouldn't read it.[42]

Despite minor social strain, the strings between Bloomsbury and Belsize Park were sufficiently tied. In the summer of 1935 Herbert and Ludo rented Vanessa Bell's farmhouse, Charleston, in Sussex while Vanessa and her children joined Duncan Grant in Rome. Ludo was playing in the orchestra at nearby

Glyndebourne. Read filed for divorce from Evelyn that summer and by the autumn both Herbert and Ludo had caught a form of infectious jaundice that 'clogs the brain & reduces one to a drowsy incapacity'. The strain of the divorce no doubt contributed to their ill health, but the divorce was eventually granted on 20 January 1936 and Herbert and Ludo were married on 12 February at the Register Office in Hampstead. They spent their honeymoon in Spain, in the rain.

Although he hadn't managed to set up a Bauhaus in Edinburgh, Read was still keen on the theories behind it. He published *Art and Industry* in 1934 which set out his ideas for collaboration between the two. On their first meeting Gropius called Read a 'kindred soul'.[43] They both believed that art should lie at the heart of education, that it should be accessible to all and that it had the power to redeem mankind during periods of instability when people seemed ready to slaughter one another. The 'highest manifestation of the immanent will of the universe', Read wrote in his memoir, is 'the work of art'.[44]

Aesthetic experiences, for Read, were profounder than religious or moral ones; they were 'related to the very structure of the universe'.[45] He later remembered the years he and Ludo had spent in the Mall Studios:

> Within this inner group that worked within five minutes' walking distance of each other in Hampstead I do not remember any quarrels, any jealousy or spitefulness. It was a 'nest' of gentle artists (I am thinking of Turgenev's *Nest of Gentlefolk*), a spontaneous association of men and women drawn together by common sympathies, shared seriousness and some kind of group criticism. There were no polemics and no programme... There was a prevailing good temper, an atmosphere in which art could grow. The war came and destroyed it all.

Such a feeling of unanimity was never to exist again after the war, but English art had come of age. Within the next

> decade it was to become, what it had not been for a century, an art of international significance.[46]

He may have smoothed over some of the cracks when it came to the 'polemics', but it was certainly true that there existed a prevailing good temper that allowed art to grow. Read wondered how, with the 'ever-present threat of the world war', they could remain so calm.[47] One way that Herbert and Ludo remained calm was by moving out of Belsize Park in 1937, 'resigning the studio to the triplets', and moving into Broom House, Read's old home in Beaconsfield. Broom House had been rented out since Herbert and Evelyn had moved to Edinburgh in 1931. Herbert commuted back to London almost daily, but Ludo took to the country 'like a squirrel to a tree'.[48]

Read found small talk difficult and even serious conversation was something of an effort: he preferred the written word. His son remembered a conversation during which someone asked him his opinion on Miró, and, after a lengthy pause, he said, 'And what do you think?' His response had been entirely in his head. Margaret Gardiner noted that his silences were 'neither arrogant nor shy – they seemed, rather, to be manifestations of an inner certainty and knowledge'.[49] For Nicholson he was a 'rare enlightened creative spirit' with a voice of 'great beauty'.[50] Hepworth said they were 'blessed by the presence of Herbert Read' and that they couldn't have lived without him because he 'coordinated the whole' and 'treated us as individuals' as well as being a 'marvellous poet and writer'.[51] And so this tall, quiet, somewhat awkward man with a 'beautiful, smiling and gentle face' and an 'impish' quality did for modern art in the 1930s what Fry had done for Bloomsbury in the 1920s.[52] He gave a voice to artists.

6
THE RISE OF SURREALISM AND THE FALL OF UNIT ONE

'I am Unit One!'

Nineteen-thirty-three was an important year for modernism in London. Herbert and Ludo moved to Belsize Park, Well Coates began sketching plans for the Lawn Road flats, Ben carved his first relief in Paris, Lubetkin's pool was taking shape at the Zoo and Moholy-Nagy taught Barbara how to make photograms. And then, on 12 June, Paul Nash published a thousand-word letter in *The Times* to launch Unit One. Like the Bauhaus, it comprised sculptors, artists and architects, eleven in total, who stood for a 'truly contemporary spirit' in art and as a result it brought together a diverse range of abstract modernism and surrealism. Nash bridged the divide, both professionally and personally. His work embodied a kind of uncluttered surrealism; it was as much about the relationship between objects and space as about his inner psyche. And yet, despite his charisma and his 'ambassadorial appearance and debonair manners', he was unable to hold the Unit together.[1] The wave of surrealism that washed over London in the mid-1930s was too powerful. Read was caught in the middle of the storm. He was keen on the idea of an artists' collective like Unit One, but he was also seduced by the anarchy of surrealism.

During the 1920s Paul Nash and his wife Margaret ('Bunty') lived in Dymchurch, Kent, then at Iden Cottage in East Sussex, before moving into Rye in 1929. They found New House Rye, with views over Romney Marsh, and enough space for Margaret's father to move in with them. They also saw a lot of the painter Edward Burra, who lived near by in Springfields, on the road to Rye. Nash suffered from severe bronchial asthma, probably due to gas inhalation when he served in the Ypres Salient as a war artist in the First World War. He also suffered a breakdown in 1921 as a result of his experiences during the war and he was advised to live in the country for his health. In 1933 he became art critic for the *Listener*, alternating each week with Herbert Read.

In early 1933 Nash invited his friends Wells Coates, Henry Moore and Edward Wadsworth to establish a group that would include artists, sculptors and architects. At first Nash wanted to call it something modest and descriptive, such as English Contemporary Group, but Coates wanted something more abstract. Coates explained his success with the 'Soviet system' of 'making up a short-clipped-word' out of the first few letters of a phrase, as he had done with the Isokon, echoing his 'system of building mass-produced houses and flats' on the basis of 'isometric unit construction'.[2] The name Unit One emerged and it suited them both: it was simple and abstract and captured the unity and individuality they were after. At first Nash did not want to include Ben Nicholson. He thought he was a 'good fellow', but did not think his judgement 'entirely sound'.[3] Nash also had a 'foolish fancy' for keeping the group all male, and Coates agreed, in the first instance 'at any rate'.[4]

Coates took Nicholson, Hepworth, Moore and the surrealist painter John Armstrong to a Japanese restaurant one Saturday night in March 1933. Discussing the Unit, the all-male 'fancy' faded as they realised that Ben would not join if Barbara was not included. They also wanted to invite the New Zealand painter Frances Hodgkins, a friend of Ben and Barbara's. Like Ben and Barbara, Hodgkins was a member of the Seven and Five Society, the group of seven painters and five sculptors set up after the First World War that had evolved into a group of entirely abstract artists after Nicholson took over in 1926. Hodgkins's work had

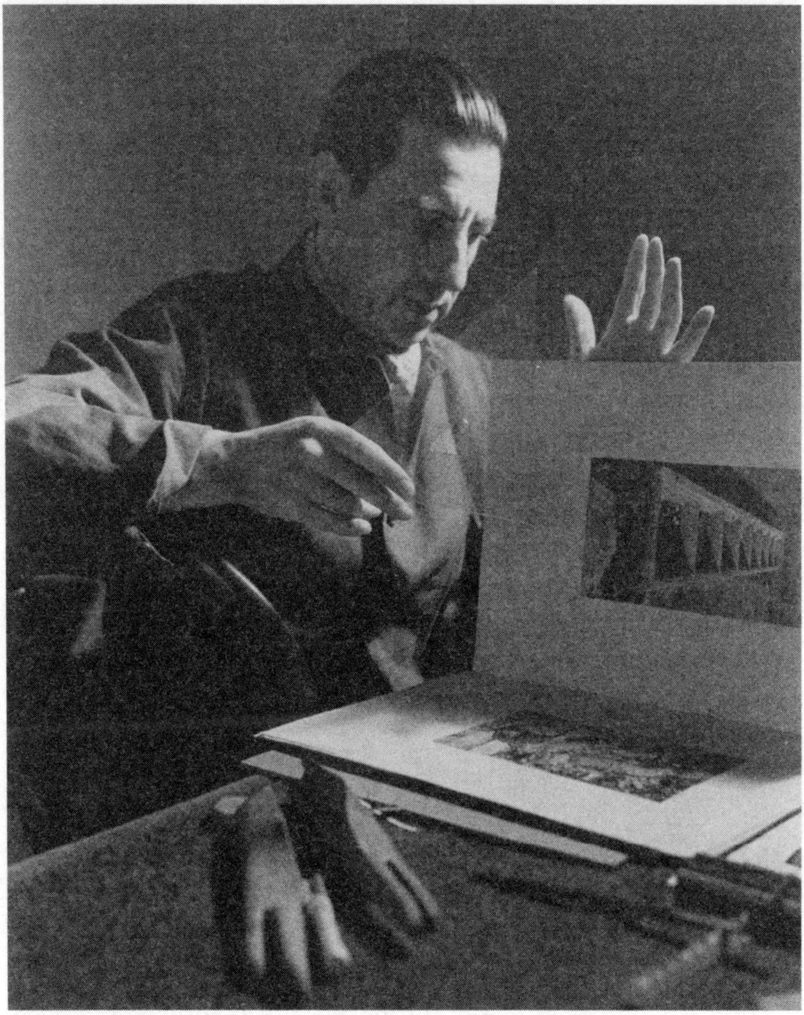

Paul Nash, 1932

become increasingly abstract in the late 1920s. They also talked about asking the artist and architect Frederick Etchells to join Unit One, as he would be a good link between the disciplines, but there was general concern that he had become 'rather gaga' and prone to long-winded discussion, so they left him out. John Bigge was suggested, but Coates was not sure. He thought that Bigge painted 'too much and thinks too quickly' and that his wife's paintings were much better than his. If they did include him, Coates suggested, they should choose his pictures for him as he was likely to select the wrong ones.[5] By spring the members were decided and both Ben and Barbara had made the cut. The architects were Wells Coates and Colin Lucas (at twenty-seven, Lucas was the youngest and least experienced of the group), the sculptors were Henry Moore and Barbara Hepworth, and the painters were Edward Wadsworth, Ben Nicholson, Paul Nash, Frances Hodgkins, Edward Burra, John Bigge and John Armstrong.

The group planned to exhibit at Tooth's Gallery and Coates agreed to spruce up the 'modern salon' for free as it was looking a bit shabby. But then they were offered Freddy Mayor's new gallery in Cork Street, which had opened in April 1933 and had become known as the 'only really modern gallery in the country'. It had white walls and modernist furniture and it had already exhibited most of the artists involved in Unit One. Its European credentials were also good. Mayor held an exhibition in October 1933 (connected with Read's publication *Art Now*), which included work by Braque, Léger, Miró, Kandinsky, Dalí, Soutine and Giacometti.[6]

Ben was frequently in Paris in 1933 seeing Winifred and the children, so he suggested, with characteristic enthusiasm, that they set up a Unit One over there. By the end of March that year Nash said that Unit One was 'oozing with ripeness', but that he wouldn't shake the tree until they'd talked everything through.[7] The tree remained unshaken a little longer: Nash fell ill and had to stay in Rye and Coates was deep in the planning stages of the Lawn Road flats. And then on 12 June Nash's letter appeared in *The Times*. It set out his vision. Nash admitted that new groups were common enough but that in England they tend to 'die hard'. He stressed that Unit One was a mature group with 'nothing naïve' about it and, although they were not all abstract artists, they were 'solid' and interested in 'architectonic' qualities. English art has suffered, he wrote, from the 'crippling weakness' of a 'lack of structural purpose'. Unlike their predecessors, he argued, Unit One artists do not paint by the 'light of nature' but stand for 'the expression of a truly contemporary spirit, for that thing which is recognized as peculiarly *of to-day* in painting, sculpture and architecture'. 'That thing' was not defined, but categorisation was less important than the 'individual forces' of Unit One that will create a 'hard defence, a compact wall against the tide'. There were eleven members, but by the opening of the exhibition in April 1934 Hodgkins had been replaced by the twenty-eight-year-old surrealist Tristram Hillier. Hodgkins had resigned, Nicholson explained, because she never felt 'wanted'; she thought she was simply there because of her friendship with Ben and Barbara.

For the last twenty-five years, Nash wrote in his column for the *Listener* in July 1933, the centre of the art scene had been Paris. 'Cézanne, Cubism, Dadaisme, Purisme, Surréalisme' had, he argued, 'astonished and inspired', whereas in England we had the 'half-remembered "Vorticist" movement'.[8] Unit One was about to change all that. Coates suggested the inclusion of an 'abstract drawing of the block of flats at Hampstead' in the *Listener* to go along with Nash's latest piece.[9] They printed it upside down. The editor was mortified and apologised for the 'disastrous blunder' of which 'any editor must be ashamed'.[10] Read backed up the idea of building blocks of artists like Unit One in the *Architectural Review*. He pointed out that artists were limited in what they could achieve on their own but as a 'band' they could do 'interesting things'. They could have a central office, he suggested, and an information bureau for the public. Their bond would be spiritual, however, and this might cause some discomfort to the average Englishman. Read was fascinated by the power of collectives.[11]

There were disagreements within Unit One even before it was launched. Ben was not happy about the 'surrealism business' and told Coates he had 'unravelled' it, by which he meant he wanted the word 'reality' in the manifesto. Whatever the process, he said, the 'outcome is reality'.[12] Nash's first draft of *The Times* announcement included the distinction between 'abstract' and 'other forms of imaginative art', but he took it out. Nash used his article in the *Listener* to make the distinction between the 'pursuit of form' (abstraction) and the 'pursuit of soul' (surrealism) in its 'devious flight'. Despite his attempt to bring them together to create the 'strength of a national art', the two factions could not coexist for long.[13] Nash's vision that the group would resemble the Pre-Raphaelite 'brotherhood' or a 'solid combination standing by each other and defending their beliefs' was short-lived.

A book to accompany the Unit One exhibition was edited, 'for no good reason' that he 'could remember', by Read. The idea was to imitate the annual publication of the Abstraction-Création group in Paris, of which Hepworth, Nicholson and Wadsworth were members. Read sent the Unit One members a series of 'emetic' questions about 'Freud, symbolism and machinery' to get things started. The results revealed that Freud and symbolism were losing out to machinery. The adulation of industrial design found an outlet in pylons: Tristram Hillier painted *Pylons* in 1933 and it was exhibited in the Unit One exhibition, Nash photographed a pylon rising out of the British countryside in 1931 and Spender captured them as nude giants without secrets in his poem of 1933, 'The Pylons'.[14]

In December 1933 Barbara asked Ben if he'd finished his text for the Unit One catalogue as she 'simply' couldn't do hers. She warned Ben that Herbert wanted their articles by the 14th. Their friend the art critic Adrian Stokes stepped in to help her with her draft. Adrian later moved into the Lawn Road flats; coincidentally he had been to the same prep school as Ben and 'attested to its squalor and severity'.[15] Margaret Gardiner had introduced Ben and Barbara to Stokes again, and he and Ben liked to play tennis at the club in Belsize Park. Stokes wore a

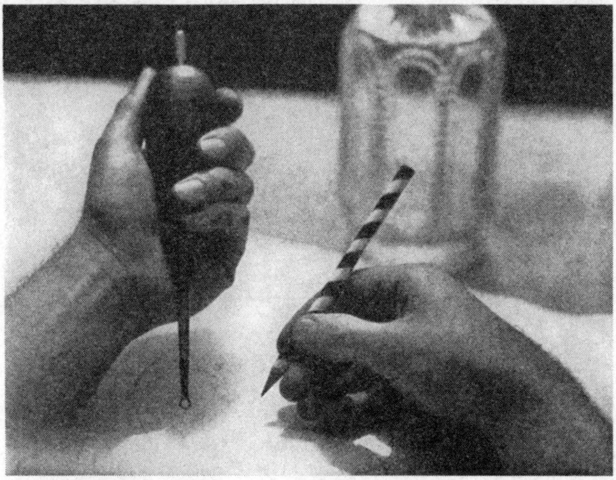

Ben's hands in Unit One *catalogue, 1934*

hairnet while he played as he was very particular about his hair. He had started analysis with Melanie Klein and was integrating psychoanalytical theories into his books on Renaissance art, particularly in the critically acclaimed *The Quattro Cento* (1932). He went on to write more than twenty books on the Renaissance, bridging the gap between sixteenth-century and contemporary art, ballet, poetry and the modern environment. 'Adrian is such a darling,' Barbara told Ben, '& is being such a help to me. He spent 3 hrs last night over my Unit One thing.'

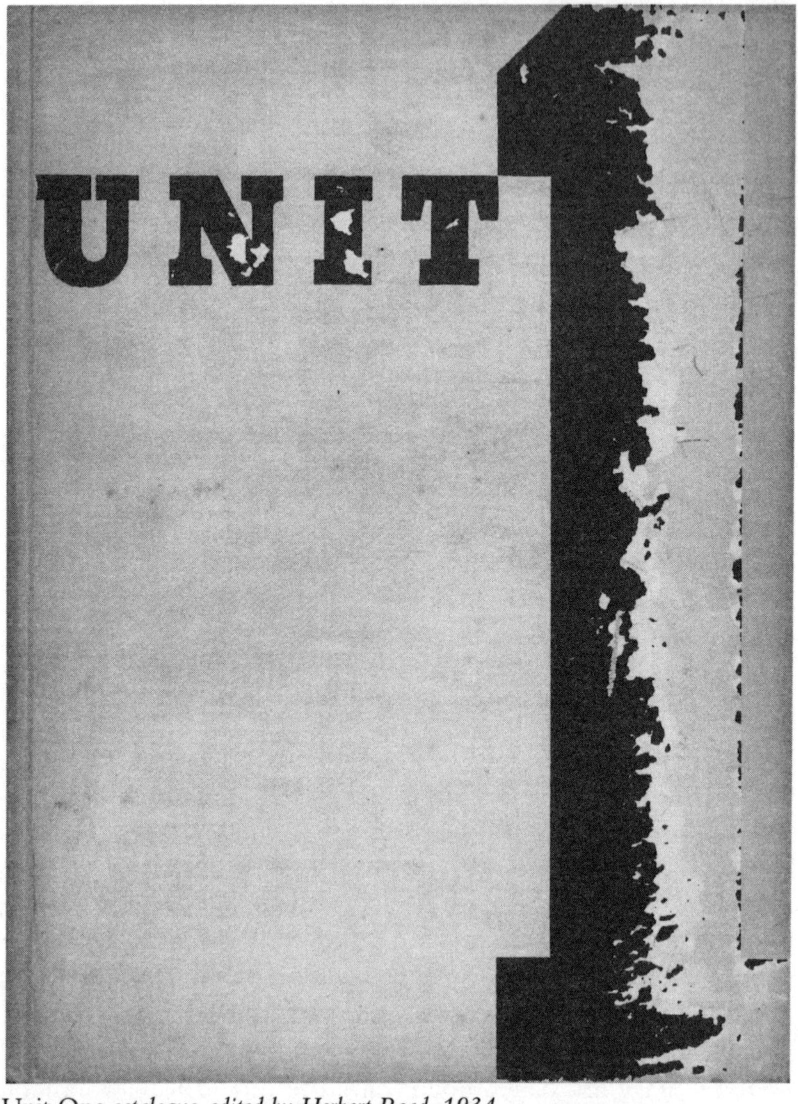

Unit One *catalogue, edited by Herbert Read, 1934*

Stokes was a fan of both Hepworth's and Nicholson's work. His help later in the decade surpassed editorial advice. At the outbreak of war in 1939 he and his wife, the painter Margaret Mellis, invited Ben, Barbara, the triplets and their nanny to their house in Carbis Bay, near St Ives in Cornwall.

Hepworth's article for the Unit One book took at least a week to write and she begrudged the time because 'I long to start carving.' But she resigned herself to it because 'if its got to be done I may as well do my best to make it nice.' She told Ben that her piece was 'very solemn & serious' because, she half joked, 'carving is you know compared with ptg.'[16] Read liked her article and she boasted to Ben a few days later that Read had said that 'people like her' always did these things well.[17] The piece included details from the time she and Ben had spent in Saint-Rémy, the train journey where she had seen 'a blue aeroplane between a ploughed field and a green field, pylons in lovely juxtaposition with springy turf'. She also added a 'stone arch' on a 'green flat space' against 'stony mountains, olives quietly growing' and a café with the wireless 'filling the air with music from some foreign station'.[18] Ben still hadn't submitted his own article by mid-December, though Herbert needed them all in so that he could write the introduction. Barbara told Ben that he was holding things up, but he wasn't the only one. Coates was so late with his draft that Douglas Cooper, co-partner of the Mayor Gallery, asked him to come over to his flat on the Brompton Road to check the draft as there was no time for proofs. 'Alcohol usually aids one on these occasions,' Cooper added.[19]

Barbara was upset about the hanging of the exhibition, which she feared would be 'appalling'. She wished she got on better with Douglas Cooper, who was curating the exhibition. He had 'tried to be nice' and said her work 'had improved', but they still had 'several little bursts'. Cooper's condescending remark about her work cannot have helped. Hepworth suggested that Ben's work be placed near her sculpture as their work was so closely related, but Cooper had 'decided long ago what ptgs to put downstairs'. He wanted a large Burra and a large Hillier. Barbara 'felt so depressed about it' and wished that Nash or Wells were there to help as Ben was in Paris. Nash was in Rye and Wells was busy at Olympia as he had a 'modern house there'. Barbara's doubts were unfounded; just before it opened on 4 April she thought the 'show is looking quite nice' and that Cooper had 'worked hard & well on it'.[20]

Between May 1934 and April 1935 the Unit One exhibition travelled around Britain. Cooper wrote to Coates 'that in 4 weeks at Liverpool they had 30,000 visitors!'[21] The reviews were lively and mixed. The critic for the *Belfast Telegraph* was 'haunted by a horrible suspicion that perhaps I wasn't a human after all, and even if I were a human … perhaps I was even more circular than I acknowledged myself to be'. The *Manchester Evening News* simply led with 'Weird, weird' and the *New English Weekly* referred to the work as 'degenerate'.[22] *Apollo* claimed that the artists took themselves 'more seriously than their exhibition seems to warrant', and news spread across the Atlantic, with the *New York Times* referring to the 'snobbish fashion of "Unit One"' which had 'done an enormous amount of justifying and explaining itself'. Nicholson didn't help matters by appearing in the catalogue as the 'complete bourgeois conception of a Hampstead artist, vivid scarf, beret and all'.[23] Geoffrey Grigson wrote in *Art Today* that the Unit One artists were 'simpletons', but that the 'cell is the simplest organism, and when art becomes loose and disorganized you must go back to the cell, to the simplest shape'. Only then, Grigson claimed, can you move on to more complicated matters.[24]

Towards the end of 1934, the divisions within Unit One were put to the test with a secret ballot to decide the future membership. Read organised things so that members would need a unanimous vote to survive, but if that failed those with ten votes would form the new group. After the results were in Moore announced 'I am Unit One!' and Cooper called him the 'sole survivor of that crazy ballot'. In fact Moore and Nash were both voted in and they invited Wells and Wadsworth to join them. Back to the original four, they felt that they were 'starting again from scratch', but the damage caused by the secret ballot had been done.[25]

Read felt the time was ripe to turn the retuned Unit One into a British Bauhaus. The Isokon was finished, Gropius was in town and they had sculptors, artists and architects lined up. Nash agreed. He had been all set to 'fade out' the Unit if only two of them had survived but then he read Read's *Art and Industry* (1934) and saw a 'glimmer of light'. Read's book advocated art and design that spoke to spiritual life. Looking back to Wedgwood and William Morris, Read idealised previous eras when art and industry appeared united. The book was an eclectic collage of contemporary design, furniture and kitchenware by Chermayeff, Mies van der Rohe and Aalto, alongside classical designs. Herbert Bayer designed the layout but he did not conform to standard editing practice, causing great distress to the typographer, Stanley Morison. Morison complained that Bayer was 'ignorant of the function of italics' and wilfully shut his eyes to the 'utility of capitals'.[26]

Read believed that the new Unit could develop itself into more or less the pattern of the German Bauhaus. Nash wondered tentatively if it could be done and recognised that it would require 'real organisation, capital and considerate concentrated devotion'. He realised they would have to work '<u>outside</u> of our own main jobs as architects, painters & sculptors'. He was ready to make the change even though the 'ways and means baffle me'.[27] Read said he was loath to interfere but wanted to keep the idea afloat. He encouraged Nash by mentioning that Gropius had told him 'the other night' that although he had 'founded the Bauhaus on an industrial basis, the first two people he asked to cooperate were a painter and a sculptor – the triad which you already have'. Although he claimed to be unwilling to interfere, Read 'talked the matter out' with Moore and thought the group should be a 'practical unit in the industrial system' and be prepared to 'undertake the designing of a building in every detail – architecture, fittings, interior decoration and furniture'.[28] Read suggested that the architect Colin Lucas and Edward Wadsworth (who had the highest number of votes after Moore and Nash) were 'unquestionably the right kind of member' of a new Unit. With Ben, he pointed out, you have a 'problem', but not one with which he was willing to interfere. He urged Nash to 'consider for a long time' before excluding Ben as it would 'confuse the public'. Besides, he predicted, if Ben were excluded he would simply go and set up his own group, 'being so vital and energetic'. Such 'division & backbiting' would be unhelpful when 'unity is so necessary and desirable'. And then if Barbara was excluded, Read continued, Ben would probably resign. So, if 'unity is the first essential', he concluded, 'I cannot see that the addition of Barbara to the Group would in any way lessen its effectiveness as a united front.' These remarks are for 'your eyes only', he wrote, but 'I have already spoken in this sense to Harry, and I don't mind if you show them in confidence to Wells, or give him the gist of them.' He promised to destroy the ballot papers, but suggested that Nash keep a record of the results.[29] Coates, Read and Moore had dinner with Gropius a week later and there's no doubt they would have discussed the new Unit with the founder of the Bauhaus.[30]

By early February 1935 they had a 'Provisional Council' with Coates, Nash, Moore, graphic designer Edward McKnight Kauffer, Read and Moholy (when he arrived in April). The Council had various 'panels', including one for engineering and one for costume design, but Ben pleaded for the retention of the old Unit One as part of the new Unit. Read agreed they ought to slow things down; the room, he said, 'was too hot the other night – something was a little wrong. The wheels were going round all right, but somehow they did not connect.'[31] Coates and Nash had fallen out and Ben's desire to keep Unit One going was too difficult to sustain. In 1935 the final dissolution notice of Unit One was signed by Moore, Nash and Coates: 'Such an association was felt to be inadequate to meet present needs, especially in view of recent developments in regard to industrial art. It was agreed therefore to end the Unit completely in form and name. The ideals embodied in Unit One, however, will find expression in a new development under another name. Details will be announced later.'[32]

The Artists' Unit was announced on 7 May 1935 at the Mayor Gallery. The aim of the new group was to connect its members with a 'new system of production' in order to promote a 'machine-made aesthetics'. They described themselves as a 'group of men concerned with design in all its aspects – architecture, engineering, painting, sculpture, cinema, publicity and all forms of manufacture'. The members included Read, Coates, Moore, Nash, Kauffer and the documentary filmmaker John Grierson. One of the more practical aims was to introduce 'more effective liaison between the factory and the art school'.[33] Meanwhile Ben was organising what was to be both the first exhibition of entirely abstract art in Britain, and the last exhibition of the '7 & 5' Society at the Zwemmer Gallery, which opened in October 1935.

Before the Artists' Unit could make any headway with their industrial aesthetics, surrealism swept them aside. Coined by Apollinaire in 1917, the term 'surrealism' was made widely known by André Breton in his *Manifeste du surréalisme* of October 1924 in which he stated that dreams and reality ought to coincide. He believed that the 'future resolution of these two states' would create a future new state, a 'surreality'. Surrealists, he wrote, must 'express thought directly' without interference from 'aesthetic and moral preoccupation'.[34] Freud's theories of the unconscious, dreams and the uncanny formed the bedrock of the movement. Although Paris was the heart of the surrealist movement, London held the first solo exhibition of de Chirico and the Mayor Gallery put on a series of surrealist exhibitions once it had opened in April 1933. But the catalyst for surrealism in London was the arrival of the artist Roland Penrose, who moved to 21 Downshire Hill in 1936. The son of Quakers, Penrose had studied at Clare College, Cambridge, where he met Roger Fry, but then, aged twenty-two, he moved to France where he became friends with Picasso, Max Ernst and Wolfgang Robert Paalen.

Read liked to refer to surrealism as 'superrealism' as a way of toning it down. Those closest to him believed he preferred the cool aesthetics of Hepworth, Moore and Nicholson. Nevertheless, Read was 'guilty of sympathetic flutters for any poor devil who is trying to be sincere', so when Penrose asked him to join the organising committee of the British Surrealism Exhibition along with Nash, Moore and Humphrey Jennings, he agreed.[35] Breton, Éluard and Man Ray made the selections on the French side and Dalí on the Spanish. Nash, Moore and Hugh Sykes Davies were also on the Objects Sub-committee. Works were chosen by artists including de Chirico, Klee, Picasso, Giacometti, Miró, Tanguy, Dalí and Ernst. Works by four ex-members of Unit One were selected, including two pieces by Bigge, eight from Burra, seven from Moore and twelve from Nash.

Nash's tilt towards surrealism began after he saw de Chirico's work at Arthur Tooth & Sons in 1928 and then again in 1931. He was taken with de Chirico's depiction of isolated objects and 'accentuated perspective', and admired the way he made 'things happen in a picture'.[36] He became further inclined when he met Eileen Agar in the summer of 1935. Agar, born in Buenos Aires, had been sent to school in England as a child, accompanied on the boat by a cow and an orchestra, because her fashionable, eccentric mother believed that fresh milk and good music were essential to her well-being.[37] She studied with the sculptor Leon Underwood along with Henry Moore in 1924, and then she went to the Slade from 1925 to 1926 before moving to Paris in 1928. In Paris she studied with the Czech painter František Foltýn until 1930 and became friends with Breton and Éluard. Agar did not believe in painting directly from dreams but she did want to paint what 'goes on inside our heads', including sexual pleasure. Art, she said, ought to be 'imaginative playfulness'. A. S. Byatt has noted that her work is never 'moody or disturbed'.[38] After a brief marriage to a fellow Slade student, Agar met the Hungarian writer Joseph Bard in 1928 and they eventually married twelve years later.

After an extended trip to the South of France, Morocco and Spain, Paul and Bunty Nash returned to London but left shortly afterwards on account of Paul's health. First they stayed with a friend in Romney Marsh, and then another friend offered them a little house on Ballard Down in Swanage, Dorset. They stayed there for a few months in 1935 before finding their

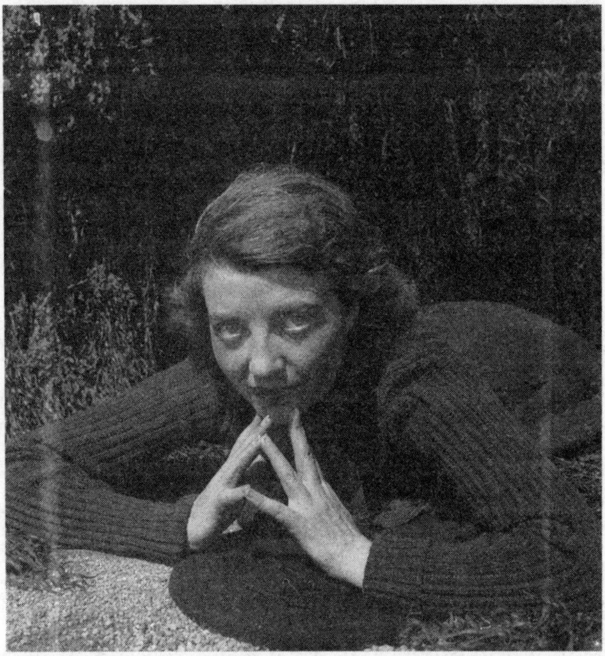

Eileen Agar

own place on the Swanage Front, at 2 The Parade.[39] Agar and Bard had rented a house near by and the two couples met. Betjeman had commissioned Nash to write the *Shell Guide* to Dorset that summer and Agar sent him a box of shells she had painted after their first meeting. He was so delighted he took some of them with him to Sussex where he was staying with friends. He told her she was 'obviously very delightful' and that it was 'refreshing' to meet someone who 'overflows with attractive actions' rather like a 'flower who could sing' or a 'stone which can fly'. He placed the shells in his tie drawer, 'bewildering the inquisitive maid'. They began an affair shortly afterwards and he wrote a poem in which he described his heart as a stone 'travelling the skies' and shaking the clouds 'till they spilled their dew'. He told her that he liked her 'best unencumbered – just as I like your pictures so'. Even though Nash was a member of the English Surrealist Group, compared to her, he said, he was 'practically a naturalist'. He loved her 'all ways and always' and sent her a Freudian drawing of a woman in garters wrapped in a snake.[40] They broke up in 1936, the same year that the Nashes moved to 3 Eldon Grove, just up the hill from Belsize Park. Paul needed to be near London doctors but away from the London smog of St Pancras, where they had been living.

Paul told Eileen that she had given him something he would never have again in his lifetime. In her, he wrote, 'is embodied for me some essence of life' which gave him 'new energy & a poignant joy', but that in 'you it remains'. He asked her not to repeat his confession as he did not want to 'wound any deeper' than he already had, adding that if they parted now, they would part at the 'peak of our flight where we have climbed dizzily like birds who make love in mid-air heedless of where they soar'.[41] A year later Nash suggested they hold hands at a 'dust up' at Roland's and, calling her a starfish, hoped to taste the brine of her 'cool wet mouth just once again'.[42] They were still arguing in their letters in 1940, the year she married Bard.

The Surrealist Exhibition opened on 11 June 1936 at the New Burlington Galleries and ran for four weeks. There were 392 works by sixty-nine artists, as well as natural objects and children's drawings, including one by 'Freddy' entitled *The Water Mug Gets Lost in the Playground*. Other pieces included Man Ray's *Lovers* (Lee Miller's red lips floating above a landscape); two walking sticks; Meret Oppenheimer's *Fur-Covered Cup, Saucer and Spoon* (which fascinated T. S. Eliot); Dalí's *Aphrodisiac's Waistcoat* (a jacket with little glasses of crème de menthe sewn all over it), and Eileen Agar's collection of *objets trouvés* including shells, rusted metal and netting.[43] Nash included a piece of driftwood which he had 'salvaged from the stream' in Romney Marsh in 1934 and which, he said, 'like a very fine Henry Moore' had been 'waiting for a bright sun to be photographed'. He called it 'Found Object Interpreted,

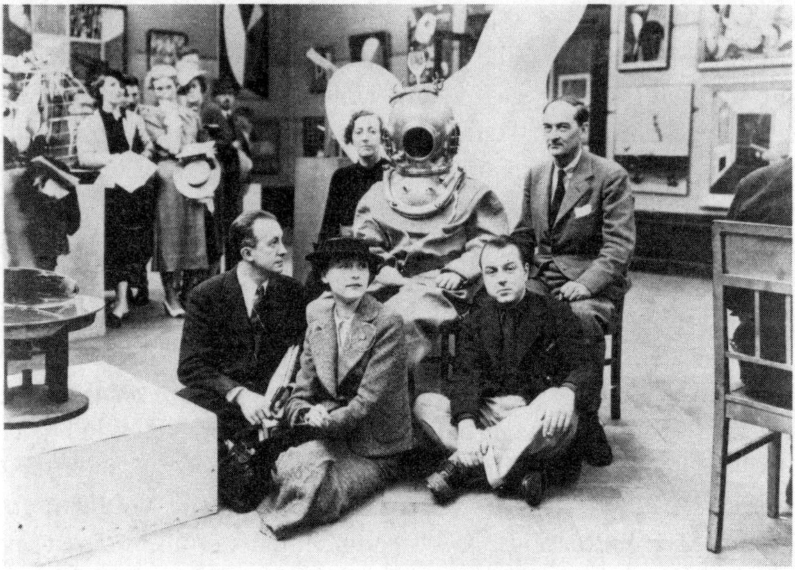

The Surrealism Exhibition at the New Burlington Galleries, London, 1936. From left to right: Paul Eluard, Nusch Eluard, Diana Brinton Lee, Salvador Dalí (in a diving suit), WLT Messens, Rupert Lee

Vegetable Kingdom' and explained that he had added a kind of 'wing appendage' that had been 'lying close by and was attached by me to complete the individual'.[44] It later became known as *Marsh Personage* and he used it as the starting point for many paintings, although it formed part of the composition only once. It did mark, however, a new stage in Nash's career in which he put together found objects in the natural landscape, photographed them and then painted them. So a tennis ball and a tree stump might have an imaginary meeting, as in *Event on the Downs* of 1934.

Over a thousand people went to the New Burlington Galleries for the opening of the Surrealist Exhibition and the police had to cordon off Bond Street because of the crowds. Breton was dressed entirely in green and declared a revolution in the relationship between perception and representation. The composer William Walton pinned a kipper on to one of Miró's paintings and Nash asked Duncan Grant to remove it on his way out. Performance artist Sheila Legge embodied a kind of surrealist phantom, her face covered in roses, like a Dalí painting, wearing a long white dress, black evening gloves and coral-red belt and shoes. She began the evening in Trafalgar Square in front of the lions with pigeons landing on her outstretched hands and then walked up to the Burlington Galleries. She wandered around the Galleries with a dummy leg in one hand and apparently a pork chop in the other. She got rid of the chop because the room was so hot. Dylan Thomas offered boiled string in tea cups and asked people if they wanted it 'weak or strong'.

All in all, 23,000 people visited the exhibition over the four weeks.[45] Reporters were baffled and some were offended. J. B. Priestley complained that the exhibition arose out of 'moral perversions' and that the 'effeminate or epicene young men, lisping and undulating', had 'strong sexual impulses' that they 'misuse or pervert'. Priestley called Read a 'nitwit' and Moore's work 'lumpy'. The *Daily Worker* concluded that they were 'a group of young people who haven't the guts to tackle anything seriously'.[46] The *Guardian* declared that good art can emerge from 'absurd' theories. Dalí, the critic argued, played with the 'very essence of things'; he made alarm clocks bend and 'sag like blankets'. Real automatic art, the critic concluded, would be the 'little drawings' one makes on blotting paper during a telephone conversation.[47] However, in general the liberal-minded middle classes were delighted by it all, and surrealism became very chic.

Read goaded the audience on the opening night: 'Do not judge this movement kindly. It is not just another amusing stunt. It is defiant – the desperate act of men too profoundly convinced of the rottenness of our civilization to want to save a shred of respectability.'[48] He was a surrealist object himself, Read continued, as Legge drifted about with her head of flowers and the prosthetic leg in her arms. Art was no longer representation, but the thing in itself. As well as talks by Read and Breton and a poetry reading by Éluard, Salvador Dalí gave the finale on 1 July. Moore remembered an empty stage for twenty-five minutes and then an 'enormous bang and great puff of smoke', and as it cleared Dalí was standing in a diving suit with a helmet.[49] The talk was called 'Authentic Paranoid Phantoms', and he held a pair of Borzois on leads. His diving helmet was tightly secured because it was so heavy that if it slipped it could break his neck.

> Dalí then began speaking, but the heat in the poorly ventilated Galleries began to overwhelm him. Edward James, the collector, who was assisting him, tried to use the billiard cue Dalí held as a pointer to unloosen the helmet. Meanwhile the two hounds had managed to tangle their leads in Dalí's legs. [The writer Ruthven] Todd finally managed to free Dalí, who finished his talk in a condition of combined paranoia and claustrophobia.[50]

In July 1937 Penrose had the use of his brother's house, Lambe Creek, just south of Falmouth, for a month. It was a large Georgian house and Penrose issued a wide invitation to join 'a sudden Surrealist invasion' of Cornwall.[51] Guests included Lee Miller, her former lover Man Ray and his new girlfriend, Ady Fidelin, Paul Éluard and his second wife, whom he called Nusch, Eileen Agar and her partner Joseph Bard, Leonora Carrington and Max Ernst, and E. L. T. Mesens. Henry and Irina Moore, who were on holiday near by, came for the day. They all signed a postcard to Éluard's ex-wife, Gala, in Paris, who was living with Dalí. Aged twenty, Carrington had run away from her family to be with the forty-six-year-old Max Ernst. Her father was so horrified by the affair that he tried to have Ernst arrested by claiming that his pictures were indecent. So as well as having fun in Cornwall Ernst was on the run from the police. Agar remembered it as a 'delightful house party', where Roland took the lead, ready to turn 'the slightest encounter into an orgy'. She recalled watching Lee Miller in a bubble bath, but noted that there was not enough room for all of them; besides, she added, 'I for one did not go to bed with everybody who asked me. When would I have time to paint?'[52]

Roland Penrose's son Antony, born ten years later, remembered stories about that summer from his parents: 'Surrealist arguments raged, interspersed with sight-seeing jaunts to Land's End, remote creeks and logan stones, the fascinating delights of Cornish pubs, and ardent lovemaking.' There were even stories of Read coming to visit and Eileen Agar and Lee Miller dancing naked around him as he stood, frozen, with the headlamps of the car shining on them.[53]

By the outbreak of the Second World War, Lee Miller had moved in with Roland Penrose in Downshire Hill. In June 1938 Penrose had bought Paul Éluard's surrealist collection of over a hundred paintings, sculptures, drawings and objects. It was one of the best collections in the world and included forty Max Ernsts, ten Picassos, six de Chiricos, eight Mirós, four Magrittes, three Dalís, three Man Rays, one Klee and one Chagall. He also commissioned Hepworth's *Two Forms (Two Figures)* for the back garden not long after moving in. Hepworth told Nicholson that it looked 'pretty fine' and very different from the way it looked in the Mall Studio garden. Not only was it surrounded by grass

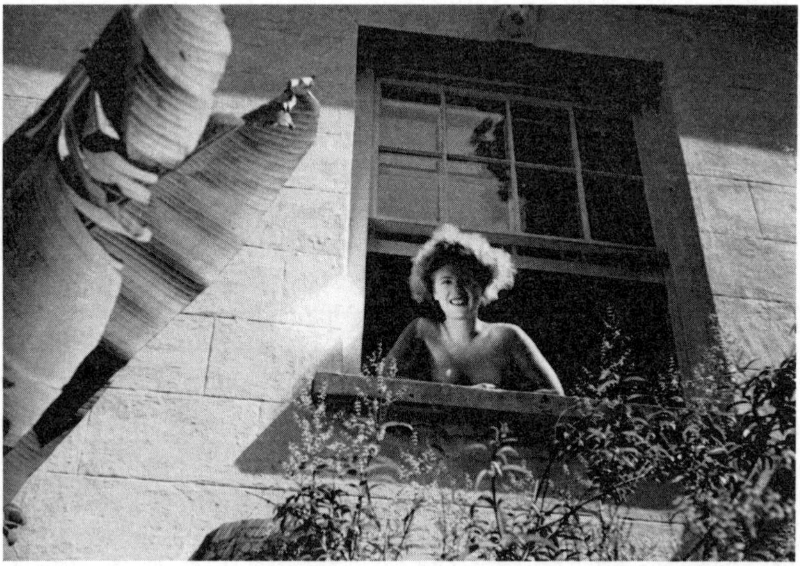

Lee Miller learning out of the top window at Lambe Greek, Cornwall, 1937

but it could be seen from above through the high windows.[54] Penrose and Miller placed Moore's *Mother and Child* in the front garden a couple of years later.

Lee had begun her career as a model in New York, but she preferred to take her own pictures, so she went to Paris, where she began working with Man Ray in the early 1930s and had a turbulent love affair with him. In Paris she was friends with Picasso, Éluard and Cocteau, and acted in the latter's film *Le Sang d'un poète* (The Blood of a Poet) in 1930. She went back to New York and her photography career continued to grow; by 1934 she was listed in *Vanity Fair* as 'one of the seven most distinguished living photographers'.[55] Then she married the Egyptian businessman and engineer Aziz Eloui Bey and moved to Egypt. In 1937 she went back to Paris, where she met Penrose at a surrealist costume ball given by the Rochas sisters, daughters of a wealthy businessman. Penrose remembered that the sisters were 'elegant high-fashion girls' and Max Ernst suggested that he and Penrose go as 'a pair of unlikely beggars'. Once there, Penrose 'found myself compelled to turn my attention to a girl dressed conventionally in a long dark robe. Blonde, blue-eyed and responsive', she seemed to enjoy the 'abysmal contrast between her elegance and my own slumlike horror'. Penrose was wearing paint-stained trousers and his right hand and left foot were painted bright blue. When he asked Max if he knew her, he said, 'Of course, let's ask her to dinner tomorrow.' Penrose and Miller spent the next few weeks together, then Penrose invited her to join them in Cornwall that summer.

Man Ray wrote to thank Penrose for the 'perfect sejour' in Cornwall and to say that the 'whole thing is now like a dream – seems very far away'. The Éluards wrote to say they were 'melancholy to have left the joy and affection' that they had 'received in Cornouailles for three weeks' and to tell 'Lee how happy we are, now, to know her well' because she was 'so sweet, so intelligent and beautiful'.[56] Miller went back to Egypt but continued to create surrealist work through Penrose. She asked him to create an object for the exhibition he was putting on at his newly opened London

Gallery in 1937. She wanted a 'beautiful wax hand' standing upright with a bracelet 'made of false teeth mounted in particularly false pink-coloured gums'. He was happy to oblige and wanted the hand to be as much like Miller's as possible and the teeth to be like his own. He found a wooden hand that he painted and then he came across two 'old men, in white coats sitting in an attic making the most rosy pearly fake jaws I've ever seen'.[57] This became *Le Baiser* (The Kiss). For maximum drama Penrose opened his Surrealist *Objects and Poems* exhibition at midnight.

In the spring of 1939 Penrose turned up in Egypt, accompanying Egyptologist Beryl de Zoëte as her photographer, and he and Miller travelled to Siwa together. Penrose returned to London and Miller followed in June. She described her first few days back in London, dinner with Man Ray at L'Étoile and then 'all went back to Hampstead – where Man was also spending the night. – Love – sleep and breakfast led to the Picasso show at the London Gallery.'[58] When the war broke out, Miller's family pleaded with her to go back to the States, and the US Embassy insisted that they would not be responsible for her safety if she did not return, but instead she became a photographer for *Vogue*. Penrose became an air-raid warden and Miller accompanied him on his rounds through Hampstead amid the searchlights and gunfire. Roland dug a small air-raid shelter in the front garden of Downshire Hill and decorated the inside in pink and blue. Roland's first wife, the poet Valentine Boué, was unexpectedly stranded in London en route to Gascony and after her hotel was bombed she moved into Downshire Hill with them for a while. By 1944 Miller was being given a significant amount of work for each issue of *Vogue* and she was also putting together a book of photographs entitled *Grim Glory: Pictures of Britain under Fire*. In 1945 she and the American *Life* correspondent David E. Scherman found their way into Hitler's secret apartments in Munich and he took the famous photo of her in the bath, with her muddy boots standing by the side. Miller and Penrose married after the war and with their son Antony, born in 1947, they moved to Farley Farm in East Sussex where they stayed for the rest of their lives.

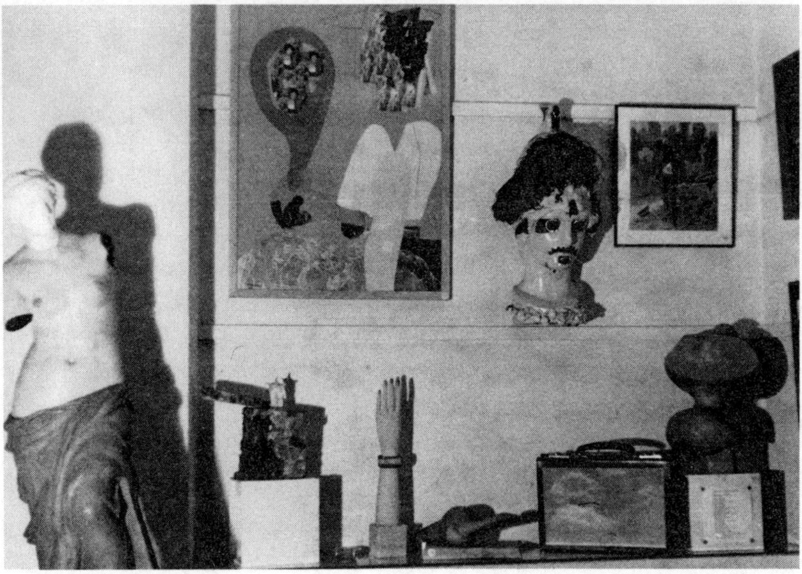

Objects and Poems *exhibition at the London Gallery, 1937 (Le Baiser in the middle)*

7
THE MOORES IN PARKHILL ROAD

'sliced out of mountain rock'

Henry and Irina Moore moved to Parkhill Road in Belsize Park in 1929. The next ten years, living around the corner from Ben and Barbara, were among the most productive of Moore's career. Moore had met Hepworth when she arrived at Leeds Art School in 1920, aged seventeen, and he was in his second year. She was like a younger sister, 'four or five years my junior in age', but this didn't stop him from becoming sweet on her and they went out together.[1] He also liked to think that he had persuaded her to become a sculptor. According to Moore she was set on taking the general art course, but after talking to him she changed her mind.[2] Hepworth's account was quite different. She knew she wanted to sculpt from the age of fifteen. Even earlier, aged seven, she remembered her head teacher giving a talk on Egyptian sculpture and that she sat 'quite rigid' because 'it was the first time I had seen a lantern slide, and both sculpture and architecture seem to exert some special kind of compulsion.'[3] The sibling-like rivalry between Moore and Hepworth continued in the 1920s and 1930s.

Moore was a stolid, handsome, ambitious young man. In later life his friend Geoffrey Grigson called him a 'good friend, a good consoler, a good adviser', and Eileen Agar said he was a 'simple and sincere man'. He was not very tall, Agar noted – like Picasso, but without his commanding presence.[4] When they first met, Barbara felt 'very young and brash' around Moore, but she joined his group of friends. They included Edna Ginesi, nicknamed Gin, and Raymond Coxon, both cheerful, ambitious young painters. Their classes finished at 4 p.m. and there was an evening life-drawing class from 7 until 9 p.m. Henry spent the time in between with Raymond, who had lodgings near by where they could have an evening meal with tea. Sometimes they went to the library to study art history books.[5] Gin and Henry usually walked to the railway station after the evening class, and it was not long before he had fallen in love with her. But Gin had her heart set on Raymond, whom she went on to marry. Despite all this, Barbara, Gin, Henry and Raymond became firm friends and remained so when they all moved to London in 1921 to go to the Royal College of Art.[6]

Moore's father was a miner in Castleford during a period of long coal strikes. He did all sorts of extra odd jobs to make ends meet, including shoe mending. He was determined that his children should have a different life from his own and put a lot of energy into helping them pass the exams for Castleford Secondary School. It took Henry three tries. Finally, he persuaded his father to let him give up the violin, so he had more time to study, and he passed. His mother was a hard-working, handsome woman with eight children. For the first eleven years of Henry's life they lived in a two-up, two-down, sleeping three or four to a bed. He remembered playing in the 'slag heaps, like pyramids, like mountains'. When he turned thirteen they moved around the corner to a more spacious end-of-terrace house at 56 Smawthorne Lane. His elder brother Raymond brought in a teacher's salary; his sister Annie had left home to get married, and his brother Alfred had emigrated to Canada, which, it seems, was to escape the scandal of getting a girl pregnant. Henry's childhood was marred by the death of his younger sister Elsie in 1913, when she was twelve. She was the closest to him in age and a very good runner. Henry blamed himself for her death because he 'encouraged her to go faster and faster and train harder and harder' and she died of heart problems. He was unhappy for many years, but as a result his family 'heaped' their love on him.[7]

Henry liked to recount two anecdotes from his childhood that formed him as a sculptor. His Sunday-school teacher told the class that Michelangelo, 'the greatest sculptor who ever lived', was once told by a passer-by that the head of an old faun he was carving in his stoneyard in Florence would have had fewer teeth and so he immediately knocked out a couple. Moore was intrigued. The second story involved his mother. He used to rub her back with a strong-smelling homemade ointment for her arthritis when he was seven or eight. He was drawn to the sensation of soft flesh and hard bone and years later tried to give 'the long-forgotten shape' of the back 'I had so often rubbed as a boy' to his sculpture *Seated Woman* (1957).[8] The headteacher at Castleford Secondary School, Mr Dawes, liked to take the pupils to local churches and point out architectural features and sculpture, and Henry particularly liked the Gothic corbels. In his second year at Castleford Alice Gostick was employed as the new art teacher. Gostick was in her mid-twenties and was kind, encouraging and enthusiastic about modern art. She invited her pupils to her house, where they saw contemporary journals like *Studio* and her wide range of art books. She had been to Italy and London and a photograph from the period shows her admiring one of Moore's pots during her evening pottery class. He was clearly a favourite pupil.

Moore tried his hand at teaching, but struggled, particularly with the girls, who would 'weep and cry and sob'. And then in 1916, aged eighteen, he decided to go to London to sign up.[9] On his way, he met Douglas Houghton, who became a Labour Cabinet minister and life peer. Both sons of working-class men, a miner and a Nottingham lace-maker, they suffered snobbery at the recruiting centres. They were eventually placed with the Civil Service Rifles because Douglas had worked as a junior civil servant. Henry wrote to Alice Gostick throughout his training and from the front. He sent home for his drawing materials, although he admitted that he did not find much time to use them.

Young men were not generally sent to the front until they were nineteen. A month after his birthday, in September 1917, he was duly posted to France and described the hallucinations that were common on sentry duty, where 'barbed wire posts' formed fours, or advanced 'in line towards your trench'.[10] Henry's battalion suffered a full-scale assault from German forces during the battle of Cambrai; he suffered mustard-gas poisoning and was ordered to a field hospital. The ten-mile walk helped to work the gas out of his system and then he was shipped back to England. While convalescing in Cardiff, he continued to write to Alice, and described going to the pictures, having tea, reading and smoking and then returning to hospital by five for singing and piano playing. The gas inhalation gave Moore a husky voice for the rest of his life. Once out of hospital he was moved to Aldershot, where he became a physical training instructor, which was useful for his understanding of the human form.

Alice Gostick continued to play a role in his life. She helped Henry to get an ex-serviceman's grant for Leeds School of Art. He took night classes over the spring and summer to prepare himself for the start of term. On his first day at Leeds he met Raymond Coxon in the lavatory. They joked that they wanted to be the next Michelangelo and Titian. Henry was not impressed by the endless copying of Greek sculptures and they were all fed up with the elderly male model who posed for them week after week. In the second year they got a female model and 'what excitement there was!'[11] Henry took sculpture in his second year and Coxon took painting. Reginald Cotterill, a Royal College graduate, was brought in to teach sculpture and he looked after Henry 'like a child. He was always breathing down my neck, but in a way this was a help, because I got through the two year course in one year.'[12]

Like Herbert Read several years earlier, Moore and Hepworth were fortunate to have been at Leeds during the period that Michael Sadler was vice chancellor. Roger Fry claimed that Sadler had 'civilised a whole population'.[13] Sadler was among the first British collectors of modern art and by this stage he had added work by Cézanne, Matisse and Van Gogh to his growing collection. Art students at Leeds would have been able to see Sadler's modernist artworks and African sculptures, and Moore remembered a

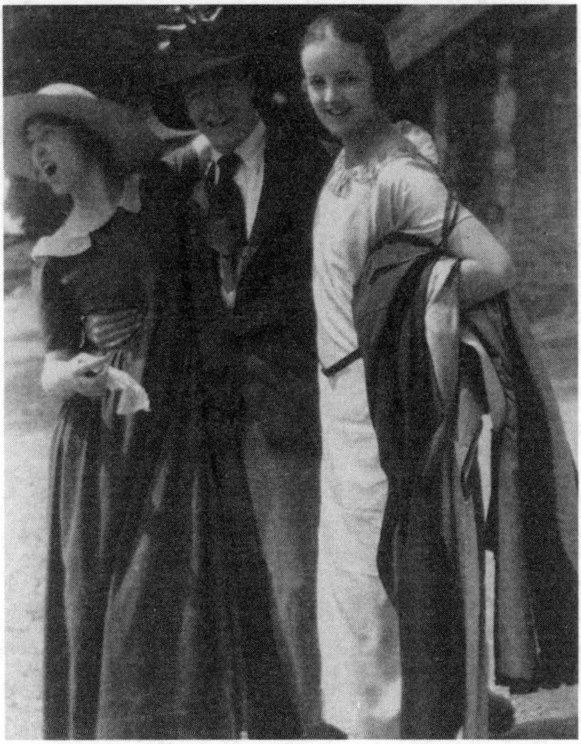

Edna Ginesi, Henry Moore and Barbara Hepworth in Paris, 1922

'wonderful Gauguin'.[14] Moore stumbled across Roger Fry's *Vision and Design* in the Leeds library, acquired just weeks after its publication in 1921. It was, he said, a 'most lucky discovery'.[15]

Moore was lucky in London too. He won an exhibition to the Royal College amounting to £90 a year and so was able to live quite comfortably. And William Rothenstein was appointed principal of the Royal College the year before Moore and Hepworth arrived. Rothenstein had been living in Paris and knew Degas, Pissarro, Whistler, Bonnard, Vuillard, Verlaine and Mallarmé, and he wanted to make the college a 'true University of the Arts' and to 'weave a garment in which to dress the living spirit in the fashion of our day'.[16] Henry rented a room in Sydney Street, just off the Fulham Road, a mile or so from the college, where his landlady gave him 'the most awful finnan haddock' every morning but from where he could walk to the British Museum, the National Gallery and the Victoria and Albert Museum. During his first term he took a train to Salisbury to visit Stonehenge, and although he got there late he decided to visit the stones straight away. In the moonlight the monoliths appeared distorted and the 'depths and distances' made the whole thing seem enormous.[17] He wrote to Nash years later: 'there's a sense of immense power about a large rough shaped lump of rock or stone.' He wanted to harness that power and dreamt of having a studio big enough to fit a 'rough-axed monolith' in the middle of it, next to the 'trunk of a big tree'. With these beside him he believed he would be less at risk of being sidetracked from 'real sculpture'.[18]

Moore's time at the Royal College was balanced between the traditional course and his own exploration of the Ethnographical Room at the British Museum. He started going there every Wednesday and Sunday afternoon and his first known 'free' carving was inspired by the Mexican sculptures he saw there. They somehow felt 'true and right' because of their 'stoniness', or 'truth to material'. Mexican sculpture formed his 'view of carving as much as anything I could do'.[19] Hepworth remembered that whenever she, Henry, Raymond and Gin managed to save 'five pounds' they 'went off to Paris to see museums'.[20] On one of the visits in 1925 Moore saw a plaster cast of a fifteenth-century Mayan Chacmool sculpture, reclining at the Musée du Trocadéro, an inspiration for many years to come.

In order to have more space to carve, he and Raymond moved further west, to a flat in Wandsworth. Their landlady, who lived above, cleaned the flat, gave Henry a silk dressing gown (which he didn't wear) and brought them ale every Saturday morning. He and Coxon travelled to Paris together, visited museums in the mornings and life classes in the afternoons and, on their last day, took a taxi to Auguste Pellerin's collection in Neuilly. The impact of Cézanne's *Grandes Baigneuses*, hanging in the hallway, was, for Moore, as powerful as Chartres Cathedral had been. The female figures appeared to have been 'sliced out of mountain rock'.[21]

Back home, Moore's father had suffered a number of minor strokes and his family moved from Castleford to Norfolk in the summer of 1922 to try and improve his health. Moore's sister Mary went with them. She became head of a primary school in Wighton, and the schoolhouse had room for their parents and also for Henry when he stayed in the holidays. Sadly, a month after their move, Henry's father died. Two of Henry's other siblings were also in Norfolk. His brother Raymond became headmaster of a school at Stoke Ferry and Betty married a teacher and settled south of Norwich, in Mulbarton.

Moore was taught by Leon Underwood at the Royal College; he was so good, Moore and a few others asked if he could hold private classes for them. Underwood emphasised form over contour, because, he explained, light changes but form does not. He taught them to learn the 'laws of light falling on a solid object' and how to reflect it 'back to the human eye'.[22] Underwood set up the private life-drawing classes in the evenings. He arranged them so that the model began by holding a still pose, and then walked slowly around the room, gradually speeding up so that the students had to capture the form of the running model. Encouraged by Epstein, Moore continued to develop his interest in African and Mexican sculpture and read Ezra Pound's book about Gaudier-Brzeska which included the poetic idea that 'sculptural energy is the mountain.'

Moore finished his degree in 1924 with a teaching qualification as well as a diploma and a six-month travelling scholarship. Just before he took up the scholarship, Rothenstein asked him to fill in for Derwent Wood, who had resigned from the Royal College. Henry held the fort for a while, before the post was filled by the Royal Academician Ernest Cole. Moore became his assistant with a salary of £240 a year. This arrangement lasted seven years, and Moore taught two days a week, allowing him to pursue his own work for the rest of the time. He 'couldn't have dreamed of better conditions'. He took up the travelling scholarship and went to France and Italy in 1925. Giotto and Masaccio made a big impression on him, but he still felt the pull of the 'paradise' of 'our National Collection' and 'our English landscape'. When he got to Florence he met up with fellow Royal College students Edna Ginesi, Norman Dawson, Robert Lyon and Eric Ravilious. Like Moore, Ravilious was overwhelmed by Renaissance art and like him took long walks along the Arno, where they sketched.

Moore realised he was still very much in love with Coxon's fiancée Gin and confessed his feelings to her. She rejected him in a kindly way and said she wanted to remain with Raymond. Henry felt terrible and wondered if his attachment to Gin was in some way an expression of his attachment to Raymond and 'almost wanting to share'. They worked things out and Henry was best man at their wedding the following year. However, Moore's trip went downhill after Florence. In Venice he stayed in a hotel that he could not afford because his scholarship money had not come through and he had to be rescued by the registrar of the Royal College, Hubert Wellington. Then, in Paris, he got a cut in his hand that became infected and he rushed back to Norfolk, unwilling to accept medical attention from French doctors. He felt later that this was the closest he had ever come to having a nervous breakdown.[23]

Things began to look up back in London. Just before his thirtieth birthday, in 1928, he held his first one-man show at the Warren Gallery in Maddox Street, he received his first public commission to carve the *West Wind* for the headquarters of the London Underground near St James's Park, and he met Irina Radetsky, a painting student at the Royal College. He first saw her walking across from the Common Room where they ate lunch and then he met her properly at a dance at the college. He had no idea that she was 'unofficially engaged': 'Leslie, her fiancé, was sitting there and I didn't realise he was anything to do with her and ignored him. Afterwards I walked her back to Kensington Station and poor old Leslie came with us – Irina and I walking together on the pavement, Leslie dragging his feet in the gutter.'[24] Irina was a painter and had 'real practical common sense'. He wrote that she 'kept my feet on the ground' and 'made the reality of life

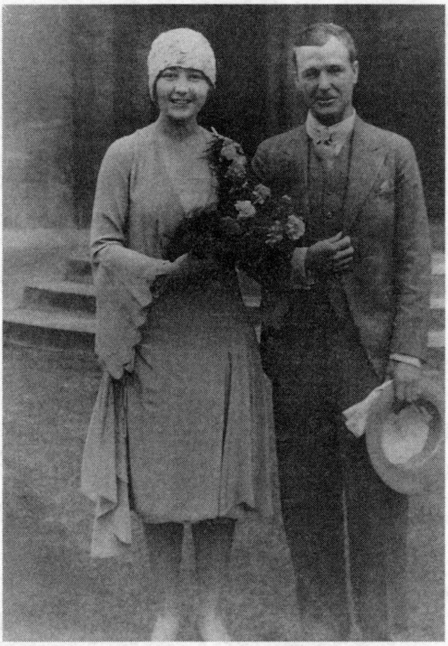

Henry and Irina on their wedding day

easier for me. It's to do with sympathy, joining in, being interested. She even moved the stones with me.'[25] He used to tease her that he had married her for her strong shoulders. A fellow student remembered her 'warm, friendly manner and peaceful charm'.[26] After a series of letters over the holidays, they were 'thick' and, having known each other for nine months, they married in July 1929. They went to Cornwall for their honeymoon, staying in a boarding house that could be reached only by boat. Then they headed to Suffolk, to a cottage near Dedham, and the Coxons joined them. Irina remembered making jam and being swarmed by wasps. When they got back to London Hepworth and Skeaping had spotted a place the Moores could rent, around the corner from the Mall Studios. They moved into 11a Parkhill Road, which had a studio on the ground floor and curved, cast-iron steps leading up to a two-roomed flat above. The move to Belsize Park and his marriage to Irina marked an important shift in Moore's work.

Henry and Irina met Ben Nicholson in the summer of 1931. When Ben and Winifred went to the Mall Studios to see Barbara and Jack for the first time that summer they also visited Henry and Irina, and lent them a couple of Ben's paintings. Henry wrote to Ben to say that he and Irina liked his paintings more than ever and especially the still life because there was so much variety in its 'big simplicity' and they found new things to enjoy in it every day. He also told Ben that the artist and poet David Jones had called Ben the 'best painter in England today'. Moore sent his best wishes and love to Winifred, and guessed it must be about time for the new baby (Andrew was born not long afterwards).[27] That September he and Irina joined Ben, Barbara and the others in Norfolk for the two-week holiday in Happisburgh.

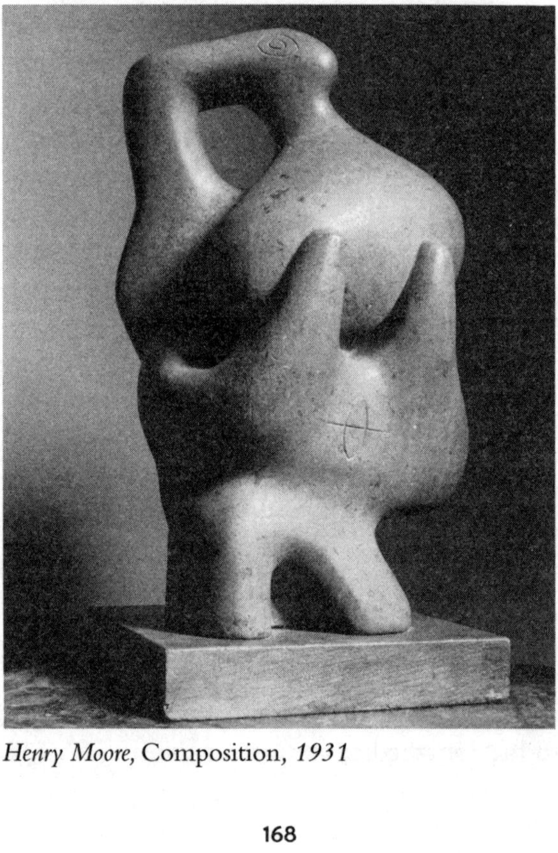

Henry Moore, Composition, *1931*

Things were coming together in 1931. Moore carved *Composition* in Hornton stone, which was, for him, a turning point in his career. He felt that he had been released from the material and it marked a shift into abstraction. Composed of three sections, it has an incised 'eye' on the head, a hole in the upper form and a symbolic incised oval shape with a line through it. He also created in 1931 a small reclining figure (about sixteen inches long) made of lead, with a hollow chest crossed with three bars. These two sculptures were his first abstract pieces, even though they retained a natural or organic feel. As his work became more abstract, Moore struggled with the traditional nature of the Royal College. He held his second solo exhibition at the Leicester Galleries in April 1931 and the resulting press controversy led to his resignation from the Royal College. The *Morning Post* headline was 'Ugliness in Art' and the president of the Society of Art Masters referred to the 'vulgar and repulsive distortions' of Moore's work.[28] Moore's friend Coxon had just started teaching at Chelsea School of Art and he suggested to the new head, H. S. Williamson, that Moore should start up their sculpture school. He was appointed in 1931.

Moore had a habit of collecting twigs, stones, bones and shells, and as he drew he let his imagination work around them, and in the spaces in between them. His friends Paul Nash and Graham Sutherland (who was also teaching at Chelsea) were making use of found objects in their work and exploring the quasi-romantic tradition of endowing nature with mystery. Nash dedicated his *Group for a Sculptor* to Moore in 1931. It included leaves, bark, seeds and a tennis ball. Moore liked to draw from imagination in the evenings and then sculpt the next morning. In the early 1930s nearly all of his sculptures were made from drawings and then in 1935 he began to work from small plaster or clay models.

Hepworth and Moore were working on similar themes in the 1930s. Moore was struck by Hepworth's *Pierced Form* of 1931 and later theorised that by connecting 'one side to the other' the hole 'can itself have as much shape-meaning as a solid mass'.[29] Even though Hepworth clearly put a hole in her sculpture first,

Jim Ede remembered them arguing about it over dinner.[30] The critic Hugh Gordon Porteus wrote in July 1935 that Hepworth suggested to Moore the possibilities of a 'new game' of 'simpler elements, disparate but juxtaposed'.[31] They also both worked on stringed sculptures, Hepworth in 1934 and Moore in 1937, and both incised their work with 'Nicholsonian' lines.[32]

Irina and Henry bought Jasmine Cottage in Barfreston, Kent, for £80 in 1931. They divided their time between the flat in Hampstead and the cottage in Kent for most of the decade. Moore's sister Betty had moved to Deal, about eight miles away, and his mother lived in Waldershare, a couple of miles further towards the coast. Moore was teaching in London but found his most productive carving was done in his studio behind the cottage. It was really two cottages knocked into one, and they built a studio at the back overlooking the sixty-foot garden that ran down to the village churchyard. They also bought a motorbike to get around the countryside. Moore worked eight-hour days and still had time to go to the beach, play tennis and make occasional trips to Canterbury or Dover. 'We get up at six and go to bed soon after 9,' he wrote to the Coxons, and 'the day seems twice as long.' In September 1933 he was not looking forward to coming back to London, to teaching at Chelsea and to his new show: 'both of 'em I hate to think about.' At this one-man show, his third, held at the Leicester Galleries, he sold £700 worth of work. The buyers included his old professor, Michael Sadler, who was now master of University College, Oxford, Fanny Wadsworth (married to Edward) and E. C. Gregory, a printer who became one of Moore's close friends. In the *Spectator* Adrian Stokes compared Moore's concrete reclining figure to Cleopatra. Later that year Anton Zwemmer (the Charing Cross Road bookseller) suggested they do a book about Moore's work. Moore was pleased and asked Herbert Read to write the text and Gregory to print it through his press, Lund Humphries. Read wrote that there had been 'no compromise' in the life of Henry Moore and that now 'in the fullness of his powers, he offers us the perfected product of his genius.'[33] He called Moore a biologist, who had 'gone beneath the flesh to the hard structure of bone'.[34] The book did not sell many copies, but it was well reviewed.

In August 1935 Henry and Irina sold Jasmine Cottage for £350 and bought a larger one, Burcroft, for £500 at Marley, near Kingston. The house was a simple bungalow, but larger and lighter and 'easier to keep clean'.[35] As before, they built a studio at the back and they went to Canterbury every Saturday for their shopping. Moore told Nash that he'd like to live full time in the country as he could carve for ten hours a day without interruption. The move to Burcroft, Moore believed,

> clinched my interest in trying to make sculpture and nature enhance each other. I feel that the sky and nature are the best setting for my sculpture. They are asymmetrical, unlike an architectural background with its verticals and horizontals. In a natural setting, the background to a sculpture changes if you move only a very small distance.[36]

But London still had its temptations. Henry and Irina spent a number of evenings at the Isobar once it was up and running. They were not members, but many of their friends were and Henry recalled 'earnest discussions' with Hampstead friends and with the new European émigrés. During one discussion about how to link art with technology Moholy suggested that it would be ideal to ring up a factory and order one's art according to specifications.

In the summer of 1935 Hepworth's cousin Jack stayed with Henry and Irina at Burcroft to learn the art of carving. He had studied at St Martin's School of Art and Ben had taught him painting for a while; he also spent some time at Mr Gumbrill's mason yard in Lismore Circus, learning carving and masonry skills. Moore asked Jack to work on the initial carving of a block of white Carrara marble that became the completely abstract *Sculpture* of 1935. Jack later exhibited with the Circle group under the name Arthur Jackson to avoid confusion with Barbara.

In July 1935 Ben invited Moore to meet Naum Gabo, who was in London for a visit. Moore was in Kent and couldn't make it, but he was very keen to meet Gabo, having heard about him from Moholy. He asked if Gabo would like to join him in Parkhill Road for a good hour or more the following Friday.[37] Moore was interested in morphology and D'Arcy Wentworth Thompson's *On Growth and Form* (1917), which argued that mathematics explains organic growth (early biomathematics). Gabo was also interested in Thompson's book, and may well have introduced Moore to the theories of his Hungarian friend the art theorist Ernő Kállai, who argued that X-rays, microscopy and other technologies paralleled modernist aesthetics.[38]

The 'Contemporary Sculpture Number' of the modernist journal *Axis* came out that summer. It led with Brâncuşis, followed by Moore, then Hepworth and finally Calder. Grigson's article on Moore described him as a mix of Brâncuşi and Mondrian because he 'can purify' and produce 'ideal harmonies', with a touch of D. H. Lawrence because he 'can soak, squirm and swim and say that life is life'. Moore's ability to 'synthesise, mix life and mind' was also like Wyndham Lewis and yet, like Auden, he found his 'mysteries' within man 'rather than in man and matter'. For Grigson, it seemed, Moore's work brought together a touch of everything.[39] But Moore himself believed that if you discuss your work too much the tension is lost. He was keen to avoid aligning himself with either the abstract or the surrealist camp. The 'violent quarrel' was 'unnecessary', he said, as all good art has both qualities.

Moore became increasingly involved in the Artists International Association (AIA), which had been set up in 1932 as the Artists International, and in 1935 it broadened its added Association and broadened its aim to promote 'Peace, Democracy and Cultural Development'. Its members' first exhibition, *The Social Scene*, took place in September 1934, in a shop off Charlotte Street, near Tottenham Court Road. The early exhibitions were Marxist in their focus and it included pieces depicting poverty and police brutality as well as works by Moore, Nash, Burra and Robert Medley. The second, larger exhibition was entitled *Artists against Fascism and War* and it coincided with Mussolini's invasion of Abyssinia. Six thousand visitors came to see the work by Moore,

Nicholson, Piper, Leger, Zadkine and others. Moore designed the front page of a broadsheet that accompanied an AIA exhibition attacking the British government's non-intervention in Spain in 1937. The AIA argued that doing nothing bred 'Fascism by deceit' at home. It called for artists, intellectuals and poets to intervene 'by violent or subtle subversion' or by 'stimulating desire'. Moore almost went to Spain in 1938, along with Jacob Epstein, Rose Macaulay, Charlotte Haldane, Stephen Spender and Paul Robeson. Their visas were refused by the British government, but Spender went anyway, slipping over the border.[40]

Global and local events played their part in politicising Moore. He helped raise funds for the Artists Refugee Committee in 1938, to assist German immigrants who were fleeing Europe. The Committee was set up in 1937 in part to rescue members of the Oskar-Kokoschka-Bund (OKB), a group of expatriate artists based in Prague. By September 1939 there were about 40,000 German refugees, 30,000 Austrian and 2,000 German-speaking Czech refugees in Britain. The German artist Fred Uhlman had arrived in London in September 1936 and two months later married Diana Croft, daughter of the Conservative politician Brigadier General Henry Page Croft. They moved to 47 Downshire Hill, where Uhlman founded the Free German League of Culture and their house became the official address for the Artists Refugee Committee. Born in Stuttgart, Uhlman had trained in law and then moved to a fishing village in Spain, Tossa de Mar, where he first met Diana. Uhlman remembered artists from Czechoslovakia 'arriving at our house all the time by ones or in groups'. Almost every day throughout 1939 'we found a newcomer in our kitchen not far from the "frig". All had escaped with great difficulty: most of them on foot, crossing the snow-covered mountains which separate Czechoslovakia from Poland.'[41] Diana was efficient, generous and spoke excellent German; the sculptor Heinz Worner said she 'restored security to the refugees'. Oskar Kokoschka came in 1938 and, after a short stay in Downshire Hill, moved to King Henry's Road in Primrose Hill. 'Charming as only a Viennese can be', he thanked Diana in particular and warned her not to overwork, as she looked 'overstrained and pale'.[42] His first commission in England was to paint a portrait of Diana's brother, and then his wife asked him to paint hers too. Kokoschka became the League's president from 1939 to 1946 and wrote several introductions to catalogues for exhibitions.

At its height the Free German League had 1,500 members. Uhlman had his first solo exhibition at the Zwemmer Gallery in 1938, and the first exhibition of the artists' section of the League opened on 20 June 1939 at the Wertheim Gallery in Burlington Gardens. It included work by Hamann, Kokoschka, Wüsten, Fritz Kraemer, Samson Schames, Feigl and Bettina Ehrlich. The reviewer for the *New Statesman* argued that this 'small exhibition gives a much more favourable view of contemporary German art than the big show last year at the Burlington Galleries'. The Free German League moved to larger premises in December 1939, at 36 Upper Park Road, and several lectures and courses were held there, as well as concerts, exhibitions and theatre performances. It was also a social centre where exiles could meet and eat together in the small restaurant. Albert Einstein declined an invitation to join the League as he believed it was unwise to be part of any organisation 'which gives the impression of belonging to a German community'.[43] Just before war was declared Uhlman was interned in the Hutchinson Internment Camp on the Isle of Man; thousands of Austrian and German refugees were held at ten camps on the island. Kurt Schwitters was also detained at the Hutchinson Camp and he and Uhlman produced an extensive body of work during their internment and helped create a strong cultural and intellectual life in the camp. Despite Diana's campaign for his release, Uhlman remained there for seven months. On 1 January 1941 he was let out and he joined Diana and his new daughter Caroline in Bamber's Green, near Great Bardfield. They bought a small cottage to escape the London bombings, but their home on Downshire Hill remained a space for artists to stay. The satirical artist John Heartfield arrived at Downshire Hill in 1938 and stayed until 1943 with his girlfriend Gertrude, known as Tutti, who remembered everyone cooked together in the evenings and discussed politics and art. The Uhlmans had a second child, Francis, in 1943, and they returned to Hampstead the following year.

The day that war was declared, 3 September 1939, Moore went swimming in Dover with Irina and his friend and protégé Bernard Meadows. When he got back to the studio he drew a picture of eight women chest high in blood-red water. Moore, aged forty-one, was unsure if his teaching would continue, unsure if he would be called up and unsure if his exhibition at the Leicester Galleries in early 1940 would take place.[44] The Chelsea School of Art was evacuated to Northampton and Moore resigned. He wrote to Herbert and Ludo on 9 October 1939 that he had about four or five months of funds left and then he would have to find work. He realised, of course, how lucky he was to be able to count that far ahead and to have a cottage where 'I can go on working as usual'. He went on:

> I'm a couple of months over the present military service age limit. But if the war goes on for long, the limit wont stay at 41, I'm sure. Having been in the trenches in the last war, not for anywhere near as long as you were, but long enough not to want it twice in a lifetime – I hope it won't come to that. But I hate Fascism & Nazism so much that if the war gets closer & more intense, & that grows into a main issue, the state of mind to go on quietly working might not be possible to keep up, & apart from necessity one might willingly seek to take some part in it.[45]

During the war Moore drew people sheltering in the Underground, and the drawings were acquired by the War Artists' Advisory Committee. Moore described these nights:

> The night-time in London is like another world – The noise is terrific & everything seems to be going on immediately over one's own little spot – & the unreality is that of exaggeration like in a nightmare.
>
> But what doesn't seem like a cinematograph reel to me, are the queues, before four o'clock outside some of the Tube

> stations, of poor looking women & children waiting to be let in to take shelter for the night – & the dirty bits of blankets & clothes & pillows stretched out on the Tube platforms – Its about the most pathetic, sordid, & disheartening sight I hope to see.[46]

In September 1940, their home and studio at 11a Parkhill Road was hit by bomb shrapnel, and Henry and Irina moved to a farmhouse in Perry Green near Much Hadham in Hertfordshire. They also took over Ben and Barbara's studio at number 7 the Mall Studios. Barbara and Ben had evacuated to Cornwall with the children and Moore could not afford the rent of £130 a year for Parkhill Road, so instead he paid £75 for number 7. He wrote to Barbara that they were 'very sorry for your sake you've had to give it up… But I'm glad it's us who are to have it so that it stays, as it were, in the family.'[47] A couple of years later, Moore was getting ready to move more of his work to Hertfordshire and spent three or four hours cursing and heaving things into the shed. There was plenty of space, he said, but he wished that Barbara had 'put her initials on her stuff' so that there was 'no danger of it getting mixed up' with his.[48] Even Moore couldn't tell some of their work apart.

Hepworth and Moore were very close in the late 1920s and Read noticed that Nicholson, 'in a sense', divided them, so that they began to 'drift apart'. Family life took over too. Moore's friend Kenneth Clark described Moore's tendency to 'look on the best side of everything and everybody'.[49] The surrealist Eileen Agar agreed; she called him 'modest and discreet' and someone who never succumbed to the temptation of getting a 'swelled head'.[50] As trustees of the Tate, Moore and Clark did not appear to see the best side of everything when they rejected one of Hepworth's wooden sculptures in 1945. The director of the Tate, John Rothenstein, recorded Moore saying that if sculpture was 'nothing more than that' then it would be a 'poor affair' and the piece was turned down. Moore did not object to the other seven sculptures bought that year by the Tate: they were all his.[51]

8

AXIS AND *CIRCLE*: FROM BELSIZE PARK TO FAWLEY BOTTOM

'a thousand battles. Left, right, black, red … Hampstead, Bloomsbury, surrealist, abstract, social realist, Spain, Germany, Heaven, Hell, Paradise, Chaos, light, dark, round, square'

In the summer of 1934 Ivon Hitchens invited Myfanwy Evans, a 'young girl just out of Oxford, full of energy and life', to join him and some friends for a weekend in his cottage in Sizewell, a small village by the sea in Suffolk. He also invited John Piper, who was in need of a bit of cheering up. Piper's marriage of three years to a fellow student from the Royal College, Eileen Holding, was breaking down and he was struggling to make a living from painting. He had abandoned a career in law and was writing for the *Saturday Review* and the *Nation and Athenaeum* to make ends meet. In 1933 he joined the Seven and Five Society, run by Ben Nicholson, and was made secretary and chairman of the Hanging Committee within the year. Ben had recently decided that the newly rebranded '7&5' would represent only abstract art, although Piper had not yet produced any.

John's wife Eileen was not too upset by the note he left on the kitchen table to say he was going away for the weekend. It seems she was already romantically involved with the Welsh artist Ceri Richards and she wrote a postcard to say that she 'had been about to take off on her own too'. John arrived in Sizewell and volunteered to pick up one of the other guests, who was arriving later at Leiston railway station. It was a warm evening, and stepping off the train Myfanwy suggested they bathe before going to the cottage. They ran up and down the strip of beach to dry off. Evans was twenty-three, with short bobbed hair and blue eyes, and she had recently graduated from St Hugh's College, Oxford. She had no idea that the tall, angular man she had just been swimming with was the author of the reviews that she enjoyed in the *Nation and Athenaeum*.

Myfanwy knew Hitchens through her old friends the Blanco Whites, who lived on Downshire Hill in Hampstead, and she had modelled for Hitchens a few times in his studio at 169 Adelaide Road. He had taken quite a fancy to her.[1] From the age of nine, she had lived in the three floors above Allchin's, a chemist on the corner of England's Lane and Primrose Gardens. She went to Camden School, then North London Collegiate, followed by Oxford. When John saw her get off the train at Leiston, he thought she was the 'cat's whiskers'.[2]

That weekend in Suffolk in 1934 was crucial for British abstract modernism. A week later, back in London, John and Myfanwy arranged to meet on the steps of the National Gallery. Not long afterwards, she introduced him to her aunt, whom she was living with in London. Myfanwy went to Devon and Cornwall for the rest of the summer and John wrote to tell her how excited he was to have met Braque, with Ben and Barbara, at Jim Ede's house in Hampstead. John thought Braque was the 'greatest of living painters'.[3] Then in August Myfanwy went to Paris, having been given the loan of a flat in rue Madame on the Left Bank, 'a lovely place to be', and £20 from her aunt.[4] She hitched a ride with a friend from Oxford. She had been to France before as an au pair, in Rennes and by the sea in Paramé, but this was her first trip to Paris. John invited her to their cottage in Betchworth, Surrey, before she left, so that she could see some of his work. Ceri Richards had been staying with them and John had found him inspirational, even if his wife was falling in love with him. Whatever the exact chronology of events, it was clear by this stage that their marriage was amicably over.

John was eager for Myfanwy to see as much contemporary art and meet as many artists as possible in Paris. He had half hoped that he and Eileen might drop in on her in Paris for a few days, but, at any rate, he urged her to go and see Jean Hélion and 'tell him you're ever so nice'. He told her to 'have tea with him and eat lots of American wife's waffles and see his pictures and Alexander Calder's wire cow that drops a cow pat'. John also told her which galleries to go to, to see work by Braque and Picasso. If she followed his advice, he said, she would have 'found out all the pictures in obscure places in Paris that are worth seeing'.[5]

Myfanwy did go and see Hélion, and she stayed 'that first day, an unconscionable time', sharing their supper and 'walking back through the unfamiliar dark streets in a state of high exaltation'. Hélion, a great 'facilitator', introduced her to Mondrian, Brâncuși, Kandinsky, Hans Arp and Giacometti. He spoke fluent English because his wife was American. Myfanwy found Kandinsky neatly dressed in a tiny flat and Brâncuși, 'half-priest, half-peasant, in his linen smock', in his studio with a 'forest of columns thrusting upward from the floor of fine stone dust'. She went to see Mondrian, who liked to play jazz records in his white studio, and they danced enthusiastically. One story is that Moore was in Paris at the same time and asked Mondrian if he might take Myfanwy out and Mondrian agreed, saying 'she's too representational for me.'[6]

Most of the artists were pleased to invite Myfanwy into their studios so that their work would be better known in London. But relations were breaking down among abstract artists in Paris in 1934. As with Unit One in London there were divisions within Abstraction-Création. It had been set up by Hélion, Arp, Albert Gleizes, Auguste Herbin, František Kupka and Georges Vantongerloo in 1931 to organise 'manifestations' of 'non-figurative art'. Their second publication was committed to 'total opposition to all oppression'.[7] Hélion suggested that Myfanwy could start up a new magazine in London dedicated to abstract art, along the same lines as the Parisian publication. At first she refused, arguing that she knew nothing about it, but he reassured her that she would learn. Her memory of the conversation fifty years later was that she told him she didn't have the money to do it, and he assured her, 'It will come.' She suggested that Herbert Read would be better placed to do it and he said, 'You are young enough to afford a failure, he isn't.' And she replied, 'So be it.'[8] This was how Myfanwy Evans became the editor of *Axis*, the first British magazine devoted to abstract art.

John Piper was delighted, writing to her that she shouldn't worry about what she didn't know because knowledge is not 'a bit of Gruyère cheese, what is needed is grit. (You might begin your first editorial like that). Hurry home and be at it.' John wanted her home for other reasons too. His divorce proceedings with Eileen had begun. Myfanwy was nervous about setting up the magazine, although a visit to Edward Wadsworth's house in Maresfield, Sussex, reassured her. He gave her £50 to help start things off and showed her a large abstract Zadkine sculpture on the lawn. This made her think the project was less 'absurd and impractical'. Wadsworth and Paul Nash became 'fathers and heralds of our hopes'.[9] Myfanwy arranged a reciprocal relationship with Geoffrey Grigson's *New Verse* whereby each would promote the other's publication. Anton Zwemmer reluctantly agreed to sell the magazine in his shop at 26 Litchfield Street, Charing Cross Road. He wanted it to look more like *Cahiers d'Art*, but for that to happen, Myfanwy told him, they'd need more money. Myfanwy also met with Herbert Read and Michael Sadler to get them on board. Like Abstraction-Création in Paris, she explained, the purpose of *Axis* was to showcase abstract art but also to give artists an opportunity to explain their work. Some were concerned that the magazine would be confused with the wartime Axis alliance, but no one came up with a new title.[10]

Myfanwy and John were waiting for John's divorce to come through, but they were very keen to live together. They had to be near enough to London for Myfanwy to get back to give her weekly lectures at Morley College in Lambeth, which she had been giving since leaving university in 1933. And although they wanted to be in the country, they both disliked low ceilings and exposed beams. They stuck a pin in a map near Turville, a pretty village in Oxfordshire (now Buckinghamshire) where Myfanwy had once stayed with a school friend. They went exploring and found Fawley Bottom Farmhouse. It had no water or electricity, but it did have a well with drinking water one field away. They rented it at once in December 1934, and the first issue of *Axis* appeared a month later. Having witnessed the disintegration of Abstraction-Création and the inner rumblings of Unit One, Myfanwy was keen to keep the doors of *Axis* wide open.[11]

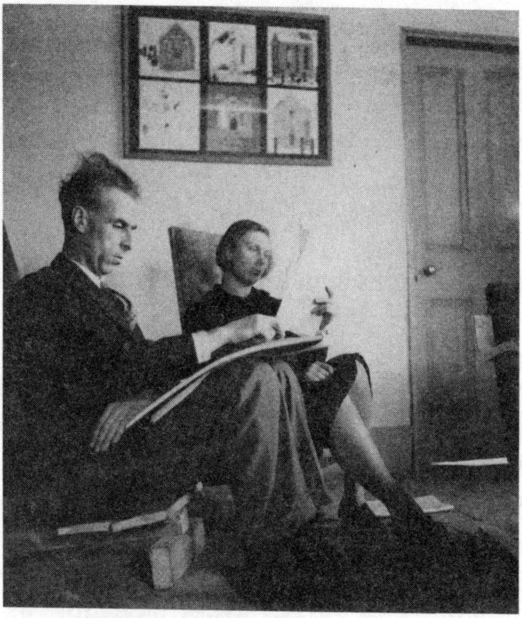

John and Myfanwy Piper

John designed the first issue, making full use of his passion for typography, setting it in sans-serif, a font generally used for advertisements. The artists and writers were listed down the right-hand side of the front cover with a large number 1 circled on the left. Myfanwy's first editorial, headed 'Dead or Alive', dealt with the idea of abstract art. She realised that it would cause controversy as a label and so put it in quotation marks in the magazine's subtitle: 'A quarterly review of contemporary "abstract" painting & sculpture'. In the first issue Geoffrey Grigson argued that Ben Nicholson's work was 'admirable in technical qualities, in taste, in severe self-expurgation' but that it was too interested in being 'art itself' and so became 'floating and disinfected'. Piper's work, he continued, was 'an attempt at biomorphic abstraction' but was 'irresolute here and there in form'.[12] Piper and Grigson had a turbulent friendship and Myfanwy remembered one occasion when they set off together on bicycles from Fawley Bottom and came back separately. Moore fared better under Grigson's pen: his 'abstraction-surrealism' was 'nearly in control' and he was the 'one English sculptor of large, imaginative power' of which he was 'almost master'. Hepworth was a 'viable abstractionist' although a 'constricted' and 'emotional' one. Wyndham Lewis and Moore were the only artists, according to Grigson, who were 'in control of enough imaginative power' to position themselves between surrealism and abstraction.[13]

Myfanwy noted that Arthur Jackson (Hepworth's cousin) was the only artist included in the first issue who didn't become famous. Plato, Read argued in the first issue, suggested that abstraction was the logical conclusion to all art, in order to divorce it from 'real' or 'natural' objects. For poetry, Read pointed out, this meant a shift to 'sound values' over 'meaning'.[14] The art critic Anatole Jakovsky wrote a series of inscriptions for some of the reproductions, including one for Mondrian that read 'final beauty exists. Beauty when breath stops. The beauty of the summit. The beauty of the iceberg.' We can see, Jakovsky declared, the 'footprints of the artist's inner life' in Kandinsky, whereas Giacometti 'transcribes the anguish of to-day'. Dalí, however, engaged in 'descriptive sadism' in which man is 'devouring himself' and Miró crucified his 'objects' with 'rusty nails'. Calder, by contrast, fixed the 'rendezvous of the planets' and Nicholson cut out 'a square, and "plays hide and seek" by himself'.[15] The prose in *Axis* was as experimental as the artwork. A piece by Kandinsky in the second issue set out the pros and cons of 'the line and the fish'. It appears, at first, to be simply absurd, but is in fact an elegant description of his preference for abstract or 'pure' art. Although they may at first seem similar, the line cannot swim, eat or be eaten, Kandinsky wrote, and so he liked it better.[16]

Jim Ede, Assistant at the Tate, explained the problems with deciding what is good art in the first issue of the magazine. Certain things, he said, 'irritate us unnecessarily, other things please us too much' and so 'our judgment is muddled by our emotion'. Botticelli, for example, might not be considered so good if you mixed his work up with some others. Ede also pointed out that 'abstract' was an unnecessary label as all art is abstract, 'in so far as it is art at all'. Artists with an 'overdose of suave technique' ought to throw open the windows and redecorate the house, he said.[17]

It is no surprise that Ede turned to domestic imagery in his criticism. He and his wife Helen had worked hard redecorating their beautiful Georgian home in Hampstead in 1928. Number 1 Elm Row was a 'rambling old' Georgian house, set back from the road, that had probably been an inn in the sixteenth century. Jim loved it because it had 'powder closets and wig cupboards' and an 'inward quiet'. Entering the garden from the corner of Heath Street one passed through a high wall, and the sudden silence felt like entering an inner sanctuary.[18] As they did it up, instead of waiting for the workmen to finish the renovations, every night after they had gone they went round with their buckets and mops so they could see the house 'clear and beautiful' each morning.

Once the house was finished, Elm Row became a place for artists, writers, actors and musicians to meet, particularly on Sunday afternoons. They sat upstairs in the double sitting room with the double door left open. The floor, Jim remembered, shone 'mysteriously … like the back of an old fiddle' and the street lights 'flickered through the vine leaves, making shadows on the white panels'. Odd leaves would blow into the room. It was sparsely furnished, with each object beautifully placed, as in Kettle's Yard in Cambridge, where Jim and Helen moved much later, in 1956. In Elm Row there was a divan with a white cover, Helen's grand piano and a few chairs. 'So many evenings', Jim remembered, they sat with 'a few painters discussing life' or listening to a pianist who wanted to practise for a concert the next day. David Jones stayed when he was writing his epic poem about the war, *In Parenthesis*. He liked to go to the pub next door to bring back a jug of beer for himself.[19] After a light supper of, say, macaroni cheese and stewed apples, Jim did much of the clearing up and took dishes out of people's hands in his haste to get things tidy again. His daughter remembered little piles of their things on the stairs that he did not want cluttering up the house. He did not encourage people to stay late as he liked to go to bed early in order to be 'bright and fit' the next morning.[20]

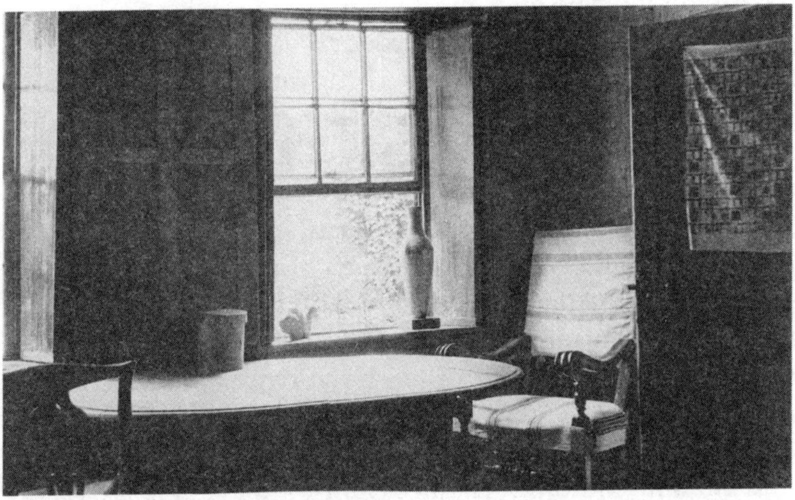

1 Elm Row

Ben and Winifred visited a few times in the late 1920s and then Ben and Barbara started to go there together in December 1931.

Jim and Ben shared a love of everyday objects, and Jim's daughter Mary remembered on a visit to the Mall Studios seeing a pot of pencils catching the light in his studio, and noted that even his 'cooking utensils' looked good. They were not beautifully clean, she thought, but you'd want to 'make a drawing' of them.[21] The Moores also visited, and in July 1934 Braque and Hélion went with Ben and Barbara and were joined by the Pipers after dinner. Braque was pleased to see that, like him, the Edes did not have a telephone. Gropius went for tea in January 1935, as did Gabo and Moholy when they got to London. For a while, Barbara's friend Margaret Gardiner rented the top floor.

Jim and Helen supported many artists over the years and Ben was among the first.[22] For Jim, Ben's work was a 'simple continuity' of the work of Giotto, Fra Angelico and Piero della Francesca. And yet, 'oddly enough', he was one of Ben's 'few admirers' at the time. Jim bought many of Ben's paintings, usually for little more than the cost of the frame and the paint. But in 1932 he generously paid him £22, giving Ben and Barbara the liberty to work again.[23] Jim and Helen continued their support for Ben and Barbara after their triplets were born, although they admitted to being a little 'dismayed' by the situation. In 1936 Ben asked Jim to 'pop' into the wastepaper basket any letters that referred to past difficulties as they were now on a 'much higher plane of understanding'.[24]

Herbert Read made a strong case for Ben's work in the second issue of *Axis*. It is so 'clean and cool' and 'alive', he argued, the public will fall in love with it and it will never 'look greasy' against the wall. He warned that the wooden boards used by Ben should stick to the 'limits of thickness we expect' of a picture, otherwise they will become sculptures. Barbara wrote to Ben in Paris that his colour reproduction in the issue was 'bloody awful' but that somehow it gave the 'feeling of the painting'. She thought the layout of the magazine was too complicated, 'with no main structure' but it looked 'popular and should sell well'. She liked the typesetting as it was not 'obvious' and on the whole, she felt, it was not too 'flashy'. She also liked Read's article on Ben and thought Hélion's long article 'very good indeed'. Hélion had written a kind of verbal montage of artists' materials: 'cork, newspaper bits, sardine tins ... screws, irons, bars, copper sheets, bulbs, wires, motors and photos'. Artists, he continued, 'mixed, glued, screwed, painted, imitated, deformed, plastered, washed, combed, sandpapered, filed, demolished, polished, adjusted with rule and compass, or malaxed with fingers'. Art was no longer simply a question of putting paint on canvas.[25]

Barbara warned Ben to 'go steady' when writing to John and Myfanwy, and reminded him that overall his work looked 'lovely' and that Winifred's painting was a 'marvellous block' and that her own work looked good, 'incidentally'. These 'intermediate stages' are necessary, she reminded him, 'as you & I know in all work'.[26] Hepworth's sculpture was given a high profile in the third issue, and by this point Myfanwy was happy to embrace abstraction wholeheartedly. She conceded that 'all good painting is abstract' in the sense that it 'translates a personal need and a universal need into one intense result that satisfies both'.[27]

Meanwhile John was quietly drifting towards ancient religious carvings and stained-glass windows. Many a 'Picasso-like profile', he wrote, is to be found on 'twelfth-century fonts and capitals'.[28] His new interest found its way into the penultimate issue of *Axis* in the autumn of 1936 in which he included a reproduction of a thirteenth-century stained-glass window originally from Salisbury Cathedral. In an article written with Grigson they decided that contemporary artists had a 'terror' of the National Gallery because it is full of paintings with 'fullness' or 'completeness', as in Constable, Blake or Turner. They came up with a plan to track the 'descent of "European painting"' from Giotto, Claude, Gainsborough, Constable and Cézanne to Mondrian. Things 'seen by human eyes' would get larger and the humans would get smaller until they eventually disappeared altogether. The only way forward, they argued, was to professionalise the whole business again, as had Picasso, Miró and Hélion. Good art, they claimed, represents the life of its time, and so a Samuel Palmer, for example, 'fixes the whole passion of his age'. There is no past, they argued, there is only 'human instinct, a *being*'.[29]

And so *Axis* mixed traditional and modern, placing Constable next to Christopher Wood or Fuseli next to Palmer. Myfanwy included a photograph of graffiti on a cement wall of a derelict tin mine in Botallack, Cornwall, on which someone had scratched their name and drawn a butterfly. This was followed by an article on 'Santhal Painting' from the 'Singhbhum district of Bihar', now the Jharkhand district of India. Adopting a colonial view of the naturalness of 'primitive' art, the authors argued that the European shift to abstraction was a return to 'natural need' rather than 'sophistication'.[30]

John was experimenting with all sorts of new ideas in his work, including collage and relief. Myfanwy and John were also slowly making Fawley Bottom more comfortable. Myfanwy felt they would stay until it is 'absolutely super, with the garden flourishing, all the rooms whitened and lovely and all the fleas flies bugs and beetles killed, and then we shall go off and leave it'.[31] In fact they stayed for the rest of their lives. They bought a small charcoal stove from Madame Cadec's in Greek Street and enjoyed peaceful weekdays followed by entertaining at the weekends. Myfanwy taught at Morley College on Thursdays and held meetings about *Axis* while up in London. The arrangement worked well as she enjoyed going to London while John preferred to stay in the country. *Axis* did not pay its authors, but it still had bills to pay. To save money, they used a small printer in Aylesbury and John invented a new method of printing which involved paramat blocks made of rubber (often used in advertising) to create large blocks of colour over black and white reproductions.

John and Myfanwy got married on 24 February 1937 at Westminster Town Hall, Marylebone, with their friends Justin Blanco White (named Justin because her parents expected her to be a boy) and Miles Marshall as witnesses. John rushed off straight after the ceremony because he was recording a television programme on modern art and stage design with the artist

Robert Medley at Alexandra Palace. The five-part series involved John leading live discussions on an aspect of art every other week. One of the discussions was on modern architecture with Serge Chermayeff and another was 'what you could see in the country from a bicycle'. Myfanwy, as one of the participants for the bicycle episode, brought in the landlord of a pub in Lower Assenden, a couple of miles up the road from Fawley Bottom.

John was interested in the way archaeologists used aerial photography. The archaeology officer of the Ordnance Survey, O. G. S. Crawford, had produced a series of 'Period Maps' on Roman Britain, Neolithic Wessex and Britain in the Dark Ages. Crawford also published *Wessex from the Air* in 1928. In 1937 John and Myfanwy went to see Crawford at his office in Southampton and he showed them how to read the landscape, to see it as a 'document that has been written on and erased over and over again'.[32] John saw how aerial views revealed the 'avenue' from Stonehenge across the downs, invisible from the ground. And, quite apart from the benefit to archaeologists, 'they are among the most beautiful photographs ever taken.' They are sharp and detailed, he wrote, but completely 'un-art-conscious'. Some of the photographs were reproduced in *Axis*. Flying, argued John, changed our 'sense of spaces and forms and vistas'. Hills are flattened out, towns are seen in an instant and the sea becomes 'something new'. But, most importantly, '*horizons vanish*'. No horizon meant no perspective, and it was as though, John wrote, the canvas had been 'tipped over backwards on to the floor'. As it was picked up again 'part of the floor' came with it.[33]

Piper, Nicholson, Klee and Kandinsky had some work exhibited in the foyer of the Experimental Theatre on Finchley Road in January 1935. Reviewing it in *Axis* Hugh Gordon Porteus called it the most impressive exhibition in London at the time. He praised Piper's 'alarmingly precise and complex "Constructions" made out of cable, rods, drums, ribbed lavatory pans, strips of perforated bluebottle-metal etc.' He likened them to 'nightmare relief maps such as a neat and gifted electrician might improvise in sleep'. Klee's work had a 'magical tactile beauty' and the

Nicholsons were 'impeccable' with 'ample feminine rhythms'. Kandinsky demonstrated a 'miracle of balance' and his work was like a 'hieroglyph of a superb vision'.[34] Inspired by the Finchley Road exhibition a young artist living in Hampstead who also taught at Morley College, Sydney John Woods, organised an exhibition of Nicholson, Hepworth, Moore and Piper at the Everyman cinema and theatre in Hampstead. Copies of *Axis* were on sale in the foyer and a brochure by Woods explained abstract art.[35] Inspired by the success of the Everyman exhibition Woods organised another at the Duncan Miller Showrooms on Lower Grosvenor Place, in April 1936. It included furniture by Marcel Breuer, a radiogram by Wells Coates, rugs and textiles by Ashley Havinden and artwork by Gabo, Brâncuşi, Giacometti, Hélion, Arthur Jackson, Miró, Moholy-Nagy, Hepworth, Mondrian, Moore, Nicholson, Paalen, Piper, Holding and Woods. Not a single artwork sold.

Myfanwy's friend from Oxford Nicolette Gray may well have gone to these exhibitions, and she would certainly have seen copies of *Axis*. Nicolette was the daughter of Laurence Binyon, keeper of the Prints and Drawings Department at the British Museum. She had spent much of her childhood going to exhibitions with her father and his expertise in non-Western art helped develop her love of abstraction. She had recently set up an art-loan scheme that she advertised in *Axis*, and through conversations with Ben they came up with the idea of bringing abstract art over from Paris. Collaborating with Myfanwy and Ben, Nicolette persuaded Helen Sutherland and Marcus Brumwell to sponsor an exhibition. This became the landmark *Abstract & Concrete* exhibition in which British and European abstract art was exhibited together. It was first held at 41 St Giles in Oxford, and then at Liverpool's School of Architecture before moving to the Lefevre Gallery in London in April 1936. Its final stop was Gordon Fraser's Gallery in Cambridge. John designed the poster, finding stencils and printing sets in a pet shop in Reading. Nicolette wrote in the catalogue that 'for the first time since the eighteenth century England is making a real contribution to an international art.'[36] Ben wrote to Jim, urging him to go:

> That Abstract-Concrete show is to be in the new white rooms at Lefevre opening about April 15. I hope you will be here to see it. The work ... 3 Mondrians alone. At Oxford where the show had to be crowded into 2 dark little rooms the Mondrians acted as a light by which the other work could be seen. There is a v. fine Giacometti too.[37]

Gray remembered that it cost seven shillings and sixpence to insure the Mondrians but that Christie's, for insurance purposes, claimed that the works by Calder, Gabo, Kandinsky, Giacometti and Miró were almost worthless. The *Daily Mail* reviewer called the exhibition 'at best, a jolly leg pull'.[38] It was the first truly international display of abstract art in Britain.

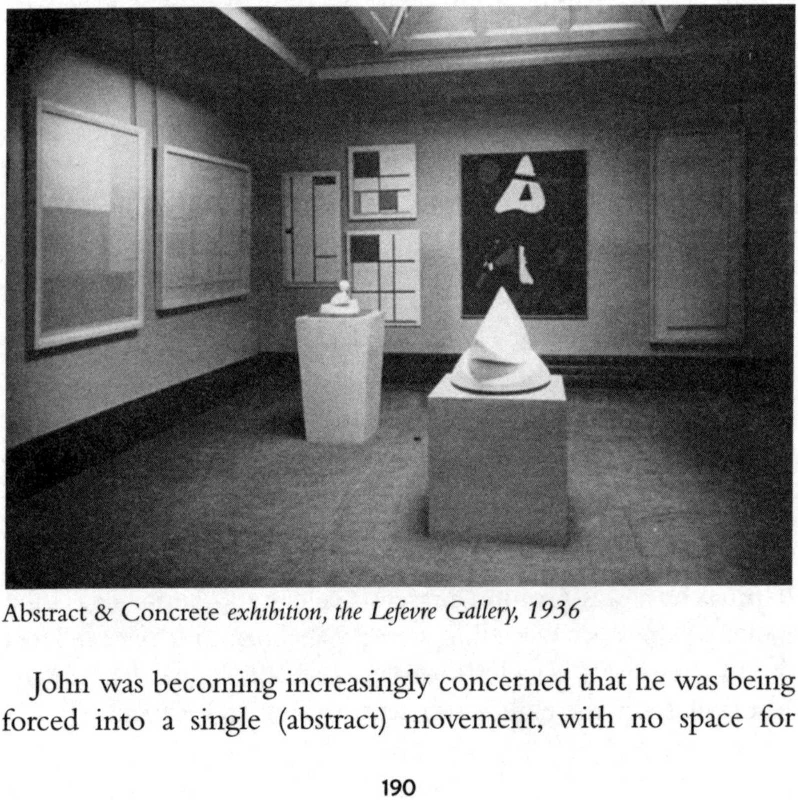

Abstract & Concrete *exhibition, the Lefevre Gallery, 1936*

John was becoming increasingly concerned that he was being forced into a single (abstract) movement, with no space for growth. He wrote to Ben that he loved being associated with him and Barbara but as 'individuals – and not as part of a movement'. He believed that movements are 'discovered afterwards' and that 'forcing them' as they emerge is to 'kill the artists in them'. The exhibition was, perhaps, a 'commercial necessity' but not an 'ideal', he concluded. Having had tea in Oxford in February just after the exhibition opened, Ben and Barbara went to visit the Pipers at Fawley Bottom in May. The visit was not a success. Myfanwy wrote succinctly in her diary: 'Ben and Barbara. Hell.'[39]

The two couples did not see eye to eye. Ben and Barbara were very serious about abstraction but this did not appeal to John and Myfanwy, who preferred those who did not take themselves too seriously. Myfanwy thought Barbara lacked a sense of humour, but years later they bumped into each other at the railway station hotel in Paddington and they had a lovely time together, with much laughter. Myfanwy decided that she had got Barbara wrong and that they could have been great friends.[40] But in 1936 it was clear that John and Myfanwy did not subscribe to abstraction for abstraction's sake. John wrote to Paul Nash a few years later that he felt a sense of release after 'an abstract period' and saw things like watercress beds with 'such new intensity!' You can hang a Ben Nicholson relief in a Cork Street gallery, he wrote, but it can't be 'hung against one's heart'.[41] But with the Surrealism Exhibition about to hit London in the summer of 1936, Myfanwy put 'Abstraction? Surrealism?' on the cover of her magazine only to reject both in her editorial: she was fed up with what she called pure form and pure daydreaming.

But Ben and Barbara were happily on the road to pure form. Having just been to the Surrealism Exhibition in Mayfair in July 1936 they went to an ABC tea shop around the corner with their friends the architect Leslie Martin and the artist Naum Gabo, who had arrived in London a couple of months earlier. They wanted to do something to 'clear the air', to pick up the baton for abstract modernism, and they came up with *Circle*, a manifesto for abstract-constructivist art, which they published the following year. The plan was to bring together art, architecture, engineering and design. Barbara later said that they came up with the idea one evening in their studio 'sitting round the fire'. Whether in a teashop or around the fire, they toyed with titles like 'Cosmos', 'Synthesis', 'New Order' and 'Document 1936' but stuck with *Circle* and work 'began on it almost at once'.[42] Barbara and Leslie Martin's wife Sadie Speight helped with the research and writing and 'did the layout, we did the corrections, proofing, everything'. Yet Ben, Leslie Martin and Gabo were named as joint editors. There was no acknowledgement of the two women 'who did the dirty work'. Gabo was more enlightened in terms of gender equality, according to Barbara, and in general the Europeans treated her like an equal. It was the English, she said, who were 'terribly patriarchal'.[43]

Naum Gabo came to live in London in March 1936. Born in Russia, he studied science in Munich and lived in Berlin, working alongside artists from the De Stijl Group, and he taught at the Bauhaus in 1928. He moved to Paris in 1932 and joined Abstraction-Création, but suffered great financial difficulty. Winifred had become a close friend, close enough for him to have proposed to her, without success. But in the summer of 1935 he became so desperate that one night he left the gas on in his apartment and went to bed. He was rescued by the concierge when he did not answer his door. In 1935 he visited Massine in London to discuss designs for the Ballets Russes and was impressed by the sense of optimism, peace and sympathy towards abstract art that he found there. He gave a lecture on constructivism, met Jim Ede and was fascinated by Herbert Read's theory that abstract artists were lying in wait for the revolution.[44]

Gabo arrived in time for the opening of the *Abstract & Concrete* exhibition at the Lefevre Gallery in April. He stayed in Bloomsbury and then Ben found him a flat at 11 Lawn Road, further along and on the other side of the road from the Isokon. Gabo thanked him for his 'careful attention to me'.[45] On one of his first visits to the Isobar Gabo saw his old friend the designer Naum Slutzky, whom he had last seen in Russia, and they 'rushed towards each other and embraced with such delight that all in the Club were entranced'.[46] In July he was introduced to Miriam Franklin. She was married to a wealthy banker and had three sons, and it was hoped she might buy some of Gabo's work.

Shortly after they met, Gabo told Miriam he had 'such a desire to tell you everything about me' without fear of being misunderstood or seeming ridiculous. She told him that she had been painting and walking on holiday and that she had scrambled up a hill through the heather, lain down on the warm earth and, 'perhaps I shouldn't tell … thought of you!' Gabo replied swiftly: 'Help me! Help me to love you quietly!' He begged her not to leave him with his 'boiling passions' and 'dreadful doubts'.[47] By October she had divorced her husband and moved in with Gabo and 'after six months we have been married!' Ben and Barbara were their witnesses. Miriam received a small income from her ex-husband and Gabo picked up some advertising work for Imperial Airways. He also designed bathroom fittings for John Gloag's agency, and some elegant plastic cabin fittings for the shipping company Cunard. He sold a few sculptures, including a commission from Winifred for *Construction in Space: Stone with a Collar* (1936–7).

In April 1937 Gabo and Miriam moved to a larger flat in Cholmley Gardens. He was delighted as he now had room for

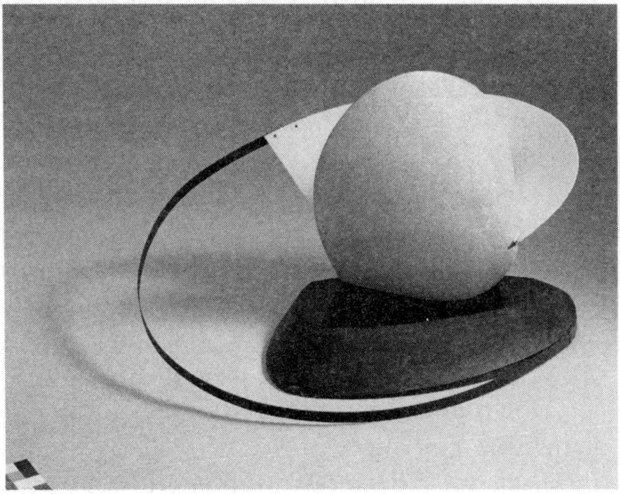

Naum Gabo, Construction: Stone with a Collar, *1936–7*

a studio, but he also had an oven where he could heat plastic sheets to bend into shape for his constructions. On a visit to the Welwyn Garden City factory in the spring of 1937 he was introduced to Perspex. He came home saying 'I have found my material!' Once Gabo was settled in London Winifred wrote to him that if he and Ben worked together with their 'vital fire', things will 'begin to move in London'. The 'dead weight of dark houses will dissolve', giving way to the 'electric purpose of the new idea'. Black railings will disappear, she said, and there will be 'order and light and freedom'.[48] Gabo held a one-man show at the London Gallery in 1938 exhibiting fifteen constructions. Eric Newton wrote in *The Times* that the sculptures fused 'mathematics and aesthetics' into a 'synthetic whole' as in a 'Bach Invention'.[49] Gabo made £134.

Gabo was fully committed to *Circle*'s constructivist aims. As one of the editors he approached Winifred for an article on colour. She agreed and wrote that 'colours wish to fly, to merge … to radiate, to shine, to withdraw deep within themselves' rather than being 'nailed down like carpets'.[50] Gabo also asked Jean Gorin for photographs of his sculpture, Michael Chekhov for an article on theatre and Sergei Eisenstein for one on film, but none of these came about. Intended as an annual review, *Circle* grew into a one-off publication about the international modernism flourishing in Britain, almost 300 pages long. The 'Art and Life' section had pieces by Gropius on 'Art Education and State', Massine on choreography, Moholy-Nagy on 'Light Painting' and Jan Tschichold on typography. They reprinted an article by the Czech architect Karel Honzík about natural form and man-made structures and Lewis Mumford on the role of machines in modern culture. They also included articles by the architect Sigfried Giedion on engineering and the physicist Desmond Bernal on sculpture. Bernal had moved in with Margaret Gardiner in Downshire Hill, and together they formed the anti-fascist organisation For Intellectual Liberty. *Circle* promoted the constructivism that had been outlawed in Germany and Russia. Leslie Martin wrote of the 'new aesthetic' that exists in 'the motor car and the aeroplane, in the steel bridge and the line of electric pylons'. The values of 'precision, economy, exact finish' were not, he argued, the result of 'technical limitation'.[51]

The aesthetics of *Circle*, unlike *Axis*, were doctrinaire. The opening editorial set out a 'new cultural unity', to 'gather here' those who were 'working in the same direction and for the same ideas'.[52] Cubism had left the art world in tatters, wrote Gabo, in a 'conglomeration of ruins'. The constructive artists would have to build things up from the beginning.[53] The book is divided into painting, sculpture, architecture and 'Life and Art', and it begins and ends with Malevich, the father of abstraction. In *Axis* Herbert Read began with Plato, and in *Circle* he turned to Hegel and Kant to explain the drive to abstraction. Le Corbusier argued that cubism opened the 'gates' of all art, and painting allowed him to 'blow open all the doors to the deep land of dreams'.[54] Nicholson offered four 'quotations', one of which was that you can't ask explorers to tell you about a country before they get there.[55] The articles in *Circle* were longer and denser than those in *Axis* and it had a stronger drive towards unity. Gabo made an ambitious claim for constructive sculpture as the 'old and glorious and powerful art re-born in its absolute form ready to lead us into the future'.[56] Constructive art, for Hepworth, revealed an 'absolute belief in man' and a belief 'in landscape and in the universal relationship of constructive ideas'. Constructive art had the power, therefore, to provide 'a solution to human difficulties'.[57] John was angry because two of his abstracts were reproduced in *Circle* without his permission.

Circle, said Read, was pure beauty. Unit One in 1934 and *Circle* in 1937 laid the foundations 'for the art that was to develop in England during the next twenty-five years', even allowing for what he called the 'Surrealist intrusion!' There was no denying, he wrote, that there was a tension between *Circle* and the surrealist group. However, 'dialectical oppositions are good for the progress of art' and the 'greatest artists (I always had Henry Moore in mind) are great precisely because they can resolve such oppositions'. Despite his clear support for abstract art, Nicholson felt betrayed by Read. Whereas Nash, Piper and Moore were open to both abstraction and surrealism, Nicholson believed there was space for only one kind of modernism. He wanted to 'squash surrealism'.[58] Moore was on the fence; he was not in favour of the pure abstract-constructivism of Gabo and, like Read, felt that surrealism had brought back a much-needed romanticism. Ben wrote that 'all the fertility and drama' in Moore's work made him an abstract surrealist rather than a constructivist.[59] John sent a painting called *Coast of Wales* to an exhibition entitled *Living Art in England*, held at the London Gallery in 1939. He was asked if he was a 'Constructivist', 'Surrealist' or 'Independent'. His response was to define himself as a 'cubist, abstract, constructivist, surrealist independent'.[60]

John wanted to do something practical, so he joined forces with Robert Wellington, who was running the Zwemmer Gallery in Charing Cross Road, to find a way to bring artwork into schools. Henry Morris, who was responsible for education in Cambridgeshire, was busy buying dull reproductions of artworks for schools, and Wellington and John came up with a way to create 'authentic' pictures. They set up Contemporary Lithographs Ltd, a scheme to produce modern art at affordable prices, and commissioned ten artists, including Ravilious, Bawden, Nash and Sutherland, to draw directly on to stones or plates. John took the artists to the Curwen Press or the Baynard Press and helped them work directly on to the plates, a process he remembered as an 'awful sweat'.[61] Their work was then printed and first exhibited at Curwen Press in Great Russell Street in 1937 before being taken into schools. The second set of commissioned prints included work by Duncan Grant and Vanessa Bell. Jack Pritchard was delighted with his 'coup' when he got hold of them to exhibit in the bar at the Isokon before they went on display at the Leicester Galleries in 1938. The prints were also intended for households with small incomes and, as they put it in an advertisement in *Studio*, they were as affordable as going to a concert or buying a book.[62]

Although the editors of *Axis* and *Circle* saw themselves at opposite ends of the aesthetic spectrum, there were many crossovers. In fact, between them, the two publications formed a pretty comprehensive overview of British and European modernism in the 1930s. In the final issue of *Axis* Myfanwy printed a photograph that had been reproduced in *Circle*, of Le Corbusier's town plan for Nemours, North Africa, from 1934. This was one of Le Corbusier's designs for an ideal city, the 'ville radieuse', based on the abstract shape of the human body. Myfanwy, quoting from *Circle*'s editorial, explained that its aim was to 'make clear a common basis' and to show 'the relationship of the work' to the 'whole social order'.[63] For Myfanwy, Paul Nash was the embodiment of all that was abstract, surreal and English. She wrote about him for the last issue, having heard him talk at the Oxford Arts Club when she was an undergraduate. 'Nash has absorbed the English climate,' she wrote, and 'By some piece of remarkable magic he has almost *become*' the climate, 'the pearly mornings and the fine pale afternoons and the irresistible charm of winter twilight'. Abstraction, in his hands, she wrote, is 'a weather-gauge' and surrealism the 'hailstones like pigeon's eggs that startle the midlands' summer sleep'. Nash's method, she explained, was not to peek behind the blindfold to see where to put the eye of the pig, but to spread his hands and declare 'This pig is all eye.' Nash could paint 3,000 years 'without turning a hair', and still belong to 'things as they are to-day'.[64]

Axis and *Circle* both published articles about Moore, Nicholson, Hepworth and Mondrian. Both had articles or reproductions by Herbert Read, Jan Tschichold, Moholy-Nagy and Winifred Dacre (Ben asked Winifred if she would use this old family name instead of Nicholson to avoid confusion during the 1930s).[65] But the cycle of competitive publishing did not end there. Myfanwy's book *The Painter's Object* came out in June 1937, partly in response to *Circle*. She included a collection of essays by Moore, Léger, Hélion, Nash, Ozenfant, Kandinsky, Trevelyan, Calder, Piper, Ernst, Picasso, Sutherland, de Chirico and Moholy-Nagy. In her playful introduction she wrote that they were in the middle of 'a thousand battles. Left, right, black, red' and, in a thinly veiled attack on Nicholson, 'white too, for the fools who won't take part'. The battles she had in mind were pretty all-encompassing: 'Hampstead, Bloomsbury, surrealist, abstract, social realist, Spain, Germany, Heaven, Hell, Paradise, Chaos, light, dark, round, square'. She mocked the banter of the art world as though eavesdropping on a private view: 'you must be a member – have you got a ticket ... have you signed the petition – haven't you a picture more in keeping with our aims – *intellectual freedom*, FREEDOM, ***FREEDOM*** – we must be allowed, we can't be bound – you can't, you must fight – you *must*. That's not abstract, sir – that's not surrealist, sir –' and so on.[66]

Patience with the art world, even within the art world, was wearing thin given the emerging political situation in Europe. One of the most famous politically engaged artworks of the twentieth century was exhibited for the first time in July 1937 at the Exposition Internationale des Arts et Techniques in Paris: Picasso's *Guernica*. The following year *Guernica* was brought to the Whitechapel Gallery in London, organised by Roland Penrose and the leader of the Labour Party, Clement Attlee. It arrived in London on 30 September, the day the Munich agreement was signed, and it came to stand as a symbol against all oppression and violence. Myfanwy reproduced a photograph of it in Picasso's studio in *The Painter's Object* in 1937, before it was exhibited in London.

9
MACNEICE, THE COLDSTREAMS AND AUDEN: KEATS GROVE AND UPPER PARK ROAD

A 'mixture of exhilaration and uneasiness'

In the autumn of 1936 Nancy Coldstream was pushing her new baby Miranda in her pram along Keats Grove when she bumped into the poet Louis MacNeice. They stood talking for a while before she 'pushed off to the heath'. As she walked away she thought, 'Aha I am warm, I have seen the fire,' her favourite bit in the Old Testament. Louis's voice sounded like velvet to her and she felt cheered and warmed for the 'next half hour'.[1]

MacNeice was renting Geoffrey Grigson's flat, 4a Keats Grove, with his two-year-old son Dan, his Borzoi Betsy and a 'dour Scot' who looked after Dan. He had just moved from Birmingham where he had been teaching classics at the university. His wife Mary had recently left him for a PhD student who had been living with them. Nancy was married to William (Bill) Coldstream, whom she had met as a student at the Slade and she was 'a long-legged bouncing girl with a lively intelligence who seemed to carry the zest of her native Bude sea breezes in her blood'.[2] W. H. Auden was lodging with Nancy and Bill in Upper Park Road and he had introduced Louis and Nancy at the Café Royal not long before.

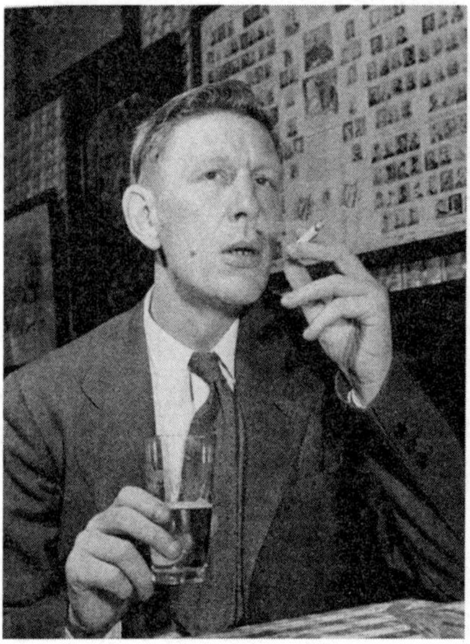
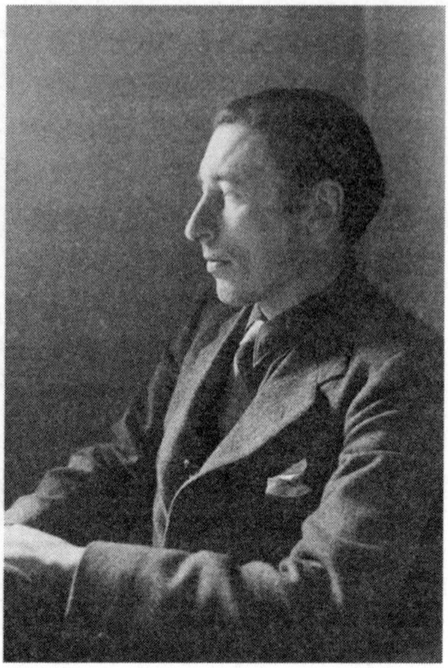

W.H. Auden and Louis MacNeice

Auden invited Louis for dinner at Upper Park Road and the four of them had a 'sort of nonsense conversation' about which of the three men had the finest hair. They all claimed their own was the best, but then Louis began to 'unwind' his like a turban. Nancy was captivated. Wystan's was 'blond and negligible', and yet somehow, despite Louis's impressive locks, Bill won the competition. Bill was 'devastatingly' handsome and funny, Nancy remembered, a 'marvellous friend' but a 'very different husband'. When she first met him he was so 'gay and cheerful' that it didn't occur to her that he might be moody behind closed doors. She soon came to realise that he was one of the 'moodiest creatures you could get'. Like her, he was quick witted, but his wit could occasionally be unkind.[3]

Shortly after dinner at Upper Park Road, Louis took Nancy to a party because Bill wasn't in the mood to go. They got quite drunk and when they arrived back at Keats Grove Louis locked the door and told her she couldn't leave. One account even suggests he bit her. She was furious, and shouted, 'Just watch me,' and left. Despite the inauspicious start they began an affair.

Auden, who was keen to spend more time with Bill, was happy to encourage the new lovers and told Bill that it would give him more time to paint. Nancy realised that Louis was a very quarrelsome drunk, and had a tendency to pick fights in the pub with 'fists and things', but still they grew fond of each other. His voice was 'very caressing' and 'splendid', but he dressed in an 'appalling dark brown suit' and 'looked like a lounge lizard' with very small feet. The 'dour' nurse, however, was extremely unhappy about Nancy's visits to Keats Grove and when she stayed over the nurse would 'wash up until 3 in the morning, dropping things ... cups and saucers'. Louis would get into a 'frenzy', ruining the liaison and making Nancy furious.[4]

As an art student at the Slade, Nancy had lived in blissful squalor on Adelaide Road, near Primrose Hill, where she and her friend Nicolette slept, ate and had parties. Nicolette Macnamara grew up in Blashford in the New Forest, near Freyn Court, home of Augustus and Ida John and his lover Dorelia McNeill. Nicolette and her siblings had little formal education and moved between the two homes. Their father, the poet Francis Macnamara, had left the family when she was young, and Augustus John helped Nicolette get a place at the Slade when she was sixteen. He also had an affair with her fifteen-year-old sister Caitlin, who later married Dylan Thomas. Nancy, by contrast, was the daughter of an eminent doctor and had been to Cheltenham Ladies' College. When they were living together, Nancy's and Nicolette's beds were like 'old dog baskets', and the washing and laundry piled up for weeks on end. In an emergency they took their underwear into the bath with them. Their stews were 'wreathed in fungus' and food 'rotted in the saucepans'. Canvases and paints and empty beer bottles lay all over the floor. 'The mice approved of our way of living,' wrote Nicolette and 'we were terribly happy'.[5]

When Nancy and Bill decided to get married, Nancy's brother was sent from Cornwall to prevent it, as the family disapproved. But he went to Marylebone instead of St Pancras and missed the ceremony by half an hour. Nancy's father told Bill that he might as well have brought her out on a stretcher after the wedding.

Instead of sticking up for their young love, Bill apologised to his new father-in-law and Nancy was disappointed. In fact her father was partly right, because Bill and Nancy were penniless in the early 1930s. At one stage Nancy made lampshades and then Bill got a teaching post at Wellington College in Berkshire.[6] They were both experimenting with their painting styles. Henry Tonks, who ran the Slade, told Bill to attend a lecture by Sickert in 1929. Bill liked Sickert's practical approach. One of his tips was to ask ten questions about the relationship between a single point and other objects, in order to plot your composition. This 'practicality around orthogonals' appealed to Coldstream and his later work reveals the measurements that became his hallmark. When David Sylvester pointed this out in a Radio 3 interview in the 1970s, Coldstream said he didn't mean for them to show and was afraid it was like leaving his 'shirt hanging out'.[7]

The economic slump of the early 1930s meant that Coldstream was even more in need of work. He had exhibited with the London Group, but he was excluded from the 7&5 Society, which had become completely abstract, and he was not interested in surrealism. He and Nancy were living in the Vale of Health in Hampstead when in the spring of 1934 he suffered something of a crisis about his work. He had seen a Degas of a girl, 'a walking stick and hoop'. This picture, he felt, had reached the logical conclusion to all art: a close-up in time. It is not clear exactly which painting this was, but it sent Bill into a terrible decline and he could see no future for his art. He did not want to paint from 'his head' because the results 'disgusted' him, and he certainly didn't want to paint from photographs which, he felt, was like 'shooting a sitting bird' with no 'sporting element'. He was 'gloomy, my goodness', remembered Nancy.[8]

With three million unemployed Bill also felt that hiding away to paint was frivolous and he wanted to do 'something of more social relevance'. When a job came up at the film unit of the General Post Office in 1934 he was pleased to do something useful. Filmmaker John Grierson, responsible for coining the term 'documentary', wanted to educate the public through film.

Coldstream helped to edit *Coal Face* in 1935, a film about the lives of a Scottish mining community, and in the same year he and Nancy moved to a maisonette on Upper Park Road in Belsize Park. Their second daughter, Miranda, was born on 18 July and in September Bill's old friend Auden moved into the basement room as their lodger. Auden had been teaching at Downs School in Colwall, Worcestershire, and he moved to London to be a full-time studio assistant for Grierson.

Auden wrote commentaries for both *Coal Face* (1935) and *Night Mail* (1936), a film about the nightly postal train from London to Glasgow. He was also the assistant director for *Night Mail*, much to the director Henry Watt's displeasure, who thought he looked like a 'half-witted Swedish deckhand'. Auden was responsible for the camera unit that shot the scenes at Broad Street station. The film includes dramatic footage of the mailbags being trapped as the train passed through small towns without stopping. The crew held on to the cameraman's legs as he leant out of the window while the train hurtled along. Narrative tension was created through the nerves of a new worker on the train who had never 'made the drop'. The three-minute coda, by Auden, sped up as the train increased speed: 'This is the night mail crossing the border, bringing the cheque and the postal order…' He wrote it in the Soho office of the GPO, in front of the footage, using a stopwatch to keep time with the shots. His verse is spoken over a score written by the twenty-two-year-old Benjamin Britten. Henry Watt told Britten that he didn't want any 'bloody highbrow stuff'.[9] The film was picked up by the Associated British Film Distributors (ABFD) and was a great success.

Auden and Coldstream had been friends since they were introduced as undergraduates, although they were at different institutions. At the GPO, along with Britten, they came up with a plan to make a film about the slave trade, but it never came off. They spent much of their time slipping out of the offices to drink coffee in Soho. In his popular *Letters from Iceland*, a travel book in prose and poetry co-authored with MacNeice, Auden wrote:

... we sat in the back passages pretending to work
While the camera boys told dirty stories ...
Till we sneaked out for coffee and discussed our colleagues

As well as sneaking out to drink coffee and discuss colleagues, Bill began to think about painting again. They'd 'scrapped Significant Form, and voted for Subject', Auden mused. Like Auden, Bill left the GPO in 1937, and found his way back into painting through portraits. Roger Fry's partner, Helen Anrep, commissioned Bill to paint her daughter, Anastasia, at Rodwell in 1936 and he later referred to it as his first Euston Road painting. He went on to paint Spender, Isherwood and Auden. He was not pleased with the portrait of Auden and wanted to throw it out, but Nancy would not let him. Auden helped Bill find his way again, pushing him back into the role of observer, the kind of painting that 'Auden himself admired', as Spender put it.

Auden, Nancy recalled, was 'a splendid lodger'. He was 'family' and 'I loved him dearly.' He was 'pale, with colourless hair and extremely clumsy', but he was excellent with the children. Bill went to his studio to paint in the mornings and she took three-year-old Juliet to nursery, leaving Miranda, aged about two months, in bed with Wystan. Miranda was still breast-fed and Wystan complained that 'she refuses to try to feed off me.' Only when Nancy came back and took Miranda would Wystan draw the blinds, get dressed, eat toffees and write poetry. They could not afford much alcohol and so after drinking a cup of cocoa in the evenings the whole household went to bed by 9.30. This suited Auden's love of routine. There was even a very brief flirtation between Nancy and Wystan. One evening, when Bill was out teaching, Wystan began to turn the lights out to create an intimate atmosphere. The front door opened and Bill walked in because his lecture had been cancelled. Auden later said that he'd been on the verge of having an affair with Nancy and remembered 'just in time' that 'all women are destructive'.[10]

Auden believed that painting, like writing, should be a form of reportage and he encouraged Bill to paint things as they were. This became the fundamental tenet of the Euston Road School, of which Bill was a founding member in 1937. It held strong parallels with the Mass Observation project, a sociological experiment that sought to document life. Mass Observation was also founded in 1937, by the poet Charles Madge, the anthropologist Tom Harrisson and the artist, poet and filmmaker Humphrey Jennings. Harrisson commissioned Bill, along with Graham Bell, to paint realist images of the city of Bolton. They worked from the top of the Municipal Art Gallery, while Humphrey Spender (Stephen's brother) took photographs around the town, with a camera concealed under his raincoat.

Bill likened painting to a game with a complex set of rules. Once you get a system, he said, you build it up 'with a certain autonomous quality in itself'. He wanted the whole canvas in balance at any given moment. He thought that Cézanne's habit of shifting an apple and propping it up with a coin was against the rules. When confronted with a large radiogram directly behind his model he simply painted it in. Although he liked the idea that he left himself out of decisions, he did concede that there are usually several motives to the things we do. In other words, as well as a 'utilitarian motive', he believed there was 'a big undertone of unconscious appendages'. This was true, he thought, even when we cross the road or climb the stairs and it was particularly important in 'those games which are called art'.[11]

In the summer of 1937 Coldstream, Victor Pasmore, Claude Rogers and Graham Bell set up a studio in Fitzroy Street, which became known as the Euston Road School when they moved to 314–316 Euston Road in early 1938. They began with a 'plan for artists' along the same lines as the London Artists' Association, but they taught a rather 'disorganised course' with no 'dogma or doctrine at all'. The only thing they impressed upon their students, according to Lawrence Gowing, who was one of them, was that 'nothing about art was wholly real apart from observation'. They had many casual members, including their friends Adrian Stokes and Stephen Spender, who signed up as 'rather incongruous art students'. The artist Thelma Hulbert remembered evenings at the restaurant Bertorelli's where Bill, Euan Uglow and Patrick George had five-minute rabbit-drawing competitions that Bill usually won. Members had breakfast at Café Conte at the corner of Goodge Street and Charlotte Street and tea at the ABC cafeteria in Tottenham Court Road.[12] One of Bill's favourite games was to guess the weight and ages of the travellers on the tube around him. He was fascinated by the subtle differences between people and liked to position his models at the Slade in the same chair, at the same angle, in order to reveal those differences. The early days of the Euston Road School overlapped with Grierson's documentaries and the Mass Observation project, and Coldstream had direct experience of both. As the School grew, supported by Kenneth Clark and Samuel Courtauld, they moved into a 'huge beautiful disused car showroom' on Euston Road, not far from Warren Street tube station.[13]

Auden introduced the artist Robert Medley and his partner, the dancer Rupert Doone, to his group of Hampstead friends. He had been at school with Medley in Norfolk, contriving to sit next to him on a school trip to Norwich, and they had a brief affair years later. Auden credited Medley with giving him the idea to become a poet. Doone and Medley set up the Group Theatre in 1932. The point of the Group, as Doone saw it, was to borrow the principles of classical ballet and transfer them to acting. Doone was interested in the 'choreographic use of space' and was keen that 'no movement or gesture could be made, and no position held that was inexpressive'. They wanted to create a collective of writers, actors, artists and musicians.[14] The first performance was staged at the Everyman Theatre in Hampstead in the spring of 1932, and the names of the actors were left out of the programme to emphasise the 'ensemble'.[15] They went on to produce left-wing poetic plays by Auden, MacNeice, Isherwood and Spender as well as folk and medieval stories and experimental productions of classics. Henry Moore designed the mask for Auden's first play, *The Dance of Death*, performed in

February and March 1934 at the Westminster Theatre. They also performed Auden and Isherwood's *The Dog Beneath the Skin* and *The Ascent of F6*.

Sensitive and creative, with a slight arrogance that masked uncertainty, Medley had studied at the Royal College and then at the Slade. His friend the surrealist painter Eileen Agar took him along to Leon Underwood's experimental life-drawing classes along with Moore, Coxon and Ginesi. But a chance meeting with the artist John Armstrong in November 1925, on the corner of Howland Street and Fitzroy Street, changed Medley's life. Armstrong persuaded him to accompany him to a birthday party for Wells Coates (the architect for the Isokon), just over the road. The party started slowly, and then his friend the actress Elsa Lanchester arrived. They danced a decadent tango and afterwards she held him at arm's length and announced, 'The trouble with you, Robert, is that you don't know what sex you are!' She had spoken loud and clear, so Robert decided to strip in front of the amused party. The artist John Banting constructed a makeshift 'fig leaf' out of a record and a piece of string as Rupert Doone arrived. He observed the action from the doorway before he made his way over to Robert and asked him to dance. Afterwards, feeling awkward, Robert dressed, and they arranged to meet again. By Christmas they were inseparable. They spent a year in Paris, and then returned in time for Robert's twenty-first birthday. His family, although far from welcoming, turned a blind eye to his relationship with Rupert. Robert and Rupert set up a studio in Shepherd's Bush, and Robert was appointed as an art teacher at Chelsea Polytechnic in 1932. They moved further north to Regent's Park.

Since the Pipers were involved in set designs for the Group Theatre they invited the whole gang to Fawley Bottom for the August bank holiday weekend in 1937. Britten was not pleased to find the 'house filled with people – I have to sleep on the floor – no accommodatory luxuries'. Altogether, he wrote in his diary, a 'pretty grim outlook'. Medley remembered Britten as a 'slim, young man, unobtrusively dressed in sports jacket and grey flannel bags, with irregular features and crinkly hair'. He wore a pair of 'owlish spectacles' which seemed to emphasise his 'watchful reticence'. Auden and Isherwood arrived shortly afterwards with a plan for their next play to be a West End production. Doone was not pleased, and they spent the day locked in a room and argued it out. 'Rows and more rows', Britten wrote in his diary. By suppertime they had agreed that *On the Frontier* would be produced by the Group Theatre.[16]

The Group Theatre performed Spender's *The Trial of a Judge* at the Unity Theatre in Goldington Street, St Pancras, in March 1938, produced by Doone and designed by John Piper. Isherwood said it was the 'greatest play of our time' but that it was 'too intricate and clogged'. The play was about the 'crisis of liberal conscience in the face of Fascism'. It was based on an incident that had taken place in Silesia in 1932: a Polish Jew had been murdered by Nazis and Nazi confederates had interfered with the trial of the murderers. Myfanwy remembered John working with Medley in the cramped basement of the theatre and said that they made 'bold use of abstract colours – Prussian blue, light blue and scarlet, with touches of black and white'. The colours were meant to represent the 'powerful – even terrifying – image of cruel and implacable forces bearing down upon vulnerable individuals'. As they worked on the scenery Myfanwy heard members of the Unity Theatre Club calling out, 'Anyone seen the banner for the Demo?' The Unity Theatre Club grew out of the Workers' Theatre Movement, which aimed to bring political and social issues to the working classes and made use of experimental dramatic forms and agitprop techniques. They tried to detach themselves, Myfanwy wrote, 'but it was not possible. There was a perpetual mixture of exhilaration and uneasiness. The fear and horror of war constantly took the attention of the only people who had any understanding or interest in modern art and literature. The rest were indifferent to both – culture and the threat of extermination.'[17] Even so, she admitted, they 'used to laugh' at 'the people who did the demos'.[18]

John Piper had the idea of an 'irregularly shaped rostrum' for the production, which could be turned to reveal different screens, making scene changes very simple. At one point the Jewish character shouts, 'They have robbed me of consciousness! They have robbed me of consciousness!'[19] The intention was to present a powerful view of communism, but the left-wing audience felt that the liberal judge was too sympathetic. Louis remembered it as an 'exhilarating evening' but added that at one point a 'pretty and ice-cold' blonde girl told the cast and audience that the play had been 'a great disappointment to herself and others in the Party'. She spoke 'precisely and quietly, never muffling a phrase (you could see her signing death-warrants)'.[20]

Louis MacNeice had married his fellow student Mary Ezra on Midsummer's Day, their last day at Oxford. Mary had 'a passion for nature', particularly for 'identifying owls'. She enjoyed telling him about the farm she grew up on in Kent and the 'baby goats she cuddled under the cherry trees'.[21] When he got the classics lectureship at the university they moved to the south, genteel side of Birmingham. For five years they lived in a cottage in the grounds of a house in Selly Park, which belonged to a professor at the university. Their son Daniel was born in May 1934. The following year, on 11 October, Louis was driving Tsalic (Charles) Katzman, a Russian Jewish postgraduate from Oxford who had been living with them, to see his tutor in Oxford. Louis fell asleep at the wheel and they collided with a large vehicle and were thrown from the car. Dazed, Louis tried to get back in to drive, only to find that all the 'little gadgets on the dashboard were hanging out by the roots as if in some picture by Dali'.[22] So he walked home caked in blood. Tsalic was taken to hospital. Louis was prosecuted for dangerous driving shortly afterwards. About a month later, a spark from their sitting-room fire burnt down the entire first floor. Louis had to smash the cement hearth to get at the burning beams below. A neighbour with a hose came to the rescue and they eventually put the fire out. The whole episode left Louis exhilarated and in 'never-again don't-care spirits', and Mary in a state of despair.[23]

Louis and Mary's relationship was already under enormous strain and this turned out to be the breaking point. Her decision to leave him for their lodger Tsalic in November left Louis shocked and devastated. Louis went to Edinburgh after she had gone, had a somewhat wild time and came back feeling purged. A letter from Mary was waiting for him saying that 'the only person who has ever shown me what I feel is real love, in an all round sense – i.e. husband, mother, father, *everything* is YOU. *That I SWEAR*.' She became pregnant in London with Tsalic's child. Louis offered to take her back but she had an abortion and stayed with Tsalic. Louis, too, moved to London at this point with Dan. At first they lived in Highgate with Louis's sister, but then Geoffrey Grigson offered him the flat in Keats Grove. Grigson remembered Louis when they had been at Oxford together, 'stalking in a cloak in the dusk of the purlieus of Merton College'.[24]

In 1932 Grigson asked Auden and MacNeice to contribute to the first issue of his new magazine, *New Verse*, published from Keats Grove in January 1933. In the editorial Grigson explained that there was no 'complex or tiring manifesto' but simply the aim to publish poems for the price of 'ten Players [cigarettes]' or a 'bus fare from Piccadilly Circus to Golders Green'. The issue opened with MacNeice's 'Turn Again Worthington (or a thought for intending mystics)', advising the day-tripper to turn inland, forget the waves, board the bus and be jolly. It was followed by Auden's poem 'Song', about having a handsome profile, having gone to a great public school, having a little money invested and yet feeling 'such a fool'.[25]

The flat on Keats Grove was beautiful and light. The south-facing sitting room at the back had a balcony with spiral stairs going down into the garden. Louis moved in on 6 November 1936, after it had been repainted. The arrival of Dan and the nurse was successful but 'Nurse wants to shift things round rather' and the 'measurement and angle problems are most difficult'. He was determined to take his dog Betsy for a walk on the heath every day, which was 'pleasant but very cold'. They were lucky, he realised, to have three 'late-open cafes which give you fried eggs if you have forgotten to lay in anything' and a cinema, although Keats Grove itself was 'most retired and residential'.[26]

On Sunday 1 November, about a week before he moved to Hampstead, the Group Theatre performed Louis's play *Agamemnon* at the Westminster Theatre. *The Times* said the verse was 'reminiscent of Mr Eliot's *Murder in the Cathedral*', but critics were not convinced by the design or the costumes. The 'chorus dressed in dinner-jackets and goggles' baffled the *Time and Tide* reviewer, as did the watchman dressed as a 'hooded monk', slaves 'dressed like the Ku Klux Klan' and Aegisthus in a 'Christmas cracker helmet'. He might have been able to tolerate all that, but the 'universal gloving of the cast' pushed him over the edge.[27]

Auden was one of Louis's first visitors at Keats Grove. They were working on *Letters from Iceland*, published by Eliot at Faber. Louis called it a 'hodge-podge, thrown together in gaiety', but it sold well. Louis and Mary's divorce was also being finalised. The process had been complicated by the fact that Louis's mother-in-law, at the last minute, tried to clear her daughter's name by hiring detectives to catch him with the nurse or the new maid, Eva, whom she herself had employed. Mary's mother also asked her husband to stop Mary's allowance (he saw no reason to) and tried to persuade Katzman to sign a document renouncing her daughter while she was preparing to leave for America. She even tried to commission a lethal curse from a rabbi and wanted her husband's friend Isaiah Berlin to deliver it. Her pleading, according to Berlin, went on for three to four hours and the 'combination of tigress, bore & femme fatale' was 'very odd'. The effect was 'violent claustrophobia & a desire for solitude'.[28] Louis was too busy to pay much attention. He launched himself into a whirl of 'narcotic engagements', including 'political meetings, private views, flirtations, the experimental theatre', but was also concerned about 'the question of my overdraft' and 'the question of Spain'. He lived next door to the writers Robert and Sylvia Lynd, who invited him to literary dinner parties where he met the 'old gang', including 'Hugh

W. [Walpole], J. B. Priestley, Oliver St. J. Gogarty, and Rose Macaulay'. They all, he said, had charm, with the 'exception of Rose Macaulay'.[29] Sylvia Lynd combined a 'whimsical brand of wit' and a way of 'flattering anyone she was talking to' in her 'clear and silver' voice. Robert's voice was husky, as if his 'cigarette ash had got into it'. They were 'politically pink in a mellow gentlemanly way', unlike their daughters who were extremely 'red' and 'got themselves injured by the mounted police in East End communist meetings'.

Nineteen-thirty-seven was a year of 'wild sensations' for Louis. He met Leonora Corbett, a musical actress who was 'very tall, very blonde, all eye-veils, furs and egotism'. She mixed her conversation with French and German and their relationship, wrote Louis, was entirely make-believe. It ended with her 'throwing a tea table' at him. The cups 'bounced about the room and the walls were spattered with tea-leaves'. They both exploded into laughter and this was perhaps their 'one real moment of communion'. And then, as he put it, he 'went about' with someone 'of whom I cannot write'. The 'someone' was Nancy, whom he found 'attractively *gamine*, with blue eyes, arched eyebrows, and a mane of honey-coloured hair'. Their affair was 'an education – or rather illumination'; she was 'so feminine that I sometimes felt like leaving the country at once' but also so easily hurt 'that to be with her could be agony'. She could be 'so gloomy as to black-out London' and yet 'so gay that I would ask myself where I had been before I knew her'. Of all the people he had known, Louis said, she 'could be most radiant'. So he did not later regret 'the hours and hours of argument and melancholy' and what he called the 'unanswerable lamentations of someone who wanted to be happy in a way that was just not practical'.[30] Re-reading Louis's account of their relationship half a century later gave Nancy a shock, reminding her of how dysfunctional they had been and why she had ended it. Louis later analysed his approach to their relationship and realised that if you decide that X (in other words Nancy) is 'all you want, you ruin X and yourself. Whoso saveth his life shall lose it.' Even psychoanalysts can't solve the problem, he decided, because they focus on the individual and that is only one half of the equation.

Louis and Nancy spent much of the spring of 1937 in the garden at Keats Grove. They lay on the grass, surrounded by tall dark trees, looking at 'wonderful daffodils' and talking. Their relationship was an antidote to the 'chaos of unhappy or dreary marriages' they saw around them. Sex in the 1930s, Louis decided, was perfunctory. He imagined 'the pounding and jingling of bedsteads but somewhere in the hearts of the couples on the beds is a reedy little voice of query: Is this enough? Or is it what I really want? Or can this possibly go on? When will it end? When will it begin?' And yet their own affair began to follow a banal pattern of clichéd agony. Freud had a lot to answer for, in Louis's view; he taught people that sexual repression is immoral and therefore fornication a virtue. It was a mistake to believe chastity had spiritual value, but Louis believed it was also a mistake to think all fornication virtuous. But 'hygienic' lovemaking advocated by 'alleged experts', he added, should be left to those 'who like everything in cellophane'. 'We are a nation of sexual frustrates,' he concluded.[31]

On the back of the success of Faber's *Letters from Iceland*, in 1937 Longmans commissioned Louis to write another travel book, about the Hebrides. He persuaded them to commission Nancy to illustrate it. At first Bill did not mind that Nancy wanted to go. In April Nancy's sister took the children to Cornwall for two weeks and Nancy and Louis caught the ten o'clock train from Euston to Edinburgh. Louis slept most of the way and Nancy drew him while he was asleep. Edinburgh was shrouded in mist when they arrived and Nancy was annoyed that when they climbed up to the castle they couldn't see much of anything. They stayed in a decent hotel where the 'mahogany [was] rather gaunt and quite nice' and then took a very early train up to the Minch, the stretch of water across to the Hebrides. The luxury of Edinburgh was well behind them. On Lewis they took a bus to Ness and found a woman who gave them a bed for the night, as there were no hotels on the island. The 'bed was streaming' because the house was so damp, and the sheets were so wet that they wore their coats all night. Nancy said it was 'vile, very sordid' and 'altogether very nasty'.[32]

It was hardly the romantic getaway they had imagined, but they managed to enjoy themselves and 'settled into a companionable rhythm, walking, talking', and their delight in each other's company went some way to compensate for 'boring food and damp beds'.[33] Louis was very taken with the barren landscape, Nancy less so. She became fed up with 'heather forever uphill and downhill' and 'boulders and things', plus the fact that they ate mostly plain bread, 'no butter or anything'. But she was fascinated by the black houses, round thatched cottages with peat between the drystone walls for insulation. Louis fell ill during the trip and although she looked after him Nancy was adamant that he recover swiftly, which he did. One night they heard a tolling bell that made Louis think about his father's church in Ulster and somehow he felt their relationship was doomed. Louis, of course, left all of this out of the book, as well as his encounter with a fortune teller who told him that he would not 'get what he wanted'. They 'had a pretty glum time after that', Nancy said. The book is an eclectic collection of observations, poems and plays, illustrated by Nancy, although the text claims to be the musings of a solitary romantic wanderer. It has been called a 'tourist suitcase' with everything thrown in at the last minute: 'wild fantasy, letters, wild energy, jokes'. Beneath the surface was a growing sense that 'the skies of Europe were darkening'.[34]

Things cheered up when they flew in a tiny plane to Barra to meet Compton Mackenzie. The pilot taxied them over the sands to Mackenzie's house where his housekeeper told them he was still in bed but to go on in. They had a good time, having a drink in his sitting room that was like a boat and he and Louis got on well. As they left Barra Louis wrote a poem to Nancy. She was alive 'beyond question like the dazzle on the sea', he wrote. They made plans for their future on the way home and Louis promised her a bullmastiff puppy as a wedding present.

When they got to Euston station Nancy called Bill. He sounded strange, so she told Louis that she'd have to go straight home to him. After spending the evening with Bill, she rang Louis to say she couldn't leave Bill after all. She and Louis had a weekend in Dieppe not long afterwards, but their affair was coming to an end. Nancy disliked Louis's obliviousness to the people around him; he failed to notice the 'ragamuffin street children' in the harbour in Dieppe where they were having lunch. She decided that painters and writers observe the world differently and that she preferred painters. She was also wary of getting 'turned into copy' when spending time with Louis.[35] But Louis did not give up that easily. He liked to wait until Bill had left to go and paint in his studio at 9.30 in the mornings and would then ring Nancy. One morning Louis asked Nancy over later that evening, but she and Bill were having dinner with the Clarks so she turned him down. He waited all evening for her, hoping she might change her mind.

As the months went by Louis became more depressed. At one point they discussed the possibility that she and the girls could move to the country with Louis and Dan; Bill could join them at weekends. But Nancy, realising it would mean looking after two households, decided against it. In May 1938 Louis moved to a maisonette on Primrose Hill Road with 'amazing views', very close to the Zoo. He sacked the nurse, who was still keeping Dan in a playpen although he was two and a half, and hired a young woman called Sophie Popper who was good at playing with him. He was teaching at Bedford College and also agreed to write a book about the Zoo (illustrated by Nancy). A more impressionistic book than Julian Huxley's guide, Louis's would be for the 'armchair reader'. He had always loved the Zoo, seeing it as a cross between music hall and museum, and felt it was like entering a 'dream-world', all for half a shilling.

In 1938 Nancy met Michael Spender, Stephen's brother, a tall handsome pianist and explorer, and Nancy and Louis's affair was finished. Louis wrote his acclaimed *Autumn Journal* in the closing months of that year. A diary in verse, it is twenty-four cantos of interwoven quatrains, full of memories. September was 'hers'; she 'left a scent on my life and left my walls / Dancing over and over with her shadow / Whose hair is entwined in all my waterfalls / And all of London littered with remembered kisses'.

The following summer, in August 1939, the Coldstreams went to Bude to visit Nancy's mother and then joined Adrian Stokes at Little Park Owles in Carbis Bay. The Nicholson-Hepworth entourage arrived shortly afterwards, including their triplets and nurse, and Nicholson was not pleased to find his 'enemy' (Bill) already there. Nancy stayed for a while but Bill returned to London alone and borrowed Vanessa Bell's studio in Fitzroy Street from November to January 1940. He and Nancy never lived together again. After the outbreak of war Nancy took the children back to her mother's house in Bude. She returned to London and became an ambulance driver and drove 'erratically and eccentrically' but with 'great courage' throughout the Blitz.[36]

10

MONDRIAN AND CALDER: PARKHILL ROAD

'The whiting has very well succeeded'

Piet Mondrian moved to Hampstead on 20 September 1938 and lived in a studio opposite Ben and Barbara for almost two years. Mondrian's studio in Paris had become a kind of pilgrimage site for modern artists across Europe in the 1930s. With no means of viewing art unless it was exhibited, the way to see new work was to visit the artist. Alexander Calder moved to Paris from New York in 1926, aged twenty-seven, and his visit to Mondrian's studio gave him what he described as the 'shock that started things'. He likened it to being slapped like a baby to get its lungs working.

Mondrian's studio at 16 rue du Départ (now the site of Galeries Lafayette) was approached through a small courtyard off the Boulevard du Montparnasse. W. F. A. Roell, the Paris correspondent for the Dutch newspaper *Het Vaderland*, wrote that it was a 'street with picturesquely neglected gardens, a verdant courtyard, a dark staircase'; on arrival he was greeted with the vision of Mondrian coming towards him 'in his overall'.[1] It was an unusual flat, built around the expansion of the railway next to Montparnasse station. The entrance was dark and you had to pass through the bedroom, up a few steps to the five-sided studio. Calder described the excitement of entering, and Mondrian's biographer Michel Seuphor said it was like

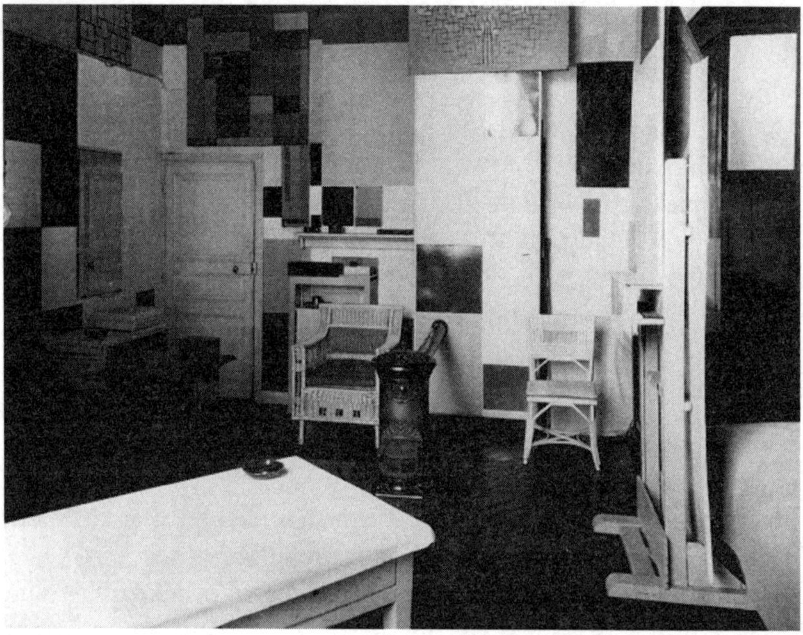

Mondrian's studio in Paris

going from 'hell to heaven. Beautiful!'[2] It was painted white, with windows on two sides, the furniture was painted white or black and the Victrola gramophone red. The gramophone is 'no frivolous means of diversion', wrote Roell, but a 'machine of mechanical music' out of which the music, of Bach for example, appears 'sublimated'.[3] The room was 'severe, businesslike', he continued, with 'limpid, cool light' where the painter 'grapples with his material in monk-like solitude in his quest for his lofty, highly controversial ideal'. The walls between the windows had 'experimental stunts with colour rectangles of cardboard tacked on'. The cardboard rectangles 'were painted in greys and blacks and different kinds of white, both shiny and matt'. Calder suggested that it might be fun to make the 'rectangles oscillate', but 'with a very serious countenance' Mondrian said, 'No, it is not necessary, my painting is already very fast.' Being in Mondrian's studio was like being in one of his abstract paintings. Roell was confused on leaving it and entering the Métro and seeing that everything was rectangular: the trains, the walls and the red and green advertisements. These were replaced by the cylinders of the tunnels, and the lights casting 'elliptical lines'. Why, he wondered, would Mondrian 'revert to the arithmetic of a child's box of bricks' instead of exploring the 'compound forms which give our world such infinite variety?'[4] Calder said that he understood 'abstraction' after his visit to Mondrian's studio in October 1930. So, aged thirty-two, he began to 'paint and work in the abstract' and for two weeks 'painted very modest abstractions'. At the end of the two weeks he 'reverted to plastic work', but his plastic work became more and more abstract.[5]

Calder and his wife Louisa, the great-niece of Henry James, arrived in London in the autumn of 1937. They had spent the summer in a rented house in Varengeville-sur-Mer, near Dieppe, between July and October. Dieppe was a favourite haunt for artists including Sickert and Ben's father, William Nicholson. The house the Calders stayed in was 'a sort of chalet, tall and shallow, facing the sun'.[6] It was a relaxing time, between exhibitions. They came from the Paris Exposition where Calder had exhibited his *Mercury Fountain* in the Spanish Pavilion (1937), alongside Picasso's *Guernica*. Calder had been called upon at the last minute because the original fountain was considered too traditional. Onlookers enjoyed throwing coins into the mercury to watch them float. For safety reasons the fountain is now kept behind glass at the Fundació Joan Miró in Barcelona. He was also gearing up for his exhibition at the Mayor Gallery in London on 1 December.

The Braques had been spending half of the year at Varengeville since the late 1920s, so Georges and his wife Marcelle visited the Calders that summer. Braque, now aged fifty-five, adopted a paternal role with the young artist. He was quite good at playing the accordion, as was Louisa, and so they enjoyed the odd duet. The art critic Georges Duthuit and Miró's dealer Pierre Loeb also had houses near by. The Mirós joined the party and stayed for a month that summer, moving between the various houses. Léger and his wife Jeanne also came for a bit, as did the Pipers, Herbert Read and Ben and Barbara (though not all at once). Ben sent Calder a plaster relief in 1936 and they were 'both very much pleased with it'. Calder found it 'much finer than the sensation any photograph has ever given me of your things'. Calder had an essay in *Circle*, as well as in Myfanwy Piper's *Axis*, and he had been a part of the *Abstract & Concrete* exhibition of 1936 in Oxford, Cambridge, Liverpool and London. Hepworth told Calder that people in London had 'enjoyed your big mobile … very much'. The summer of 1937 was like being on an island, wrote Calder. They took trips into Dieppe in their Ford sedan, they bought sailors' shirts and red handkerchiefs, and there was plenty of dancing and jazz.[7]

In September 1937 Sandy (short for Alexander) and Louisa Calder sold their Ford, and with their daughter Sandra took a boat to England from Dieppe. Myfanwy helped to find them a flat in Belsize Park. Sandy 'set to work whitewashing the walls', and when their things arrived he added 'a big red Moroccan rug I had bought at the Paris exposition'. Sandra was two and a half and had picked up head lice from some local children in France, so a hairdresser came to the house and doused them all with kerosene. Sandy was sorry they had to cut off Sandra's long blonde curls.[8] He found himself a studio in Camden Town and got hold of some second-hand lumber to make a workbench. They spent a weekend at the Pipers' farmhouse at Fawley Bottom with Léger, who had begun work on the decor and costume design of Alexander Korda's film of H. G. Wells's *Things to Come* (1936). The film was set in a futurist city, devastated by war. Eventually Moholy took over Léger's role, but it was a 'landmark in cinematic design'.[9]

They all had a cheerful weekend, and Myfanwy remembered Léger's 'huge form and jovial presence gambolling about with Sandy Calder's equally huge one', which made our meals 'like a Normandy wedding feast'.[10] The Clarks, Kenneth and Jane, were regular visitors to Fawley Bottom. Kenneth enjoyed poking the ashes of the dying fire, 'while the children rammed one in the stomach', and sleeping in a room 'full of dark brown books on Gothic churches with a heavy heraldic banner on the bed'. He called John and Myfanwy 'two of the most completely humanized people I have ever known'. It was, he explained, the 'perfect antidote to life in London', even though 'Jane did once find a mouse drowned in the glass of icy water beside her bed.'[11]

The Calders had met the Clarks in New York in 1936 and introduced the Pipers to them. Myfanwy and Kenneth had a good argument about abstract art on their first meeting and they became firm friends. Clark was then director of the National Gallery and he and Jane cut glamorous figures in the art world. Calder was similarly in fashion. *Vogue* promoted him as the 'young American abstract sculptor' who 'occasionally makes jewelry of great charm and originality'.[12] Peggy Guggenheim opened her Guggenheim Jeune Gallery in 1938 on Cork Street while sporting a pair of Calder's earrings to match the Calder in the exhibition.

Sandy was particularly famous, in the international art crowd, for his wire circus. His love of the circus began years earlier when he was working as an illustrator for the *National Police Gazette* in New York. He regularly went to the Ringling Brothers Circus to draw for the weekly gazette. The magic of the whole thing and the 'vast space' captivated him.[13] But he was keenly aware of the reality of the performers' lives. One artiste, who performed a hundred 'flops' hanging by her wrist from a wire, was killed in an accident. The Art Students League, where Calder studied, at the south end of Central Park, was also very close to Central Park Zoo. He published *Animal Sketching* in 1926, a book of lively drawings in pen and ink, of lionesses, birds and monkeys, among other animals. He offered practical tips in the book: for example, not to draw sequentially or even the right way up on your paper, and if an animal moves 'leave what you have drawn and start a new sketch.' Monkeys, he noted, should be drawn doing something, and deer should be observed for their alertness and grace. When a horse is doing something with one leg, pay attention to what the other three legs are up to. And, he pointed out, cows are much neglected but make 'splendid and inexpensive models'.[14]

When he got to Paris he created his own miniature Cirque Calder out of found objects and bits of wire. He packed it into two suitcases and began to give performances to friends; then it grew to five suitcases and he started to charge an entrance fee for performances at his studio in rue Daguerre. Calder planned to stop performing the circus in Paris in 1930. Then *Vogue* featured a performance photographed professionally in their studio and so, thanks to popular demand and financial good sense, he ran four nights in November 1930 and charged 25 francs a head. His audiences included Mondrian, Léger, Van Doesburg, Le Corbusier, Man Ray and Cocteau. One performance was claimed to have attracted every member of the disbanded Abstraction-Création group. Performers from the local circus, Cirque Medrano, also enjoyed it. The audience sat on champagne crates, while Calder knelt on the floor and played songs on the phonograph for the different acts. There was wild applause for the 'tossing, from one man to another, of the acrobats' white handkerchief or the picking up of the dung after the chariot race'. A wooden horse galloped around the ring (propelled by an egg beater), dogs ran in and out of the spokes of the carriage wheels, a flock of white paper pigeons descended on to the shoulders of a large lady. Acrobats moved from one trapeze to another. What had begun as a fifteen-minute show became a two-hour performance with about seventy figures, each only six inches tall.[15]

He gave a number of performances of the circus during his time in London, including one at Mayor's gallery to accompany his exhibition. The reviews of the exhibition were excellent and Clark bought a large standing stabile known as the 'pagoda' for his private collection. (Duchamp gave the label 'mobiles' to Calder's moving work, and Arp called his static sculptures 'stabiles'.) The *Manchester Guardian* reviewer wrote that Calder had the 'ingenuity of a mechanical engineer' and his sculptures were both 'trivial and cosmic'.[16] A photograph from the exhibition shows Calder's head between two spheres, hanging off wire arcs. The lighting and angle creates a spherical shadow on the ceiling. Calder hung 'wire drawings' around the cornice, creating further shadows. The *New Statesman and Nation* critic wrote that the shadows were like infinite 'abstract drawings by Picasso' as the wires 'turn about on their strings'.[17] The *Architects'*

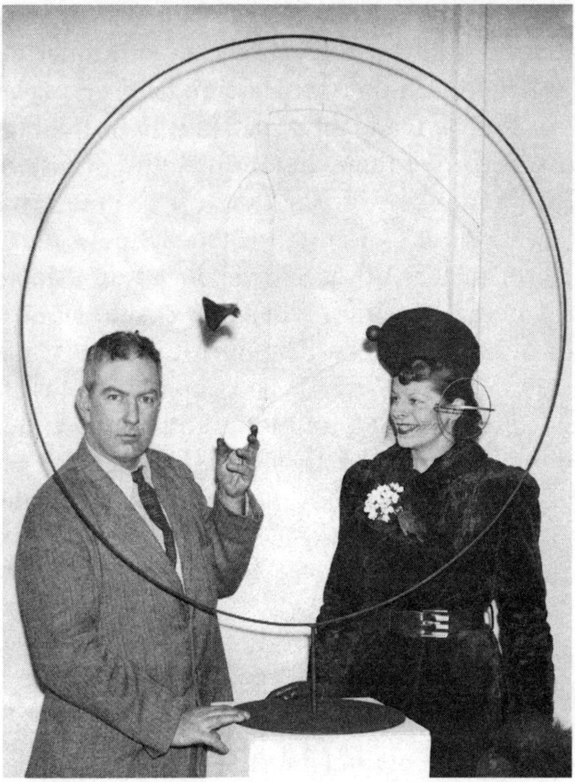

Calder at his exhibition at the Mayor Gallery, London, 1937

Journal wondered whether the 'preoccupation with the abstract movements of a mechanical ballet, or something very like it, together with Moholy-Nagy's theories of light, and Auden's experiments with sound' might 'one day revolutionize cinema and raise it to its place as one of the arts'.[18] Calder's moving sculptures opened up possibilities across the arts.

Margaret Gardiner remembered an 'enchanting' performance of the circus in Cecil Stephenson's studio in London, next door to Ben and Barbara. The 'ring' was strewn with sawdust, and there was a 'barrel of beer'. They all sat, 'mugs in hand', on the floor. The 'little creatures' of 'wire, wood and rag' seemed 'incredibly alive' as they 'pranced, pirouetted and clowned'.

Calder himself was a 'great, burly, rather rough-shod man' who 'contrasted oddly with the delicacy of his early mobiles'. Gardiner watched him on one occasion hammering a 'splendid necklace' for her; he made metal earrings to match but she kept losing one or other of them and eventually, after asking him to remake them a number of times, she banged out a pair herself 'on the kitchen floor'.[19] Louisa helped with the music for the London performances of the circus. But at the Mayor Gallery she recalled being horrified when she caught sight of herself in a mirror in her new dress. The mirror in their flat in Belsize Park was behind the bin, so she had not realised that her white dress billowed out like a voluminous tent. Calder and his family sailed to New York in the spring of 1938. They had been in Belsize Park for only about six months, but they made a lasting impression and lifelong friends.

Not long after the Calders left Belsize Park, Mondrian arrived. Winifred and Mondrian had become close in Paris and she accompanied him on his journey to London in the autumn of 1938, when he was sixty-six. Mondrian hadn't left Paris for almost twenty years and as the train sped through the Normandy landscape he murmured, 'Isn't it wonderful?' Aware of his dislike of the countryside Winifred was surprised at his delight in the scenery until she realised that he was referring to the regular beat of the telegraph poles as they bisected the horizon. When he first arrived in London he stayed for two weeks at the Ormonde Hotel at 12 Belsize Grove, recommended by Gabo. Then Ben found him a room on the ground floor in a communal house at 60 Parkhill Road, just opposite his own studio. Ben and Barbara lent him a bed and Gabo and his wife Miriam took him shopping in Camden Town for cheap kitchen furniture, including some drum-shaped stools, which he painted white. He brought his red Victrola with him, a trunk filled with personal papers, a suitcase and some canvases. Gabo lent him a pair of slippers, and he was very pleased.

Mondrian had the brown walls of the studio painted white with patches of red, and Barbara remembered his 'wonderful squares of primary colours [which] climbed up the walls'. He also painted some orange boxes white and placed them around the room. He wrote to his brother Carel on 2 October that the 'landlord has had my room cleaned by Snow White and the squirrel has whitewashed the walls with its tail'. They had been to see the Disney film of *Snow White and the Seven Dwarfs* (1937) together earlier in the year and Mondrian liked to call his brother 'Sneezy' and to sign his letters to him 'Sleepy'. He often listened to the soundtrack of the film. He told Ben that 'the whiting has very well succeeded' and Ben thought that 'no one could make a white more white than Mondrian'. The effect, he said, 'of entering his room on a foggy Hampstead night was indeed something'.[20] Barbara thought his studio 'so very beautiful' and his company 'always inspiring'. But he liked the domestic side of Barbara's studio. Whereas his and Ben's were most austere, Barbara's 'was a jumble of children, rocks, sculptures, trees, importunate flowers and washing'.[21]

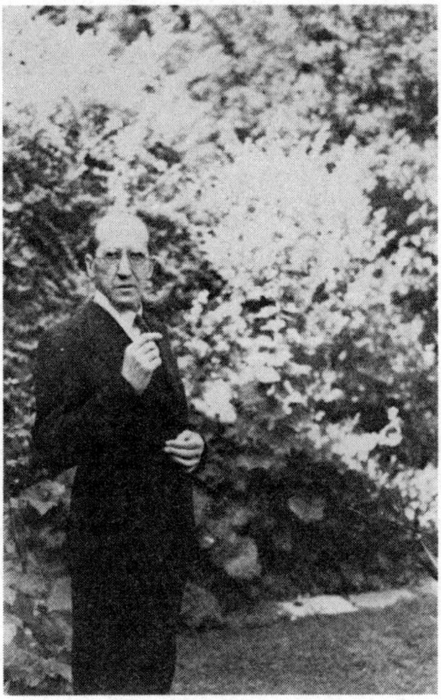

Mondrian in Hampstead

Mondrian did not mix with his housemates at 60 Parkhill Road. He shared it with a policeman and his wife, office workers and a businessman. He noticed the smell of delicious roast beef or fish from the shared kitchen, but he preferred to cook for himself on a stove in his room and he used his own basin for washing. He was a follower of the American diet created by Dr William Howard Hay, which involved keeping starch and protein separate. His copy of the diet manual was annotated with lists of possible foods, and he wrote 'mince pie', perhaps hopefully, at the top of one of the pages. Mondrian liked London; he took pleasure in the wide streets, the mansion blocks in Belsize Park and the tourist sites. He visited the Houses of Parliament, the Royal Exchange, the Bank of England, the Tower of London and St Paul's Cathedral. He told his brother that 'the buildings are so spaciously placed, that it combines countryside and city… I like it very much indeed here.' He sent postcards to his brother and called Paris a 'toy city' by comparison. Mondrian befriended Nicholson's lawyer Robin Ody and his girlfriend Jean and they spent many evenings together. She often darned his socks. Jean remembered that he was extremely fond of women's shoes, the brighter the colour the better. Mondrian served as the witness at their wedding in July 1940 and he gave them one of his paintings as a present.[22]

But London in 1938 began to feel unsafe. Mondrian wrote in his deadpan way that he had 'very kindly' been given a 'gasmasque' by the 'gouvernment' which was 'not very encouraging'.[23] In March Ben and Barbara took the triplets to stay with Ben's sister Nancy outside Oxford and Winifred wrote to Mondrian to invite him to Cumberland to stay with her and the children at Bankshead. He refused, as Winifred remembered later, because it was 'too green'. Apart from the threat of war, Mondrian was quite content in his Hampstead studio. He wrote to his brother that it 'has the advantage over my studio in Paris that the windows are on the long side so that I have more space to work with'. He had more space for the rectangles he placed on the wall between the two windows, as he had done in Paris. He wrote to some Dutch friends in April 1939 that it 'suits me very well here, but who knows for how long?' Things were better in London than in Paris, he wrote, but it was still better 'not to read the papers too much. Bombs etc., and preparations for war...' Fortunately, he reassured himself, 'we know that the way of the world is good in the end: greater perfection.'[24] Even the trees in London caught his eye, and he described them to his brother.

Mondrian enjoyed dancing in London as he had done in Paris. He asked Peggy Guggenheim to recommend a nightclub and she remembered he was a 'very fine dancer'. Miriam Gabo had a different recollection. She and Virginia Pevsner used to take it in turns to dance with him as they both 'hated it'.[25] Seuphor, his biographer, admitted he suffered watching Mondrian dance as it seemed to him 'that he danced very badly', and he pitied his partners.[26] Mondrian sometimes went for tea with Ben and Barbara. He could go to the end of his garden where there was a small gate to reach the path to the Mall Studios. The triplets were delighted that he licked the jam off the end of his knife. Barbara wrote in her autobiography that 'red-letter days were when Gabo or Calder, and later, Mondrian, came to share nursery tea. Three pairs of eyes would watch every movement and three pairs of ears listen to every word.'[27] He wrote to Winifred that the air was 'good for my health' but that 'above all the spiritual surrounding is here better than in Paris to me.' His friends, he told his brother, had carried him 'to a very good spot' because he could 'get going better with my work here. I see that my work is greatly influenced by these different surroundings.' He was in the middle of what became *Trafalgar Square*, which he completed in New York in 1943. Although the artistic situation was similar to Paris, he told the artist Jean Gorin, he was more 'free' in London as it was so much bigger. This freedom is perhaps reflected in the larger white rectangles and smaller squares of colour in *Trafalgar Square*.

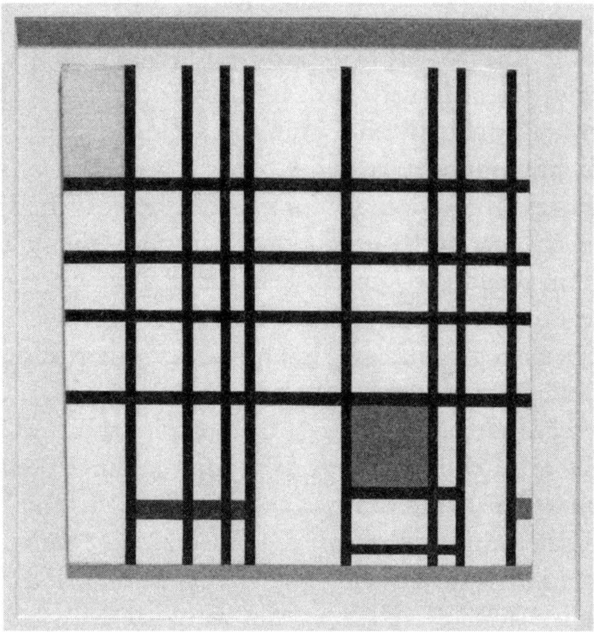

Piet Mondrian, Composition with Yellow, Blue and Red, *1937–42*

Although he was enjoying the sense of space and freedom Mondrian was still an awkward presence in new company. Margaret Gardiner remembered him as a 'Dutch puritan' when she met him in Barbara's studio. He 'stood very stiffly, with straight arms pressed close to his sides as though defending himself against some dangerous intrusion'.[28] He was thin, 'bespectacled and carefully dressed', but Hélion described him as 'that lovable, gentle and silent man' who has 'remained for me an example of the self-demanding artist whose devotion to his art shaped his life'.[29] He was 'casually elegant with a bright scarf round his neck' and, although he was extremely courteous, he did not smile very often. It is easy to conflate Mondrian's personality with his art. His work came to represent the logical conclusion of abstract art for the Hampstead modernists. Ben wrote to Margaret that one could 'take Cézanne & Picasso & Mondrian & know all about contemporary ptg without having seen anything else. The Mondrian vision is an altogether smaller thing but it is vital because it supplies an element missing from the others.'[30]

The days for international abstract modernism in London were short-lived. Hepworth wrote to Sandy and Louisa Calder in Roxbury, Connecticut, that life was 'hell *here*. Work goes so well + more + more people are interested + care about it; but what can one do with "stark reality" in the shape of Hitler + A.R.P. [Air Raid Precaution volunteers] stalking the streets? Every week more of the nice things disappear.'[31] In late August 1939 Hepworth and Nicholson bundled the triplets into their recently acquired small car, which had cost them £17, and drove to St Ives. Adrian Stokes and Margaret Mellis had a 'beautiful house' in Carbis Bay and invited them for a holiday, adding that 'if war broke out' they would give shelter to the children, 'as a glass-roofed studio in London was no place for them'. And so for four months Adrian and Margaret 'gave us shelter, warmth and kindness until we found a way to live'. Ben and Barbara begged Mondrian to come too, 'in our battered old car', or to follow after by train, but he preferred to stay in his studio.[32] 'I know by experience how much time garden-culture takes,' he told them, and besides, 'the country upsets me.' He would move only in an 'utmost emergency'. Barbara and Ben had dug a trench at number 3 Mall Studios and they told Mondrian to use it during air raids. As they drove away, 'The last person we saw was Piet Mondrian in the street.'

They arrived in Carbis Bay 'at midnight with very weary children, in pouring rain', by which time Barbara's 'spirits were at zero'. Things looked better in the morning, and she realised how beautiful the surroundings were and the 'sense of community'. She decided it would be possible to 'find some manual work and raise the children'. War was declared at the start of September, and they 'set about finding ways of working and helping the war effort'. Naum Gabo and his wife Miriam arrived shortly afterwards, expanding the community of modernists in Cornwall. They were planning to cross the Atlantic, but when the liner *Athena* was sunk they cancelled their tickets. For Barbara 1938 and 1939 became the 'years of attrition' as it had become 'harder and harder to sell any work or get jobs of any kind'. And yet somehow the lack of time, money and space in St Ives gave Barbara ideas for large artworks. Large works were obviously impractical or impossible, and so, although she had made three works over ten feet high between 1934 and 1937 (all of which were damaged during the war), she now had to 'work imaginatively in maquette form and dream up some future monument'.[33]

Herbert Read, having visited Mondrian on 31 October 1939, wrote to Nicholson and Hepworth that he 'seemed very happy' and had received a cheque from Peggy Guggenheim for *Composition with Red*. He hadn't finished it but he promised he would, even though he had been unable to work since the outbreak of war. Mondrian was stoical about his position and told Ben and Barbara that 'in this imperfect world we – imperfect too – must find our life by work, and we have a great privilege that our work is a nice and good work.' On Christmas Eve he wrote to Winifred that 'I am still always glad having come here. And having remained. My work goes better than ever. In spite of all.' The German invasion of Holland in May 1940 shook Mondrian, and he was very concerned for his two brothers and his friends. He kept working, 'inspite of the events', but after the fall of Paris in mid-June he stopped. On 4 July he wrote to Barbara, 'I am very pessimist,' though he often thought of her and Nicholson. He wrote to Winifred on the same day to reassure her that 'I did not lose my confidence in Human's future and Progress.'[34]

Life in St Ives was hectic. Barbara was too busy to work and 'could only draw at night and make a few plaster maquettes'. Her days were filled with 'running a nursery school, double-cropping a tiny garden for food, and trying to feed and protect the children'. She did not 'resent the war effort or the hard work, but I did begin to worry about the future: we were picking our salads in the hedgerows, and mushrooms in the fields, while the children's appetites grew bigger and bigger'. It was Stokes, their 'life-long friend', who made the first three years of the war supportable.[35]

Mondrian applied for permission to leave London with the help of Robin Ody; his friend Harry Holtzman in New York advanced him the money for the crossing. His passport was stamped on 26 June, but he had to wait for a berth. He sent his work on ahead to New York. On the night of 8 September he was lying in bed when a bomb hit Parkhill Road a few doors down. He wrote to Ben and Barbara that his shutters were blown half open but that fortunately his blackout meant that as he lay in bed he had 'only dust in a eye. Lucky!' There was, he said, 'still quite near a time-bomb', but as he reported to Winifred, 'happely' his pictures 'were already gone'. Forty-nine people were killed in Hampstead in the first month of the bombing. Feeling anxious, on 12 September Mondrian moved into the Ormonde Hotel where he had first stayed in London two years earlier. He was there for two weeks and did not undress at night but sat in an 'armchair in the basement'. At last a place became available on a boat from Liverpool.[36]

Ody drove him to the port to see him off. On the crossing to New York the boat suffered a night attack from U-boats in the Atlantic. But he made it and wrote to Winifred that he was happy, although his health was 'yet always not what it ought be'. But he could work again and 'life here is not much different from that in Europe and persons also', but he admitted that 'in those two years I had learned to love London very much.' He wanted to tell his 'dear friends' that he would 'feel always grateful to you for your help in coming to London'. He said to Winifred, 'it was good you brought me from Paris to London after Nicholson's good help.'[37]

And so the struggles in love, friendship, ambition and the future of British art dissolved as the people at the centre drifted apart. The threat of war became a reality. Mondrian fled to New York, the Calders to Connecticut, Ben and Barbara and the Gabos to St Ives, the Moores to Hertfordshire, Winifred to Cumberland, the Pipers to the Chilterns, Ivon and Mary Hitchens to a caravan in Sussex, the Moholy-Nagys to Chicago and the Gropiuses and Breuer to Massachusetts. London's moment as the centre of international modernism had passed.

EPILOGUE

It was dark and raining when Barbara, Ben, the triplets, their nanny and their cook arrived at Adrian Stokes and Margaret Mellis's house in St Ives on 25 August 1939. Barbara remembered it being midnight, Margaret remembered it was mid-afternoon. Ether way they could not see the view of Carbis Bay or Godrevy Lighthouse (the one Woolf based her novel on) when they piled out of the car after the long drive from Belsize Park. They went into the house, Little Park Owles, and found that Bill and Nancy Coldstream and their girls were also staying. Ben and Barbara were at opposite ends of the spectrum from Bill in terms of their art, but arguments about realism and abstraction didn't seem so important in the face of war. There was a big garden with palm trees and peach trees, but the house itself had four bedrooms. Nancy stayed on for a while before taking the children to her mother's in Bude, and Bill went back to London. Ben and Barbara were given the guest room, but they were not used to sharing as Barbara smoked and Ben had asthma. The triplets and nanny slept in Margaret's studio and Adrian gave Ben his studio to work in. Barbara used their bedroom to draw in when she got the chance. Ben knew St Ives well and because he had Adrian's studio he could get to work straight away. It was less straightforward for Barbara. She was delighted, however, when she saw the view and found the landscape 'unconquerable and strange, & my God how sculptural'.[1]

War was declared nine days later and so a return to London was out of the question. Barbara got stuck in helping Adrian create a market garden. The artist Sven Berlin, who had recently moved to St Ives, earned some extra money by digging vegetables for them, looking 'marvellous' stripped to the waist, 'just like Samson', Adrian thought. Berlin also enjoyed sitting on the veranda eating Margaret's Cornish saffron buns.[2] Barbara and Ben had very little money, which meant they had no independence. There were a lot of people living in a small space and it began to take its toll. Ben wrote to Read that Barbara had been unable to do any sculpture and had been 'laid up a great deal lately'.[3] One morning Margaret found Barbara crying because Ben had thrown her alarm clock out of the window: he hated being woken up by it. When Ben found the house too crowded he went to bed and Barbara brought him meals on trays, or he simply took off and cycled around the countryside. Traditional roles ran deep, so while Barbara did most of the childcare, Margaret was responsible for feeding the household, which was not easy with food shortages. The fear of being unable to work began to engulf Barbara. She had only pencils and gouache at her disposal and began to draw crystals in her bedroom with complicated networks of strings, inspired by Desmond Bernal's crystallography. Bernal, living in Downshire Hill in Hampstead with Margaret Gardiner, had pioneered the use of X-ray crystallography.

Naum and Miriam Gabo moved to St Ives just after the war broke out. Although they had planned to stay for only a few weeks, they ended up staying in Cornwall until 1946. They lived in a small bungalow called Faerystone, almost at the end of the Stokeses' driveway. The three couples spent most of their evenings together, and argued about which records to play. But by Christmas 1939 Adrian and Margaret were ready to have their own space, particularly as Margaret was pregnant. Ben and Barbara found a small house near by called Dunluce, and Adrian paid the rent for them for a while. Barbara's sister arranged for their furniture to be sent from the Mall Studios and

Ben persuaded Margaret Gardiner to pay for a few of Barbara's sculptures and for his big paintings to be transported down to St Ives. They were also receiving a little money from Barbara's father and getting rent from number 3 Mall Studios.

Barbara painted Dunluce white and planted vegetables; she had grown 600 tomatoes by the end of 1940. She taught drawing and painting to the triplets as well as to some neighbouring children and encouraged them all to express themselves freely. In September 1942 they moved to a bigger house, Chy-an-Kerris, or 'sky-and-cherries' as Ben called it, higher up the cliff, on Headland Road. Herbert Read and Margaret Gardiner came to visit in the summer of 1942, and a photograph shows them playing croquet with Nicholson on the lawn at Little Park Owles. With seven bedrooms at Chy-an-Kerris Barbara could now have her own studio. But they still had little income, and two careers and triplets to care for. Paul, who was at boarding school in Wales, also came to stay with them for some of the holidays. Alfred Wallis died in August 1942, having been transferred to a workhouse. Ben, Adrian and Sven Berlin fell out over what they could have done to help and how much Ben had paid Wallis for his work. Adrian arranged for Wallis's burial in St Ives Cemetery, with a 'sea view', as Barbara put it. As well as this conflict, Ben grew apart from Gabo and began to spend more and more time in London. Ben and Barbara grew further apart and by the Christmas of 1949 they had agreed to separate.

Ben wrote to Winifred during the war, telling her how much he missed her and the children. Winifred had moved to Boothby at the beginning of the war and stayed there until after her father's death in 1959, when she moved back to Bankshead. Winifred had also taken on a small farmstead called Banks Side and she was running a small school for about a dozen local children and was keeping bees. She wrote to Ben, to tell him how she had ploughed two ten-acre fields but then, through 'bitter tears', declared that he had 'cut the roads' on which they could meet on this 'human plane'.[4] Ben went to Paris in 1956 for an exhibition and he and Winifred decided to go on a drawing trip to Mallorca with their daughter, Kate. Ben developed asthma and left after a week. Her last letter to Ben, over a year before she died, thanked him for 'all you gave me'.[5]

Barbara stayed in St Ives. She moved into Trewyn Studio in December 1950 (now the Hepworth Museum and Sculpture Garden), which she had bought the previous year. Ben moved to Switzerland in 1958 with his third wife, the journalist and photographer Felicitas Vogler, who had come to St Ives to report on the Cornish artists. He and Vogler separated in 1971 and he moved back to England, first to Cambridge and then to Pilgrim's Lane in Hampstead, where he had lived for a while as a child. Barbara wrote to Ben, not long before she died, telling him that her life now centred on her bed, her television, radio and telephone. She hoped he would come and visit her. She died a year later in a fire in her studio in 1975. Ben died in Hampstead in 1982.

□

The Moores took over Ben and Barbara's studio in the Mall Studios after the war broke out as it was cheaper than their flat on Parkhill Road. They had put a strain on their finances by buying a new car, a Standard 8, and Moore needed money to frame his work for an upcoming exhibition at the Leicester Galleries. Chelsea School of Art stopped all teaching in the autumn of 1939 and, although it resumed in 1940 for two terms, it evacuated all students to Northampton, and Moore stopped teaching there altogether. The Clarks had abandoned their house at Lympne on the Kent coast and rented a Georgian house near Tetbury in Gloucestershire; after France fell to the Germans they urged Henry and Irina to do the same. The Moores spent a couple of weeks with the Clarks' friends in Gloucestershire, but they didn't find a place to rent. One evening in London, their car broke down, so they took the tube into town. They had not realised how many people were using the tube platforms as an air-raid shelter. 'I had never seen so many reclining figures,' Henry wrote; 'even the train tunnels seemed to be like the holes in my sculpture.'[6] He made some sketches and showed them to Clark, who persuaded him to join the War Artists' Advisory Committee. After an evening's drawing at Hampstead or Belsize Park tube station, he often dropped in on Jack Pritchard at Lawn Road for a drink.

One weekend in October 1940 Henry and Irina Moore went to stay with their friend the Labour MP Leonard Matters, in Perry Green near Much Hadham in Hertfordshire. When they got back to the Mall Studios, it was cordoned off and a policeman told them it had all been bombed. In fact number 7 was still standing, although it had suffered some damage and one sculpture was destroyed. They went back to stay with Matters and looked for a place to rent near by. They found half of a run-down seventeenth-century house called Hoglands, and Henry wrote to Jane Clark that he thought they might 'stay here for some time'.[7] Once they were settled, Jack sometimes took a train to have lunch with them, bringing a bottle of wine. He and Henry liked to have a snooze on a pile of hay in the garden after lunch. Not long after they moved in, Henry sold an elmwood sculpture to the surrealist Gordon Onslow Ford for £300, which was exactly what the owner of Hoglands wanted for a deposit, and so they were able to buy the house. The place was big enough to allow Henry the freedom to work on a much larger scale and he could rig up temporary outdoor studios when scaling up his sculptures. Irina gave birth to their daughter Mary in 1946 and they stayed at Perry Green for the rest of their lives.

□

Like Moore, John Piper was working for the War Artists' Advisory Committee, but his first commission was not a success. It was a series of pictures based on the Air Raid Precaution Control Rooms at Bristol and after two paintings Piper asked if he could work on something else. So he and Clark came up with the idea of a series of paintings of churches damaged by war. Given his newfound fascination with aerial photography Piper also offered his services to the Central Interpretation Unit of photographic intelligence, run by the RAF at nearby Medmenham. The Pipers became close to John and Penelope Betjeman during the war. By 1942 John and Myfanwy had two small children, Edward aged four and Clarissa, a baby, so Penelope helped Myfanwy find a housemaid and a horse and cart to get around the countryside. Betjeman nicknamed Myfanwy 'Goldilocks' and enjoyed swimming with her in the Thames. He began to compose poetry to her, including a nostalgic poem about being at Oxford, where they had never met. He called her his 'darling Prefect' in one letter, but after his death she 'dismissed outright any notion of love'.[8] The Pipers stayed at Fawley Bottom. John died there in 1992 and Myfanwy five years later.

□

Paul Nash, an important First World War artist, was given a full-time salary by the War Artists' Advisory Committee for his work with the Royal Air Force when the Second World War broke out. His initial drawings were rejected but he went on to produce four paintings, including *Totes Meer*, *Battle of Britain* and *Battle of Germany*, which are considered to be some of the best paintings of the war. Nash began to suffer from increasingly severe bouts of illness related to his asthma. He and Margaret moved from Eldon Grove in Hampstead to Oxford just before the war broke out, staying first at the Randolph Hotel and then in Holywell Street, before moving to a flat in Banbury Road. When they came to London they stayed at the Russell Hotel, and enjoyed the sense of camaraderie. On one occasion they went to Dover so that Paul could see the Spitfires fighting over the Channel. After the war Paul was advised by doctors to get some sea air, so they went to one of their favourite places, Boscombe, and visited Corfe, Swanage and Worth Matravers. On 11 July 1946 Nash died of a heart attack in his sleep at the hotel they were staying in. He was buried next to his father's grave at Langley Church. Margaret ensured that his unfinished autobiography, *Outline*, was published, and she organised a memorial exhibition at the Tate in 1948. Margaret died in a car accident in Oxfordshire in 1960.

□

Herbert and Ludo Read settled in Broom House, Beaconsfield, in 1937, just before their son Thomas was born. Their second child, Sophia, was born in October 1939, their third, Piers Paul, in 1941, and their fourth, Ben, in 1945. Ludo was ready for another but Herbert said it was time to 'call a halt'.[9] In April 1941, during one of the worst raids of the Blitz, when German aircraft dropped 100,000 tons of bombs and a thousand people were killed in one night, Read made his way to the Routledge office in Ludgate Hill, where he was a literary adviser and director. There was no transport so he walked, and he was struck by the way that, 'after a night of relentless bombing', people were not 'even bad-tempered' but simply 'normal, unnaturally normal', as was he.[10] Two months later Read described a domestic scene with Ludo spring-cleaning a bookshelf, the children running about 'naked in the garden' and 'only an occasional aeroplane to remind us of the war'. Friends from London came to stay, simply to get a good night's sleep.[11] T. S. Eliot asked if he could keep a suitcase of clothes at Broom House so that if his place was bombed he wouldn't lose all of his clothes at once.

Read had been keen to establish a contemporary art museum in London for some time. After several months of negotiation, in March 1939 he and Peggy Guggenheim seemed to have a feasible plan for a permanent collection with Read as director. He created a list of artworks and Clark told him he could borrow anything he liked from his private collection. Guggenheim requested that Read give up his post at the *Burlington* magazine, so he did. But in December 1939 she paid him £2,500 and told him it was all off. She had decided to set up an artists' colony in France instead. Read was extremely frustrated, and concerned about the future of contemporary art in Britain. Things did not improve when Clark told him, in passing, that abstract art and functional architecture were dead, and a 'damned good job too'. Read wrote to Ben in St Ives that he dreaded the revival of the 'picture with a story' and the 'Coldstream Guards forming fours behind their Führer'.[12] Ben was less concerned; he had faith in the power of abstract art. Read and Roland Penrose, among others, founded the Institute of Contemporary Art (ICA) in 1947.

On 21 March 1939 Louis MacNeice left his son Dan and the nanny, Miss Popper, with his sister in Highgate and went to America to give a series of lectures, organised by T. S. Eliot.[13] He, Isherwood and Auden gave a reading in New York. MacNeice met the writer Eleanor Clark during the trip and arranged a temporary lectureship at Cornell in order to spend more time with her. He was planning to bring his son over to America but in the end he left him with his father and stepmother in Ireland. Just before going back to the States for the Cornell job he took Margaret Gardiner to Belfast for the weekend and they ended up in bed together after a party. MacNeice felt guilty as he liked her 'very much' but hadn't 'even the beginnings of any romantic feelings for her'. She told him she would be back to normal soon enough.[14] Auden stayed in the US, teaching at Michigan, Swarthmore and Smith College, and became a US citizen in 1946. Thereafter he spent his summers in Europe and his winters in New York. Appointed professor of poetry at Oxford University in 1956, he gave three lectures a year. He died in his farmhouse in Austria in 1973 just after giving a reading at the Austrian Society of Literature.

MacNeice came back to London in 1940 and, unable to join the military services due to his eyesight, joined the features department at the BBC. At Stephen Spender's wedding in April 1941 Margaret Gardiner found Louis with a tearful Nancy, asking him, 'How *could* you? With that woman?' Later that evening Nancy found Louis and her new partner Michael Spender deep in conversation about polar exploration.[15] By 1942 Louis had married the Group Theatre actor and singer Hedli

Anderson. One morning Nancy found a note saying 'Darling, Hedli and I are getting married this afternoon' but it 'won't change anything between you and me'. Hedli was 'free' and 'dashing' and, according to Nancy, she wanted someone who would write her songs.[16] Over the years MacNeice began to drink more heavily and by the late 1950s, with their marriage under strain, Hedli eventually asked him to leave. In August 1963 MacNeice went caving in Yorkshire to gather sound effects for a radio play he was working on. He caught pneumonia and died in London, aged fifty-five. Nancy married Michael Spender in 1943 and they had one son before he died in a plane crash in 1945 in Germany. Nancy lived until she was ninety-one. Two of her portraits are held at the National Portrait Gallery and one at Sir John Soane's Museum.

□

Gropius and Ise arrived in New York on 17 March 1937. Josef and Anni Albers met them at the dock. On their first evening they went to the Cotton Club where Duke Ellington was playing. Joseph Hudnut from Harvard sent a telegram to say, 'Welcome to America where happiness and success await you.' He arranged for them to have lunch at the top of Radio City Music Hall and dinner with MoMA director Alfred Barr. There were already plans for a Bauhaus exhibition in honour of Gropius at MoMA. Ise wrote to the Pritchards that Hudnut and his wife were looking after them very well, 'almost like Jack and Molly'. It was an extremely sociable time. 'We were out every single night,' Ise remembered, and 'all the other nights we had to give parties to all these people.'[17] Then, a wealthy art patron and philanthropist, Mrs Storrow, offered Gropius a plot of land on her estate in Massachusetts, to build a house and rent it back from her. It seemed, Ise told Molly and Jack, 'a fairy tale', but when Walter started to plan the location of the lavatories she began 'to think it is real'.[18] Walter and Ise were given permission to bring all their furniture over from Germany and Ati enrolled in a local school in Concord. Gropius was pleased that the house was close to Walden Pond and Thoreau's simple hut.

Not long after they arrived Gropius negotiated with Hudnut to bring Marcel Breuer over from London. He came first for a visit, along with Herbert Bayer, and they all took a holiday on Planting Island, near Cape Cod. Moholy joined them, as did the curator Alexander Dorner (who became director of the Rhode Island School of Design) and his wife Lydia, who called it a 'Summer Bauhaus'. They all sent Ben and Barbara a postcard of New Bourne Bridge over Cape Cod Canal, signed Breuer, Gropius, Dorner, Bayer and 'heartiest greetings' from Moholy.[19] Moholy was in the process of establishing 'The New Bauhaus, American School of Design' in Chicago. He wanted Mondrian to join him, but as it wasn't set up yet Mondrian went to London. The New Bauhaus closed after one year due to financial difficulties, but in 1938 Moholy reopened the school in a former bakery on East Ontario Street, calling it the School of Design in Chicago. By 1944 it became simply the Institute of Design. His wife Sibyl became Moholy's editor and she ran the summer school. She felt that the spirit of openness they felt in Lawn Road was lacking in Chicago. Moholy began to write an account of his design curriculum, but in 1945 he was diagnosed with leukaemia and died the following year. His book, *Vision in Motion*, was published posthumously in 1947 and Sibyl wrote his biography. Moholy, she said, found a 'unique English capacity for friendship' where conversations were warm and stimulating and yet objective and unemotional.[20] Sibyl became an architectural historian and held teaching positions at the Rudolf Schaeffer School of Design in San Francisco, the University of California and then the Pratt Institute in New York before becoming a visiting professor at Columbia University.

□

Breuer had his farewell dinner in London at the Isobar in December 1937. He taught at Harvard from 1938 to 1946, before moving to New York. He was popular with his students who appreciated his 'spatial aesthetic' and his 'disarmingly simple' solutions to 'planning and structural problems'.[21] Gropius's house was such a success that Mrs Storrow offered Breuer the same deal. He was delighted and set to work. As a starting point, he used the fan-shaped living room and curved stone wall of the Gane Pavilion he had designed in Bristol in 1936. He wrote to Jack that it was a kind of 'cave with central heating'. When he and Constance Leighton got married in 1940 Calder gave them a large mobile as a wedding present, and it hung in the double-height living room. Constance was the secretary for Breuer and Gropius's architectural practice on Harvard Square – Walter Gropius and Marcel Breuer Associated Architects – set up in 1937 and disbanded in 1941. Breuer wrote to Jack in January 1939 and told him how busy they were. They had completed a large house in Pittsburgh that cost 'about $110,000', and they had designed the 'Pennsylvania-State Pavilion for the N.Y. World's Fair' and were busy with 'competitions, teaching, – and Isokon. No time to be bored.'[22]

□

The Isokon building in London survived the war; it was painted brown to prevent the Luftwaffe from using it as a navigation aid. In November 1939 Jack Pritchard wrote to the members of the Isobar to say that, in these difficult times, they were planning to rent out furnished flats on a short-term basis for at least one month and unfurnished flats for a year or more. The building was constructed out of reinforced concrete, the statement went on, and it 'has a high bank and trees at the back' so it is 'particularly safe'. The clubroom served as an inbuilt air-raid shelter, which meant that inhabitants could sit out air raids in comfort and style. And so 'if you or any of your friends have had to close your house and are looking for comfort and security with the possibility of companionship or privacy, ring us up.'[23] Jack also advertised in *The Times*, mentioning that it was a club 'renowned for cuisine in private air raid shelter'.[24] Jack desperately needed rent from the flats to cover the rates and the compulsory war damage insurance, which was £200 per annum. Two months after the war broke out he was £528 in debt.

Jack took out a life-insurance policy and closed the Isokon Furniture Company. Not long afterwards, the residents received a notice from Philip Harben, who had taken on a managerial role in the building, to say that 'for one night only' the warden for the area was coming to the Isobar at 6 p.m. to fit gas masks, and given the urgency of the situation he asked for full cooperation.[25] Harben later left to join the RAF, as did Wells Coates, who helped develop fighter aircraft, for which he was awarded an OBE.[26] There were some strange scenes in the Isobar during the Blitz. Some tenants 'brought down their bedding' and some liked to claim 'a particular patch as their own', but this was not always easy to arrange with those who wanted to dance.[27] The windows on the top floor were blown out on the second day of the Blitz in September 1940.

Agatha Christie and her husband, the archaeologist Max Mallowan, were among the respondents to the ad in *The Times*. Christie's home in South Kensington had been bombed, so they moved, first into flat 20 of the Isokon and then into flat 22. Christie volunteered at the chemist's dispensary at University College Hospital, a job that gave her useful material for her detective fiction. When Max had to go to Cairo with the intelligence branch of the RAF Christie was happy to have the company of the 'kindly people' at the Isokon, and she liked the 'informal and happy atmosphere' of the restaurant. All in all she spent six years in Lawn Road and published nine novels while she was there.

The Austrian architect Egon Riss arrived in 1939, when the Architects' Czech Relief Fund introduced him to Pritchard. He moved into flat 2 in February 1939 and became known as Chips. His brother Erwin also came, straight from a concentration camp in Germany in June 1939, but at the outbreak of war he was interned by the British authorities. As well as doing odd jobs, Egon Riss took over design at the Isokon Company as Breuer and Gropius had left. During the few months before the Company closed, Riss designed the 'Penguin Donkey' plywood shelf for holding paperbacks for Allen Lane of Penguin Books. Lane promised to promote it in 100,000 leaflets inside Penguin books. The first fifty 'Donkeys' were snapped up but production stalled because of the difficulty in getting hold of plywood. Riss also designed the 'Gull', a smaller bookstand that could be hung on a wall, and the 'Bottleship', which was closely related to the 'Donkey' but carried several bottles and glasses. Prototypes were made for these two but they were not put into production. Isokon Plus, the reincarnation of the Isokon Company, now sell the 'Donkey' mark two and three for over £500 each. As the war developed, Riss helped to protect the flats by creating what he called the 'Isokon Line' out of sandbags to preserve the windows and the open-air restaurant.[28]

When Paris fell to the Germans in June 1940 the British government began a mass evacuation scheme to remove children to safety. Jack and Molly agreed that she should take Jonathan and Jeremy to Canada. Beatrix Tudor-Hart, Jack's former lover, arranged for her daughter Jennifer to go to Canada to stay with her grandfather in Quebec. Molly found school places for the boys at Upper Canada College in Toronto and then she herself moved in with Walter and Ise Gropius in Massachusetts. She lived there on and off for the next two years, moving to a flat in Cambridge when the Gropius House became too crowded with visitors. Walter and Molly enjoyed riding together, and he helped her to get a post at the Psychological Clinic at Harvard where she worked on the structure and development of personality. Molly and Breuer did their best to get Isokon furniture made and sold in the US, but the timber restrictions during the war made it impossible. Molly returned to London in 1942 and the boys stayed at boarding school in Canada.

In 1962 Jack and Molly asked Jack's daughter Jennifer, who was by then an architect, to design them a holiday house on a plot of land in Blythburgh, Suffolk. They called it the Isokon. When they were in London they stayed in Lawn Road, but in December 1968 they sold the flats to the *New Statesman* for £67,500, hoping the magazine would continue to run the building as they had. Jack and Molly rented the penthouse flat. In 1972 the *New Statesman* sold the Isokon to Camden Council for £157,500, more than doubling their money. Two years later Molly and Jack moved permanently to Blythburgh. Almost twenty years later, Ken Livingstone, then chairman of housing for Camden Council, wanted to demolish the Isokon and build high-rise flats in its place. English Heritage stepped in and gave the building a Grade II listing. But in the 1990s the building was in a terrible state and the Labour councillor Gerry Harrison described the situation as a 'disgrace'. Sewage flowed 'down the balconies', the fabric was 'damp and crumbling' with no 'effective heat or sound insulation'. The building was, he said, 'simply a disaster'.[29] Nothing had improved by the late 1990s, there were burnt-out cars in the car park and a murder took place on one of the balconies. The last tenant moved out in November 1999. Camden Council put the building on the market. After an exhibition at Hampstead Town Hall (*Belsize 2000: A Living Suburb*), Camden decided to go with the £1.5 million bid from the Isokon Trust, Notting Hill Housing Group and Avanti Architects. Twenty-five of the units were ring-fenced for key workers (80 per cent for teachers and 20 per cent for the police) and eleven were sold on the open market. The beautifully renovated flats were officially reopened in 2005.

□

One of the most famous Hampstead residents of the 1930s was Sigmund Freud. In 1938 Freud reluctantly left Vienna and came to London, a move triggered in part by the questioning of his daughter, Anna, by the Gestapo. His son Ernst and family were already settled in London. He was eighty-two when he arrived and dying of cancer. He gave an interview for the BBC in which he said he had left his home in Vienna as a result of the German invasion and had come to England where he hoped to 'end his life in freedom'. At first he lived at 39 Elsworthy

Road in Primrose Hill, before moving to Maresfield Gardens in Hampstead. The Woolfs visited him and Leonard said there was something about him of 'a half-extinct volcano, something sombre, repressed, reserved' and that he gave him the feeling of 'great gentleness, but behind that, great strength'.[30] Dalí persuaded his friend Stefan Zweig to introduce him to his idol. Dalí sketched Freud's head, which he likened to a snail's shell, but Zweig wasn't sure if they should show Freud the results.

□

And so, as Read put it, 'the displacement due to the rise of the Nazis' created 'a continual stream of foreign artists passing through London'. They came to Hampstead and Belsize Park because we had 'prepared the way for them'. So, when 'Gropius, Moholy-Nagy, and Gabo and Mondrian came, they came to a situation that already existed and where they found, well, comrades'.[31] For Hepworth, their arrival made England seem suddenly 'alive and rich – the centre of an international movement in architecture and art'. It gave the British artists a new lease of life, and they felt 'carried on the crest of this robust and inspiring wave'. Because of the impending war they 'worked the harder to lay strong foundations for the future' and sought 'an understanding of the true relationship between architecture, painting, and sculpture'.[32]

After the war they all dispersed, 'never to reassemble', wrote Read, but the scattered artists had a sense of 'confidence and a courage' they would not have had if they hadn't come together with 'spontaneous enthusiasm' generated when an 'arbitrary chance' brings together 'spirits with the same ideals and aspirations'.[33] At his eighty-fifth birthday party in Harvard, after cutting the cake Gropius raised a glass to Molly and Jack 'for saving our lives'.[34]

ACKNOWLEDGEMENTS

Writing a group biography involves a large number of people who have helped in many different ways. I first want to thank my editor Michael Fishwick and my agent Anna Webber for their expert guidance and support throughout. I am extremely grateful to friends and colleagues who have read drafts of the book and have helped to shape it into its current form. In particular Dawn Ades, Sarah Bilston, Sophie Bowness, Ophelia Field, Judith Jammers, Jeremy Lewison, Jovan Nicholson and Piers Paul Read. Their comments and suggestions have been invaluable.

Copyright holders have been very generous with their permissions — in particular Sophie Bowness, Jovan Nicholson, Sally Pritchard, Susan Wright and Peter Suschitzky. So many librarians and archivists have helped but I would especially like to thank Bridget Gillies at UEA, Frieda Midgley at Kettle's Yard and the curators and archivists at the Tate Gallery Archive. I am very grateful to Sarah Turner at the Paul Mellon Centre for inviting me to give a talk about the project and to the experts who have steered me along the way, including Ana Nyburg, Michael Paraskos, Charmian Brinson, Celia Scott, Robert M. Maxwell, Alan Powers and Elizabeth Darling. And thanks to everyone at Bloomsbury and in particular, Lauren Whybrow for her tireless efforts and enthusiasm and to Lilidh Kendrick and Peter James.

Friends and colleagues have helped me so much. I would like to thank Rebecca Hyam and Adam Pettit at Highgate for giving me the time to write and to all my colleagues in the English and Art History Departments for their warmth, generosity and intellect. And for their support, encouragement and conversation over the years I would like to thank Rebecca Beasley, Corinna Csáky, Ben Bond, Nicola Kohn, Chris Taylor, Kitty Sellars, Theo Tait, Jessica Ferm, Imogen Slaughter, Lottie Moggach, Lucy Jeal, Eliane Glaser, Adam Smyth, Eleanor Birne, Lara Feigel, Alex Harris, Devorah Baum, Josh Appignanesi, Lisa Appignanesi, Haidy Geismar, Joanna Kavenna, David Dwan, Aida Edemariam, Roland Chambers, Susan Chambers, Jenny McCartney, Dennis Duncan, Nikita Lalwani, Vik Sharma, Yasmin Hai, Paul Berczeller, Paul Myerscough, Ananda Rutherford, Sam van Schaik, Chloe Houston Mandy, Rachel Donadio, Melissa Katsoulis, Aimée Brown Price, Rosanna Gardner and Hannah Westland. And finally, thank you to my family: to my parents Mavis and Robert Maclean, for everything, including taking me to the Ben Nicholson exhibition at the Tate in 1993, and to my sister Sarah and all of my extended family for their wonderful support. Most importantly, thank you to my husband Ben and my children Gwen and Henry. Life and work overlap and I dedicate this book to them.

ILLUSTRATION CREDITS

xii: Barbara in Happisburgh, Norfolk, 1931; Tate Gallery Archive, Barbara Hepworth © Bowness

xiv–xv: On the beach in Happisburgh, Ivon Hitchens, Irina Moore, Henry Moore, Barbara Hepworth, Ben Nicholson and Mary Jenkins (originally Stannard); reproduced with permission of the Henry Moore Foundation

xvi: Barbara in the farmhouse, Happisburgh, Norfolk, 1931; Tate Gallery Archive, Barbara Hepworth © Bowness

3: Ben and Winifred Nicholson, Westmoreland, early 1920s; Tate Gallery Archive © Tate

9: Alfred Wallis and Ben Nicholson at 3 Back Road West, St Ives; Tate Gallery Archive

11: John Skeaping and Barbara Hepworth playing musical instruments; © Hulton-Deutsch Collection/ CORBIS/Corbis via Getty Images

13: Barbara Hepworth and John Skeaping, 1928; © Fox Photos / Getty Images

14: Barbara Hepworth, *Doves (Group)*, Parian marble, 1927 (BH 3); Manchester City Galleries / Bridgeman Images, Barbara Hepworth © Bowness

16: Frognal Lane, Hampstead; © Hulton Archive / Getty Images

20: Henry and Irina in the studio at Parkhill Road, Hampstead; © reproduced with permission of the Henry Moore Foundation

26: Barbara Hepworth, *Pierced Form*, Pink alabaster, 1932 (BH 35), destroyed in war, photograph by Paul Laib; courtesy of Witt Library, Courtauld Institute of Art, London, Barbara Hepworth © Bowness

28: Winifred Nicholson, *The Artist's Children, Kate and Jake, Isle of Wight*, 1931-2, purchased from the artist, with the assistance of the Friends of Bristol Art Gallery, 1971; Bridgeman Images © Winifred Nicholson Estate

29: Barbara and Ben on the Serpentine; Tate Gallery Archive

30: Ben and Kate Nicholson; Tate Gallery Archive © Tate

34: Ben Nicholson in Dieppe; Tate Gallery Archive, Barbara Hepworth © Bowness

34: Barbara Hepworth in Dieppe; Tate Gallery Archive © Tate

36: Ben and Barbara in the Mall Studios; Tate Gallery Archive © Tate

37: Photographs from Barbara Hepworth's photograph album of the exhibition *Carvings by Barbara Hepworth, paintings by Ben Nicholson* at Arthur Tooth & Sons in London (October-November 1932); Barbara Hepworth © Bowness

41: Barbara Hepworth, *Self-portrait photogram*, c. 1932-3; Tate Gallery Archive, Barbara Hepworth © Bowness

43: Ben Nicholson, *Relief (1934)*; © Angela Verren Taunt 2018. All rights reserved, DACS

46-7: Page from Barbara Hepworth's photograph album; Barbara Hepworth © Bowness

52–3: Lawn Road Flats by John Maltby; UEA Pritchard Papers

55: Wells Coates, 1937, by Howard Coster; © National Portrait Gallery

58: Cresta Silks dress shop Brompton Road, 1930; © Architectural Press Archive / RIBA Collections

62: Molly and Jack with their children Jonathan and Jeremy on Hampstead Heath, 1934; UEA Pritchard Papers, courtesy of Sally Pritchard.

65: Weissenhof Estate, Stuttgart; © Freunde der Weissenhofsiedlung e.V.

68: Floor plans for Lawn Road Flats, Wells Coates, 1933; UEA Pritchard Papers © Wells Coates Estate

70: Ursula and Ernő Goldfinger, photograph by Eileen Agar; Tate Gallery Archive © Tate

77: The opening of Lawn Road Flats, 9 July 1934; UEA Pritchard Papers © Edith Tudor Hart, courtesy of Peter Suschitzky

78: Furnished studio sitting room at Lawn Road Flats; © Hulton Archive / Getty Images

85: The Sun House, Frognal Way, Hampstead; © Estate of Jack Howe, courtesy of Susan Wright

86: Bauhaus campus, Dessau; © Ullstein bild / Getty Images

89: Walter and Ise Gropius, 1929; © SZ Photo / Scherl / Bridgeman Images

99: Isokon Furniture Company 'trademark' designed by László Moholy-Nagy, 1936; UEA Pritchard Papers © Pritchard Estate, courtesy of Sally Pritchard

100: László Moholy-Nagy by Lucia Moholy; © Lucia Moholy

103: Barbara, Ben and the triplets in the Moholy-Nagy's garden; private collection © Moholy-Nagy

105: Breuer, Ise and Walter Gropius on the terrace of the Lawn Road Flats, July 1935; UEA Pritchard Papers

106: Page from a leaflet advertising Breuer's Long Chair designed by László Moholy-Nagy 1935; © The Stapleton Collection / Bridgeman Images

110: The Isobar, designed by Breuer and Yorke; Dell & Wainwright/RIBA Collections

111: Isobar menu, 26 May 1938; UEA Pritchard Papers, courtesy of Sally Pritchard

116: Ise and Walter Gropius leaving London; UEA Pritchard Papers © Jack Howe, courtesy of Susan Wright

120: Herbert Read at the Mall Studios, by Howard Coster; National Portrait Gallery

137: Paul Nash by Helen Muspratt, 1932; © National Portrait Gallery

141: Photograph of Ben's hands from *Unit One* catalogue, from the collection of Dawn Ades

142: *Unit One* catalogue, from the collection of Dawn Ades
149: Eileen Agar, Tate Gallery Archive
151: The Surrealist Exhibition, 1936; Tate Gallery Archive
154: Lee Miller at Lambe Creek, 1937; © Roland Penrose Estate, England 2020
157: *Objects and Poems* exhibition at the London Gallery, 1937; © Lee Miller Archives, England 2020
163: Edna Ginesi, Henry Moore and Barbara Hepworth in Paris, 1922; © reproduced with permission of the Henry Moore Foundation
167: Irina and Henry Moore on their wedding day, July 1929; © reproduced with permission of the Henry Moore Foundation
168: Henry Moore, *Composition*, LH 99, Blue hornton stone, 1931; © reproduced with permission of the Henry Moore Foundation
181: John and Myfanwy Piper; © E H McCormick Papers, E H McCormick Research Library, Auckland Art Gallery Toi o Tāmaki, gift of Linda Gill, 2015
184: 1 Elm Road, Kettle's Yard Archive
190: *Abstract & Concrete* exhibition, Lefevre Gallery, 1936, Tate Gallery Archive
193: Naum Gabo, *Construction: Stone with Collar*, 1936-7 Tate Gallery Archive; © Gabo Estate, represented by the Tate
200: W.H. Auden; © Eileen Darby / Getty Images
200: Louis MacNeice; © Kurt Hutton / Getty Images
218: Mondrian's studio in Paris; © ullstein bild/ullstein bild / Getty Images
223: Alexander Calder's exhibition at the Mayor Gallery, 1937 © SZ Photo / Scherl / Bridgeman Images
225: Mondrian in Hampstead photographed by John Cecil Stephenson, Tate Gallery Archive © Estate of John Cecil Stephenson
228: Piet Mondrian, *Composition in Yellow, Blue and Red*, 1937-42, Tate Gallery Archive

SELECTED BIBLIOGRAPHY

Christopher Andreae, *Winifred Nicholson* (Farnham: Lund Humphries, 2009)

Shulamith Behr and Marian Malet (ed.s), *Arts in Exile in Britain 1933-45* (Amsterdam/New York: Editions Rodopi 2005)

Roger Berthoud, *The Life of Henry Moore* (London: Faber & Faber, 1987)

Sophie Bowness (ed.), *Barbara Hepworth: Writings and Conversations* (London: Tate Publishing, 2015)

Sophie Bowness and Christopher Green, *Sculpture and Painting in the 1930s* (London: Hazlitt Holland-Hibbert, 2019)

Sophie Bowness, *The Sculptor in the Studio* (London: Tate Publshing, 2017)

David Burke, *The Lawn Road Flats* (Woodbridge, The Boydell Press, 2014)

Sherban Cantacuzino, *Wells Coates: A Monograph* (London: Gordon Fraser 1978)

Andrew Causey (ed.), *Paul Nash: Writings on Art* (Oxford: Oxford University Press, 2000)

Emma Chambers (ed.), *Paul Nash* (London: Tate Publishing, 2016)

Sarah Checkland, *Ben Nicholson: The Vicious Circles of his Life and Art* (London: John Murray, 2000)

Eleanor Clayton (ed.) *Lee Miller and Surrealism in Britain* (London: Lund Humphries, 2018)

Laura Cohn, *The Door to a Secret Room: A Portrait of Wells Coates* (Aldershot: Scolar Press, 1999)

Penelope Curtis and Chris Stephens (ed.s), *Barbara Hepworth: Sculpture for a Modern World* (London, Tate Publishing, 2015)

Elizabeth Darling, *Wells Coates* (London: RIBA Publishing, 2012)

Leyla Daybelge and Magnus Englund, *Isokon and the Bauhaus in Britain* (London: Pavilion, 2019)

Sally Festing, *Barbara Hepworth: A Life of Forms* (London: Penguin, 1995)

Juliet Gardner, *The Thirties: An Intimate History* (London: Harper Press, 2011)

Mark Glazebrook, *Unit One: Spirit of the 30's* (London: Mayor Gallery, 1984)

Christopher Green and Barnaby Wright (ed.s), *Mondrian II Nicholson in Parallel* (London: Courtauld Gallery, 2012)

Alastair Grieve, *Isokon* (London: Isokon Plus, 2004)

Martin Hammer and Christina Lodder, *Constructing Modernity: The Art and Career of Naum Gabo* (New Haven/London: Yale University Press, 2000)

Alexandra Harris, *Romantic Moderns: English Writers, Artists and the Imagination from Virginia Woolf to John Piper* (London: Thames and Hudson, 2014)

Reginald Isaacs, *Gropius: An Illustrated Biography of the Creator of the Bauhaus* (London: Bullfinch, 1983)

James King, *The Last Modern: A Life of Herbert Read* (London: Weidenfeld & Nicolson, 1990)

Bruce Laughton, *William Coldstream* (Hew Haven: Yale University Press, 2004)

Jeremy Lewison *Henry Moore* (London: Taschen, 2006)

Jeremy Lewison, *Ben Nicholson* (London: Tate Publishing, 1993);

Jeremy Lewison, *Ben Nicholson: The Years of Experiment 1919-39* (Cambridge: Kettle's Yard Gallery, 1983)

Fiona MacCarthy, *Walter Gropius: Visionary Founder of the Bauhaus* (London: Faber & Faber, 2019)

Francesco Manacorda and Michael White (eds), *Mondrian and his Studios: Colour in Space* (London: Tate Publishing, 2014)

Joan Marter, *Alexander Calder* (Cambridge: Cambridge University Press, 1991)

Robert McCarter, *Breuer* (London: Phaidon Press, 2016)

Jovan Nicholson, *Art and Life 1920–1931: Ben Nicholson, Winifred Nicholson, Christopher Wood, Alfred Wallis, William Staite Murray* (London: Philip Wilson, 2013)

Jovan Nicholson, *Winifred Nichoslon: Liberation of Colour* (London: Philip Wilson Publishers, 2016)

Michael Paraskos (ed.), *Rereading Read* (London: Freedom Press, 2007)

Antony Penrose, *The Lives of Lee Miller* (London: Thames and Hudson, 1985)

Jed Perl, *Calder: The Conquest of Time: The Early Years, 1898–1940* (New Haven/London: Yale University Press, 2017)

Alan Powers, *Modern Art and Design in Britain and America* (London: Thames and Hudson, 2019)

Benedict Read and David Thistlewood (ed.s), *A British Vision of World Art: Herbert Read* (London: Lund Humphries, 1993)

Richard Read, *Art and its Discontents: The Early Life of Adrian Stokes* (Aldershot: Ashgate, 2002)

Michel Seuphor, *Piet Mondrian: Life and Work* (London: Thames & Hudson, 1957).

Michael J Sidnell *Dances of Death 'The Group Theatre of London in the Thirties'* (London: Faber and Faber, 1984)

Frances Spalding, *John Piper, Myfanwy Piper: Lives in Art* (Oxford: Oxford University Press, 2009)

Jon Stallworthy, *Louis MacNeice* (London: Faber & Faber, 1995)

Nigel Warburton, *Ernö Goldfinger: The Life of an Architect* (London: Routledge, 2003)

NOTES

PROLOGUE

1 Cumberland became Cumbria in 1974.
2 TGA (Tate Gallery Archive) 8717.1.1.46.
3 TGA 8717.1.1.47.
4 TGA 8514.1, Memories of Ben Nicholson by Douglas Jenkins, writing to Sir Alan Bowness (16 November 1982).
5 Barbara Hepworth, *A Pictorial Autobiography* (Bath: Adams & Dart, 1970), p. 19.
6 TGA 8514.2, Memories of Ben Nicholson by Anthony Lousada.
7 Hepworth, *Pictorial Autobiography*, p. 20.
8 TGA 8514.1, Memories of Ben Nicholson by Douglas Jenkins, writing to Sir Alan Bowness (16 November 1982).
9 Sarah Checkland, *Ben Nicholson: The Vicious Circles of his Life and Art* (London: John Murray, 2000), p. 98.
10 Barbara Hepworth, 'Contemporary English Sculptors' (April 1930), in Sophie Bowness (ed.), *Barbara Hepworth: Writings and Conversations* (London: Tate Publishing, 2015), p. 14.
11 Ben Nicholson's statement for Unit One, quoted in James King, *The Last Modern: A Life of Herbert Read* (London: Weidenfeld & Nicolson, 1990), p. 120.
12 TGA 8717.1.1.52, Hepworth to Nicholson (27 September 1931).
13 TGA, 8717.1.1.52; TGA 8717.1.1.53.
14 TGA 8717.1.1.52 (28 September, postmarked 29 September).

CHAPTER ONE

1 Letter 5 October 1914, quoted in Jeremy Lewison, *Ben Nicholson* (London: Tate Publishing, 1993), p. 14.

2 Winifred Nicholson, *Unknown Colour: Paintings, Letters, Writings* (London: Faber & Faber, 1987), p. 32.
3 Ibid., pp. 31–2.
4 Sarah Checkland, *Ben Nicholson: The Vicious Circles of his Life and Art* (London: John Murray, 2000), p. 32.
5 Winifred Nicholson to E. J. Hooper, Easter Monday 1921, quoted in Jovan Nicholson, *Art and Life 1920–1931: Ben Nicholson, Winifred Nicholson, Christopher Wood, Alfred Wallis, William Staite Murray* (London: Philip Wilson, 2013), p. 12.
6 Checkland, *Ben Nicholson*, pp. 49, 51.
7 Nicholson, *Unknown Colour*, p. 36.
8 Winifred to E. J., 25 January 1922, quoted in Nicholson, *Art and Life*, p. 13.
9 Checkland, *Ben Nicholson*, p. 49.
10 Ibid., p. 51.
11 Ibid., p. 54. The whereabouts of the painting of the mandolin is unknown but a photograph of it is reproduced in Christopher Andreae, *Winifred Nicholson* (Farnham: Lund Humphries, 2009), p. 53.
12 Andreae, *Winifred Nicholson*, p. 59.
13 Nicholson, *Unknown Colour*, p. 36.
14 *Daily Mail*, 7 March 1924.
15 David Alan Mellor, 'A Spectral Modernity', in Emma Chambers (ed.), *Paul Nash* (London: Tate Publishing, 2016), pp. 23–33 at p. 24.
16 Nicholson, *Unknown Colour*, pp. 38, 64.
17 Andreae, *Winifred Nicholson*, p. 70.
18 Quoted in Lewison, *Ben Nicholson*, p. 24.
19 Nicholson, quoted in Elizabeth Fisher and Andrew Naine (eds), *Alfred Wallis: Ships and Boats* (Cambridge: Kettle's Yard, 2012), p. 14.
20 Checkland, *Ben Nicholson*, p. 82; Nicholson, *Unknown Colour*, p. 50; Ben Nicholson to Helen Sutherland, 30 September 1929, Helen Sutherland Archive, TGA.
21 Eleanor Birne, 'At Kettle's Yard', *London Review of Books*, vol. 36, no. 8, 17 April 2014, p. 18.
22 Quoted in Richard Ingleby, *An English Painter* (London: A&B, 1995), p. 273.
23 Quoted in Nicholson, *Art and Life*, p. 42.
24 Ibid., p. 54.

25 Rachel Smith discussed this at a conference on Hepworth at the Henry Moore Institute in a paper entitled 'Becoming Barbara Hepworth' on 14 February 2018.
26 Leo Walmsley, *So Many Loves* (Glasgow: Pan Books, 1947, first published 1944), p. 258.
27 Barbara Hepworth, *A Pictorial Autobiography* (Bath: Adams & Dart, 1970), p. 12.
28 Walmsley, *So Many Loves*, p. 275.
29 'New Studios, The Mall Park Road, Haverstock Hill', *Architect*, 17 August 1872, quoted in *Belsize 2000: A Living Suburb* (London: Belsize Conservation Area Advisory Committee, 2000), p. 76.
30 Richard Carline, Foreword, in *Hampstead Artists Past and Present* (London: Hampstead Artists Council, 1946), exhibition catalogue, p. 3.
31 'Belsize: A Living Suburb 2000', in *Belsize 2000: A Living Suburb*, p. 56.
32 It was succeded by the London Borough of Camden in 1965.
33 Geoffrey Grigson, *Recollections: Mainly of Writers and Artists* (London: Chatto & Windus/The Hogarth Press, 1984), p. 56.
34 Margaret Gardiner, *Barbara Hepworth: A Memoir* (Edinburgh: The Salamander Press, 1982), pp. 21, 10.
35 Hepworth, *Pictorial Autobiography*, p. 17.
36 John Skeaping, *Drawn from Life: An Autobiography* (London: Collins, 1977), pp. 91, 94.
37 Hepworth, *Pictorial Autobiography*, p. 17.
38 Roger Berthoud, *The Life of Henry Moore* (London: Faber & Faber, 1987), p. 51; Sally Festing suggests that Hepworth and Moore had an affair – see her *Barbara Hepworth: A Life of Forms* (London: Penguin, 1995), p. 73; interview with Nick Skeaping, quoted in Checkland, *Ben Nicholson*, p. 116.
39 Skeaping, *Drawn from Life*, pp. 81, 91.
40 Ibid., pp. 91–2.
41 TGA 8717.1.1.49.
42 TGA 8717.1.4 (early August? 1931).

CHAPTER TWO

1 Mary Baker Eddy, *Science and Health with Key to the Scriptures* (Boston: Christian Science Publishing Company, 1875), 234:27.

2 Margaret Gardiner, *A Scatter of Memories* (London: Free Association Books, 1988), p. 1.
3 KYA (Kettle's Yard Archive) Helen Sutherland to Jim Ede (November 1931).
4 TGA 8717.1.1.55.
5 Hepworth owned two copies of Eddy's *Science and Health* as well as a complete concordance to that work. She also owned Eddy's *Miscellaneous Writings* (1924, first published 1896) and a later edition of her *Prose Works* (*c.* 1966). All held in the Tate Archive, currently being catalogued. She also gave a pocket-book version of *Science and Health* dedicated to Jack Skeaping with love when they were in Florence in April 1925.
6 Eddy, *Science and Health*, 310:6.
7 TGA 8717.1.56 (postmarked 2 October).
8 TGA 8717.1.1.57 (3 October? postmarked 4 October); TGA 8717.1.1.58 (postmarked 5 October, readdressed to 15 St Leonard's Terrace, Chelsea, London SW3).
9 TGA 8717.1.1.62 (postmarked 27 October 1931).
10 TGA 1.1.1715 (postmarked 13 December 1931).
11 TGA 9323.1.41 (postmarked Fishbourne, December 1931).
12 Sarah Checkland, *Ben Nicholson: The Vicious Circles of his Life and Art* (London: John Murray, 2000), p. 102.
13 TGA 9323.1.41; TGA 9323.1.42.
14 TGA 8717.1.1.64 (postmarked 1 February 1932).
15 TGA 8717.1.1.64 (postmarked 1 February 1932).
16 TGA 9323.3.8.
17 TGA 20321.1.144.7 (15 May 1932 from Par, Cornwall).
18 TGA 20321.1.144.9 (18 May 1932).
19 TGA 8717.1.1.68 (postmarked 16 May 1932 to Penpillick House).
20 TGA 8717.1.1.72 (postmarked 23 May 1932 to Penpillick House).
21 TGA 20132.1.144.11 (21 May 1932).
22 KYA Ben Nicholson to Jim Ede (1932), File 4.
23 TGA 20132.1.144.12 (19 July 1932); TGA 1.1.1718 (30 July 1932).
24 TGA 8717.1.1.88 (postmarked 25 July 1932, 11.30 p.m.).
25 TGA 8717.1.1.95.
26 TGA 8717.1.1.74 (no envelope, no date, Thursday).
27 TGA 8717.1.1.72.
28 TGA 8717.1.1.82 (postmarked 22 July 1932).

29 TGA 8717.1.1.105.
30 Sophie Bowness, 'Ben Nicholson and Georges Braque: Dieppe and Varengeville in the 1930s', in Caroline Collier and Julia MacKenzie (eds), *The Dieppe Connection: The Town and its Artists from Turner to Braque* (Brighton: Herbert Press, 1992), pp. 44–52.
31 Ben to Nicolette Gray, 14 January 1966, in Penelope Curtis and Chris Stephens (eds), *Barbara Hepworth: Sculpture for a Modern World* (London: Tate Publishing, 2015), p. 24.
32 TGA 8717.1.1.104 (5 September 1932).
33 TGA 20132.1.144.21 (6 September 1932).
34 TGA 8717.1.1.106 (7 September 1932).
35 TGA 8717.1.1.103 (3 September 1932).
36 Quoted in Checkland, *Ben Nicholson*, p. 111.
37 Adrian Stokes, *Spectator*, 3 November 1933, quoted in James King, *The Last Modern: A Life of Herbert Read* (London: Weidenfeld & Nicolson, 1990), p. 124, and in Barbara Hepworth, *A Pictorial Autobiography* (Bath: Adams & Dart, 1970), pp. 21, 29.
38 Quoted in Barbara Hepworth, 'Contemporary English Sculptors' (April 1930), in Sophie Bowness (ed.), *Barbara Hepworth: Writings and Conversations* (London: Tate Publishing, 2015), p. 17.
39 Quoted in Checkland, *Ben Nicholson*, p. 112.
40 TGA 20132.1.44.25 (17 December 1932).
41 TGA 20132.1.44.26; 27.
42 TGA 8717.1.1.118 (20 December 1932).
43 TGA 20132.1.44.124 (25 December 1932).
44 TGA 8717.1.1.119 (21 December); 123 (24 December); 124 (25 December 1932).
45 Bowness, 'Ben Nicholson and Georges Braque', p. 46.
46 TGA 20132.1.144.33 (6 January 1933).
47 Quoted in Checkland, *Ben Nicholson*, p. 117.
48 Hepworth, *Pictorial Autobiography*, p. 23.
49 Sophie Bowness, 'Carved with Light', www.tate.org.uk/context-comment/articles/carved-light.
50 TGA 8717.3.1.19 (30 November 1966), https://www.tate.org.uk/art/archive/items/tga-8717-3-1-19/first-draft-of-an-article-by-ben-nicholson-with-editing/2.
51 Christopher Green, 'Hepworth/Nicholson: Sculpture and Painting in the 1930s – "A Perfect Unity"', in *Barbara Hepworth/*

Ben Nicholson: Sculpture and Painting in the 1930s, curated by Sophie Bowness and Christopher Green (London: Hazlitt Holland-Hibbert, 2019), p. 20.

52 TGA 8717.1.1.156 (5 December 1933).

53 TGA 20132.1.144.57 (12 December 1933).

54 23 December 1933, in Checkland, *Ben Nicholson*, p. 129.

55 Ibid., p. 130.

56 Roger Berthoud, *The Life of Henry Moore* (London: Faber & Faber, 1987), p. 126; John Summerson, *Ben Nicholson* (London: Penguin, 1948).

57 Quoted in Checkland, *Ben Nicholson*, p. 137.

58 Margaret Gardiner, *Barbara Hepworth: A Memoir* (Edinburgh: The Salamander Press, 1982), p. 36.

59 TGA 8717.1.1.191.

60 Gardiner, *Barbara Hepworth*, p. 36.

61 Hepworth, *Pictorial Autobiography*, p. 31.

62 Gardiner, *Barbara Hepworth*, p. 41.

63 Quoted in Checkland, *Ben Nicholson*, pp. 139–40.

64 Quoted in ibid., p. 140.

65 TGA 8717.1.1.203 (postmarked 12 January 1935).

66 TGA 8717.1.1.201 (postmarked 4 January 1935).

67 TGA 8717.1.1.206; TGA 8717.1.1.206.214.

68 www.tate.org.uk/context-comment/video/barbara-hepworth-and-ben-nicholson.

69 TGA 8717.1.1.217 (24 December 1935).

70 Cindy Nemser, 'Conversation with Barbara Hepworth', *Feminist Art Journal* (Brooklyn), vol. 2, no. 2, Spring 1973, quoted in Hepworth, 'Contemporary English Sculptors', pp. 251, 252.

CHAPTER THREE

1 The name Isokon came from the idea of isometric unit construction favoured by Coates and was the name of Coates and Pritchard's company.

2 TGA 9120.71 Ben Nicholson to Wells Coates (2 August 1934).

3 Jack Pritchard, *View from a Long Chair: The Memoirs of Jack Pritchard* (London: Routledge, 1984), p. 78.

4 Alastair Grieve, *Isokon: For Ease, For Ever* (London: Isokon Plus, 2004), p. 13.

5 Letter to Marion Grove, 5 December 1927, quoted in Sherban Cantacuzino, *Wells Coates: A Monograph* (London: Gordon Fraser, 1978), p. 11.
6 Letter to Marion Grove, 30 March 1926, quoted in Cantacuzino, *Wells Coates*, p. 11.
7 Patrick Heron, 25 February 1973, quoted in Cantacuzino, *Wells Coates*, p. 43.
8 Leyla Daybelge and Magnus Englund, *Isokon and the Bauhaus in Britain* (London: Pavilion, 2019), p. 34.
9 Letters quoted in Laura Cohn, *The Door to a Secret Room: A Portrait of Wells Coates* (Aldershot: Scolar Press, 1999), pp. 64, 65, 68, 71.
10 Cantacuzino, *Wells Coates*, p. 16; Farouk Hafiz Elgohary, 'Wells Coates and his Position in the Beginning of the Modern Movement in England', PhD thesis, University of London, 1966.
11 Deirdre Sharp, 'Jack Pritchard: A Design Classic and the (Second) Most Ugly Building in England', in *Belsize 2000: A Living Suburb* (London: Belsize Conservation Area Advisory Committee, 2000), pp. 88–96 at p. 89.
12 Pritchard, *Long Chair*, pp. 38, 39.
13 Daybelge and Englund, *Isokon*, p. 17.
14 Pritchard, *Long Chair*, p. 42.
15 Ibid., pp. 68, 69, 70.
16 David Burke, *The Lawn Road Flats: Spies, Writers and Artists* (Woodbridge: Boydell Press, 2014), p. 22.
17 Dora to Bertrand, 6 October 1927, in Nicholas Griffin (ed.), *The Selected Letters of Bertrand Russell*, vol. II: *The Public Years, 1914–1970* (London: Routledge, 2013), p. 267.
18 Bertrand Russell, *Autobiography* (London: Routledge, 1998, first published 1971), p. 390.
19 Pritchard, *Long Chair*, pp. 73, 75.
20 Ibid., pp. 60, 61.
21 Grieve, *Isokon*, p. 5; Burke, *The Lawn Road Flats*, p. 18.
22 Quoted in Cohn, *The Door to a Secret Room*, pp. 134, 135.
23 13 July 1930, to Jack Pritchard, quoted in Fiona MacCarthy, Introduction to Pritchard, *Long Chair*, p. 12.
24 Daybelge and Englund, *Isokon*, p. 8; Pritchard, *Long Chair*, p. 57.
25 Pritchard, *Long Chair*, p. 79.
26 Letter from Wells to Jack, UEAA (University of East Anglia Archive) PP (Pritchard Papers) 23/1 (12 August 1931).

27 Jack Pritchard, 'The Making of the Lawn Road Flats', in *Belsize 2000*, pp. 82–7 at p. 82.
28 Sharp, 'Jack Pritchard', p. 91.
29 Pritchard, 'The Making of the Lawn Road Flats', p. 82.
30 Nigel Warburton, *Goldfinger: The Life of an Architect* (London: Routledge, 2003), p. 82.
31 Pritchard, *Long Chair*, p. 80.
32 UEAA PP 16/1/2/43 (15 July 1932).
33 UEAA PP 16/1/1/16 Wells to Molly (5 October 1932).
34 UEAA PP 16/1/1/22 Wells to Jack (26 November 1932).
35 UEAA PP 16/1/2/2 Isokon Company to Wells (8 February 1933).
36 UEAA PP 16/1/2/3 Wells to Graham Maw (9 February 1933).
37 UEAA PP 16/1/2/6 Wells to Molly (20 March 1933).
38 UEAA PP16/1/2/21 Wells to Jack (19 May 1933).
39 UEAA PP 16/1/2/31 (14 June 1933).
40 UEAA PP 16/1/2/36 (3 July 1933).
41 UEAA PP 16/1/2/87 (29 December 1933).
42 UEAA PP 16/1/3/33 (17 February 1934).
43 UEAA PP 16/1/3/34 (20 February 1934).
44 UEAA PP 16/1/3/38 (27 February 1934).
45 UEAA PP 16/1/3/46 (5 March 1934).
46 UEAA PP 16/1/3/51 (7 March 1934).
47 UEAA PP 16/1/3/68 (26 March 1934).
48 UEAA PP 16/1/3/71 (28 March 1934).
49 Cantacuzino, *Wells Coates*, p. 16.
50 Hilary Spurling, *Anthony Powell: Dancing to the Music of Time* (London: Hamish Hamilton, 2017), p. 170.
51 Pritchard, *Long Chair*, p. 83.
52 Burke, *The Lawn Road Flats*, p. 34.
53 Grieve, *Isokon*, p. 13.
54 UEAA PP 16/1/3/80 (10 April 1934).
55 UEAA PP 16/1/3/176 (1 June 1934); UEAA PP 16/1/3/184 (4 June 1934).
56 UEAA PP 16/1/3/225 (4 July 1934).
57 UEAA PP 16/2/23/3 (Molly's speech).
58 *Yorkshire Observer*, 10 July 1934; *Birmingham Post*, 14 July 1934; *New Statesman and Nation*, 13 July 1934; *Daily Mirror*, 13 November 1934; *Cabinet Maker*, 14 July 1934.

59 UEAA PP 16/1/3/335 (30 October 1934).
60 UEAA PP 16/1/3/338 (3 November 1934).
61 UEAA PP 16/1/3/250 (28 August, 1934); UEAA PP 16/1/3/238 (1 August 1934).
62 UEAA PP 16/1/3/277 (4 October 1934).
63 UEAA PP 16/1/3/262 (17 September 1934); UEAA PP 16/1/3/240 (10 August 1934).
64 UEAA PP 16/1/3/259 (7 September 1934).
65 UEAA PP 16/1/4/26 (23 January 1935).
66 Daybelge and Englund, *Isokon*, p. 77.

CHAPTER FOUR

1 Gropius to his daughter, quoted in Fiona MacCarthy, *Walter Gropius: Visionary Founder of the Bauhaus* (London: Faber & Faber, 2019), p. 291.
2 Ise to Walter Gropius, quoted in ibid., p. 278.
3 TGA 8717.1.1.188 (n.d., but probably early May 1934).
4 Maxwell Fry, *Autobiographical Sketches* (London: Elek, 1975), p. 147.
5 Jack Pritchard, *View from a Long Chair: The Memoirs of Jack Pritchard* (London: Routledge, 1984), p. 102.
6 Jack Pritchard, 'The Making of the Lawn Road Flats', in *Belsize 2000: A Living Suburb* (London: Belsize Conservation Area Advisory Committee, 2000), pp. 82–7 at p. 86.
7 McCarthy, *Gropius*, p. 279.
8 UEAA PP/32/1/5 Fry to Gropius (3 July 1934).
9 UEAA PP/32/1/6 Gropius to Fry (6 July 1934).
10 UEAA PP/24/3/2 Pritchard to Gropius (20 June 1934).
11 UEAA PP/32/1/6 Gropius to Fry (6 July 1934).
12 Pritchard, 'The Making of the Lawn Road Flats', p. 86.
13 Quoted in Nicholas Fox Weber, *The Bauhaus Group: Six Masters of Modernism* (New York: Knopf, 2009), p. 63.
14 UEAA PP/24/1/3 Gropius to Mr Weidemann (2 February 1934).
15 UEAA PP/24/1/5 (27 March 1934).
16 UEAA PP/24/2/23 (16 September 1934).
17 UEAA PP/32/1/15.
18 UEAA PP/32/1/16 Pritchard to Fry (23 October 1934).
19 UEAA PP/24/3/52 Pritchard to Gropius (4 December 1934).

20 Quoted in Leyla Daybelge and Magnus Englund, *Isokon and the Bauhaus in Britain* (London: Pavilion, 2019), p. 87, and in Reginald Isaacs, *Gropius: An Illustrated Biography of the Creator of the Bauhaus* (London: Bullfinch, 1983), p. 193.
21 UEAA PP/24/4/2 (9 April 1935).
22 UEAA PP Pritchard to Gropius (31 July 1935).
23 Gropius to Martin Wagner, quoted in Isaacs, *Gropius*, p. 192.
24 UEAA PP/24/4/10 Gropius to Pritchard (29 October 1935).
25 UEAA PP/24/3/40 R.C.S. to Pritchard (2 November 1934).
26 MacCarthy, *Gropius*, p. 307.
27 Ibid., p. 150.
28 Alastair Grieve, *Isokon: For Ease, For Ever* (London: Isokon Plus, 2004), p. 29.
29 Sibyl Moholy-Nagy, *Moholy-Nagy: Experiment in Totality* (New York: Harper, 1950), pp. 120–1.
30 Hauserwirth.com, exhibition notes by grandson.
31 Moholy-Nagy, *Experiment*, p. 126.
32 Ibid., p. 129.
33 Ibid., p. 134.
34 Ibid., p. 137.
35 Terence A. Senter, 'Moholy-Nagy: The Transitional Years', in Achim Borchardt-Hume (ed.), *Albers and Moholy-Nagy: From the Bauhaus to the New World* (London: Tate Publishing, 2006), pp. 85–91.
36 Moholy-Nagy, *Experiment*, p. 145.
37 MacCarthy, *Gropius*, p. 333.
38 Pritchard, *Long Chair*, p. 111.
39 UEAA PP 25/1/4 Breuer to Isokon Company (8 July 1937).
40 Pritchard, *Long Chair*, p. 111.
41 Grieve, *Isokon*, p. 27.
42 Pritchard, *Long Chair*, p. 112.
43 Daybelge and Englund, *Isokon*, p. 142.
44 Grieve, *Isokon*, p. 26.
45 UEAA PP 16/1/5/155 Jack to Wells (24 September 1936).
46 UEAA PP 17/6/12 (19 May 1938).
47 UEAA PP 17/6/15 (9 June 1938).
48 UEAA PP/17/6/16 (7 July 1938).
49 David Burke, *The Lawn Road Flats: Spies, Writers and Artists* (London: Boydell Press, 2014), p. 109.

50 UEAA PP/39/1/35/30.
51 Fiona MacCarthy, Introduction to Pritchard, *Long Chair*, p. 18.
52 Pritchard, *Long Chair*, p. 111.
53 15 December 1936, quoted in Isaacs, *Gropius*, p. 216.
54 UEAA PP/24/5/10.
55 UEAA PP/24/5/9.
56 UEAA PP/24/5/11 Gloag to Pritchard (10 March 1937).

CHAPTER FIVE

1 TGA 8514.2 Ben Nicholson in conversation with Anthony Lousada (21 February 1980).
2 Ludo Read, 'Moving into the Mall Studios: Lady Read talks to Leonie Cohn', in *Belsize 2000: A Living Suburb* (London: Belsize Conservation Area Advisory Committee, 2000), pp. 78–81 at p. 78.
3 Sarah Checkland, *Ben Nicholson: The Vicious Circles of his Life and Art* (London: John Murray, 2000), p. 124.
4 Barbara Hepworth, *A Pictorial Autobiography* (Bath: Adams & Dart, 1970), p. 30.
5 Read, 'Moving into the Mall Studios', pp. 79, 81.
6 Conversation with Robert Maxwell and Celia Maxwell Scott, November 2017.
7 Herbert Read, *Annals of Innocence and Experience* (London: Faber & Faber, 1940), pp. 17, 18, 19, 30, 60.
8 Ibid., pp. 61, 72.
9 James King, *The Last Modern: A Life of Herbert Read* (London: Weidenfeld & Nicolson, 1990), p. 25.
10 Charles Marriott, 'Here and Now', *Evening Standard and St. James's Gazette*, 6 December 1911, p. 5, quoted in Ysanne Holt, 'The Camden Town Group: Then and Now', in Helena Bonett, Ysanne Holt and Jennifer Mundy (eds), *The Camden Town Group in Context* (London: Tate Research Publication, May 2012), https://www.tate.org.uk/art/research-publications/camden-town-group/ysanne-holt-the-camden-town-group-then-and-now-r1105679.
11 Read, *Annals*, p. 80.
12 King, *Last Modern*, p. 40.

13 Alan Bowness, Foreword, in Benedict Read and David Thistlewood (eds), *A British Vision of World Art: Herbert Read* (London: Leeds City Art Galleries and Lund Humphries, 1993), p. 3.
14 Herbert Read, 'A Nest of Gentle Artists', in Read and Thistlewood (eds), *Herbert Read: A British Vision of World Art*, pp. 59–63 at p. 60.
15 Piers Paul Read, interview in *To Hell with Culture*, a film about Herbert Read directed by Huw Wahl (2014, 56 minutes).
16 Herbert Read, 'Auguries of Life and Death', quoted in King, *Last Modern*, p. 54.
17 Read, *Annals*, p. 157.
18 King, *Last Modern*, p. 45.
19 Ibid., p. 47.
20 Read, *Annals*, pp. 176, 177.
21 Piers Paul Read claims that his father met Eliot on the night before his investiture at Buckingham Palace at the Carlton Restaurant ('Father and Son: The Herbert Read I Knew', *Standpoint*, December 2014). King claims that Rutter introduced them at Café Monico in Piccadilly Circus, that Read had come straight from the Palace and that Eliot was a little overawed by him (King, *Last Modern*, p. 56).
22 King, *Last Modern*, p. 70.
23 BLSA (British Library Sound Archive) Stephen Spender talking to Sir Alan Bowness for *Recollections of Herbert Read*.
24 King, *Last Modern*, pp. 80, 90, 91.
25 Richard Aldington to Read, 27 November 1930, quoted in ibid., p. 97.
26 T. S. Eliot, 'The Function of Criticism', in *Selected Essays* (New York: Harcourt, Brace & World, 1964), p. 15.
27 Christos Hadjiyiannis, 'Romanticism versus Classicism in 1910: T. E. Hulme, Edward Storer and *The Commentator*', *Literature and History*, vol. 22, no. 1, 2013, pp. 25–41 at p. 25.
28 Read, *Annals*, p. 192.
29 King, *Last Modern*, p. 99.
30 Ibid., p. 114.
31 Benedict Read, '"I'm Burlington Bertie": Herbert Read and the Burlington Magazine', in Michael Paraskos (ed.), *Rereading Read* (London: Freedom Press, 2007), pp. 88–101 at p. 90.
32 *Listener*, 6 April 1932, 11 January 1933, quoted in Checkland, *Ben Nicholson*, pp. 110, 123.

33 Geoffrey Grigson, *Recollections: Mainly of Writers and Artists* (London: Chatto & Windus/The Hogarth Press, 1984), pp. 56–7.
34 Read, 'Moving into the Mall Studios', p. 80.
35 BLSA Stephen Spender talking to Sir Alan Bowness for *Recollections of Herbert Read.*
36 Benedict Read, 'Herbert Read: An Overview', in Read and Thistlewood (eds), *Herbert Read: A British Vision of World Art*, pp. 11–20 at p. 14.
37 Read, *To Hell with Culture* film interview.
38 King, *Last Modern*, pp. 96, 121.
39 Anne Olivier Bell (ed.), *The Diary of Virginia Woolf*, 5 vols, vol. IV: *1931–1935* (London: The Hogarth Press, 1982), 20 February 1935, pp. 280–1.
40 Quoted in King, *Last Modern*, p. 146.
41 Ibid.
42 Bell (ed.), *Diary of Virginia Woolf*, vol. IV, 20 June 1935, p. 324.
43 Quoted in Robin Skelton (ed.), *Herbert Read: A Memorial Symposium* (London: Methuen, 1970), p. 27.
44 Read, *Annals*, p. 10.
45 Ibid., p. 202.
46 Quoted in Read, 'A Nest of Gentle Artists', p. 61.
47 Herbert Read, 'British Art 1930–40', in *Art in Britain 1930–40 Centred around Axis, Circle, Unit One* (London: Marlborough Fine Art, 1965), pp. 5–6.
48 King, *Last Modern*, p. 172.
49 Margaret Gardiner, *A Scatter of Memories* (London: Free Association Books, 1988), p. 176.
50 'Draft for an article on Herbert Read by Ben Nicholson', August–September 1968, TGA 8717/3/1/21.
51 Barbara Hepworth, 'In Memoriam Herbert Read', 15 June 1968, in Sophie Bowness (ed.), *Barbara Hepworth: Writings and Conversations* (London: Tate Publishing, 2015), p. 217.
52 Gardiner, *A Scatter of Memories*, p. 28.

CHAPTER SIX

1 *Paul Nash: Paintings and Watercolours* (London: Tate Publishing, 1975), p. 43.

2 TGA 9120.1 Paul Nash to Wells Coates (19 January 1933). Coates replied on 29 January 1933, TGA 9120.3.
3 Sarah Checkland, *Ben Nicholson: The Vicious Circles of his Life and Art* (London: John Murray, 2000), p. 121.
4 TGA 9120.3 (29 January 1933).
5 TGA 9120.7 Coates to Nash (3 March 1933).
6 Mark Glazebrook, *Unit One: Spirit of the 30's* (London: Mayor Gallery, 1984), p. 12.
7 TGA 9120.17 Nash to Coates.
8 Paul Nash, *Listener*, 5 July 1933, reprinted in Glazebrook, *Unit One*, pp. 41–3 at p. 43.
9 TGA 9120.34 Coates to Nash (21 June 1933).
10 TGA 9120.40 Letter from editor of the *Listener* to Wells Coates.
11 Herbert Read, 'Unit One', *Architectural Review*, October 1933, reprinted in Glazebrook, *Unit One*, pp. 45–9 at p. 45.
12 TGA 9120.38 Nicholson to Coates.
13 Nash, *Listener*, 5 July 1933, reprinted in Glazebrook, *Unit One*, p. 43.
14 Glazebrook, *Unit One*, p. 21; Stephen Spender, 'The Pylons', in *Poems* (London: Faber & Faber, 1933).
15 Richard Read, *Art and its Discontents: The Early Life of Adrian Stokes* (Aldershot: Ashgate, 2002), p. 7.
16 TGA 8717.1.1.160; 8717.1.1.166 Hepworth to Nicholson (12 December 1933).
17 TGA 8717.1.1.163 Hepworth to Nicholson (16 December 1933).
18 Barbara Hepworth, Unit One statement, in Barbara Hepworth, *A Pictorial Autobiography* (Bath: Adams & Dart, 1970), p. 30.
19 TGA 9120.65 (23 February 1934).
20 TGA 8717.1.1.182 (3 April 1934); TGA 8717.1.1.183 (4 April 1934).
21 TGA 9120.81.
22 *Belfast Telegraph*, 21 March 1935; *Manchester Evening News*, 22 June 1934.
23 *Apollo*, 13 April 1934; *New York Times*, 5 August 1934.
24 Geoffrey Grigson, 'The Modern Point of View', *Art Today*, 13 April 1934.
25 Roger Berthoud, *The Life of Henry Moore* (London: Faber & Faber, 1987), p. 126; TGA 9120.88 Coates to Nash (14 November 1934).
26 In Gwen Finkel Chavzit, *Herbert Bayer and Modernist Design in America* (Ann Arbor: UMI Research Press, 1987), p. 108; James King, *The Last Modern: A Life of Herbert Read* (London: Weidenfeld & Nicolson, 1990), p. 142.

27 TGA 9120.96 Nash to Coates (28 November 1934).
28 TGA 9120.97 Read to Nash (23 November 1934).
29 Ibid.
30 TGA 9120.98 (30 November 1934).
31 TGA 9120.130 Read to Coates (11 February 1935).
32 TGA 9120.141.
33 TGA 9120.143, 2nd draft of 'Artists' Unit' statement.
34 Guillaume Apollinaire, *Les Mamelles de Tirésias* (1903, first performed in 1917); Eleanor Clayton, 'Lee Miller and Surrealism in Britain', in Eleanor Clayton (ed.), *Lee Miller and Surrealism in Britain* (London: Lund Humphries/The Hepworth Wakefield, 2018), pp. 13–75 at p. 14.
35 Read to Wyndham Lewis, 9 December 1934, MS Cornell, quoted in King, *Last Modern*, p. 129.
36 Paul Nash, *Listener*, 29 April 1931, reprinted in Andrew Causey (ed.), *Paul Nash: Writings on Art* (Oxford: Oxford University Press, 2000), p. 60.
37 A. S. Byatt, 'Angel of Anarchy', *Guardian*, 26 November 2004.
38 Ibid.
39 For an account of these years and Paul's bouts of illness see Margaret Nash, 'Memoir', in Paul Nash, *Outline: An Autobiography*, ed. David Boyd Haycock, new edn (London: Lund Humphries, 2016).
40 TGA 8712.1.2 (18 July 1935); TGA 8712.1.9 Poem to Eileen; TGA 8712.1.10.
41 TGA 8712.1.18 (15 July 1936).
42 TGA 8712.1.23 (6 April 1937); TGA 8712.1.27 (14 June 1937).
43 Juliet Gardiner, *The Thirties: An Intimate History* (London: Harper Press, 2010), p. 335.
44 Anthony Bertram, *Paul Nash: The Portrait of an Artist* (London: Faber & Faber, 1955), p. 220, quoted in Chambers (ed.), *Paul Nash*, p. 36; TGA 769.1.31 Nash to Dudley Tooth (November 1943).
45 Michael Remy, *Surrealism in Britain* (Aldershot: Ashgate, 1999), p. 78.
46 King, *Last Modern*, p. 163.
47 *Guardian*, 12 June 1936.
48 King, *Last Modern*, p. 161.
49 Henry Moore and John Hedgecoe, *Henry Moore: My Ideas, Inspiration and Life as an Artist* (London: Ebury Press, 1986), p. 72.

50 Paul C. Ray, *The Surrealist Movement in England* (Ithaca, NY/ London: Cornell University Press, 1971), p. 139.
51 Clayton, 'Lee Miller and Surrealism in Britain', p. 13.
52 Ibid., p. 42.
53 Antony Penrose, *Lives of Lee Miller* (London: Thames & Hudson, 1985), p. 75.
54 *Barbara Hepworth/Ben Nicholson: Sculpture and Painting in the 1930s*, curated by Sophie Bowness and Christopher Green (London: Hazlitt Holland-Hibbert, 2019), p. 24.
55 Clayton, 'Lee Miller and Surrealism in Britain', p. 22.
56 Ibid., p. 47.
57 Ibid., pp. 52, 53.
58 Penrose, *Lives of Lee Miller*, p. 94.

CHAPTER SEVEN

1 *The Times*, 2 November 1967, quoted in Alan Wilkinson (ed.), *Henry Moore: Writings and Conversations* (London: Lund Humphries, 2002), p. 49.
2 Henry Moore and John Hedgecoe, *Henry Moore: My Ideas, Inspiration and Life as an Artist* (London: Ebury Press, 1986), p. 31.
3 Barbara Hepworth, January 1952, reprinted in Sophie Bowness (ed.), *Barbara Hepworth: Writings and Conversations* (London: Tate Publishing, 2015), p. 58.
4 Geoffrey Grigson, *Recollections: Mainly of Writers and Artists* (London: Chatto & Windus/The Hogarth Press, 1984), p. 98; TGA 9222.2.2.8 Notes by Eileen Agar on her memories of Henry and Irina Moore (19 November 1988).
5 Roger Berthoud, *The Life of Henry Moore* (London: Faber & Faber, 1987), p. 50.
6 Barbara Hepworth, *A Pictorial Autobiography* (Bath: Adams & Dart, 1970), p. 15.
7 Moore and Hedgecoe, *Henry Moore*, p. 14.
8 Wilkinson (ed.), *Henry Moore: Writings and Conversations*, p. 32.
9 Berthoud, *Henry Moore*, p. 33.
10 Letter to Alice Gostick, 6 October 1917, quoted in Wilkinson (ed.), *Henry Moore: Writings and Conversations*, p. 41.
11 Moore and Hedgecoe, *Henry Moore*, p. 31.
12 Berthoud, *Henry Moore*, p. 57.
13 Ibid., p. 55.

14 Wilkinson (ed.), *Henry Moore: Writings and Conversations*, p. 44.
15 Berthoud, *Henry Moore*, p. 56.
16 Ibid., p. 61.
17 Stephen Spender, Introduction to Henry Moore, *Stonehenge* (London: Ganymed, 1974), quoted in Wilkinson (ed.), *Henry Moore: Writings and Conversations*, p. 49.
18 TGA 8313.1.2.153 (15 September 1933).
19 Wilkinson (ed.), *Henry Moore: Writings and Conversations*, p. 45.
20 Barbara Hepworth, *A Pictorial Autobiography*, p. 15.
21 Quoted in Berthoud, *Henry Moore*, p. 66.
22 Moore and Hedgecoe, *Henry Moore*, p. 45.
23 Berthoud, *Henry Moore*, pp. 70, 75, 79, 81.
24 Wilkinson (ed.), *Henry Moore: Writings and Conversations*, pp. 56–7.
25 Moore and Hedgecoe, *Henry Moore*, p. 152; Wilkinson (ed.), *Henry Moore: Writings and Conversations*, p. 57.
26 Berthoud, *Henry Moore*, p. 99.
27 TGA 8717.1.2.3019.
28 Quoted in Berthoud, *Henry Moore*, pp. 106, 107.
29 Henry Moore, 'The Sculptor Speaks', *Listener*, 18 August 1937, quoted in Berthoud, *Henry Moore*, p. 141.
30 Jim Ede, *Way of Life: Kettle's Yard* (Cambridge: Cambridge University Press, 1984), p. 70.
31 Hugh Gordon Porteus, 'New Planets', *Axis*, 3, July 1935, pp. 22–3 at p. 22.
32 Berthoud, *Henry Moore*, p. 102.
33 Ibid., pp. 127, 128.
34 Herbert Read, *Henry Moore: Sculptor* (London: A. Zwemmer, 1934), p. 15.
35 Berthoud, *Henry Moore*, p. 134.
36 Wilkinson (ed.), *Henry Moore: Writings and Conversations*, p. 59.
37 TGA 8717.1.2.3020 (9 July 1935).
38 Edward Juler, 'Life Forms: Henry Moore, Morphology and Biologism in the Interwar Years', www.tate.org.uk/art/research-publications/henry-moore/edward-juler-life-forms-henry-moore-morphology-and-biologism-in-the-interwar-years-r1151314.
39 Geoffrey Grigson, 'Henry Moore and Ourselves', *Axis*, 3, July 1935, pp. 9–10 at p. 9.
40 Berthoud, *Henry Moore*, p. 146.

41 Fred Uhlman, *The Making of an Englishman* (London: Victor Gollancz, 1960), p. 214.

42 Anna Müller-Härlin, 'It All Happened in This Street, Downshire Hill', in Shulamith Behr and Marian Malet (eds), *Arts in Exile in Britain 1933–1945* (Amsterdam/New York: Editions Rodopi, 2005), p. 245; Uhlman, *The Making of an Englishman*, p. 213; Müller-Härlin, 'It All Happened in This Street', p. 246.

43 Uhlman, *The Making of an Englishman*, p. 216.

44 Berthoud, *Henry Moore*, p. 166.

45 Wilkinson (ed.), *Henry Moore: Writings and Conversations*, p. 60.

46 Moore to Arthur Sale, scholar, poet and Fellow at Magdalene College, Cambridge, 10 October 1940, quoted in ibid, p. 60.

47 Ibid., p. 59.

48 TGA 8717.1.2.3024.

49 Kenneth Clark, *Another Part of the Wood: A Self-Portrait* (London: John Murray, 1974), p. 256.

50 TGA 9222.2.2.8 Notes by Eileen Agar on Moore (19 November 1988).

51 Dalya Alberge, 'Henry Moore Rubbished Barbara Hepworth Sculpture, diaries say', *Guardian*, 25 March 2018.

CHAPTER EIGHT

1 BLSA Myfanwy Piper in conversation with Margaret Garlake, 21 November 1994, part of the National Life Stories series, C466/25/01-03.

2 See Frances Spalding, *John Piper, Myfanwy Piper: Lives in Art* (Oxford: Oxford University Press, 2009), p. 51.

3 Ede's logbooks record that on 6 July Gallatin, Hélion, Ben, Barbara and Braque came over for dinner and that 'Mr and Mrs Piper joined them after dinner'. KYA Ede File 6 Diaries and Visitors Books. Braque came to London in connection with his exhibition at the Lefevre Gallery.

4 BLSA Myfanwy Piper in conversation with Margaret Garlake.

5 Quoted in Spalding, *John Piper, Myfanwy Piper*, p. 60.

6 Ibid., p. 62.

7 Editorial statement, 1933, reproduced in Charles Harrison and Paul Wood (eds), *Art in Theory 1900–2000: An Anthology of Changing Ideas* (Oxford: Blackwell Publishing, 2001), p. 375.

8 Spalding, *John Piper, Myfanwy Piper*, p. 62.
9 Ibid., pp. 63, 64.
10 BLSA Myfanwy Piper in conversation with Margaret Garlake.
11 Spalding, *John Piper, Myfanwy Piper*, p. 67.
12 Ibid., p. 70.
13 Geoffrey Grigson, 'Comment on England', *Axis*, 1, January 1935, pp. 8–10 at p. 10.
14 Herbert Read, 'Our Terminology', *Axis*, 1, January 1935, pp. 6–8 at p. 7.
15 Anatole Jakovski, 'Inscriptions under Pictures', *Axis*, 1, January 1935, pp. 14–20 at pp. 16, 17.
16 Wassily Kandinsky, 'Line and Fish', *Axis*, 2, April 1935, p. 6.
17 Jim Ede, 'Modern Art', *Axis*, 1, January 1935, pp. 21–3 at pp. 21, 23.
18 Jim Ede, *Way of Life: Kettle's Yard* (Cambridge: Cambridge University Press, 1984), p. 57.
19 Ibid., p. 58.
20 KYA Elisabeth Ede, recording, MYKY 06.
21 KYA Mary Ede, recording, MYKY 25.
22 Ede did not buy Hepworth's work in the 1930s, a source of sadness to her, expressed later. I am grateful to Sophie Bowness for pointing this out.
23 KYA Ben Nicholson to Jim Ede (1932), File 4.
24 KYA Ben Nicholson to Jim Ede (9 July 1936), File 6.
25 Hélion, 'From Reduction to Growth', *Axis*, 2, April 1935, pp. 19–24.
26 TGA 8717.1.1.207 Hepworth to Nicholson (18 January 1935).
27 Myfanwy Evans, 'A Review and a Comment', *Axis*, 3, July 1935, p. 25.
28 Quoted in Spalding, *John Piper, Myfanwy Piper*, p. 74.
29 Geoffrey Grigson and John Piper, 'England's Climate', *Axis*, 7, Autumn 1936, pp. 5–9 at pp. 5, 6, 9.
30 W. G. and M. Archer, 'Santhal Painting', *Axis*, 7, Autumn 1936, pp. 27–8.
31 Spalding, *John Piper, Myfanwy Piper*, p. 79.
32 Ibid., p. 99.
33 John Piper, 'Prehistory from the Air', *Axis*, 8, Early Winter 1937, pp. 5–8 at p. 5.
34 Hugh Gordon Porteus, 'Exhibition of Abstract Painting at the Experimental Theatre', *Axis*, 1, January 1935, p. 27.

35 Spalding, *John Piper, Myfanwy Piper*, p. 83.
36 Ibid., p. 88.
37 KYA Ben Nicholson to Jim Ede (17 March 1936), File 6.
38 BLSA Nicolette Gray interview with Andrew Forge, 'The Thirties in Britain: Art; Innovation and Commitment' for BBC Third Programme; Frances Spalding, 'Abstract Art: From the Radical to the Everyday', *Guardian*, 10 January 2015.
39 Spalding, *John Piper, Myfanwy Piper*, p. 89.
40 BLSA Myfanwy Piper in conversation with Margaret Garlake.
41 John Piper to Paul Nash, 12 January 1943, quoted in Spalding, *John Piper, Myfanwy Piper*, p. 131.
42 Barbara Hepworth, *A Pictorial Autobiography* (Bath: Adams & Dart, 1970), p. 37.
43 In Sophie Bowness (ed.), *Barbara Hepworth: Writings and Conversations* (London: Tate Publishing, 2015), p. 255.
44 Herbert Read, 'What is Revolutionary Art?', in Betty Rea (ed.), *Five on Revolutionary Art* (London: Wishart, 1935), pp. 11–22.
45 Postcard from Gabo to Nicholson, 1936, https://www.tate.org.uk/about-us/projects/gabo-archives.
46 Jack Pritchard, *View from a Long Chair: The Memoirs of Jack Pritchard* (London: Routledge, 1984), p. 92. Slutzy was interned on the Isle of Man between June 1940 and February 1942. He moved into the Lawn Road flats after his release and remained there until 1946.
47 Letter from Gabo to Miriam Franklin, 1936; postcard from Miriam Franklin to Gabo, 1936; letter from Gabo to Miriam Franklin, 1936, all https://www.tate.org.uk/about-us/projects/gabo-archives.
48 Quoted in Martin Hammer and Christina Lodder, *Constructing Modernity: The Art and Career of Naum Gabo* (New Haven/London: Yale University Press, 2000), p. 234.
49 'A Visit to Mars', *Sunday Times*, 16 February 1938, quoted in ibid., p. 255.
50 Winifred Dacre, 'Unknown Colour', in J. L. Martin, Ben Nicholson and N. Gabo (eds), *Circle: International Survey of Constructive Art* (London: Faber & Faber, 1937), pp. 57–60 at p. 59.
51 Martin, 'The State of Transition', in Martin et al. (eds), *Circle*, pp. 215–19 at p. 216.

52 Editorial, in Martin et al. (eds), *Circle*, p. v.
53 Naum Gabo, 'The Constructive Idea in Art', in Martin et al. (eds), *Circle*, p. 6.
54 Le Corbusier, 'The Quarrel with Realism', in Martin et al. (eds), *Circle*, pp. 67–74 at p. 73.
55 Ben Nicholson, 'Quotations', in Martin et al. (eds), *Circle*, p. 75.
56 Naum Gabo, 'Sculpture: Carving and Construction in Space', in Martin et al. (eds), *Circle*, pp. 103–11 at p. 111.
57 Hepworth, 'Sculpture', in Martin et al. (eds), *Circle*, p. 116, quoted in Hepworth, *Pictorial Autobiography*, p. 33.
58 James King, *The Last Modern: A Life of Herbert Read* (London: Weidenfeld & Nicolson, 1980), p. 131.
59 Conference, 'Becoming Barbara Hepworth', at the Henry Moore Institute, 14 February 2018.
60 Spalding, *John Piper, Myfanwy Piper*, p. 117.
61 Roger Berthoud, *Graham Sutherland* (London: Faber & Faber, 1982), pp. 76, 84–5.
62 Advertisement, *Studio*, vol. 116, 1938, p. 301.
63 'The Town Plan for Nemours, North Africa, 1934', *Axis*, 8, Early Winter 1938, p. 30.
64 Myfanwy Evans, 'Paul Nash, 1937', *Axis*, 8, Early Winter 1938, pp. 12–13.
65 Winifred used the name Dacre for *Circle* and when exhibiting abstract works but continued to use Nicholson for her naturalistic paintings and for her solo show at Leicester Galleries in 1936. She went back to using Nicholson consistently in the 1950s. See Christopher Andreae, *Winifred Nicholson* (Farnham: Lund Humphries, 2009), p. 19.
66 Myfanwy Evans, 'The Painter's Object', in Myfanwy Evans (ed.), *The Painter's Object* (London: Curwen Press, 1937), pp. 3–13 at p. 5.

CHAPTER NINE

1 BLSA *A Gift of Autumn*, BBC Radio 3 programme, 2 November 1990, Nancy Spender in conversation with Jon Stallworthy.
2 Nicolette Devas, *Two Flamboyant Fathers* (London: Collins, 1966), p. 158.

3 BLSA *A Portrait of the Artist William Coldstream*, BBC Radio 3 programme, 19 October 1990, written and presented by Christopher Cook, C798/120.
4 BLSA *A Gift of Autumn*, BBC Radio 3.
5 Devas, *Two Flamboyant Fathers*, p. 159.
6 Bruce Laughton, *William Coldstream* (New Haven/London: Yale University Press, 2004), p. 18.
7 BLSA William Coldstream talking to David Sylvester, BBC Radio 3, 20 October 1976.
8 BLSA *A Portrait of the Artist William Coldstream*, BBC Radio 3.
9 Blake Morrison, 'Stamp of Excellence', *Guardian*, 1 December 2007.
10 'Nancy Spender's Recollections of Wystan Auden', in *The W. H. Auden Society Newsletter*, nos. 10–11, September 1993, written up from conversations with Kathleen Bell and approved by Nancy Spender, http://audensociety.org/10-11newsletter.html.
11 BLSA William Coldstream talking to David Sylvester, BBC Radio 3, 20 October 1976.
12 Laughton, *William Coldstream*, p. 49.
13 BLSA *A Portrait of the Artist William Coldstream*, BBC Radio 3.
14 Frances Spalding, *John Piper, Myfanwy Piper: Lives in Art* (Oxford: Oxford University Press, 2009), p. 102.
15 Michael Sidnell, *Dances of Death: The Group Theatre of London in the Thirties* (London: Faber & Faber, 1984), p. 51.
16 Spalding, *John Piper, Myfanwy Piper*, pp. 102, 103.
17 Myfanwy Piper, 'Back in the Thirties', *Art and Literature: An International Review*, Winter 1965, p. 148, quoted in Spalding, *John Piper, Myfanwy Piper*, pp. 103, 104, 118.
18 BLSA Myfanwy Piper in conversation with Margaret Garlake, 21 November 1994, part of the National Life Stories series, C466/25/01-03.
19 Spalding, *John Piper, Myfanwy Piper*, p. 105.
20 Louis MacNeice, *The Strings are False: An Unfinished Autobiography* (London: Faber & Faber, 1965), p. 167.
21 Ibid., p. 129.
22 Jon Stallworthy, *Louis MacNeice* (London: Faber & Faber, 1995), p. 170.
23 MacNeice, *Strings are False*, p. 151.
24 Stallworthy, *Louis MacNeice*, p. 154.

25 Grigson, *New Verse*, 1, January 1933, pp. 2–3.
26 MacNeice to Mrs E. R. Dodds, 18 November 1936, in Jonathan Allison (ed.), *The Letters of Louis MacNeice* (London: Faber & Faber, 2010), pp. 287–8.
27 Stallworthy, *Louis MacNeice*, p. 195.
28 Ibid., pp. 198, 176.
29 MacNeice, *Strings are False*, p. 165.
30 Ibid., p. 171.
31 Ibid., p. 172.
32 BLSA *A Gift of Autumn*, BBC Radio 3.
33 Stallworthy, *Louis MacNeice*, p. 205.
34 BLSA *A Gift of Autumn*, BBC Radio 3.
35 Ibid.
36 John Margetson, Nancy Spender obituary, *Guardian*, 25 June 2001.

CHAPTER TEN

1 W. F. A. Roell, 'A Visit to Piet Mondrian' (1920), in Francesco Manacorda and Michael White (eds), *Mondrian and his Studios: Colour in Space* (London: Tate Publishing, 2014), pp. 34–7 at p. 34.
2 Seuphor (an anagram of Orpheus, his real name was Fernand Berckelaers) quoted in Jed Perl, *Calder: The Conquest of Time: The Early Years, 1898–1940* (New Haven/London: Yale University Press, 2017), p. 339.
3 W. F. A. Roell, 'At Piet Mondrian's: His New Philosophy of Life' (1932), in Manacorda and White (eds), *Mondrian and his Studios*, pp. 103–4 at p. 104.
4 Roell, 'A Visit to Mondrian', pp. 34, 37.
5 Alexander Calder, *An Autobiography with Pictures* (London: Penguin, 1967), p. 113.
6 Perl, *Calder*, p. 537.
7 Ibid., pp. 544, 539.
8 Calder, *An Autobiography with Pictures*, p. 164.
9 Christopher Frayling, *Things to Come* (London: British Film Institute, 1995), p. 56.
10 Perl, *Calder*, p. 552; Myfanwy Piper, 'Back in the Thirties', *Art and Literature: An International Review*, Winter 1965, p. 149.
11 Kenneth Clark, *Another Part of the Wood: A Self-Portrait* (London: John Murray, 1974), pp. 255–6.

12 Perl, *Calder*, p. 549.
13 Quoted in Joan M. Marter, *Alexander Calder* (Cambridge: Cambridge University Press, 1991), pp. 64, 63.
14 Alexander Calder, *Animal Sketching* (New York: Bridgman, 1926, reissued 1941), pp. 11, 39, 47.
15 Quoted in Howard Greenfeld, *The Essential Alexander Calder* (New York: Harry Abrams, 2003), pp. 41, 40.
16 Quoted in Marter, *Alexander Calder*, p. 194.
17 'Alexander Calder, at the Mayor Gallery', *New Statesman and Nation*, 11 December 1937, p. 1016, quoted in Perl, *Calder*, p. 550.
18 Perl, *Calder*, p. 551.
19 Margaret Gardiner, *Barbara Hepworth: A Memoir* (Edinburgh: The Salamander Press, 1982), p. 47.
20 Simon Grant, 'Hello Sleepy', https://www.tate.org.uk/tate-etc/issue-20-autumn-2010/hello-sleepy.
21 Barbara Hepworth, *A Pictorial Autobiography* (Bath: Adams & Dart, 1970), p. 39.
22 Grant, 'Hello Sleepy'.
23 Sophie Bowness, 'Mondrian and London', in Christopher Green and Barnaby Wright (eds), *Mondrian || Nicholson in Parallel* (London: Courtauld Gallery, 2012), p. 53.
24 To Mrs and Mr Hoyack, 4 April 1939, in Herbert Henkels, *Mondrian: From Figuration to Abstraction* (London: Thames & Hudson, 1987), p. 225.
25 Grant, 'Hello Sleepy'.
26 Michel Seuphor, *Piet Mondrian: Life and Work* (London: Thames & Hudson, 1957), p. 168.
27 Hepworth, *Pictorial Autobiography*, p. 39; Perl, *Calder*, p. 551.
28 Gardiner, *Barbara Hepworth*, p. 186.
29 Perl, *Calder*, pp. 343, 344.
30 Gardiner, *Barbara Hepworth*, p. 46.
31 Perl, *Calder*, p. 551.
32 Hepworth, *Pictorial Autobiography*, p. 41.
33 Ibid.
34 Bowness, 'Mondrian and London', p. 58.
35 Hepworth, *Pictorial Autobiography*, p. 45.
36 Bowness, 'Mondrian and London', pp. 58, 63 n. 112.

37 Mondrian to Winifred, 4 January 1941, in Henkels, *Mondrian: From Figuration to Abstraction*, p. 226.

EPILOGUE

1 Quoted in Sally Festing, *Barbara Hepworth: A Life of Forms* (London: Penguin, 1995), p. 141.
2 Sarah Checkland, *Ben Nicholson: The Vicious Circles of his Life and Art* (London: John Murray, 2000), p. 191.
3 James King, *The Last Modern: A Life of Herbert Read* (London: Weidenfeld & Nicolson, 1980), p. 187.
4 Checkland, *Ben Nicholson*, p. 188.
5 Ibid., p. 395.
6 Roger Berthoud, *The Life of Henry Moore* (London: Faber & Faber, 1987), p. 171, quoted in Henry Moore and John Hedgecoe, *Henry Moore: My Ideas, Inspiration and Life as an Artist* (London: Ebury Press, 1986), p. 134.
7 3 November 1940, quoted in Berthoud, *Henry Moore*, p. 173.
8 Frances Spalding, *John Piper, Myfanwy Piper: Lives in Art* (Oxford: Oxford University Press, 2009), p. 166.
9 Herbert Read to Rayner Heppenstall, 7 April 1945, quoted in King, *Last Modern*, p. 237.
10 King, *Last Modern*, p. 197.
11 Herbert Read to Douglas Cooper, 25 June 1941, quoted in King, *Last Modern*, p. 188.
12 Checkland, *Ben Nicholson*, p. 189.
13 Jon Stallworthy, *Louis MacNeice* (London: Faber & Faber, 1995), p. 230.
14 Ibid., p. 265.
15 Ibid., p. 297.
16 BLSA *A Gift of Autumn*, BBC Radio 3 programme, 2 November 1990, Nancy Spender in conversation with Jon Stallworthy.
17 Fiona MacCarthy, *Walter Gropius: Visionary Founder of the Bauhaus* (London: Faber & Faber, 2019), p. 366.
18 Ibid., p. 368.
19 TGA 8717.1.2.268 (1 September 1937).
20 MacCarthy, *Gropius*, p. 22.
21 Quoted in Robert McCarter, *Breuer* (London: Phaidon Press, 2016), p. 76.

22 UEAA 25/1/13 (11 January 1939).
23 UEAA 17/1/3/97 (6 November 1939).
24 Leyla Daybelge and Magnus Englund, *Isokon and the Bauhaus in Britain* (London: Pavilion, 2019), p. 166.
25 UEAA 17/6/34.
26 Wells Coates eventually moved to Canada, where he died, in Vancouver, in 1958.
27 Jack Pritchard, *View from a Long Chair: The Memoirs of Jack Pritchard* (London: Routledge, 1984), p. 95.
28 Ibid., p. 115.
29 Daybelge and Englund, *Isokon*, p. 214.
30 Adam Sonin, 'Sigmund Freud met his greatest admirer Salvador Dalí at Primrose Hill home', *Hampstead & Highgate Express*, 16 April 2013.
31 BLSA Herbert Read interview with Andrew Forge, 'The Thirties in Britain: Art, Innovation and Commitment'.
32 Barbara Hepworth, *A Pictorial Autobiography* (Bath: Adams & Dart, 1970), p. 37.
33 Read, 'British Art 1930–40', in *Art in Britain 1930–40 Centred around Axis, Circle, Unit One* (London: Marlborough Fine Art, 1965), pp. 5–6.
34 Pritchard, *Long Chair*, p. 183.

INDEX

Aalto, Alvar, 105, 145
Abstract & Concrete exhibition, 103, 189–90, 192, 220
Abstraction-Création, 44, 140, 179–81, 192, 222
Adelphi, 130
Agar, Eileen, 148–50, 153–4, 159, 176, 207
Albers, Anni, 241
Albers, Josef, 88, 105, 241
Aldington, Richard, 125, 127
Alfieri, Dino, 90
Allied Artists' Association, 121, 128
Anderson, Hedli, 240
Anrep, Helen, 204
Apollinaire, Guillaume, 147
Apollo, 144
Architects' Czech Relief Fund, 244
Architects' Journal, 222–3
Architectural Review, 57, 83, 112, 139
Armstrong, John, 136, 138, 207
Armstrong, Louis, 32
Arp, Hans, 179
Arp, Jean, 40
Art and Letters, 123
Art Now, 138
Art Students League, 221
Art Today, 144
Artists International Association (AIA), 103, 172–3
Artists Refugee Committee, 173
Artists' Unit, 104, 146–7
  see also Unit One
Arup, Ove, 70
Associated British Film Distributors (ABFD), 203
Attlee, Clement, 198
Auden, W. H., 172, 199–201, 203–4, 206–8, 210–11, 223
Axis, 46, 172, 180–2, 185–9, 195, 197, 220

Ballets Russes, 192
Banting, John, 57, 207
Bard, Joseph, 148–9, 153
Barr, Alfred, 241
Bartlett, Ethel, 32
Batterbury, Thomas, 15
Bauhaus, 41, 67, 80, 84–95, 97, 100, 103–5, 110, 116, 135, 192
  and America, 241–2
  and Read, 104, 127–8, 132, 144–6
Bawden, Edward, 196
Bayer, Herbert, 85, 241–2
Baynard Press, 196
Beacon Hill school, 61–3, 96
Beardsley, Aubrey, 126
Beaux Arts Gallery, 7, 15
Bell, Clive, 130
Bell, Graham, 205

Bell, Vanessa, 113, 131, 196, 216
Benedetta, Mary, 101
Berg, E. & L., 77
Berlin, Isaiah, 211
Berlin, Sven, 234–5
Berlin Olympic Games, 103
Bernal, Desmond, 194, 234
Bernini, Gian Lorenzo, 125
Betjeman, John, 101, 237–8
Betjeman, Penelope, 237
Bevan, Robert, 122
Bigge, John, 138, 148
Binyon, Laurence, 189
birth control, 63
Blake, William, 1, 186
Blanco White, Justin, 178, 187
Bliss, Arthur, 39
Bloomsbury Gallery, 10, 21
Bonnard, Pierre, 163
Book of Psalms, 7
Borgeaud, Alfred, 56–7, 59
Botticelli, Sandro, 183
Boué, Valentine, 156
Brâncuşi, 40, 125–6, 172, 179, 189
Brandt, R. A., 80
Braque, Georges, 39–40, 128, 138, 178–9, 185, 219
Braque, Marcelle, 219
Braunfels, Munza, 129, 131
Braunfels, Walter, 126
Breton, André, 147–8, 152
Breuer, Marcel, 104–9, 112, 114, 129, 189, 231
  long chairs, 106–7, 109, 112
  and the war, 241–5
British Museum, 164, 189
British Surrealism Exhibition, 148, 150–3, 191
Britten, Benjamin, 203, 207
Broadcasting House, 67, 73
Brooke, Henry, 71
Brown, Ford Madox, 16
Brumwell, Marcus, 32, 189
Burlington magazine, 127–8, 239
Burra, Edward, 136, 138, 143, 148, 172
Byron, Lord, 16

Cadec, madame, 187
Cahiers d'Art, 180
Calder, Alexander, 17–18, 45, 172, 179, 183, 190, 197, 217–24, 227, 229, 231
Calder, Louisa, 219–20, 229, 231
Calder, Sandra, 220
Cambridge University, 60–1
Camden Council, 245–6
Camden Town Group, 122
Carlisle, Earl and Countess of, 1–2
Carrà, Carlo, 4
Carrington, Leonora, 153
Castleford Secondary School, 160–1
Cave of Harmony, 56
Cazalet, Thelma, 78
Central School of Art and Design, 97
Cézanne, Paul, 122, 139, 163, 165, 186, 205, 228
Chagall, Marc, 154
Chartres Cathedral, 165
Chekhov, Michael, 194
Chelsea Polytechnic, 207
Chelsea School of Art, 169, 175
Chermayeff, Serge, 67, 69, 96, 145, 188
Children's Group, 62
Christian Science, 6, 10, 23–5, 33–4
Christie, Agatha, 244
Churchill, Winston, 79
Circle, 191–8, 220
Clark, Eleanor, 240
Clark, Jane, 215, 220–1, 237
Clark, Kenneth, 127, 176, 206, 215, 220–2, 236–7, 239
Claude, 186

Clausen, George, 15
Coade, T. T., 63
Coates, Harper Havelock, 54
Coates, Wells, 43, 51, 54–7, 59, 64–70, 72–81, 95, 110, 189, 207, 243
and Unit One, 135–6, 138–40, 143–4, 146–7
Cocteau, Jean, 7–8, 155, 222
Coldstream, Miranda, 199, 203–4
Coldstream, Nancy, 199–204, 212–16, 233, 240–1
Coldstream, William (Bill), 199–206, 213, 215–16, 233
Cole, Ernest, 165
Committee for Social Investigation and Reform, 6
Communist Party of Great Britain, 56
Conant, James, 114–15
Constable, John, 16, 121, 186–7
Contemporary Lithographs Ltd, 113, 196
Cooper, Douglas, 143–4
Corbett, Leonora, 212
Cotterill, Reginald, 162
Council for Art and Industry, 93
Courtauld, Samuel, 206
Coxon, Raymond, 113, 160, 162, 164, 166–7, 169–70, 207
Crawford, O. G. S., 188
Criterion, 124, 127
Croft, Diana, 173–4
Crossley and Porter School for Orphans, 119
Crysédе, 57
Cubism, 5, 139, 195
Cummings, Constance, 96
Curwen Press, 196

Dacre, Winifred, *see* Nicholson, Winifred
Dadaism, 139
Dalí, Salvador, 118, 138, 148, 150, 152–4, 182, 246
Daumier, Honoré, 88
Davies, Hugh Sykes, 148
Dawes, Mr, 161
Dawson, Norman, 166
de Chirico, Giorgio, 4, 147–8, 154, 197
De La Warr Pavilion (Bexhill on Sea), 67
De Stijl Group, 192
Degas, Edgar, 163, 202
Delvaux, Paul, 123
Derain, André, xiii, 4
Deustscher Werkbund, 65
Diaghilev, Sergei, 7
Dicky, E. M. O'Rorke, 93
Donaldson, Jack and Frances, 96
Doone, Rupert, 56, 206–8
Dorland Hall exhibition, 69, 73
Dorner, Alexander, 241–2
Doyle, Arthur Conan, 60
Duport, Jean, 75
Duthuit, Georges, 219

Eddy, Mary Baker, 6, 24
Ede, Helen, 32, 39, 183–5
Ede, Jim, 10, 32, 39, 170, 178, 183–5, 190, 192
Ede, Mary, 185
Ehrlich, Bettina, 174
Einstein, Albert, 174
Eisenstein, Sergei, 194
Eliot, T. S., 56, 124–5, 127–8, 131, 150, 211, 239–40
Ellington, Duke, 241
Elmhirst, Leonard and Dorothy, 92
Eloui Bey, Aziz, 155
Éluard, Paul, 148, 152–5
English Heritage, 245
English Surrealist Group, 150
Epstein, Jacob, 165, 173

Ernst, Max, 147–8, 153–5, 197
Etchells, Frederick, 138
Eumorfopoulos, George, 15
Euston Road School, 204–6
Evans, Myfanwy, *see* Piper, Myfanwy
Everyman Theatre, 77, 189, 206
Experimental Theatre, 188
Exposition Internationale des Arts et Techniques, 198

Faber, Geoffrey, 115
Fantin-Latour, Henri, 121
Ferguson, Mrs, 23
Fergusson, Bernard, 101
Fidelin, Ady, 153
Florence, Philip Sargent, 92
Flower, Gerald, 71
Foltýn, František, 148
For Intellectual Liberty, 194
Ford, Ford Madox, 124
Ford, Gordon Onslow, 237
found objects, 169
Fra Angelico, 185
Franchetti, Alberto, 90
Frank, Ati, 95–6, 241
Frank, Hertha, 88, 95
Franklin, Miriam, 193
Fraser, Gordon, 189
'Freddy', 150
Free German League of Culture, 173–4
Freud, Anna, 246
Freud, Sigmund, 140, 147, 213, 246
Friedlander, Eileen, 19
Fry, Maxwell, 83–4, 91, 96–7, 115
Fry, Roger, 121, 127–8, 133, 147, 162–3, 204
Fuseli, Henry, 187

Gabo, Miriam, 224, 227, 229, 231, 234–5
Gabo, Naum, 102, 171–2, 185, 189–96, 224, 227, 229, 231, 234–5, 246
Gainsborough, Thomas, 16, 186
Gane Pavilion, 109, 242
Gardiner, Margaret, 33, 44–5, 49, 71, 133, 140, 185, 194, 223–4, 228, 234, 240
Garnett, David, 57
Gathorne-Hardy, Hon, Ralph Edward, 79–80
Gaudier-Brzeska, Henri, 165
Gauguin, Paul, 1–2, 121–2, 163
General Post Office (GPO), 102, 202–4
George, Patrick, 206
Gertler, Mark, 17
Giacometti, Alberto, 138, 148, 179, 182, 189–90
Giedion, Carola, 108
Giedion, Siegfried, 105, 108, 194
Gill, Eric, 126
Gilman, Charles, 122
Ginesi, Edna, 160, 164, 166, 207
Ginner, Charles, 122
Giotto, 90, 166, 185–6
Gleizes, Alber, 179
Gloag, John, 116, 193
Goepfert, Louise, 64
Gogarty, Oliver St J., 212
Goldfinger, Ernő and Ursula, 71–2
Gorin, Jean, 194, 227
Gostick, Alice, 161–2
Grant, Duncan, 113, 131, 151, 196
Gray, John, 126
Gray, Nicolette, 189–90
Gregory, E. C., 170
Grierson, John, 101–2, 112, 147, 202–3, 206
Grigson, Geoffrey, 17, 128–9, 144, 159, 172, 180, 182, 186, 199, 210

Gropius, Ise, 80, 83–5, 88–96, 105, 115, 231, 241, 245
Gropius, Manon (Mutzi), 88, 93
Gropius, Walter, 65, 67, 80–1, 83–5, 88–98, 104–5, 108–10, 185, 194, 231
  and Nazis, 88–90, 93–4
  and Read, 128–9, 132, 144–5
  and the war, 114–16, 241–7
Group Theatre, 206–8, 211, 240
Grove, Laura, 59, 75–6
Grove, Marion, 56–7, 59, 75–6
Guggenheim, Peggy, 221, 227, 230, 239
Gumbrill, Mr, 171
Gurdjieff, George, 64

Haldane, Charlotte, 173
Half Hundred Club, 114
Hamann, Paul, 174
Hampstead, 15–17
Hampstead Heath and Old Hampstead Protection Society, 71–2
Hampstead Spanish Relief Committee, 113
Hampstead Town Hall, 246
Harben, Philip and Kathie, 112–14, 243
Harrison, Gerry, 245
Harrison, Harry and Jill, 66
Harrisson, Tom, 205
Harvard School of Design, 114
Havinden, Ashley, 189
Hay, Dr William Howard, 226
Heal, Ambrose, 69
Heartfield, John, 174
Hegel, G. W. F., 195
Hélion, Jean, 128, 179, 185–6, 189, 197, 228
Hepworth, Barbara, xi–xvii, 6, 10–15, 17, 19–29, 31–50
  and *Axis*, 182, 189
  and Calder and Mondrian, 217, 219–20, 223–7, 229–30
  and *Circle*, 192, 195, 197
  and the Edes, 184–5
  and Gropius, 83
  and Moholy-Nagy, 103–4
  and Moore, 159–60, 162–3, 168–70, 172, 176
  photograms, 41, 135
  and Piper, 178, 186, 191
  pregnancy and triplets, 43–9, 103–4
  and Read, 117–18, 126, 128–9, 133
  and surrealism, 147, 154
  and Unit One, 136, 138–43, 146
  and the war, 230–1, 233–6, 241, 246
Hepworth, Elizabeth, 45
Hepworth, Jack (Arthur Jackson), 31–3, 38, 171, 182, 189
Hepworth, Paul, xii, xvi, 19, 32, 38, 43
Herbin, Auguste, 179
Heretics Society, 63
Heron, Patrick, 57
Heron, Tom, 57
Highpoint, 71, 109–10
Hillier, Tristram, 139–40, 143
Hinterglasmalerei, 121
Hitchens, Ivon, xii, 5, 20, 177–8, 231
Hitchens, Mary, 231
Hitler, Adolf, 90, 156, 229
Hodgkins, Frances, 136, 138–9
Holding, Eileen, 177, 179–80, 189
Holtzman, Harry, 231
Hönig, Professor Eugen, 89–90, 93–4
Honzík, Karel, 194
Hooper, E. J., 31
Hornbostel, Professor Erich von, 80
Houghton, Douglas, 161

Howard, Lady Cecilia Maude, 1
Howe, Jack, 84, 97
Hudnut, Joseph, 114, 241
Hulbert, Thelma, 206
Hulme, T. E., 124, 127
Huxley, Julian, 72, 114–15, 215

Ideal Home Exhibition, 109
Impington Village College, 96–7
Ingres, Jean-Auguste-Dominique, xiii
Institute for the Harmonic Development of Man, 64
Institute of Contemporary Art (ICA), 239
International Textiles, 98, 100
Isherwood, Christopher, 204, 206–8
Isokon, 51–4, 66–81, 91–3, 95–6, 98, 104, 108–10, 112, 115, 192, 207
  Isobar, 110–14, 243–4
  Isokon chairs, 98–9, 109
  and Unit One, 135–6, 138–40, 144
  war damage and renovation, 243–6

Jackson, Arthur, *see* Hepworth, Jack
Jackson, Holbrooke, 121
Jakovsky, Anatole, 182
James, Edward, 153
James, Henry, 219
Jenkins, Douglas, xi–xiii
Jennings, Humphrey, 148, 205
John, Augustus, 121, 201
John, Ida, 201
Jones, David, 168, 184
Jowett, Percy, 93
Jung, Carl, 129–30

Kállai, Ernő, 172
Kandinsky, Wassily, 88, 105, 121–2, 128, 138, 179, 182–3, 188–90, 197
Katzman, Tsalic (Charles), 209–11
Kauffer, Edward McKnight, 146–7
Keats, John, 16
Kepes, György, 100
Keyserling, Count Herman, 54
Klee, Paul, 40, 88, 105, 148, 154, 188
Klein, Melanie, 141
Kokoschka, Oskar, 173–4
Korda, Alexander, 96, 102, 220
Korn, Arthur, 80
Kraemer, Fritz, 174
Kupka, František, 179

Lamb, Henry, 1 6
Lanchester, Elsa, 56, 207
Lane, Allen, 244
Laski, Harold, 56
Laurana, Luciano di, 125
Lawn Road, *see* Isokon
Lawrence, D. H., 17, 172
Layton, Thomas, 112
Le Charivari magazine, 88
Le Corbusier, 44, 65, 72, 105, 125, 195, 197, 222
Leeds School of Art, 17, 162–3
Leeds University, 117, 119, 121–2, 127, 162
Lefevre Gallery, 15, 21, 189–90, 192
Léger, Fernand, 138, 173, 197, 219–20, 222
Léger, Jeanne, 219
Legge, Sheila, 152
Leicester Galleries, 113, 169–70, 175, 196
Leighton, Constance, 242
Lescaze, William, 92
Lewis, Wyndham, 56, 172, 182
Listener, 76, 127, 130, 136, 139–40
Livingstone, Ken, 245
lobsters, 102
Loeb, Pierre, 219
London Artists' Association, 202, 205

London County Council, 74
London Gallery, 103, 155–6, 194, 196
London Underground, 101, 166, 175–6
London Zoo, 70–1, 102, 114, 135, 215
Lörcher, Carl Christoph, 94
Lubetkin, Berthold, 69–71, 102, 135
Lucas, Colin, 138, 145
Ludwig, Margaret (Ludo), *see* Read, Margaret (Ludo)
Ludwig, Maymay, 131
Lund Humphries, 170
Luterma furniture company, 64
Lynd, Robert and Sylvia, 211–12
Lyon, Robert, 166

Macaulay, Rose, 173, 212
Mackenzie, Compton, 214
Macnamara, Francis and Nicolette, 201
MacNeice, Daniel, 199, 209–10, 215, 240
MacNeice, Louis, 112, 199–201, 203, 206, 209–15, 240
MacNeice, Mary, 209–11
McNeill, Dorelia, 201
Madge, Charles, 205
Magritte, René, 154
Mahler-Werfel, Alma, 88, 93
Malevich, Kazimir, 195
Mall Studios, 15, 17, 20, 26, 29, 31, 103, 118, 127, 132, 154, 176, 185, 235–7
Mallarmé, Stéphane, 164
Mallowan, Max, 244
Manchester flats, 84–5, 92–3
Mansfield, Katherine, 17
Marriot, Charles, 122
Marshall, Miles, 187
Martin, Leslie, 191–2, 194
Masaccio, 166
Mass Observation, 205–6
Massine, Léonide, 192, 194
Mathias, John, 101–2
Matisse, Henri, 4, 122, 163
Matters, Leonard, 237
Maw, Graham, 73
Maxwell, Robert, 118
Maxwell Scott, Celia, 118
Mayor, Freddy, 138
Mayor Gallery, 143, 146–7, 219, 222, 224
Meadows, Bernard, 175
Medley, Robert, 172, 188, 206–7
Mellis, Margaret, 142, 229, 233–4
Mendelsohn, Erich, 67, 96
Mesens, E. L. T., 153
Meynell, Francis, 57, 114
Michelangelo, 161–2
Middleton Murry, John, 17
Miller, Duncan, 189
Miller, Lee, 71–2, 150, 153–6
Miró, Joan, 133, 138, 148, 151, 154, 182, 189–90, 219
Modern Architectural Research Group (MARS), 54, 70, 73, 103
Moholy, Hattula, 98
Moholy, Lucia, 97–8
Moholy-Nagy, László, 41–2, 71, 88, 94, 97–104, 108, 115, 146, 189, 194, 197, 220, 223
  and Moore, 171–2
  and the war, 231, 242, 246
Moholy-Nagy, Sibylle (Sybil), 98, 101–4, 108–9, 128, 135, 231, 242
Mondrian, Piet, 44, 179, 186, 189–90, 197, 217–19, 222, 224–31, 242, 246
Monsarrat, Nicholas, 80
Moore, Alfred, 160
Moore, Annie, 160
Moore, Betty, 165, 170
Moore, Elsie, 160–1

Moore, Henry, xii–xiii, xvii, 12, 19–21, 26, 103, 112, 115, 159–73, 175–6
and AIA, 172–3
and *Axis*, 182, 189
and *Circle*, 195–7
and the Edes, 185
and the Pipers, 179
and Read, 117–18, 126, 128–30
and surrealism, 147–8, 150, 152–3, 155
and theatre, 206–7
and Unit One, 136, 138, 144–6
and the war, 231, 236–7
Moore, Irina, xii, 20, 117–18, 128, 130, 153, 159, 166–8, 170–1, 175–6, 185
and the war, 231, 236–7
Moore, Marianne, 56
Moore, Mary, 165, 237
Moore, Raymond, 160, 165
Morandi, Giorgio, 4
Morison, Stanley, 145
Morris, Cedris, 7
Morris, Henry, 97, 196
Morris, William, 145
Morton Shand, Philip, 83–5, 91, 97
Mumford, Lewis, 194
Municipal Art Gallery, 205
Munter, Frosca, 10
Münter, Gabriele, 121
Murray, William Staite, 10
Musée du Trocadéro, 164
Museum of Modern Art (MoMA), 102, 241
Mussolini, Benito, 90, 172

Nash, Margaret ('Bunty'), 6, 135–6, 148, 150, 238
Nash, Paul, 1, 6, 35, 37, 44–5, 56, 135–40, 143–51, 180, 191, 238
and *Circle*, 196–7
and Moore, 164, 169, 171–2
Nation and Athenaeum, 177–8
National Gallery, 127, 164, 178, 186, 241
National Police Gazette, 221
New Burlington Galleries, 151–2, 174
New Statesman, 79, 174, 222, 245
New Verse, 17, 210
Newton, Eric, 194
Nicholson, Andrew, xi, 30
Nicholson, Ben, xi–xiii–xvii, 1–10, 21–49
and Abstract & Concrete exhibition, 190
and *Axis*, 182–3, 185, 188–9
'Ben Theory', 24
and *Circle*, 192, 195–8
and Coldstream, 216
and the Edes, 184–5
and Gabo, 192–4
and Gropius, 83
and Half Hundred Club, 114
and Moholy-Nagy, 103–4
and Mondrian and Calder, 217, 219–20, 223–7, 229–30
and Moore, 159, 168, 171, 173, 176
and the Pipers, 177–8, 186, 191
and Read, 118, 123, 125, 128–9, 133
reliefs, 42–4
and surrealism, 147, 154
and Unit One, 136, 138–46
and the war, 230–1, 233–6, 239, 241
Nicholson, Edie, 5
Nicholson, Jake, xi, 7–8, 27, 30–1, 42, 45, 48
Nicholson, Kate, xi, 8, 27, 30, 42, 236
Nicholson, Kit, 42
Nicholson, Mabel, 1–2
Nicholson, Nancy, 129

Nicholson, William, 1, 121, 219
Nicholson, Winifred, xi–xvii, 1–10, 21–33, 35, 38–9, 43–5, 48, 138, 168, 184, 186, 192–4, 197, 216, 224, 226, 230–1, 235–6
Nicholson-Hepworth, Rachel, Sarah and Simon (triplets), 45–9, 51, 83, 103–4, 133, 142, 185, 216, 226–7, 229, 233, 235
1917 Club, 57
Nonesuch Press, 57

Ody, Robin, 226, 231
Oppenheimer, Meret, 150
Orage, Alfred, 121, 124
Oskar-Kokoscha-Bund (OKB), 173
Oxford Arts Club, 197
Ozenfant, Amédée, 197

Paalen, Wolfgang Robert, 147, 189
Paepcke, Walter, 104
Palmer, Samuel, 186–7
Paris Exposition, 219–20
Paroissien, Harry F., 101
Pasmore, Victor, 205
Pater, Walter, 126
Paterson's Gallery, 5
Pellerin, Auguste, 165
Pelman Institute, 59
'Penguin Donkey', 245
Penrose, Antony, 154, 156
Penrose, Roland, 71, 147, 150, 153–6, 198, 239
  Objects and Poems Exhibition, 155–7
Perspex, 194
Pevsner, Nicolaus, 97
Pevsner, Virginia, 227
Picasso, Pablo, xiii, 4, 7, 40, 122, 147–8, 154, 156, 160, 179, 186, 197, 228
  Guernica, 198, 219
Pick, Frank, 93–4
Piero della Francesca, 125, 185
Piper, Clarissa, 238
Piper, Edward, 238
Piper, John, 113, 173, 177–81, 185–91, 195–7, 207–9, 219–21, 237–8
Piper, Myfanwy, 177–82, 185–9, 191, 197–8, 207–8, 219–21, 237–8
Piper, Penelope, 238
Piscator, Erwin, 90
Pissarro, Camille, 163
Plato, 182, 195
Popper, Sophie, 215, 240
Porter, Cole, 129
Porteus, Hugh Gordon, 170, 188
Postgate, Raymond, 114
Pound, Ezra, 165
Powell, Anthony, 75–6
Pre-Raphaelite Brotherhood, 140
Priestley, J. B., 152, 212
Pritchard, Clive, 59
Pritchard, F. C., 98
Pritchard, Jack, 51, 54, 57, 59–62, 64–7, 69–70, 72–7, 80–1
  and Breuer, 108–9
  furniture designs, 95
  and Gropius, 84–5, 91–2, 94–7, 115–16
  and Isobar, 110–14, 196
  and the war, 237, 241–5, 247
Pritchard, Jennifer, 62, 65, 245
Pritchard, Jeremy, 61, 245
Pritchard, Jonathan, 61, 245
Pritchard, Rosemary 'Molly', 51, 54, 60–2, 64–70, 72–6, 78, 81, 109
  and Gropius, 91–3, 96, 115–16
  and Isobar, 112, 114
  and the war, 241, 245, 247
Puvis de Chavannes, Pierre, 121

Raffalovich, Marc-André, 126
Ravilious, Eric, 166, 196

Ray, Man, 148, 150, 153–6, 222
Read, Ben, 239
Read, Charles, 123
Read, Evelyn, 117, 122–4, 126, 132–3
Read, Herbert, 37, 43, 49, 104, 112, 115, 117–33, 219, 230
and *Axis*, 182, 185, 195
and *Circle*, 192, 195–7
The Green Child, 118, 129–30
and Moore, 162, 170–1, 175–6
and romanticism, 125–6
and surrealism, 147, 152
and Unit One, 135–6, 139–40, 143–7
and the war, 234–5, 238–9, 246–7
Read, John, 117, 127
Read, Margaret (Ludo), 43, 117–18, 126–33, 135, 175, 238–9
Read, Piers Paul, 123, 239
Read, Sophia, 239
Read, Thomas, 238
Read, William, 123
Reilly, Paul, 113
Reynolds, Sir Joshua, 16
Rhode Island School of Design, 241
Rhodoid plastic, 102
Rhythm, 121
Richards, Ceri, 177–8
Ringling Brothers Circus, 221
Riss, Egon, 244
Riss, Erwin, 244
Roberts, Charles Henry, 1
Robeson, Paul, 173
Rochas sisters, 155
Rochester Folk Art Guild, 64
Roell, W. F. A., 217–18
Rogers, Claude, 205
romanticism–classicism debate, 125–6
Rothenstein, John, 176
Rothenstein, William, 93, 163, 165
Rousseau, Henri, 2
Royal Academy, 12
Royal College of Art, 11–12, 17, 93, 160, 163–6, 169, 177, 207
Royal Institute of British Architects (RIBA), 83
Russell, Bertrand, 61–3
Russell, Dora, 61–3
Russell, Kate, 63
Rutter, Frank, 121–3

Sadler, Michael, 121–2, 162, 170, 180
St Mark's Gospel, 7
St Martin's School of Art, 171
Salisbury Cathedral, 186
Sanderson, F. W., 59
Savinio, Alberto, 4
Schames, Samson, 174
Scherman, David E., 156
Schwitters, Kurt, 174
Seuphor, Michel, 217
Seven and Five Society, 5, 8, 136, 147, 177, 202
Shand, Philip Morton, 70
Shaw, George Bernard, 122
Shelley, Percy Bysshe, 16
Sickert, Walter, 202, 219
Simpson, Alexander, 100, 103
Sir John Soane's Museum, 241
Skeaping, Jack, xii, 11–15, 17, 19–22, 24–5, 33, 35, 39, 168
Slade School of Art, 17, 201–2, 206–7
Slutzky, Naum, 192
Society of Art Masters, 169
Sommerfeld, Adolf, 115
Soutine, Chaim, 138
Spanish Civil War, 112–13, 173
Speight, Sadie, 192
Spencer, Stanley, 16
Spender, Humphrey, 205
Spender, Michael, 215, 240–1

Spender, Stephen, 130, 140, 173, 204–6, 208, 240
Stannard, Mary, xii
Steer, Philip Wilson, 121
Stephenson, Cecil, 17, 223
Stokes, Adrian, 37, 42, 80, 140–2, 170, 205, 216, 229–30, 233–5
Stonehenge, 91, 164, 188
Storrow, Mrs, 241–2
Studio, 37, 161, 196
Sullivan, Louis, 54
Summer, Gerald, 98
Sun House (Hampstead), 84–5
surrealism, 118, 123, 135, 139–40, 147–57
  and *Circle*, 195–6
Sutherland, Graham, 169, 196–7
Sutherland, Helen, 7, 24, 31, 44, 189
Sylvester, David, 202
synaesthesia, 121

Tanguy, Yves, 148
Tate Gallery, 10, 176, 183
Teapot and Pavement Club, 60
Tecton Group, 70–1, 102
Thomas Caitlin, 201
Thomas, Dylan, 152, 201
Thompson, D'Arcy Wentworth, 172
Times, The, 135, 138, 194, 211, 243–4
Titian, 162
Todd, Ruthven, 153
Tonks, Henry, 202
Tooth's Gallery, 21, 24, 35, 138, 148
Toulouse-Lautrec, Henri de, 122
Trevelyan, Julian, 197
Tschichold, Jan, 194, 197
Tudor-Hart, Beatrix, 61, 65, 245
Turgenev, Ivan, 132
Turner, J. M. W., 186

Uglow, Euan, 206
Uhlman, Fred, 173–5
Underwood, Leon, 148, 165, 207
Unit One, xvii, 44, 49, 118, 135–6, 138–46, 179, 181, 195
  becomes Artists' Unit, 104, 146–7
Unity Theatre, 208

van der Rohe, Ludwig Mies, 65, 88, 145
van Doesburg, Theo, 44, 222
Van Gogh, Vincent, 122, 163
Vantongerloo, Georges, 179
Venesta Plywood Company, 51, 57, 61, 64, 77
Ventris, Dorothea, 109
Verlaine, Paul, 163
Victoria and Albert Museum, 124, 164
Vogler, Felicitas, 236
Vogue, 112, 156, 221–2
Vorticism, 139
Vuillard, Édouard, 163

Wadsworth, Edward, 113, 136, 138, 140, 144–5, 180
Wadsworth, Fanny, 170
Wagner, Martin, 92
Wallis, Alfred, 8–10, 31–2, 129, 235
Walmsley, Leo, 13
Walpole, Hugh, 211–12
Walton, William, 151
War Artists' Advisory Committee, 175, 237–8
Warren Gallery, 166
Watt, Henry, 203
Waugh, Evelyn, 56
Wedgwood, Josiah, 145
Weissenhof Estate, 65, 67
Wellington, Hubert, 166
Wellington, Robert, 196
Wells, H. G., 102, 115, 220
Werfel, Franz, 88
Wertheim Gallery, 174

Westminster Theatre, 211
Whistler, J. A. M., 163
Whitechapel Gallery, 198
Wilde, Oscar, 126
Williamson, H. S., 169
Wintemute, Agnes, 54
Wohnbedarf furniture, 105, 108
Women's Tax Resistance League, 6
Wood, Christopher 'Kit', 7–8, 10, 187
Woods, Sydney John, 189
Woolf, Leonard, 130–1, 246
Woolf, Virginia, 130–1, 246
Wordsworth, William, 119, 125
Workers' Birth Control Group, 63
Workers' Theatre Movement, 208
World League for Sexual Reform, 63
Worner, Heinz, 173–4
Wüsten, Johannes, 174

Yeats, W. B., 122
Yorke, Francis Reginald Stevens, 108–9, 112

Zadkine, Ossip, 126, 173, 180
Zoëte, Beryl de, 156
Zweig, Stefan, 246
Zwemmer, Anton, 170, 180
Zwemmer Gallery, 147, 174, 196

A NOTE ON THE AUTHOR

Caroline Maclean studied English and History of Art at Oxford University before completing her PhD at the University of London. She worked in film and television and lived in New York and Boston before moving back to London where she combines writing with teaching. She has written for the *London Review of Books* and the *Times Literary Supplement.*

A NOTE ON THE TYPE

The text of this book is set in Bembo, which was first used in 1495 by the Venetian printer Aldus Manutius for Cardinal Bembo's De Aetna. The original types were cut for Manutius by Francesco Griffo. Bembo was one of the types used by Claude Garamond (1480–1561) as a model for his Romain de l'Université, and so it was a forerunner of what became the standard European type for the following two centuries. Its modern form follows the original types and was designed for Monotype in 1929.